By the same author

Guide to the Archives of the Spanish Institutions in or concerned with the Spanish Netherlands, 1556–1706
(Brussels, Archives Générales du Royaume, 1971)

The Army of Flanders and the Spanish Road, 1567–1659. The logistics of Spanish victory and defeat in the Low Countries' Wars
(Cambridge University Press, 1972, 1975; Spanish edition, *Revista de Occidente*, Madrid, 1976)

The emergence of modern finance in Europe, 1500–1730
(Collins, 1974)

Introduction to the Sources of European Economic History, 1500–1800, Volume 1, *Western Europe*
(with Charles Wilson, Weidenfeld, 1977)

The private world of Philip II
(Little, Brown & Co., Boston, 1977)

European Soldiers, 1550–1650
(with Angela Parker, Cambridge
University Press, 1977)

Geoffrey Parker

THE DUTCH REVOLT

Allen Lane

ALLEN LANE
Penguin Books Ltd,
17 Grosvenor Gardens, London SW1W 0BD

First published in 1977

Copyright © Geoffrey Parker, 1977

ISBN 0 7139 1032 1

Set in Monotype Bell

Printed in Great Britain by
Ebenezer Baylis and Son Ltd,
The Trinity Press, Worcester, and London

FOR JACK PLUMB

Contents

8   Contents

List of maps and diagrams

Acknowledgements

I wish to thank the Master and Fellows of Christ's College, Cambridge, the Research Committee of the Leverhulme Trust and the Travel and Research Fund of St Andrews University for their generous financial support.

I also wish to thank those who helped with the writing of this book. I am indebted above all to Mr Alastair Duke, Mrs Angela Parker, Professor J. H. Plumb and Professor K. W. Swart, all of whom read the entire typescript for me, giving generously of their time and knowledge in trying to save me from error. Mr James S. Coonan, one of my research students, Dr D. M. Fenlon, and Professors J. H. Elliott, H. G. Koenigsberger, P. D. Lagomarsino, B. A. Vermaseren and C. H. Wilson gave me useful advice and information, for which I am most grateful. Finally I must mention the eleven generations of students, at Cambridge and St Andrews, who have suffered from my interest in Dutch history; I have benefited greatly from their incisive criticisms and suggestions – especially the comments of Helen Bannatyne, John de Quidt, Patrick Rayner and Catherine Stewart.

Note on spelling, usage, currency and dates

Where there is a recognized English version of a foreign place-name (Ostend, The Hague, Brussels and so on) I have used it. Otherwise I have preferred the style used in the place itself (Ieper, not Ypres; Aalst, not Alost). I have followed the same system with personal names: where there is an established English usage (William of Orange, Don John of Austria, Philip II) I have adopted it. In all other cases the style and title employed by the person concerned have been used.

The terms 'Flanders' and 'Holland', which in the sixteenth century were sometimes used to refer to the entire Netherlands, are here employed only to designate the individual provinces.

To avoid confusion and to make comparisons possible, all sums of money mentioned in the text have been converted to florins of twenty pattards, the principal money of account used in the Netherlands, equivalent to the *livre de 40 gros* also used as a money of account. There were about ten florins to the pound sterling during the later sixteenth century; there were two florins to the ducat, two florins also to the escudo until 1578 and thereafter two and a half or three.

On 24 February 1581 Pope Gergory XIII ordered that the calendar should be advanced by ten days and, although Spain and the Netherlands obeyed, they did not do so at the same time: Spain adopted the new calendar on 4/15 October 1582; the States-General on 14/25 December 1582; Holland (by itself) on 1/12 January 1583; the 'Spanish Netherlands' on 11/22 February 1583. All dates in the text of this book are in New Style from October 1582 onwards, and throughout I have assumed that the calendar year began on 1 January (and not on 25 March, as in the Julian Calendar).

Foreword

To write another book about *the* Dutch Revolt may seem perverse to some, for it has been convincingly argued that there was not one revolt in the sixteenth-century Netherlands but many. Historians have been warned to 'stop treating the Revolt as a *bloc* and become aware that there were a number of revolts, representing the interests and ideals of various social, economic and ideological groups: revolts which sometimes run parallel, sometimes conflict with one another, and at other times coalesce into a single movement'.[1] The great problem is to find a credible framework which is flexible enough to fit the experience of all the seventeen provinces of the Low Countries where, in the sixteenth century at least, particularism was more potent than patriotism. Local loyalties were the more tenaciously defended because the 'privileges' or 'liberties' of each town and province pre-dated the 'state'. A central government appeared relatively late on the scene in the Low Countries. There was no political or dynastic union to embrace the entire area until 1548–9, and even then the large principality of Liège was not included, although it lay in the geographical centre of the new union.

The defence of local privilege against the encroachments of the new central power proved to be the mainspring of the early opposition to Philip II. The various provinces, and the different social groups within them, were drawn together by the threat to their corporate 'liberties' posed by the 'novelties' introduced by Philip II and his ministers: the Spanish garrisons, the control of policy by Cardinal Granvelle, the 'new bishoprics' scheme and the rigorous persecution of heretics by a special Inquisition. Religion played its part in all this, but support for the Protestants came principally from those who were not themselves prepared to join the Reformed church. Calvinism was exploited by politicians for their own ends and the small band of devoted Protestant ministers who made many converts in 1566, while they enjoyed the support of the political leaders, were to see most of their flocks executed or exiled when their political support evaporated in 1567.

Interference with the privileges also played a part in sparking off the next outbreak of rebellion in the Netherlands in 1572. One of the first acts of the defiant States of Holland in that year was to send a deputation to the provincial archives at Gouda castle in order to draw up a list of the privileges and liberties which had been overridden by 'the Spanish tyranny'.[2] Religion too was a factor in this second revolt: many of the Calvinist exiles of 1566–7 returned to their homeland, determined to turn it into an impregnable citadel of God's Word which would never again succumb to papal power. However, neither of these issues was capable of generating massive popular support as they had in 1566; for many people it was a case of 'once bitten, twice shy'. Too many heads had rolled in the earlier outbreak; too many leaders had fallen or fled. The different geography of rebellion in 1566 and 1572 is striking. The heart of the first revolt lay in the south Netherlands; that of the second revolt lay in the north. Even there the centres of disaffection were different: the towns which had remained obedient in 1566 – Gouda, Rotterdam, Dordrecht and Haarlem, for example – led the defections in 1572; conversely, some of the most unruly towns of the 1560s – such as Middelburg and Amsterdam – remained loyal in 1572 and long after. The new troubles thus involved new persons, motivated principally by a new grievance: the government's attempt to impose illegally a 10-per-cent Value Added Tax on all sales. The 'Tenth Penny' dominated all the rebels' propaganda; it was the rallying cry of the revolt.

The rebellion of 1576 was different again. It began in Brussels, a town which had remained loyal both in 1566 and in 1572, and found initial support in provinces like Hainaut and Artois which had been little involved in the earlier unrest. Practically all those involved were convinced Catholics. This time the target of the 'rebels' was the mutinous Spanish army which was running amok in the (loyal) southern provinces and threatening their entire well-being with destruction. This time it was a question of defending the 'Fatherland' from subversion. Although after 1576 the different elements in the three revolts coalesced to some extent, their initial distinction appears in most sources. To give one visual example, the different motives of each uprising were embroidered on their military banners. The soldiers who fell in the 1566–7 rebellion fought under flags bearing a picture of a beggar's scrip and the motto *Vive les Gueux* (Long Live the Beggars); the Sea Beggars in 1572 flew a standard with a picture of ten coins, alluding to the Tenth Penny; in 1576 the troops who fought the Spaniards had banners inscribed *Pro Fide et Patria* (For Faith and Fatherland), *Pugno pro Patria* (I fight for the Fatherland) and *Pro Fide et Pace* (For Faith and Peace).[3]

Most contemporaries were able to see that there was not one Dutch Revolt, but three. Don Luis de Requesens, the Spanish commander in the Netherlands from 1573 to 1576, regularly distinguished in his dispatches between the causes of the first and second revolts, and he predicted (correctly) that a third would soon follow. Baron Champagney, a leader of the Catholic nobles of the south Netherlands, likewise emphasized the different motives of the troubles of the 1560s and those of the 1570s.[4] The Dutch, however, were reluctant to share this outlook. On the contrary, they – and subsequent Dutch historians – have tended to stress the continuity of the conflict with Spain. This attitude was exemplified by the decision of the States-General to hold a thanksgiving day for the peace of Münster on 10 June 1648 because that was the eightieth anniversary of the execution of Egmont and Hornes by 'the tyrant Alva' and his depraved master, Philip II.

The present book is not an attempt to correct this imbalance by writing a Spanish 'official history' four hundred years too late! However, the attempt must be made to see the revolt from the point of view of the Spaniards as well as from that of the Dutch. It is important to see how developments in the Netherlands appeared in Spain. This is particularly important in 1566-7 when it might seem that Philip II overreacted to the first revolt by sending the duke of Alva with permission to mobilize 60,000 men. Philip II, however, was separated from the Netherlands by 1,000 miles; news reached him at second-hand and about two weeks late. If we consider only the information at the king's disposal in the winter of 1566-7, we are compelled to agree with Professor H. G. Koenigsberger that no sixteenth-century ruler could have 'acted differently when faced with the double opposition of the high nobility (albeit a constitutional opposition) and a revolutionary religious movement with a military organization (albeit only in its infancy)'.[5] Later on in the struggle we find Netherlands policy influenced by Spain's financial problems. Money – or rather lack of it – is the key to many tergiversations in Spanish policy towards the Netherlands: the Spanish financial crisis of 1575 explains in large measure the 'Spanish Fury' at Antwerp the following year; the financial crisis of 1596 preceded the transfer of power from Philip II to the Archdukes in 1598; the financial crisis of 1607 paved Philip III's way towards a settlement, albeit temporary, with the Dutch in 1609. As the Belgian historian, Hubert Lonchay, wrote long ago: 'The fate of the Netherlands was thus tied to that of Spain, and often one cannot understand the political history of the one without knowing the financial situation of the other.' The minutiae of Spanish finance may seem trivial but, as Dr Juliaan Woltjer has recently pointed out, there is always a tendency among historians to assume that major events must have major causes whereas, in reality, small beginnings often have large consequences.[6]

*   *   *

'The King of Spain', observed an English writer in 1652, 'hath now got a command so wide, that out of his Dominions the *Sunne* can neither rise nor set.'[7] My last book, *The Army of Flanders and the Spanish Road*, to which this volume is in some ways a sequel, was criticized by one eminent Dutch historian for being pro-Spanish and pro-Catholic.[8] It was not intended to be either. I love Spain and the Netherlands equally and, although I always take the religion of sixteenth-century people seriously, I am indifferent to both Protestantism and Catholicism today. What I say in the pages which follow is not the product of partiality for either side in the struggle, nor for either religion. Although I cannot hope to fulfil the demand of the late Jan Romein for an 'objective, global history' of the Dutch Revolt,[9] in writing this book I have tried constantly to see the troubles of the Low Countries in a wider setting: secular as well as religious, economic as well as political; French, German and English as well as Spanish and Dutch. The Revolt of the Netherlands studied in passion or in isolation makes no sense at all.

⌈1⌋

PRELUDE

The Netherlands in 1549

A casual visitor to the Netherlands in the summer of 1549 would have
been astonished to find in every major town a series of triumphal
arches, large and splendid, some depicting mythological subjects or
classical stories, others showing scenes of martial exploits. Plays were
staged by the local 'chambers of rhetoric'; processions and presenta-
tions took place; there were lion-fights and bull-fights; the chivalric
romance *Amadis of Gaul* was acted out in the grounds of the castle
of Binche and special illustrated books were commissioned to describe
all the festivities. But 1549 was not a normal year for the Netherlands.
Between April and September Crown Prince Philip, son and heir of
the Emperor Charles V, ruler of the Netherlands, paid a state visit
to his father's northern inheritance: all the arches, pageants and
processions were in his honour. It was the first time that the prince
had left Spain, the country of his birth and education, and the Low
Countries were the last point on a 'grand tour' through his father's

19

vast European empire, covering most of Italy and much of Germany as well as all of Spain and the Netherlands. The voyage had taken six months, pleasantly punctuated by memorable excesses at the table (at one dinner the company ate and drank so much that the dancing had to be delayed for several hours to allow the guests to recover) but the prince and his entourage survived until they reached Brussels on All Fools' Day 1549. There they were met by Charles V, the sovereign ruler of the Netherlands, who was anxious to introduce his subjects to their future lord.

The Low Countries made quite an impact on the prince and his entourage, so much so that two members of the party were moved to write down their impressions of the journey. Of course, like all tourists in all periods, they paid most attention to the things which were different from the situation at home – differences of physiognomy, of social habits, of climate. They noted with astonishment the natives' massive consumption of beer, which was cheap and plentiful – recent research reveals an average daily consumption per adult of three pints – and the enormous quantities of food eaten (at least by the rich). It was not unknown, one Spaniard reported, for a banquet which began at lunchtime to last late into the night, the guests eventually too drunk to move, urinating on the floor rather than get up and go outside. This incontinence was surprising, he noted, in view of the meticulous cleanliness of the Dutch women who, even in 1549, made a strong impression on visitors with their spotless homes (although, it must be admitted, the praise of a Spaniard may be suspect: most visitors to the peninsula commented on the filth and squalor of Spanish homes!). The Dutch women also impressed the Spaniards with their capacity for gossip, with their 'miniskirts' (which only came down to the ankle) and with their big coarse hands and big black teeth. But above all, the men from the Mediterranean noted that Dutch women were 'naturally cold and little given to pleasure, sexual or otherwise'; they thus anticipated by more than a century the celebrated judgement of Sir William Temple: 'In general, All Appetites and Passions seem to run lower and cooler here, than in other Countreys where I have converst . . . I have known some among them that personated Lovers well enough but none that I ever thought were at heart in love; Nor any of the Women that seem'd at all to care whether they were so or or no.'[1] The visitors had less to say about Dutch men: apart from their semi-permanent inebriation, the Spaniards were impressed by their rosy cheeks, their superior stature (some men, they observed, were over six feet tall) and their delight in doing things with machines rather than by hand.

Naturally the Spanish visitors did not confine their attention to these crude anthropological data. They also noted the widespread literacy of the Netherlanders. One of Prince Philip's entourage, Vicente Alvarez, noted in his journal that 'almost everyone' knew how to read and write, even women, and further investigation lends his surprising claim considerable support. There were 150 schools in Antwerp alone in the mid-sixteenth century and there was a flourishing schoolteachers' guild (founded in the 1460s). Other towns were likewise well endowed with schools, many of them founded since 1500: Ghent had forty schools (twelve of them grammar schools), Flushing had six and Veere (with a population of only 2,000) had three; Breda had fourteen schoolmasters, Tournai had eleven and Poperinghe had seven. At least fourteen towns in the province of Flanders had grammer schools. Although we lack similar quantitative data for other areas, the town school at Zwolle, which had 2,000 pupils by 1500, was famous over the whole north-east Netherlands, and the general high regard for education in an isolated province like Friesland appears in such casual evidence as the will of a sixteenth-century farmer which stipulated that 'of the three brothers [who were to inherit], he who turns out the most learned will have the major part of the property'. We only have proper statistics on schools in a rural area for the diocese of Tournai in the south Netherlands. Here a survey of 141 parishes conducted in 1569 revealed only three entirely lacking someone to teach the children basic literacy; there were eight grammar schools in the area and two Sunday Schools 'teaching those who, on account of their manual employment and life-style, have not the time to come to school to learn to read and write'. It is doubtless no accident that Tournai – like the two other areas of extremely high educational provision, Antwerp and west Flanders – was to play a central role in the religious opposition to Philip II. In the sixteenth century book-learnin' led to Calvinism.[2]

The Spanish visitors were also impressed by the political and economic strength of the Low Countries. The Habsburg Netherlands, they noted, covered a large area. In fact the provinces extended over

34,000 square miles, an area not much smaller than neighbouring England (51,000 square miles). Like England, there was a compact core of territories at the centre – a 'heartland' consisting of the rich provinces of Flanders, Brabant, Hainaut and Artois – to which outlying areas were attached. To the north lay the prosperous provinces of Friesland, Utrecht, Holland and Zealand, almost surrounded by the sea and separated from the 'heartland' by the rivers, dikes and lakes which lay squarely across the narrow centre of the Netherlands. To the east and north-east lay the sparsely populated provinces of Luxemburg, Limburg, Gelderland, Overijssel, Drenthe and Groningen, cut off by the dunes, heaths and bogs around the great rivers and by the independent principality of Liège. Far to the south, separated from the rest of the Netherlands by the independent duchy of Lorraine, lay the oldest province of Charles V's inheritance: the Franche-Comté of Burgundy.

These physical and political obstacles were important, for they seriously impeded communications. The normal route from Friesland to the south was by boat across the Zuider Zee: the lakes and marshes made it virtually impossible for a horse – let alone a horse and cart – to get across. However the sea voyage was also appallingly slow and so in September 1566, when the provincial governor of Friesland required to send an urgent message to the central government in Brussels, he sent a runner overland: 'Messengers on foot go fastest' he observed. Even short distances could take many hours in the sixteenth century. A chronicler describing his native city of Breda, right in the centre of the Low Countries, situated it 'eight hours west of 's Hertogenbosch [twenty-five miles away], seven hours east of Bergen-op-Zoom [twenty-two miles away] ten hours north-east of Antwerp [thirty miles] and three hours south of Geertruidenberg [nine miles]' – an average speed of three miles an hour in every direction. And this was written in the mid-eighteenth century! It was only farther south that communications became better, thanks to the network of commercial routes which centred on the towns of the south Netherlands. It was possible for a letter posted in Antwerp to reach Ghent, Brussels or Lille in a day; there was a regular weekly postal service which connected the Netherlands cities with Spain and Italy (the courier took between two and three weeks). Even freight could be sent from Antwerp to Cologne in ten days and from Antwerp to Venice in seventy days. Brussels and Antwerp were in many ways closer to Paris and Cologne than they were to Amsterdam and Groningen.

The Netherlands of 1549 were relatively thickly populated. There were roughly three million people, the same as the estimated population of the somewhat larger England and Wales. The majority of the inhabitants lived in the western provinces – Holland, Zealand, Hainaut, Flanders and Brabant – where the population density was the highest in Europe (between thirty and thirty-five people per square kilometre) and an unusually large proportion lived in towns. There were about 200 towns in the Netherlands, some of them very large. Antwerp had 80,000 inhabitants; Ghent, Brussels, Lille, Valenciennes and Amsterdam each had over 30,000. In all, nineteen Netherland towns had a population of more than 10,000; in the whole of the British Isles there were only four.

It was not only the dense population which made the Netherlands such a jewel in the Habsburg crown. There were also the attractions of nature, such as the long summer evenings which enabled the visitors from Spain to read out of doors until 10 p.m., the long groves of trees laid out along the boundaries of the fertile fields and the vast expanses of flat countryside with low horizons and towering skies. There were also man-made attractions: the Low Countries were famous for the beauty of their towns, the splendour of their country houses and formal gardens, the skill of their numerous artists and musicians, and the ingenuity of their engineers and architects. The future Philip II was to see the best of everything, and he was to see it in the company of his father Charles V, his aunt Mary of Hungary (regent of the Netherlands), his principal Spanish advisers (the duke of Alva and Ruy Gómez da Silva) and a number of leading Netherlands nobles (the prince of Orange, the marquis of Berghes, Counts Egmont and Hornes). Most of the principal actors in the first phase of the Dutch Revolt thus travelled together.

From Brussels the royal party proceeded first to Flanders, a province famous for its weaving industry in both town and country, then to the frontier provinces of Artois and Hainaut, the principal agricultural centre of the Netherlands. The Italian merchant and writer Lodovico Guicciardini, who lived in Antwerp most of his life, noted in 1567 that most crops would grow in the Netherlands, even peaches, cherries and apricots although (except for pears and apples) 'the fruits lack

1. *Philip II's tour through the Low Countries in 1549*

Prince Philip entered the Netherlands, after his long overland voyage from Italy, in mid-March 1549. He arrived in Brussels on 1 April. In July and August the prince toured the southern provinces; in September and October he visited the north. In each provincial capital he was sworn in as heir apparent.

Source: Cristobal Calvete de Estrella, *El felicissimo viaje del mvy alto y mvy poderoso principe don Phelipe* (Antwerp, 1552): 'Itinerario breue del Principe'.

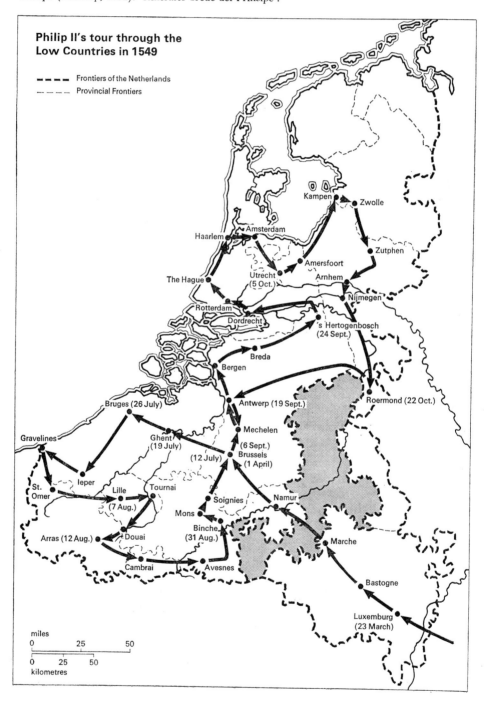

entirely the delightful taste and flavour they have in Italy. They are not so good because there is not enough warm weather.' Likewise, he complained, the local wine was 'rather coarse and tart because the grapes are not able to ripen fully'. The main problem with the food of the Netherlands, however, was not quality but quantity. Despite the variety of agricultural produce, and despite widespread land reclamation and improvement, the Low Countries could not supply enough food to satisfy all their needs. Roughly one quarter of the total food consumed in the Netherlands had to be imported, and imports ranged from basic items such as grain to luxuries such as fine wines, spices and Mediterranean fruit. The Spaniards who accompanied Prince Philip were surprised to find masses of Spanish oranges on sale in Brussels – and selling cheaper than they did in Valladolid, so efficiently was the city's food supply organized. But the poor could not feed on oranges and spices. Their staple diet was a bowl of salt soup with black rye-bread – so black that it could not be sold in Spain, noted Vicente Alvarez (who had a professional interest since he was responsible for supplying the prince's household with its daily bread). Perhaps half the income of the average poor family went on bread. This could increase to three quarters or more with the violent fluctuations in the price of grain, which could sometimes increase threefold within a period of weeks. The practice of reducing the size of the loaf, sometimes to almost half, in an attempt to disguise price rises, did not mitigate the difficulties of the poor in obtaining enough food to survive. Every town in Europe contained a hard core of people who were permanently unable to make ends meet and who therefore had to beg or subsist on charity. There is no evidence that the Netherlands had an above average number of permanent paupers. But at times of high food prices or of low employment, and especially when both coincided, this reservoir of indigent citizens was swelled by those in temporary need. The industrial towns of Flanders and Brabant were particularly vulnerable to economic difficulties, and therefore to sudden poverty crises. The number of people receiving poor relief doubled at Brussels and tripled at Leuven between 1437 and 1526; in the 1540s the number of poor in Ghent sometimes reached 6,000 (one seventh of the total population), in Ieper 3,000 (one fifth of the inhabitants) and in Bruges 7,700 (one quarter of the town). The towns created public bakeries to dispense free bread during crises, municipal pawn-shops (*monts de piété*) to give small loans free to those in need (the first opened at Ieper in 1534) and special boarding-schools for destitute children to take them off the streets (the poor school at Bruges had 230 children by 1550). But such measures – although noted with approval by foreign visitors – were insufficient to solve the poverty problem which was probably worse in the great towns of the southern Netherlands than anywhere else in Europe.

The royal party spent three months on its tour of the rich southern provinces and in September they passed through Brussels again on their way to see the lands in the north. The first major town on their route was Antwerp, one of the largest cities in Europe, with 212 streets, 13,500 houses, a vast new chain of fortifications (five miles round) and some of the best new buildings in Europe. Every week, according to the contemporary historian Scribanius, there were 2,500 vessels in the port of Antwerp; sometimes 500 ships entered and departed in a day; and 10,000 carts laden with merchandise left every week for all parts of Europe. The streets of Antwerp were perpetually choked with merchandise, carts and people, for the city offered the businessman unique commercial opportunities. The French printer, Christopher Plantin, first came to Antwerp (like Philip II) in 1549 and there he stayed to publish and bind books because, as he put it, 'No other town in the world could offer me more facilities for carrying on the trade I intended to begin. Antwerp can be easily reached; various nations meet in its market-place; there too can be found the raw materials indispensable for the practice of one's trade; craftsmen for all trades can easily be found and instructed in a short time.' Plantin's claim is vindicated by the publication record of the Antwerp printers between 1500 and 1540: 2,250 editions, half of them in Latin and the rest in Dutch, French, English, German, Greek, Spanish and Italian, covering almost every subject from religion and theology (900 titles) to geology, botany and romantic fiction. Plantin himself helped to increase these production figures: by 1561 he had created the largest printing house in northern Europe and published twenty major works in a year. Over his thirty-four years of activity, Plantin produced 1,500 different works in Antwerp and in 1574, his best year, he had sixteen presses in operation and employed fifty-five craftsmen and specialists.[3]

Antwerp was, above all, a town of specialists. There were 300 artists practising in the city by 1560 – compared with only 169 bakers and seventy-eight butchers! -- organized in a powerful craft guild with its own sale room, the first organized art market in northern Europe. Antwerp was also famous for its music and specialist musicians. Guicciardini, in his *Description of all the Low Countries* (Antwerp 1567), made special mention of the popular habit of singing in the streets on summer evenings and indeed at most other times as well: 'At all hours one sees weddings, feasting, dancing and recreations. On all street corners one hears the sound of musical instruments, singing and general rejoicing.' The Antwerp magistrates themselves paid five municipal musicians (*Stadsspellieden*) to compose and play music on festive and official occasions. During the trade fairs they played continuously in the great Market Place; for the ceremonial entry of Prince Philip in 1549, on which the Antwerp corporation spent 250,000 florins, there was ceaseless music, some of it composed by one of the *Stadsspellieden*, the music printer Tielman Susato.[4]

Specialists like Plantin and Susato thrived in Antwerp because of its commercial prosperity. Antwerp's trade was large enough to support many wealthy men who could afford the services of professional artists and musicians. The city handled seventy-five per cent of the total trade of the Netherlands: goods from the Baltic, Germany and England were exchanged for commodities from Spain, Italy, France, Portugal and the Orient. This trade was impressive both in volume and in value. The total exports of the Netherlands were worth around twenty-two million florins (just over two million pounds sterling; at the same time English foreign trade was worth less than half of this). Almost all the exports were textiles; against this, roughly equal quantities of raw materials, industrial goods and (surprisingly) food were imported. The majority of it passed through Antwerp (see figure, p. 28). The city also acted as the clearing house for the commercial and public finance of most of northern Europe, pioneering many financial innovations. The negotiable bill of exchange, endorsement, discounting and bill-broking, all standard techniques of modern finance, were invented by merchants and brokers trading in the Beurs, the new Exchange built in 1531 to house Antwerp's money market. On a single day ten million florins might change hands. There was not only trading, there was also gambling. In 1555 and again in 1559 there was a lottery on the identity of the next pope: the names of the sixty-three cardinals were set up 'upon the Bourse . . . in manner of a lottery, at three crowns

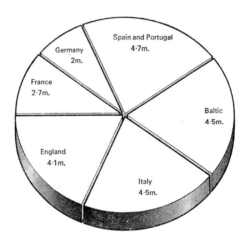

2. The pattern of Anwerp's trade c. 1550
The value and provenance of goods imported are shown in millions of florins.

a head; whoso chances upon him that shall be pope shall win the lot'.
The Antwerp brokers took bets on everything: on the safe return of
ships, on the outbreak of war (or peace) between states, on the death
dates of the great.[5] It was all noted down with respectful wonderment
by the visitors from Spain before they moved on to the provinces
farther north.

First the royal party went to Zealand, where they made a brief
boat trip to marvel at the massive sea-dikes and to view the church
spires of some of the twenty villages 'drowned' in the terrible floods
of St Elizabeth's Day, 1421. The menacing presence of the sea became
increasingly obtrusive as the royal progress continued. Everywhere
the prince could see the evidence of the rising water level of the North
Sea which periodically burst through the sea defences to widen estuaries
and flood coastal plains: the Zuider Zee, inundated in 1287, the 'Braak-
man' of north Flanders (1404), the Biesbos of south Holland (1424),
the Dollard estuary by Groningen (1509). In 1570 the sea was to re-
claim the newly drained Zijpe estuary of north Holland and flood parts
of Flanders and Friesland. Besides the sea, there were lakes. Holland
in particular was full of them, ranging in size from a few acres to the
enormous Harlemmermeer (about 17,000 acres by 1550) and the even
larger Purmer-Beemster-Schermer complex north of Amsterdam. Even

the province's dry land was made up mostly of 'polders' (drained lakes) and land recovered from the sand dunes during the Middle Ages. The activities and settlements of the people of Holland and Zealand had been profoundly affected by the sea. There were relatively few villages in the provinces, but a large number of towns: about half of Holland's population inhabited towns, some of them working in the textile factories of Haarlem and Leiden, others manning the 700 fishing boats and 1,400 carrying-ships of Holland's enormous merchant fleet. The rest worked on the land, but not to till the earth: Holland's fields were famous for their cattle. According to Guicciardini, the largest sheep and cows in the world were raised in Holland and Friesland, supplying meat, milk and cheese for export. Recent research has confirmed this observation: the normal size of a live cow in the sixteenth century appears to have been under 1,000 lbs; the average Friesian weighed 1,600 lbs, and one beast weighed a magnificent 2,528 (but, it must be admitted, this was so remarkable even for a Friesian that its proud owner commissioned a life-size portrait). Likewise the average milk yield of a cow in the sixteenth century was around 700 litres a year, but some Friesians produced 1,300 litres.

The Grand Tour of the future Philip II, which had included almost all the 'sights' recommended by later visitors to the Netherlands, ended with a rapid progress through the declining cities of the eastern provinces – Zwolle, Deventer, Zutphen, Arnhem and Nijmegen – their trade and industrial output all but eclipsed by Flanders and Brabant. In a last foray in the spring of 1550, Prince Philip saw Limburg and the sparsely populated flat lands of north Brabant known as the 'Campine' or 'Kempen'. In six months of intensive travelling the prince had seen the entire Netherlands and their people, with the exception of the remote provinces of the north-east. He had met the principal nobles and stayed in their stately homes. And he had been sworn in as heir apparent to every province of the Low Countries ruled by his father. The Grand Tour had in fact been an exercise in public relations, a piece of careful propaganda designed to stress the solidarity of the Habsburg Netherlands, their political stability and their enthusiasm for the ruling dynasty. Alas, as Prince Philip was soon to discover, the carefully engineered impressions of unity and harmony which he received in his visit were sadly misleading. The Low Countries were politically fragmented, highly volatile and, even in 1549, somewhat restless under Habsburg rule.[6]

The seeds of discontent (1549–59)

It is important to remember that the provinces visited by Philip II in 1549 had only been welded into a single political unit the previous year. On 26 June 1548 Charles V persuaded the Diet of the Holy Roman Empire, assembled at Augsburg, to permit him to make all his Netherlands provinces – which formed part of the Empire – into a separate administrative unit. Although they continued to pay taxes and send troops to the Holy Roman Emperor in emergencies, the 'Augsburg Transaction' freed the Netherlands from imperial legislation and jurisdiction. The provinces ruled by Charles V – sometimes known as the *pays de par deçà*, sometimes as 'the seventeen provinces' – became virtually independent and autonomous, only nominally within the empire. In November 1549 Charles V consolidated this separation by persuading the States (the representative assembly) of each province to ratify a document known as the 'Pragmatic Sanction', which ensured that, after the emperor's death, all the provinces would continue to obey the same ruler and the same central institutions. Prince Philip, following his Grand Tour, was solemnly accepted by the States as heir apparent.

These constitutional events marked the consummation of many years of patient endeavour by Charles V and his servants. The emperor had inherited from his father, Philip I, only the hereditary estates of the duke of Burgundy: apart from Franche-Comté, these were Mechelen and Flanders (acquired by the House of Burgundy in 1384), Namur (1421), Hainaut, Holland and Zealand (all acquired in 1428), Brabant and part of Limburg (1430) and Luxemburg (1451). To this core of hereditary lands Charles V added by conquest the city-states of Tournai in 1521 and Cambrai in 1543 and he conducted a relentless and eventually successful struggle with the duke of Gelre for control of the lands north of the river Rhine. Underpopulated and fairly poor, the lands of the north-east Netherlands had never been effectively governed. They formed, in a sense, a political vacuum. Friesland was annexed in 1523–4; Utrecht and Overijssel in 1528; Groningen, the Ommelanden and Drenthe in 1536; finally Gelderland itself in 1543.

The predominance of the Dutch language even in the Habsburg Netherlands is here apparent; Walloon, Frisian, 'Oosters' and Low German were all minority languages. The Dutch-language area also contained the majority of the large towns of the Low Countries. The total of 'seventeen' provinces was only arrived at by omitting Cambrai (which remained part of the Holy Roman Empire until 1678) and by combining Groningen with the Ommelanden and Drenthe with Overijssel.

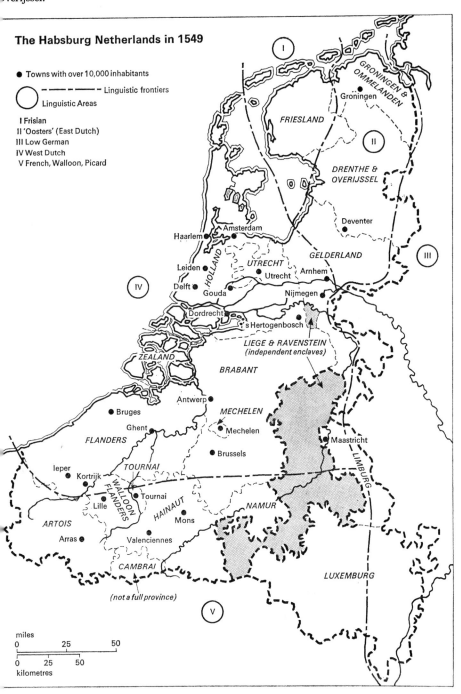

The Habsburg Netherlands in 1549

● Towns with over 10,000 inhabitants

--- ------- Linguistic frontiers

◯ Linguistic Areas

I Frisian
II 'Oosters' (East Dutch)
III Low German
IV West Dutch
V French, Walloon, Picard

GRONINGEN & OMMELANDEN
Groningen

FRIESLAND

DRENTHE & OVERIJSSEL

Deventer

Haarlem
Amsterdam
Leiden
UTRECHT
HOLLAND
Delft
Utrecht
Arnhem
GELDERLAND
Gouda
Nijmegen
Dordrecht
's Hertogenbosch
LIEGE & RAVENSTEIN
(independent enclaves)
ZEALAND
BRABANT
Antwerp
MECHELEN
Bruges
Ghent
Mechelen
FLANDERS
Brussels
Maastricht
Ieper
Kortrijk
TOURNAI
WALLOON FLANDERS
Lille
Tournai
HAINAUT
NAMUR
LIMBURG
ARTOIS
Mons
Arras
Valenciennes
CAMBRAI
LUXEMBURG
(not a full province)

miles
0   25   50

0   25   50
kilometres

Upon this ill-assorted collection of provinces, many of them with a long history of mutual hostility, the Habsburgs imposed a measure of cohesion. There was to begin with dynastic union – all provinces owed obedience to Charles V, albeit under different titles – and there was a considerable measure of geographical compactness. However, the large principality of Liège and one or two imperial enclaves in Gelderland remained entirely free of Habsburg rule, and there were one or two lesser anomalies: thus in Brabant there was the sovereign lordship of Aerschot which had its own representative assembly and an independent ruler (the duke) who only did fealty to the duke of Brabant through choice. The province of Cambrai remained a part of the empire and subject to imperial jurisdiction until 1678. In Gelderland and Limburg there were many prominent landholders, the *vrijheeren*, who claimed to be direct vassals of the Holy Roman Empire like the Imperial Knights of Germany. On the whole, however, they – like the rest of the inhabitants of the Netherlands – obeyed the orders of the Brussels government (a representative of the sovereign advised by a council of state for high policy, a council of finance for fiscal affairs and a privy council for justice) and respected the judgements of its law-courts (a 'council' in each province and a 'great council', or supreme court, at Mechelen).

Scrutinizing the orders and judgements of these government agencies were the 'States' (États or Staten). Every province of the Netherlands and even some smaller areas had a representative assembly of their own, most of them dating back to the thirteenth century. The States normally included delegates from the clergy, the nobility and the leading towns, but these were rarely democratically chosen. In some provinces one of the three orders was not represented at all (the States of Holland had no clergy and only one representative of the nobles; the States of Flanders were reduced to delegates from Bruges, Ghent, Ieper and the 'Brugse Vrij', the rural area between Bruges and the Scheldt), and even where they were, representatives tended to be drawn from the same ecclesiastical institutions, the same noble families and the same towns. Nevertheless the States were powerful: they possessed powers to raise troops and taxes and to pass laws; in some provinces (Flanders for example) these activities could only take place with their consent; and they were the watch-dogs of the constitution, protecting local privileges against erosion. The Burgundian dukes' practice of convening joint meetings of delegates from the States of all the provinces they ruled, a practice which began in the 1420s, did not diminish in any way the powers of the local assemblies. Each provincial delegation to the States-General was strictly bound by instructions issued by their States and they had to refer back before taking any major decision (a practice known as *ruggespraak*). Each provincial delegation also had to reach its decision unanimously for it to be binding, and all the provinces had to give their approval before a motion in the States-General could be put into effect. On the whole the States-General met every three years, mainly to discuss tax demands and there might be several meetings before the necessary unanimity was achieved. In the course of the haggling and debate a certain degree of unity and cooperation grew up among the delegates from the main provinces who habitually attended – perhaps ten clerics, ten nobles and fifty magistrates representing twenty-five major towns formed a hard core of permanent deputies (a figure to be compared with the English Parliament around 1550 with perhaps 100 peers and 400 commoners). Until 1549 attendance was limited to the hereditary provinces of the house of Burgundy, of which nine or ten regularly sent deputations; after 1549 the right to attend the States-General was thrown open to all the provinces united by the 'Augsburg Transaction' of the previous year. In 1555, to witness and ratify the transfer of power from Charles V to his son Philip, over 312 deputies representing eighteen provinces attended the States-General: an impressive witness to the Habsburgs' progress in creating a unified policy in the Netherlands.[7]

Further evidence of unity came from the Netherlanders themselves, who began to speak of their *patrie* or Fatherland, meaning their country, not their town or province. When they went abroad to study or travel, they stuck together, no matter what province they came from, and they regarded the emblems of the dukes of Burgundy – a red St Andrew's cross and a lion holding a sword and a sheaf of seventeen arrows – as their 'national' emblems. Foreigners regarded them as a collective entity: the study of the Italian merchant Lodovico Guicciardini, *A description of all the Low Countries*, first published in 1567, proclaimed their unity and corporate status.[8]

A sort of 'United Netherlands' was thus created by 1550, for the first time. In normal circumstances the empire-building of the

2

Habsburgs might have formed the basis for a permanent political unit, much as the Swiss *Eidgenossenschaft* of 1291 or the Spanish Union of Crowns of 1479 had done. But the sixteenth century was not a normal time, and the Low Countries, as noted above, were not normal provinces. Coupled with their economic strength and their enormous population were strong local institutions and traditions, different fiscal and legal systems, even separate languages. There were comprehensive customs barriers between some of the provinces; it was possible to escape judicial proceedings just by crossing the frontier between one province and the next; even within a province offences and penalties differed according to the customs of the place in which they were tried – the province of Artois alone had 248 separate legal codes and there were about 700 different codes in the whole Netherlands. In Brabant there was a law that no one might hold public office unless he were a native (or a Knight of the Golden Fleece, a highly exclusive group rather like the Knights of the Garter in England). Holland retaliated by forbidding the employment of Brabanders in offices in the province. Local laws like these, 'liberties' or 'privileges' as they were called, might seem unreasonable and unnecessary today, but in early modern times they were the life-blood of politics. 'Whoever touches the privileges' wrote the royalist, Maximilian Morillon, 'cuts to the quick'.[9] In a society where government was irresponsible, without restraints, where the subject had no real protection against abusive or arbitrary exercise of power, the existence of guaranteed privileges, however illogical, was of vital importance. They were worth fighting for and rebellion in defence of the privileges was, as the Habsburgs came to realize, nothing new in the Netherlands. Don Luis de Requesens, governor-general of the Low Countries from 1573 to 1576, was discouraged to find that 'in the history books we read that there have been thirty-five revolts against the natural prince, and after each of them the people remained far more insolent than before'.[10] The fourteenth and fifteenth centuries had been punctuated by revolts of the great towns of Flanders, Brabant, Holland and Zealand against their rulers, each rising commemorated by a charter of liberties and rights extorted from the 'sovereign' (like the 'Joyous Entry' of Brabant first granted in 1356 and accepted on oath by every ruler at his accession). In the sixteenth century revolts were also common. Brussels and 's Hertogenbosch publicly defied the government in 1523–5; Ghent staged an open rebellion in 1539–40 (which, for once, was firmly crushed – the city lost all its privileges); there was serious rioting at Antwerp in July 1554. The provinces of the north-east annexed by Charles V also had turbulent histories. Friesland had never been sub-jected to an overlord before 1498 and thereafter spent seventeen years opposing the attempts of the dukes of Saxony (Charles V's predecessors in the province) to exercise any part of their 'sovereign powers'. Gelderland only accepted Habsburg rule in return for solemn guarantees that local laws and liberties would be preserved intact (the Treaty of Venlo, 12 September 1543).

The 'new provinces', like Gelderland, annexed by Charles V pre-sented the central government with special problems. They were further away from Brussels and, unlike the equally distant provinces of the north-west, they did not have any experience of union with the south (Holland and Zealand had been united with Hainaut since 1299). Friesland had never been united at all until 1498. The recent wars had also left a legacy of feud, bitterness and hatred: Gelre might have lost the struggle for the north-east, but it left behind it numerous partisans who never entirely accepted the necessity for Habsburg rule. Even those who had opposed Charles of Gelre, such as the families of Culemborg, Batenburg and van den Berg, always remained restless under Habsburg rule. All the former Gelre territories eventually renounced their allegiance to Philip II; all but southern Gelderland retained their independence.

Reinforcing these divisive influences was the potent badge of linguistic individuality. The sixteenth century saw the use of language as a political tool. Sebastian Munster, the noted geographer, wrote in his *Cosmography* of 1552: 'Formerly regions were bounded by mountains and rivers . . . but today languages and lordships mark the limits of one region from the next, and the limits of a region are the limits of its language.' There were only two languages in the hereditary provinces of the Netherlands: French and Dutch (or dialects based on them: Walloon and Picard, east and west Flemish, 'Hollands' and so on) and the Brussels government carried on its administrative tasks in both languages. In the east, however, there were the areas colonized by the Saxons in the Middle Ages where Low German was spoken and written. In the north, in Friesland, virtually isolated by bogs and heaths and water, Fries was spoken. And in between Fries and German there was a large area where 'Oosters' or East Dutch (as distinct from the West Dutch, parent of modern Dutch, used in the west Netherlands) was spoken. In the sixteenth century 'Oosters' was still a language apart, like Lowland Scots or Provençal, and it was written (even printed) as well as spoken. The influential religious writings of Menno Simons, Andreas Veluanus and Hendrik Niclaes were heavily impregnated with eastern dialect and later some books were printed entirely in Oosters, such as the *Over-Ysselsche Sangen en Dichten* (*Songs and Poems of Overijssel*, 1630) and the *Over-Ysselsche Boere-Vryagie* (*The Overijssel Peasants' Courtship*, 1641). Although it was more developed, with its first dictionary and first grammar published in 1553, West Dutch did not triumph totally for a long time and the linguistic diversity of the Low Countries in the sixteenth century was a real aid to particularist feeling (see map, p. 31).[11]

Particularism and language were but two of the problems facing the enlarged Habsburg Netherlands. Another equally serious challenge to unity was the rise of Protestantism. The sixteenth century was a time of religious ferment, and it started early in the Netherlands: Lutheranism was condemned by government edict in October 1520, a year before Luther's confrontation with the emperor at Worms, but even so about eighty books by Luther were found, and burnt at Leuven the same year. In 1522 Charles V set up a state-run inquisition to supplement the efforts of the long-established episcopal inquisition and in 1523 the first Protestant martyr in the world was burnt at Antwerp. Despite these efforts, and despite repeated book-burnings and perhaps thirty burnings of heretics, by 1530 at least thirty works by Luther had appeared in Dutch translation (compared with three in England) and there were fifteen complete or partial versions of Luther's Bible in Dutch. By 1525 already 'Luther had become a household name in the Netherlands'.[12] Before long other 'heretics' were also familiar. First came the Anabaptists, who gained ground in Holland, Flanders and Friesland; then came the disciples of Martin Bucer, the Strasburg Reformer, and of Heinrich Bullinger, Zwingli's successor at Zurich; finally there were other influential religious figures who did not belong to any of these 'main-stream' creeds – Joris Cassander (born at Bruges, who preached the need to reconcile all the Christian churches), David Joris (who claimed to be the 'Third David' a new Messiah) and Hendrik Niclaes (founder of the spiritualist 'Family of Love'). The works of all of them were published in French, Flemish or Oosters by the numerous printers of the Netherlands and elsewhere.

The first four decades of the Reformation have aptly been described as a period of 'magnificent anarchy'. The dogma of the various churches had not yet been defined; the frontiers of the different creeds had not yet been fixed. There were only a few beliefs shared by all – rejection of the Mass, of the role of the priest; insistence on the need for individual Bible study and for Biblical justification for church organization – and the government revealed its general confusion about the nature of heresy by referring to those suspected of heterodox views indiscriminately as 'sectaries', 'Lutherans' and 'Anabaptists'. The government was certain enough to sentence people to death for religious deviation, however: during the reign of Charles V at least 2,000 Netherlanders were executed for their beliefs, probably two thirds of them Anabaptists, and a larger number were punished by fines, confiscations or banishment. Persecution was particularly intense in 1536–8 (as a reaction to the Anabaptist 'Kingdom of Münster' which involved many Netherlanders) and in 1544–5 (following the conclusion of peace with France and the arrest of a personal emissary from Bucer and Calvin, Pierre Brully, at Tournai). As the figure on p. 63 below shows, however, there was a constant stream of accusations, trials and condemnations. There is a clear impression that from 1544 until about 1554 the heretics were losing ground in the Netherlands. Although the great cities like Antwerp or Ghent, the marshy wastes of Friesland, or the handful of semi-independent *vrijheeren* estates in the eastern provinces still offered some shelter to heretics, on the whole Charles V's edicts against the Protestant movement were enforced and its leaders were either dead or driven into exile. By the time of the emperor's abdication heresy was a Netherlands problem which was well on the way to being solved.

The only outstanding problem which Philip II inherited from his father in the Low Countries was financial. Charles V had been a warrior king and the cost had been enormous: wars with Gelre sporadically from 1515 until 1543, war with France (fought in Italy and the Netherlands) 1521–9, 1536–7 and 1542–4, war with the Turks 1521–38 and 1541–7, war with the German Protestants 1546–7. Then in 1551 war began again when France, allied this time with the German Protestants and the Turks, attacked Charles V. With the exception of the brief Truce of Vaucelles (February–July 1556) the conflict lasted until April

1559. The Netherlands paid dearly. Apart from the direct damage inflicted by the armies of France and Gelre, there was a mounting burden of taxation. In the small village of Boussoit-sur-Haine (Hainaut) taxes of nine florins were levied in the fiscal year 1463–4; they grew in steady instalments to 116 florins in the fiscal year 1534–5 – a twelvefold increase. In the 1460s central taxation absorbed one third of the communal budget; by the 1520s it absorbed one half; and by the 1530s it absorbed two thirds. Yet even tax increases on this scale were not enough to pay for Charles V's wars: in 1545, theoretically a year of peace, the revenue of the central treasury was 300,000 florins but its expenditure exceeded 1,000,000. To bridge this gap, the emperor borrowed furiously on the Antwerp money market, paying up to 30 per cent interest in return for money to pay his army. The government's short-term debt, which totalled two million florins in 1544, rose to five million in 1553 and seven million in 1556.[13]

Not unnaturally, this persistent and heavy expenditure by the government provoked considerable ill-feeling among the taxpayers. The resistance of Brussels and 's Hertogenbosch in the 1520s and of Ghent in the 1530s had centred around their unwillingness to pay for a war which they did not feel was in their own interests. In the 1550s this unrest came to a head when the Netherlands were asked to pay larger sums than ever for a war fought expressly to defend Spanish Milan and Naples from the French. Although in fact Spain sent large quantities of money to the Low Countries to pay for the war – twenty-two million florins between 1551 and July 1556 alone – the Netherlanders became firmly convinced that they were subsidizing Spain. In November 1556 the governor-general of the Low Countries, Emanuel Philibert of Savoy, warned Philip II of 'the impression held by the subjects of these provinces that the late wars were fought mainly for Naples, Milan and Navarre, although the Low Countries have borne the principal burden'. Although the king immediately produced detailed figures of the money paid out by Spain to demonstrate that this assertion was untrue, the impression of the Netherlands taxpayers remained unchanged. In August 1557, just before the victory of St Quentin, the acting governor-general, Count Lalaing, wrote: 'We would not be at this last extremity if the kingdoms of Spain, for whom this war is also being fought, had paid in proportion only the half of what we have paid.'[14]

With such deeply ingrained misconceptions among even senior ministers, it is small wonder that the less well-informed representatives of the taxpayers, summoned to the States-General in March 1556, should be equally convinced that any money they voted would immediately be shipped off to Spain and Italy. In addition the States were aware of the serious economic situation among the taxpayers: French privateering was affecting trade, the harvest had failed and a mysterious lethal epidemic (probably influenza) was spreading fast. The records of the rich and populous county of Hainaut reveal the extent of the crisis: of 306 villages there was a population loss between 1540 and 1560 in 140 communities. Fields were abandoned, settlements deserted, and as people moved out the wolves moved in: by 1562 even the council of state was called in to take steps to control the 'large number of wolves' in Hainaut. It was doubtless much the same elsewhere.[15] In this situation there was determined opposition to any suggestion of new taxes, and it was led by the States of Brabant and especially by the deputies from the town of Brussels. According to a charter of 1421 the nine principal craft guilds of the city each elected two of their members to form a committee of eighteen, and 'The Eighteen' became a powerful voice in city government, especially on matters of taxation. Without the consent of 'The Eighteen', Brussels could not agree to the new taxes demanded by the government; and without Brussels the States of Brabant were paralysed. The ability of these eighteen artisans to sabotage his plans irritated Philip II. He felt that his regal dignity had been slighted and he soon displayed that impatience and insensitivity towards these, his first Netherlands opponents, that he would later display against critics in the 1560s. He tried to get the 1421 charter revoked. This was totally unconstitutional – it was blatantly against the 'Joyous Entry' – and it failed. In the end (July 1557) the States agreed to the taxes but only in return for a promise from the government that they themselves would supervise the collection and distribution of all the money voted (to make sure none of it was sent abroad). No sooner had this undignified wrangle ended than another began. Charles V had borrowed money as heavily in Spain as in Antwerp: the Spanish government's short-term debt in 1556 stood at 7,000,000 ducats (14,000,000 florins), seven times the crown's annual revenue. There was no way of repaying this sum, and the interest payments absorbed almost all available revenues. Therefore on 10 June

1557 Philip II took the only possible way out: he decreed that no money, neither interest nor capital, was to be repaid to his creditors until further notice; he ordered all crown revenues to be paid direct to the central treasury and he ordered all the treasure aboard the Indies fleet to be seized at Seville and sent to the Netherlands. Unfortunately for him, by the time his orders arrived at Seville the Indies treasure was already ashore and in the pockets of its owners. There was no money to send to the Netherlands.

The States-General therefore had to be reconvened on 3 August 1557 and asked to provide more money. For the first time the delegates of the various provinces began to act in unison. Warmed by the success of Brabant in 1556–7, the other provinces also began to insist that they should control the taxes to be voted. In November they proposed an *aide* of 7,200,000 florins, an enormous sum, to be spread over nine years; they also agreed that 2,400,000 of this sum should be provided immediately, as a loan to be repaid from the yield of the *aide* in future years; but they demanded absolute control over all the funds raised. This proposal was bitterly resisted by the government, which correctly foresaw that the States would thus gain the power of withholding their money if their grievances were not redressed. But, with a war to win, there was no alternative. In January 1559 the 'Nine Years' Aid' was voted and a standing committee of the States-General was set up to coordinate collection and distribution of the money; the committee was chaired by the Antwerp banker and magistrate, Antoon van Stralen, a friend (and probably the creditor) of many prominent noblemen.

Although the price had been high, the government made good use of the money voted by the States-General. The French were routed at Gravelines (13 July 1558) and military pressure was maintained until October 1558 when a ceasefire was signed. Negotiations began and on 3 April 1559 a definitive peace was made at Cateau-Cambrésis on the Franco–Netherlands frontier. The settlement gave Philip II almost all he could have hoped for: he kept most of his conquests and his predominant position in Italy was recognized. 'Truly', wrote Cardinal Granvelle, 'these peace negotiations have been directed by God himself because, although we have settled things so much to our own advantage, the French are delighted with it.'[16] The costly wars were over at last. Philip II now had the chance to win the hearts of his Netherlands subjects amid the euphoria which followed the peace.

The erosion of royal power 1559–64

Charles V left his son to face difficult problems when he abdicated in 1555–6, but he had also taken care to see that his son was well equipped to cope. Philip II in 1559 was already an experienced ruler: he was better prepared for the responsibilities of kingship than almost any other monarch of the sixteenth century. Born in 1527, he had been regent of Spain from 1543 until 1548 and from 1551 until 1554, when he took over the government of Italy and became king of England. When he replaced his father as ruler of the Netherlands in 1555 he already knew the country well from first-hand experience and he knew its political leaders. But Philip also had his faults, and they too were the fruits of his long apprenticeship: his deep sense of responsibility and his almost pathological anxiety to do the right thing made him slow to make up his own mind and resentful of those who tried to make it up for him. Time and again a vital decision was postponed, sometimes for weeks, because the king could not bring himself to embrace any of the limited number of possibilities open to him. His actions in 1559 were a case in point. Philip II was well qualified to face and solve the problems besetting the Netherlands, but he chose not to solve them at once. Instead, as soon as he had arranged peace with France, he strained every nerve to get back to Spain at the earliest opportunity.

Spain was the centre of the Habsburg monarchy. As early as 1543 Charles V had admitted that 'I cannot be sustained except by my kingdoms of Spain', and it became even more true in the last years of his reign: Spain, and especially Castile (which made up three quarters of the whole), provided the Habsburgs with the men and the money necessary to carry out their imperial policies. It was Spanish troops who drove back the Turks in Hungary in 1532 and at Tunis in 1535; it was Spanish troops again who defeated the German Protestants at Mühlberg in 1547 and the French at St Quentin in 1557. Castilian soldiers defended Spanish Italy and Castilian administrators governed it. Spain's money was even more important. Charles V had won his wars not only by having better soldiers than his adversaries but by having more of them. In 1552 he had had 150,000 men mobilized; they all required paying and their wages came overwhelmingly from the taxpayers of Castile. It was therefore of critical importance that Castile remained peaceful and law-abiding. Any unrest or disturbance might interupt the flow of taxation and therefore disrupt imperial finance. The situation was already delicate: the government was living to a dangerous degree on borrowed time, since future revenues had been sold up to 1561 in order to raise cash loans. Attempts were made to raise new taxes, but in 1558 both the Cortes (representing the lay taxpayers) and the Church Assembly (representing the clergy) refused to vote more money. The nobles, exempt from taxation, gathered together in order to wrest more privileges from their absentee ruler. There were riots in the province of Aragon and the provincial estates, the Cortes, met illegally to resolve the crisis. Then in 1558 Protestant cells were discovered in Valladolid and Seville, one of them centred on the king's own chaplain, Dr Constantino de la Fuente, who had been with him on his tour of Germany and the Netherlands in 1548–51. There was a risk that the royal household was infected with heresy. These developments were dangerous, but by themselves they were not disastrous. There was no open opposition, and although a current of discontent and disaffection was clearly visible, by itself it would probably not have brought Philip II home so soon.

There were pressing reasons for the king to remain in the north. The Netherlands were restless after the long wars, and the death of Henry II of France in July brought with it the risk that his successor, Francis II, a boy of fifteen dominated by the belligerent duke of Guise, would repudiate the recent peace so unfavourable to France. There was also the 'British question'. Spain needed to maintain an interest and an influence in England, where Queen Elizabeth (only six months on her throne) was moving rapidly towards a Protestant stance which might lead to a papal bull ordering her deposition in favour of the Catholic Mary Stuart, her next of kin. Mary, married to Francis II and therefore queen of France as well as queen of Scotland, already had a French army deployed around Edinburgh. In view of this tense situation, soon to be further complicated by the revolt of the Scottish Protestants against Mary and the French, Philip II's advisers feared that the king's departure for Spain would mean the neglect of 'developments which could do irreparable damage to His Majesty and his successors. It cannot be a good thing for him to leave the Netherlands with English affairs as they are at present and the relations with France not settled. I am not sure that the needs of Spain are such that they are greater than ours.'[17] It was not, however, merely domestic difficulties which drew the king back to Spain in 1559. There was also a serious problem of defence: war had broken out again in the Mediterranean.

The war which began with the Ottoman sultan in 1551 had gone badly for Spain. Tripoli fell almost as soon as hostilities commenced, and Bougie followed in 1555. In 1558 a Spanish army was badly mauled outside Oran. Negotiations for a ceasefire were started by Philip II at the end of 1558, at the same time as the talks with the French, but on 8 April, six days after the Peace of Cateau-Cambrésis, it was all called off. 'Peace has just been concluded with the king of France', Philip II informed his ministers, 'which leads one to suppose that the Turks, deprived of assistance and lacking any port in the West Mediterranean to accommodate their fleet, will not send it against Christendom.' The king had been persuaded by the Knights of Malta to mount an expedition to recover the town of Tripoli, and by June 1559 he was issuing detailed orders and instructions from Brussels.[18] The king wished for a swift surprise attack by a small expeditionary force but, 1,500 miles from the theatre of operations – letters took over four weeks to reach the field commanders – he could not impose his will. The men on the spot wished to send a larger force against Tripoli, in order to be sure of success, but they failed to realize how long such an army would take to assemble. As delay followed delay, it became clear that only the presence of the king could ensure that his orders were carried out and possible disaster averted. Preparations for the royal departure from the Netherlands were therefore expedited. Philip left Brussels for the last time on 5 July 1559; he embarked at Flushing on 24 August and landed in Spain on 8 September.

As soon as he reached his motherland, and could see for himself, the king realized that the state of his monarchy was far worse than he had imagined. The crisis of authority in Spain had proceeded further than he had supposed and his financial resources were all squandered. The king realized that many of his orders had displayed total ignorance of the true situation and that he had become a laughing-stock to his advisers. 'I have to admit'. he confided in December, 'that I never thought while I was in the Netherlands that things could be so bad here' in Spain.[19]

Before long, things were even worse because in the spring of 1560 the Tripoli expedition was ambushed *en route*: twenty-seven galleys and 10,000 men fell into the hands of the Turks. These included Spain's most seasoned veterans, men who were accustomed to galley warfare, men who could not be swiftly replaced like the galleys (new ones were in service within a year). The veterans lost before Tripoli represented a whole military generation which would take years to replace. It was a disaster of the first magnitude: the western Mediterranean was denuded and at any moment the Ottoman fleet, vastly superior to anything the Christian powers could muster, might violate the coast of Spain. The king's presence on the scene was indispensable; he could not afford to leave the peninsula until the Turkish menace had passed. Philip II made complex administrative arrangements for his absence. His half-sister Margaret of Parma, six years his elder and born in the Netherlands of a casual liaison between Charles V and a servant, was appointed regent and governess-general. She was to be advised by the council of state (on foreign and domestic policy), the council of finance (for money matters) and the privy council (on judicial matters), three bodies created in 1531 and manned by experienced ministers, foremost amongst them Antoine Perrenot, bishop of Arras and later Cardinal Granvelle, who possessed a long experience and an impressive competence in public affairs.

Nevertheless these appointments were not entirely happy ones. Margaret of Parma had no practical experience of government and had spent most of her life since 1535 in Italy. Somewhat timid by nature, she proved unable to cope with any serious challenge to her authority. Anxious not to offend the king, at first she played down the extent of the discontent and unrest in the Netherlands, lulling Philip II into a false sense of security; then, after April 1566 when the collapse of royal power could no longer be disguised, she exaggerated the danger and provoked the king to overreact. Yet Margaret had not been expected to cope with such problems. Philip had intended her to serve as his puppet: all executive power was retained by him, even though he was in Spain. On his departure in August 1559 he gave Margaret a list of candidates who were to be appointed in strict order of seniority to ecclesiastical benefices as and when they fell vacant;

he also instructed his sister to write and inform him of every matter of note and to take no decision without consulting him first. To ensure that these orders were carried out, Antoine Perrenot was given a special position of trust in the Brussels government, maintaining a direct correspondence with the king and conveying the royal intentions to his colleagues.

Perrenot, however, was far from perfect. Born at Besançon in 1517 (and thus ten years older than the king), Perrenot was the son of Charles V's leading councillor and grew up at Court. There the future Cardinal Granvelle made many enemies through his favour with the emperor, through his somewhat domineering manner (particularly galling in one so young) and through his extensive use of government patronage to advance and favour the financial interests of his family and friends. Alongside these old enemies at the king's Court, of whom the leader was Francisco de Erasso, secretary of the Spanish Council of Finance, Perrenot was soon to make new ones in Brussels. The Netherlands politicians, who had played an important role during the war against France and during the king's residence in the Low Countries were distressed to find that after his departure their voice carried no weight. It was evident that all decisions were being taken in secret by Margaret, Perrenot and the king.

There was nothing new in this government by remote control. Charles V, who had only spent ten years in the Netherlands after he became king of Spain in 1516, never slackened his grip when he left the country of his birth for Germany, Italy or Spain. However, the situation in the 1560s was less susceptible to outside control than in the emperor's day. First, although Charles V had moved around a great deal in his earlier years, he had resided in the Netherlands from 1547 until his abdication with only one short break; Philip II was likewise in Brussels from 1555 until 1559 with only one small gap. The Netherlands had become accustomed to the personal presence of their 'natural prince'. Second, in spite of the fact that he was going away, Philip II was determined to make certain changes in the govern-ment of the Low Countries, and he left a corps of trustworthy Spanish officials – secretaries, financial experts, political and religious advisers – behind him to ensure that his plans were put into effect. The 'advisers' were carefully placed. Margaret of Parma was given a confidential secretary, Tomás de Armenteros (after 1564 assisted by his brother

Alonso), who was the cousin of Philip II's own secretary of state, Gonzalo Pérez; two members of the king's household, Alonso del Canto and Cristóbal de Castellanos, were left in Antwerp to handle royal funds and keep an eye on heretics, particularly Spanish ones, in the city. The French ambassador was only exaggerating slightly when he described Margaret as 'surrounded by Spanish minds, which are hated here to the death . . . nothing here is well said, well done or well considered unless it comes in Spanish and from a Spaniard'.[20]

The king also intended to leave 3,000 Spanish veterans behind to garrison the strategic towns of the southern frontier in case of attack by France. To the king this might seem an eminently reasonable step, but everyone in the Netherlands knew that 3,000 Spaniards were enough to enforce Spanish control in Lombardy, Naples and Sicily. One of the great fears of the Netherlanders during this period was that their country would be reduced to the status of a Spanish colony. As Perrenot put it some years later: 'People here universally display discontent with any and all Spaniards in these provinces. It would seem that this derives from their suspicion that one might wish to subject them to Spain and reduce them to the same condition as the Italian provinces which are under the Spanish crown.'[21] The presence of the Spanish garrisons after the king's departure therefore became an issue charged with very great political significance. The States of the provinces, which now had control of the money voted under the Nine Years' Aid, refused to release any funds until the Spaniards were repatriated. The king naturally resisted this sort of blackmail: the political troubles in France, England and Scotland made the presence of a dependable Spanish regiment in the Netherlands highly desirable. However the States were adamant and, without any funds to pay their wages, the troops became mutinous and the civilians among whom they lived became restless. The Spaniards embarked in Zealand on 10 January 1561 and went straight to the Mediterranean where they took the place of some of the men lost on the Tripoli expedition of the year before. It was a major victory for the Netherlands politicians, the significance of which was apparent to all. Philip II's secretary of state was appalled: 'I will say nothing about the departure of the Spaniards, so necessary or rather so obligatory', he told Perrenot, but he hoped that 'God will maintain our affairs in such a way that we shall not some day regret it. But as the saying goes: out of the frying pan into the fire.' Perrenot was less sanguine: 'There will be trouble here sooner or later on some other pretext,' he warned the king as the Spaniards prepared to leave.[22] His forecast soon proved true. The States began to attack the government on a new issue in 1561: the 'new bishoprics' scheme.

In the 1550s there were still only four bishoprics in the entire Habsburg Netherlands, an area with a population of 3,000,000. For some years this situation had caused concern in government circles. Several remedies were proposed during the reign of Charles V, but only in May 1559 was agreement reached between pope and king on a scheme which would create fourteen new bishoprics. All the Netherlands would be under the ecclesiastical control of the new archbishop of Mechelen, who would become primate of the Low Countries, and the jurisdiction of all other sees outside the Netherlands – Cologne and Rheims, for example – would be excluded.[23] A joint royal-papal committee of five was set up in secret to decide the practical details of the scheme, and by March 1561 the boundaries of the new dioceses had been drawn (they followed linguistic not political frontiers) and a method of financing them had been worked out. Instead of levying a tax on all church revenues for the new bishops, it was proposed to unite ten of the new bishoprics with abbeys in the vicinity, allowing the bishop to become abbot *in commendam* and pocket the abbot's revenues. Thus the archbishopric of Mechelen, which was to be incorporated with the great Brabant abbey of Afflighem, would receive the abbot's revenues of 90,000 florins. There were certain other innovations in the 'new bishoprics' project. Most notable was the proposal that two canons of each new episcopal chapter were to serve as inquisitors in their diocese. There was violent opposition to this measure from the magistrates of Antwerp (Antwerp was to be one of the new sees) on the grounds that the inquisition was contrary to the privileges of Brabant and that, more specifically, so many heretics came to Antwerp to trade that its prosperity would be ruined if a resident inquisition were introduced. The magistrates put up a good case and in 1563, with great reluctance, the king agreed to suspend the appointment of a bishop for Antwerp until his next visit to the Netherlands. The 'privileges' had triumphed again.

Resentment against the 'new bishoprics' scheme was not confined to Antwerp, but elsewhere the opposition was more overtly political, stemming in large part from the secrecy in which the scheme had been hatched. Hardly anyone in the Netherlands knew about it until the first bishops were appointed by papal briefs in March and August 1561, and at the head of the list, as archbishop of Mechelen and abbot-designate of Afflighem in Brabant, was Antoine Perrenot, created at the same time Cardinal Granvelle. The king's principal minister inevitably became the target of some of the animus directed against the ecclesiastical innovations. Resistance to the new bishops was keenest in the provinces annexed by Charles V (where it was feared that the scheme was merely a device for increasing royal control) and in Brabant. There the provincial States had three chambers, of which the senior comprised the deputies of the clergy. Most of the abbots of Brabant sat in this chamber and, by ancient tradition, the abbot of Afflighem acted as the spokesman of the entire clerical order. This was precisely the post to which Granvelle had been appointed: 'the king's man' in the Low Countries was suddenly promoted to a leading role in the States of Brabant, the most powerful in the Netherlands.[24]

This created for the first time a point of focus for several groups of opponents of the regime in the Netherlands. The abbots of Brabant made heroic efforts to alert their colleagues in the provincial assembly to the threat posed by the incorporation clause, and by the end of 1561 they had succeeded: the nobles and the towns were won over to the same cause. This was a remarkable achievement since, throughout the reign of Charles V, there had been conflict between the nobles and the towns of many provinces, mainly about taxation, with the nobles trying to gain exemption, despite the bitter opposition of the towns. The struggle had been particularly intense in Holland and in Brabant. There was also resolute opposition to the appointment of any nobleman to local government office unless he was a native of the province (or a Knight of the Golden Fleece). In 1559 and 1560 the collection of the 'Nine Years' Aid' was paralysed by the wrangling of nobles and towns over privileges and vested interest. After 1561, however, this antipathy moderated and the initiative came from the nobles. There were about 4,000 nobles in the Netherlands in the 1560s, an élite comprising just over 1 per cent of the total population. Inevitably there was a wide spread of wealth, power and ability within the élite, ranging from great nobles like William of Orange at the top (with an income of 150,000 florins from his Netherlands estates and probably

as much again from his public offices and from his sovereign principality
of Orange) down to minor gentry like the Marnix brothers, John and
Philip, whose small estates in the south Netherlands provided only
1,800 florins and 1,400 florins respectively per year. Most noblemen
of limited means like this lived either in the towns, participating in
trade or industry, or in the household of some greater lord. In between
Orange and the Marnix brothers came the marquises, counts and barons
of the various provinces, some with extensive territorial rights, rents
and jurisdictions, others with scarcely more than their titles. Although
there was some tension between the great and the small, on the whole
there was a strong homogeneity and cohesion among the nobles of the
Netherlands, based upon inter-marriage, government service and
patronage. A surprisingly large number of noblemen in the hereditary
Burgundian provinces belonged to the houses of Croy, Lalaing or Ligne;
many more were related to them (see the genealogical tables pp.271–3).
In the eastern lands the houses of Egmont, van der Mark and Batenburg
were prominent and were proud of their power and ancient lineage
(so proud that the lords of Batenburg, anxious to convince the world
of the longevity of their line, placed stones around their castle inscribed
with dates such as '127 B.C.' [*sic*]).[25] Family solidarity explains the
political choices made by many noblemen during the crisis of authority
in 1565–6: a man chose the same side as his cousins and brothers.
Often the ties of blood were strengthened by those of gratitude. The
great nobles in particular possessed extensive resources of patronage
either in their own right or in the administration. Orange was provincial governor of Holland, Zealand, Utrecht and, after 1562, of Franche-
Comté. Lamoral, count of Egmont, related to the former dukes of
Gelderland, possessed numerous hereditary clients in the eastern
provinces while in the west, as governor of the provinces of Flanders,
Walloon Flanders and Artois, he could make many appointments to
minor government posts. He was also responsible for supervising the
annual elections of the magistrates in every town within his provinces.
Finally Egmont, like Orange, was the captain of a *bande d'Ordonnance*,
a troop of heavy cavalry made up of noblemen chosen by their leader
and paid (rather poorly) by the state. There were fifteen *bandes*, all
commanded by prominent noblemen, with a total strength of 1,800
men – thus including almost half the total nobility of the Netherlands.
They met regularly, sometimes went on manoeuvres and occasionally

saw active service either as part of an expeditionary force (for instance in France in 1562 and again in 1567) or to enforce an unpopular government order (it is in this role that they appear in the background to Pieter Breughel's *Massacre of the Innocents*, painted in 1565). The *bandes* thus provided a forum where the nobles could exchange ideas and discuss grievances. In the years after 1559 there was plenty of both.

Count Egmont, who had gloriously defeated a French invasion at Gravelines in 1558, was one of the first to announce his unease about the new order which the king proposed to leave in his absence. On 1 July 1559 he complained in particular about the Spanish garrisons and confided to William of Orange: 'I do not believe that people are particularly happy with so many novelties.' Egmont, born in 1523, was ten years older than Orange and at this stage was definitely the dominant figure among the Brussels nobility by virtue of his estates and his military prestige. At first he had no particular grievance against Granvelle, being more interested in pensions and property than in political intrigue and influence. However, the secrecy with which the new bishoprics scheme was announced – unknown even to the members of the Council of State – was a humiliation, and it was rubbed in by Granvelle's appointment as cardinal which at once gave him precedence at council meetings, a precedence formerly held by himself and Orange. Both men were affronted and Orange decided to write a formal letter of protest to the king. He signed it on 23 July 1561 and immediately rode off to Germany leaving Egmont to sign, seal and post the missive. Egmont hesitated. On 27 July he concocted a covering note to his friend, Francisco de Erasso, one of Granvelle's most bitter enemies at the Court of Spain. In it he claimed that Granvelle 'would take no less notice of me if I was not there', but despite his sense of outrage Egmont still did not dare to post the two letters until 15 August.[26]

Egmont's co-signatory, William of Nassau, was born in Germany in 1533, the heir to the small but ancient county of Nassau. In 1544 his whole life was changed by the unexpected inheritance of the vast lands of the house of Orange in Brabant, Luxemburg, Holland and Burgundy as well as the independent principality on the south-eastern borders of France. His sudden elevation to one of the greatest Netherlands landowners secured the young prince a place at the court of Charles V, where he came into contact with the great and was befriended by Antoine Perrenot and his father. After 1559, although ambitious and able, Orange accepted the superiority of Granvelle with a good grace; he could not afford to do otherwise. His father died in 1559 and left debts amounting to almost one million florins, mostly owing to the landgrave of Hesse. At a family conclave in October the same year it was decided that the Nassau family's only escape lay in Orange's marriage with a rich heiress. After some false starts the prince's choice fell upon Anna, niece of the Lutheran Elector, Augustus of Saxony. Her dowry was estimated at 250,000 florins and it was in her favour that her grandfather was the landgrave of Hesse, to whom so much was owed. In February 1560 Orange notified the king of the intended match. The discovery that Anna was the daughter of Maurice of Saxony, the man who had 'betrayed' Charles V in 1551, and granddaughter of the landgrave, an inveterate enemy of the Habsburgs, made Orange's position at court most uncomfortable. The regent, the king and Granvelle did all they could to dissuade Orange and to sabotage his marriage plans; they even had the matter discussed by the Council of State. Orange was humiliated, but he persevered; and in August 1561 he married Anna of Saxony at a glittering ceremony in Dresden, attended by the king of Denmark and many other potentates. He also pocketed the dowry, which gave him a degree of financial independence which he had previously lacked. An English agent in Germany observed that the marriage made Orange a person of international standing at a stroke. This was true enough, but at the same time it ruined his standing at Court: the prince no longer deferred to or trusted Granvelle, and he forfeited the confidence of the king, whose expressed wishes he flouted. The Saxon wedding made him an enemy of Granvelle, and also gave him the funds to make his enmity effective.[27] In December 1561 he received an ally with the arrival in Brussels of Count Hornes.

Philippe de Montmorency, related to the powerful French family of that name (cf. the table on p. 271), was thirty-seven years old in 1561. Since 1549 he had been in constant attendance on Philip II as captain of his personal bodyguard and in 1559 he returned with his sovereign to Spain to be 'superintendent of Netherlands affairs' at Court. Hornes soon discovered, however, that the important decisions were all being taken without him and, after two years, he decided that he had had enough of being a useless ornament in Madrid. In the autumn of 1561 he made himself unpopular with the king by an intemperate attack on the new bishoprics scheme and he was given permission to return home. Immediately he launched into a campaign against Granvelle, whom he blamed for his neglect. On 19 December he complained from Brussels to his friend Erasso at Court: 'The Cardinal is in charge of everything [here] and if things go wrong His Majesty should attribute the blame to him alone.'[28]

It was no accident that Hornes chose to write to Erasso: the powerful secretary had long battled to destroy the influence of Granvelle. During the 1550s he and Ruy Gómez, aided by a Burgundian, Simon Renard (formerly Granvelle's protégé), competed with the duke of Alva and Granvelle for control of the young Philip II. By 1559 Erasso and Ruy Gómez had won: Alva retired from public affairs and Granvelle was left behind in Brussels. However, the Cardinal was able and experienced, and he still had some friends at Court. He might have been able to retain his power and influence but for the extremely delicate international situation in Europe.

In July 1559 the death occurred of Henry II, king of France; he was succeeded by his son Francis II, a sickly and indecisive youth who died in December 1560. This left his brother Charles IX, aged ten, as king, and a regency became necessary. After some animated intrigue and a number of plots, the young king's mother, Catherine de Medici, emerged as regent, but her position as a foreigner and a woman, complicated further by the exhaustion of the French treasury, was weak. In June 1562 civil war broke out between the two great aristocratic families of France, the house of Guise-Lorraine (supported by the Catholic church) and the house of Bourbon (supported by the nascent Protestant church). Philip II promised aid to the French king, who was also (since 1559) his brother-in-law, and he ordered the immediate despatch of 4,000 veterans from Spain and 1,500 troopers from the *bandes d'Ordonnance* of the Netherlands. Margaret of Parma hesitated. If she intervened in France against the Protestants, there was the risk that she might provoke a Huguenot counter-attack which she had neither the men nor the money to repel. Trapped between the commands of the king and the safety of the Netherlands, Margaret summoned a meeting of all the Netherlands noblemen who belonged to the exclusive Order of the Golden Fleece; they were to come to Brussels on 26 May and give their opinion on the French situation. The meeting took several days and it provided for the first time a forum for the prince of Orange to sound out his peers on the current state of the Netherlands. He called them all to his house and tried to forge a common anti-Granvelle policy. In this he failed, but he did persuade the government not to send troops into France – instead Charles IX was to receive 100,000 florins – and it was agreed to send Hornes's brother Floris, baron of Montigny, to Spain in order (among other things) to persuade the king that more money was required for the defence of the Netherlands.

Money, however, was something which Philip II could not spare. In November 1560 he issued a new decree of bankruptcy which 'consolidated' his short-term debts – worth about 7,000,000 ducats (14,000,000 florins) – reducing the interest payable and freeing future revenues. There was a serious attempt to reorganize the royal treasury, centralizing payments to creditors through the Casa de Contratación (House of Trade) at Seville, but the truth of the matter was that there was not enough money to go round. In September 1560 the king himself estimated his expenditure at 3,000,000 ducats and his revenues at 1,300,000. In 1561–2 the royal factor in the Netherlands received only 325,000 crowns (650,000 florins) from Spain; in 1563 only 59,000 crowns. Montigny's mission had failed.[29]

Montigny might not have brought back money when he returned to Brussels in December 1562 but he certainly brought back a clear impression of Spain's debility and of her preoccupation with Mediterranean affairs. He had been at Court in October 1562 when news arrived of the destruction of twenty-five more Spanish galleys in a freak tempest off Málaga, which meant that the king's resources would continue to be tied down in the Mediterranean. In April 1563 the Algiers pirates profited from this disaster by laying siege to Spanish Oran; the expedition to relieve it was said to have cost 1,200,000 florins.[30]

It was at the height of the Oran crisis that Orange, Egmont and Hornes made their decisive attack on Granvelle. On 11 March 1563 they sent an ultimatum, informing the king that Granvelle must go, or else they would all resign. At Hornes's suggestion those opposed to the cardinal formed a solemn 'league', each member dressing himself and his servants in a livery of a single colour with badges on the sleeves – first a fool's cap and bell (a parody of the cardinal's hat), then a bundle of red arrows – and they held a riotous sequence of meetings and banquets at which Granvelle was execrated and maligned. It became apparent that the League enjoyed a wide measure of support from the other Knights of the Fleece, but the king stood firm and in his reply to the three nobles, dated 6 June, he asked one of them to come to Madrid to explain the situation to him. Until then Granvelle was to stay in office. When this letter arrived in Brussels, the three co-recipients convened a meeting of all their supporters, at which it was resolved that all three should cease attending the Council of State until Granvelle was removed. They communicated their decision to the king in a letter dated 29 July and thereafter they kept away from the Court. At the same time the States of Brabant decided to withhold all taxes until the cardinal went.

Margaret realized that this spelled the paralysis of her administration and, with France still in turmoil, a trade war with England imminent and the Baltic closed to Netherlands shipping, she could not afford to let the crisis of authority continue. There may also have been personal reasons for abandoning the cardinal. Margaret was aware that he was in the habit of writing reports on her behaviour to the king, reports that were sometimes critical and occasionally somewhat flippant and offensive. She also suspected that Granvelle had not done his utmost to further her efforts to marry her only son, Alexander Farnese, to one of the Austrian Habsburgs. Above all she was unpleasantly aware that she was commonly regarded as the cardinal's supporter and that, as such, a measure of the abuse and criticism directed against him was also coming towards her. On 12 August 1563 she therefore gave her trusted private secretary, Tomás de Armenteros, a set of detailed instructions on how to persuade the king that the recall of Granvelle was both desirable and unavoidable. Armenteros was told to play upon the obvious affront to royal authority which the league and the liveries represented, and upon the Mediterranean situation which made trouble in the Netherlands so embarrassing. He was also told to argue, somewhat bizarrely, that the departure of Granvelle would enable the government to intensify and improve its campaign against heresy in the Low Countries.

It is unlikely that these threadbare arguments would have made any impression on Philip II but for a chance concentration of Granvelle's enemies at court. The duke of Alva, the cardinal's friend and an implacable enemy of concessions to Netherlanders, was absent from Court, leaving the king's ear open to the hostile insinuations of Erasso and Ruy Gómez da Silva, aided by the reports of loyal Spaniards in the Netherlands who described with alarm the disintegration of royal power. The events in Madrid and Brussels were closely allied: one French observer in 1563 went so far as to suggest that the machinations against Granvelle in the Netherlands reflected and were encouraged by the rivalries of Alva, Erasso and Ruy Gómez at the king's Court.[31] By 14 December the pressure from the Netherlands and from his immediate entourage had broken Philip II's resistance. Unable to come to the Low Countries himself in the foreseeable future, he had to sacrifice Granvelle for the sake of domestic peace. The cardinal was ordered to leave Brussels on the pretext that he needed to visit his aged mother in Burgundy. He rode out of the capital of the Low Countries, never to return, on 13 March 1564.[32]

The collapse of royal power (March 1564–October 1565)

The fall of a ministry in the sixteenth century, as today, meant not only the disgrace of the principal adviser but of his friends and his policies as well. As Granvelle went to his exile in Burgundy, the various planks of his policy, and his supporters, were removed. On 30 July 1564 the government came to an agreement with the abbots of Brabant whereby the 'incorporation' plan was dropped, and instead the new bishops would receive a fixed stipend. The 'inquisition' proposal was also dropped. In return the States of Brabant increased their grant. The noblemen who had felt excluded from power under Granvelle now monopolized business, attending the Council of State regularly after 18 March 1564 (when it was clear that the cardinal had gone for good) and working closely with Margaret, who praised their diligence in her letters to the king. After so many months of frustration and hostility, it was good to feel popular and powerful again. Even the king seemed contented: he ceased writing to Granvelle, preferring instead to concentrate his energies on a new Mediterranean campaign – a fleet of 100 galleys attacked and captured the Turkish stronghold of Peñón de Vélez near Tetuán in north Africa (September 1564) – and between January 1564 (when he recalled Granvelle) and October 1565 the king scarcely intervened in Netherlands affairs.

This long period of royal silence was certainly not uneventful. In the first place the new rulers of the Netherlands were faced with grave difficulties in the field of foreign policy. Relations between Queen Elizabeth and the Netherlands had been deteriorating for some time. Piracy in the Channel, harassment by customs officials and sudden increases in the rates of duty by the English created much bad blood until in December 1563, in the hope of teaching Elizabeth and her advisers a lesson, the Brussels government imposed a temporary ban on the importation of certain English goods. Unchastened, Elizabeth retaliated by transferring all her wool and cloth exports to Emden in north Germany, depriving thousands of Flemish textile workers of their traditional raw material. Widespread unemployment ensued until the English reversed their decision in January 1565. At the same time difficulties occurred with another of the Netherlands' principal trading partners: the Baltic states. In June 1563 Denmark declared war on Sweden and the Hanseatic towns; Poland and Russia were soon involved in the struggle and before long the Baltic was sealed off from the rest of Europe. Between January and June 1565 only thirty-six ships left the Baltic for the Netherlands – scarcely one tenth of the normal total. The closing of the Baltic was serious for the Low Countries in all sorts of ways since so many of its people were dependent on it both for food and for employment: there were those who worked with the raw materials produced in the Baltic, those who manned the 2,000 or so Dutch ships which sailed through the Danish Sound every year and those who ate Baltic grain – the latter perhaps 15 per cent of the entire population (the Netherlands managed to produce only about three quarters of its total grain consumption; the rest had to be imported).

This unfavourable economic situation was made far worse by the weather. The winter of 1564–5 was one of the coldest of the century. Pieter Breughel painted his famous *Hunters in the Snow*, with a background of vast frozen wastes, at this time, and enormous icebergs entered the North Sea and even blocked the port of Delfshaven on the Maas. The bad weather continued and ruined the harvest of 1565. Coupled with the closing of the Baltic, this inevitably meant that bread became scarce and more expensive. At Diksmuide in Flanders a 'hoet' of wheat cost 150 groats in March, 230 groats in May and 440 groats in December. On 6 August there was a riot at the corn

market of neighbouring Ghent, and shortly afterwards the magistrates
of the city noted with alarm 'the evident danger from the dearth of
corn and the large number of paupers, coupled with the arrival in this
town of about 300 people from the region of Armentières who, it is
to be feared, are infected with heresy'. Farther north the States of
Holland noted in mid-November that people were 'murmuring and
voicing criticisms which might tend towards sedition, and also singing
songs with the same end' because of the dearth of corn. In Brussels
a government minister lamented the coincidence of high unemployment
and 'the shortage of grain which grows worse every day. I do not
know . . . if it will prove possible to restrain the common people,
who are discontented and protest loudly . . . If the people rise up, I
fear that the religious issue will become involved.'[33]

The government had good reason to fear the spread of heresy.
Since the accession of Philip II the Protestant movement had made
great progress. The persecution of 1544 and the following years had
changed the face of heresy in the Netherlands: many Reformed communities were destroyed and whole areas were lost to the Protestant
cause, so that the heterodox cells which survived tended to be more
uniform, more disciplined and more determined. The 'magnificent
anarchy' of the early period gave way, under the pressure of persecution,
to a more streamlined organization dominated by the Anabaptist
leader Menno Simons and the Genevan reformer John Calvin. After
the Munster persecution the Anabaptist cells were reorganized by
two 'bishops', Gillis van Aken, executed in 1557, and Lenaert Bouwens,
who survived until 1582 (keeping invaluable registers of those he
'baptized' into his faith). The numbers of the Anabaptists were kept
down by constant persecution, however: often whole families were
arrested together and sent to the stake. The family of Jan de Zwarte,
to take but one example, most of them weavers at Hondschoote,
provided eighteen martyrs for Anabaptism between 1558 and 1567.
In the end it would seem that the Catholic authorities exterminated
the entire family.[34] In the whole of Flanders only forty-four places
were reported to have Anabaptist cells between 1550 and 1566, compared with over 100 known to have had Reformed communities, and
most of them were very small: Ghent, the largest in Flanders, numbered
around seventy Anabaptists in 1557 and probably did not exceed 100
before 1566.[35]

The impact of John Calvin on the Netherlands came relatively late. His name did not appear on an Index of eighty-four forbidden books (by thirty-five authors) prepared for the bishop of Liège in 1545, but he was mentioned in the Index of 1546 for one book and on the Index of 1550 for eight. In the same year he was condemned by name in Charles V's 'blood edict' against heresy. As in France, however, there were still no established Calvinist churches in the Netherlands until 1555 or 1556. Even as late as 1561, when there were (according to Coligny, the French Huguenot leader) 761 established Calvinist churches in France, there were still only a score or so in the Netherlands and there was public worship only at Tournai and Valenciennes (where *chanteries* or public psalm-singing took place in September 1561; *presches*, or open-air services followed only in autumn 1562 and spring 1563). The massacre of Vassy in 1562 and the persecution of Protestantism which followed in France changed the situation. Many Calvinists took refuge in the towns of the south Netherlands, where many magistrates were prepared to turn a blind eye to heresy. New 'churches under the cross' (sc. in hiding) were formed and existing ones increased in size until by 1566 there were perhaps 300 places which had a nucleus of Reformed Protestants in their midst. There were synods held at Antwerp in 1561 and 1562, and two synods were held annually from 1563 until 1566. The rapid spread of Calvinism in the Netherlands contrasts strongly with the stagnation of Lutheranism: in the 1560s there were only five Lutheran groups – at Amsterdam, Antwerp, Breda, Mechelen and Woerden.

There were many reasons for the triumph of Calvinism. First and most important was the presence of so many Huguenots across the border, able to advise, teach and preach to their Netherlands co-religionists. Heresy, wrote Margaret of Parma in May 1561, 'grows here in proportion to the situation in our neighbours' countries'. The existence of properly constituted refugee churches for Netherlanders abroad was also important: they provided, among other things, training and instruction in the orthodox dogma of the Reformed faith. Although only twelve Netherlanders attended the university of Geneva between 1559 and 1563 (and only twenty-four attended between 1564 and 1568), many more received a training in theology at Heidelberg (Calvinist from February 1559), London (openly Protestant from May 1559), Emden (a haven of refuge since 1554) and elsewhere. It was in exile that men like Guy de Brès, who played a leading part in organizing the Reformed church in the south Netherlands, received Calvinist training.

Despite the efforts of the churches in exile and their dedicated members, Calvinist doctrine was imperfectly understood by many in the Netherlands in the 1560s. Even prominent leaders of the opposition movement, professed Protestants like the Bronkhorst brothers or Jan Denys (who commanded the Calvinist army in West Flanders and led the iconoclasm there), revealed when interrogated by the government how little they knew about the articles of the faith for which they were to die. They only knew what they were against. They deplored the wealth and the fiscal immunity of the Catholic church; they resented its jurisdiction, which could imprison, fine and even maim those who insulted the clergy; they criticized the absenteeism among the priesthood (which reached 40 per cent in some areas); and they ridiculed the concubinage, the drunkenness and the ignorance of many ecclesiastics. These ideas, however, did not necessarily come from Calvin and his ministers: the humanists had long made the same complaints. There was indeed a considerable overlap between humanism and reformation. It is striking how many children of prominent humanists of the generation of Erasmus became supporters of Protestantism.

Very often the bridge by which the educated passed from Erasmus to Calvin was provided by a curious Netherlands institution: the chambers of rhetoric. These were debating clubs, amateur dramatic societies and leisure centres all at the same time. Most important towns had at least one, and they were especially popular in the Dutch-speaking areas, where there were at least 187 *rederijkerkamers* (eighty-five in the province of Flanders). There were far fewer chambers in the French-speaking provinces, but some of them were important. The *chambre de rhétorique* at Tournai, for example, possessed a theatre which could seat 3,500 people. Lenaert Bouwens, David Joris and many other prominent Protestants belonged to the local chamber of rhetoric in their early days: they found in the discussions and in the plays staged by the chambers a platform for the expression and development of their early ideas. Not for nothing did some of the 'churches under the cross' take the name of their local chamber of rhetoric ('the vine', 'the rose' and so on). It would be wrong to see the chambers purely as crucibles of heresy (although that was the government's

view), for most of their members remained Catholic; the chambers
were important to the spread of Reformed ideas because they provided
an enlightened and tolerant milieu in which heterodox opinions might
flourish. There were others. The Jewish community of Antwerp,
composed of perhaps 300 Spanish and Portuguese *marranos* (Jews
who were only nominally Christians), flourished amid the anonymity of
Antwerp. Many *marranos* favoured the Protestants, and some even
joined the Calvinist church, providing ideas on how to avoid detection,
on how to gain toleration from the authorities and, eventually, on
how to resist persecution.[36] The gentry who supported the Reformation
played much the same role as havens of protection and encouragement.
Although there were few who went so far as to give Protestants open
protection – the van Boetzelaar lords of Asperen and the Bronkhorst
lords of Borculo were notable exceptions from the 1540s onwards –
many gentlemen, like the Marnix brothers, belonged to a Reformed
community and offered their fellow-worshippers a measure of protection,
prestige and respectability simply by their presence. The gentlemen
made it safe for others.

Thanks to all these influences, the Reformed opinions were able to
reach all social classes, and one of the striking facts to emerge from
any analysis of the social origins of the Protestants is the movement's
evident appeal to almost all groups, from the highest to the lowest.
Of 2,793 persons accused of heresy between 1521 and 1565 in the
province of Flanders (population about 350,000) we know the social
backgrounds of 1,518. If we divide them between the two 'phases' of
the Reformation in the Low Countries, we find the following pattern:[37]

Totals of persons accused of Protestant opinions in the province of Flanders, 1521–65

| | First phase: 1521–44 | | Second phase: 1545–65 | | |
Social class	'Lutheran'	Anabaptist	'Reformed'	Anabaptist	Total
Clergy	20	1	39	0	60
Nobles	2	0	5	0	7
Middle class	67	1 (or 4)	456	83	607
Lower class	71	24 (or 20)	489	260	844
Totals	160	26	989	343	1,518

These totals are impressive in more ways than one. Although they demonstrate the broad-based appeal of Protestantism, they also reveal that the government possessed adequate machinery with which to destroy the heresy it detested. At the highest level there was an agreement between the kings of France and Spain that they would join forces against the Protestants, intensifying persecution and repatriating (under custody) any heretics who tried to take refuge across their mutual border. The agreement reached between the kings at Crépy in 1544 preceded a purge on heresy in the Netherlands; a new agreement appears to have been reached at Cateau-Cambrésis in 1559.[38] Charles V and Philip II also took steps to deal with the heretics once they were caught. A stream of edicts and proclamations were issued condemning all forms of Protestant belief from October 1520 onwards and all magistrates were instructed to root out heresy by all means available. To help them in this, a special apostolic inquisition was created by Charles V and the pope in 1522. It was expanded and reorganized in 1546, and the inquisitors were given the right to question anyone, even magistrates, to arrest anyone and to commit them for trial anywhere they chose.

These innovations created several problems of practical politics. The new heresy laws of Charles V created a new legal offence. Besides the traditional offence of holding heterodox opinions (punishable by the ecclesiastical courts) there was now the criminal offence of breaking the laws enacted to extirpate heresy (punishable by the secular courts). Moreover the new offence was classed by the government as treason (*crimen lesae majestatis divinae*, treason to God) and this challenged an important part of the legal system of the Netherlands: the *jus de non evocando*, the right of many towns and most provinces to try persons accused of criminal acts committed within their boundaries. The only agreed exceptions to this rule were crimes which touched the prince's prerogative, such as treason or forgery. However, whereas cases of treason and forgery were infrequent, cases involving heresy were legion – there were literally tens of thousands of them – and it was therefore of some importance to the local authorities to stand fast upon their right to deal with such cases themselves. The claims of the inquisitors to arrest and try heretics where they chose had to be resisted. The town authorities were firmer in their opposition to the inquisitors after 1549 because the government began to insist that the goods of condemned heretics, who might be men and women of considerable local standing, should be confiscated. If they were tried outside the town, the town lost all right to the confiscated goods. Perhaps the most potent reason for the opposition to the inquisition and the heresy legislation on the part of the magistrates was moral, however: many of them were repelled by the torture, the mutilation and the eventual incineration which accompanied serious heresy accusations.

For this variety of reasons no heretics were condemned to death in the province of Holland after 1553 and few were executed in Friesland after 1557. Brabant mounted a major campaign against the inquisition with some success, ensuring that arrests were on the whole made only in rural areas where the local authorities were too weak to resist. In Flanders the town of Bruges successfully excluded the inquisition and in August 1564 they even arrested and imprisoned two officials of the provincial inquisitor, Peter Titelman, who managed to enter their jurisdiction. Titelman, however, was not the man to be discouraged by such reverses. He had been a part-time inquisitor since 1545 and became full-time after 1550; he had no doubts about the justice of his cause and about the need to harass and hound down all heretics. For twenty years, aided by only three or four assistants, he rode ceaselessly all over his territory in search of his prey, lying in wait for hours in a suspected area, plotting with informers, following up anonymous tips, making arrests even at the dead of night and during thunderstorms in order to avoid ugly scenes, interrogating and condemning those accused (up to and including sentences of life imprisonment). Between 1550 and 1566 Titelman tried 1,600 cases of heresy in the province of Flanders alone, an average of 100 a year or one every three working days.[39]

This was a grimly impressive record, but it was simply not enough to stem the tide of heresy after 1559. One man and his three assistants could not be on the spot everywhere. The new bishoprics scheme, which promised to strengthen the almost defunct episcopal inquisition, might have helped, but even then two 'inquisitor' canons per diocese would scarcely have sufficed. In 1562 the pastor of Eeklo was woken from his slumbers several nights running 'by heretics assembling in front of my windows and singing abusive songs about the sacraments and the clergy'. In the summer of 1563 there was dancing in the streets of Ostend; when the dancers sat down to rest they found themselves being entertained by 'scandalous songs about the Whore of Babylon

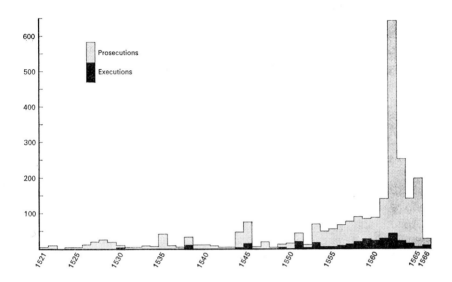

4. *Persecution of heresy in the province of Flanders 1521–66*

Source: J. Decavele, *De dageraad van de Reformatie in Vlaanderen*, II (Brussels, 1975), appendices I and II.

and other things'. In July 1564, at Ieper, again street dancing was punctuated by 'scandalous songs', this time about a Protestant 'martyr' executed earlier in the year.[40] Incidents like these, all of them in Titelman's province, could only have been stopped by the magistrates and, in Flanders, as in other parts of the Netherlands, by the early 1560s the magistrates were no longer prepared to proceed against heretics who did not also disturb the peace. In this they were merely reflecting public opinion, which tended to support the captured heretics in spite of the authorities. There were riots at the execution of Protestants in Valenciennes in 1562 and at Antwerp in 1564; there were many attempts, some of them successful, to free heretics from prison; and there was an end to denunciations for heresy. The last was, from the government's point of view, the most serious for, as the king himself was forced to admit, 'without informers and denunciations, all the penalties which one decrees are superfluous and illusory because they are never put into effect'.[41] As the figure above makes clear, after the departure of Cardinal Granvelle in the early months of 1564, there were fewer heresy trials and very few executions. The law was clearly no longer being observed. There was a growing case for changing it.

The government decided in December 1564 to approach the king about the possibility of 'moderating the placards' – that is to say, about reducing the penalties in the hope of making them more acceptable to those responsible for putting them into effect. After some discussion the council of state in Brussels resolved that Count Egmont should go to Spain to present the case to King Philip in person. While there he could also ask for formal recognition of the new-found role of the council of state as the effective ruler of the Netherlands and for more money from Spain. Egmont left Brussels at the end of January 1565 and arrived at Court on 20 February, where he remained until 6 April.

The king had certainly not wanted Egmont to come – it might force him to declare his views on the Netherlands before he was ready. There was a meeting to arrange at Bayonne between his wife Isabella, and his mother-in-law, Catherine de Medici, at which a new Franco–Spanish entente could be worked out; there was also certain news that the Turks would launch a major naval offensive against the west in 1565. 'I have so much on my mind', he confided to his secretary while Egmont was being particularly importunate, 'that I scarcely know what I am saying or doing.' However, the king had to make the best of a bad job. He went out of his way to impress Egmont with his confidence and he gave him some handsome personal gifts; but he also made certain demands. He insisted that the wearing of the anti-Granvelle livery should cease at once (it did) and that there should be no precipitous change in either the religious or the political structure which he had left at his departure in 1559. Instead he promised to set up a committee of theologians (the *junta de teólogos*) to consider whether the heresy laws could be modified without encouraging heresy to spread. He made it clear to his secretary, Gonzalo Pérez, who was to draw up Egmont's instructions, that he was not becoming 'soft' on heretics:

'Under no circumstances do I wish the punishment to stop: I only wish the method [of punishment] to be examined. And although it seems to me that Egmont wants the punishments to be mitigated, I do not wish this to be considered or interpreted in that way. Only the method is to be discussed.'

This forthright statement is particularly interesting in view of Egmont's subsequent claim that the king had told him that heretics were no longer to be burned. Finally the king promised to think about making the council of state supreme and appointing more (anti-Granvellist) members to it. As he explained to his secretary:

'I have drafted the answer in this way, so that Egmont will not be able to force me into a decision . . . My intention is, as you will have gathered, neither to resolve these demands of the Count, nor to disillusion him about them, for then he would worry us to death and we would never be finished with him.'[42]

Egmont was completely taken in by the treatment he received at Court. He returned to the Netherlands in high spirits and, despite the fact that he had brought no firm resolution in writing, he assured his colleagues that the king had expressed his verbal consent to a relaxation of the heresy laws and to the supremacy of the council of state. In any case, Egmont continued, 'being preoccupied with the war against the Turks, who are expected to attack Malta, His Majesty finds it impossible to come to the Low Countries this year'.[43] The council, encouraged by this news, felt free to proceed as it wished without fear of interruption from Madrid, and on 29 May the *junta de teólogos* was convened and given its brief to find ways of 'moderating' the heresy laws (which was not what Philip II had wished it to do).

Egmont's deception – whether self-induced or deliberately intended by the king – was revealed just the next day when letters arrived from the king, dated 13 May, one of which ordered the execution of six repentant Anabaptists. This proved that the king intended to make no change in the heresy laws. Egmont was totally discredited; he was made to look a fool. The fact that the *junta de teólogos* recommended a moderation of the placards made no difference: the final decision remained with the king in Spain, and everyone could see what it would be.

Baron Henry de Brederode, a prominent opponent of Granvelle, had suspected for some time that the king of Spain would always continue to sing 'the same old song. However,' he continued, using a pun that does not translate into English, 'it would be welcome if the note could change for once so that in place of the B major (*B dur*) which we have heard until now we could hear a B minor (*B moll*).'[44]

But, Brederode realized, even a change of key was unlikely and so, in secret, a number of noblemen held a series of informal meetings in July and August 1565 at the town of Spa in the politically 'safe' principality of Liège. There they discussed what action should be taken if the king chose to disregard the advice of the council and the *junta de teólogos*. No firm decision was taken, partly because there was too much difference of opinion among the nobles, but also because until the king communicated his decision the heresy laws were virtually in abeyance and the council of state 'usurped the sovereign control of all business'.[45] The nobles believed that the king could do no other than approve of their actions. Since the departure of Granvelle they had become much better informed about the general position of Philip II's monarchy, and they fully appreciated that the Turkish siege of Malta, which lasted from March until September 1565, would keep the king fully occupied. 'The Turks press us hard this year,' Orange wrote to his brother in April, 'which will mean, we believe, that the king will not come to the Netherlands this year.' In August the magistrates of Ghent jubilantly informed a government official that, since the Turks were besieging Malta, the king would have to conform to the seigneurs' demands. But on 8 September Malta was relieved; on 24 September the news reached the Spanish Court and everyone realized that a decision from the king on the Netherlands question could not be long delayed.[46]

As the king's draft of Egmont's instructions in March and his letters of 13 May had made clear, Philip's mind had been made up for a long time. The duke of Alva, whose advice against recalling Granvelle in 1563–4 had been ignored, was coming back into favour. In June 1565 Alva had accompanied the queen, Isabella de Valois, to see her mother, Catherine de Medici, queen-regent of France, at Bayonne. Besides the family reunion and some spectacular festivities, there was much important and secret political discussion between Alva and the leading French councillors, at which certain misunderstandings between France and Spain were removed and a common determination not to compromise with heresy was expressed. The Bayonne meetings were a considerable success for Alva. They vindicated his policy of firmness in domestic issues and friendship with Catholics abroad, and they prepared the French government for the firm measures which the king intended to take in the Netherlands. At the same time, those who had advocated compromise in the Netherlands and the recall of Granvelle – Ruy Gómez and Erasso in particular, the allies at Court of Egmont and Orange – were discredited by the stream of reports coming from the Netherlands concerning the growing strength and daring of the heretics and concerning the peculation and inefficiency of the government of the grandees. Erasso was put on trial, accused of massive fraud; Ruy Gómez was kept out of the king's council for several weeks and was apparently not consulted at all about the multiple letters which were laboriously composed to deal with every outstanding point concerning the government of the Netherlands. The final drafting took place in Philip II's new country house of El Bosque de Segovia (the Segovia Woods) and they were signed on 17 and 20 October 1565.[47]

The letters from the Segovia Woods were, without doubt, the work of the duke of Alva, whose policy towards the Netherlands was to prevail (as we shall see) for almost a decade. They gave an uncompromising restatement of the king's arrangements made in 1559: the king dismissed out of hand the advice of the *junta de teólogos* – the heresy legislation was not to be touched – and there was to be no change in the powers of the council of state. Moreover the duke of Aershot, a supporter of Granvelle and an enemy of Orange, was appointed to the council instead of the anti-cardinalists recommended by Egmont. Although there were one or two minor concessions and favours to the nobles, there was no disguising the fact that the letters from the Segovia Woods constituted a direct challenge to the nobles and their supporters. They could either obey and recommence the vigorous persecution of heretics, or else they could leave the placards as they were – in abeyance – and become guilty of gross disobedience, if not treason. The decision was theirs.

[2]

THE FIRST REVOLT
(1565–8)

The crisis

The letters from the Segovia Woods arrived in Brussels by special messenger on 5 November, just a week before the projected marriage of Alexander Farnese, Margaret of Parma's only son, to Princess Elizabeth of Portugal. In order not to ruin the festivities, Margaret only laid the letters before the Council of State two days after the wedding, on 14 November. Everyone realized the significance of the king's orders, and it was decided to leave a fortnight for consideration. It was not until 30 November that the Council saw to the enforcement of every decision communicated by the king in his letters (even though Egmont still expressed his resentment that some of the orders were 'contrary to what his Majesty had said to him by word of mouth in Spain'). This caused more delays and it was not until 20 December that the proclamation calling upon all provincial authorities to enforce the heresy laws was approved and published. By then, those opposed to the king's decision were already well on the way to organizing resistance.

After the furtive meetings at Spa in July and August, which involved only minor nobles and gentry, the grandees held a conference of their own at Brederode's castle of Vianen on 8–12 September, 1565: Egmont, Hornes, Orange, Hoogstraten and Culemborg stayed with Brederode and his eminent German guests: the duke of Cleves, and the counts of Schouwenburg and Neuenar (related to Orange, Brederode and Hornes). It seems highly probably that the possibility of resistance was discussed at this assembly. On 15 October the grandees met again at Montigny's wedding in Tournai and again on 12 November at Alexander Farnese's wedding in Brussels. On both occasions it seems likely that political developments were discussed; but nothing was decided. A more important meeting was held at the house of Count Culemborg in Brussels on 2–3 November 1565. Those involved were minor noblemen of openly Calvinist sympathies: John and Philip Marnix, both Geneva-educated, Count Louis of Nassau and others – twenty in all – addressed by the French-born Calvinist preacher, François du Jon or Junius. A decision was taken to form a solemn league to secure the abolition of the inquisition and the moderation of the heresy laws. The publication of the letters from the Segovia Woods merely confirmed this resolve. John Marnix took the lead and drew up a document later known as the Compromise of the Nobility, which was to serve as the basis of a confederation against the inquisition. It was signed by some nobles at Marnix's country house near Brussels in December 1565 and six identical copies were made to be circulated throughout the Netherlands for signatures. Brederode, Louis of Nassau and Charles de Mansfelt were among the first to sign.

In the end perhaps 400 signatures were secured for the Compromise, almost all of them from lesser nobles. It was noticeable that support for the Compromise was greatest in the outlying provinces where the government's authority was weakest (as in Friesland) and in the provinces governed by one of the dissident grandees (Artois and Franche-Comté, for example). The grandees themselves would not sign the petition, but they did refuse to carry out the king's orders to enforce the placards in their own provinces: Berghes resigned on 8 January 1566 rather than comply; Egmont, Meghen and Mansfelt warned the regent that they would be unable to enforce the king's commands; Orange asked to be relieved of his governorships for the same reason on 24 January. In March the confederate leaders (those who had organized the Compromise) came to Breda, Orange's main palace, to confer with Orange, Berghes, Hornes and Hoogstraten. Marnix read out a document of six or seven sheets which he proposed should be presented to the regent. Count Louis criticized its prolixity and it was reduced in length and also made to sound less aggressive. The nobles then went on to Hoogstraten to meet Egmont and Meghen and enlist their support for submitting a petition to the regent. Meghen, however, an ardent member of the anti-Granvelle league, took fright at the project of a formal request and went back to Brussels to forewarn Margaret. He was soon followed by Egmont. In a way this forced the confederates' hand. They now resolved to present their 'Request', with as many signatures as possible, to the regent early in April. The document was read out again in Culemborg's house and was actually presented on 5 April by Brederode, supported by some 300 confederates, all armed. The tone of the Request was overtly loyal, its demands – for the moderation of the placards and the abolition of the inquisition – apparently moderate; but the event itself was revolutionary. Three hundred armed men had forced their way into the presence of the king's sister and supreme representative and no one, neither grandees nor government, had been able to stop them. The confederates had seized the initiative.

Gaspar Schetz, a shrewd if slightly dishonest civil servant, correctly viewed the presentation of the Request on 5 April, 1566 as *Pandorae pinxit* – Pandora's Box. By challenging the government openly and, in the event, successfully, the confederates (who began to call themselves 'the Beggars', 'les Gueux', the derogative term used of them by a government minister) unleashed a tempest which neither they nor anyone else in the Netherlands had the power to control. Margaret's authority was critically compromised. She was powerless to refuse the confederates' demands and on 6 April, by her 'Apostil' (reply) to the Request, she agreed to instruct all magistrates and judges to be more lenient towards heretics until further notice. This concession was reiterated in Margaret's circular letter to provincial magistrates and tribunals (9 April) and in the text of the *Moderation*, a document mitigating the heresy laws, which was communicated in secret to the estates of each province. Although official publication was to be delayed until the king gave his formal approval, the tenor of the government's concessions soon became known: in plain terms, no one was now to be persecuted for their private beliefs, although public meetings by the heretics were still prohibited.

As the government had intended, the *Moderation* appealed to moderates. Almost all the provincial estates tabled a resolution which warmly welcomed the concessions, and in this they were often led by their prelates: the bishops of Arras and St Omer were among the first to signify their approval in the States of Artois, the bishop of Ieper in the States of Flanders, and so on. It was supported even by government advisers of indubitable loyalty – Aerschot and Mansfelt, Viglius and Assonleville – and there seemed to be a good chance that it might therefore prove a satisfactory compromise on the vexed religious question. However, it did not completely satisfy two important groups: the court opposition and the committed Calvinists.

On 9 April, the day on which Margaret signed the order which authorized local magistrates to be more lenient towards heretics, the prince of Orange announced at a meeting of the Council of State that he was disgusted by the treatment he had received from the king. He complained about the rumours which, as everyone knew, circulated about him at the Spanish Court – that he and his family were heretics; that he was hatching plots in Germany against the king – and he resented the fact that the king never wrote to ask his advice or to give him news of public affairs. Orange therefore declared that he had decided to abandon the Netherlands and the service of Philip II. His bags were packed and he planned to depart from his family home at Dillenburg the following day. After Orange's announcement, Egmont and Hornes spoke in much the same terms and affirmed their intention to go to Germany as well. The grandees had chosen their moment well. Margaret was totally dependent on their support in order to restrain the confederates and enforce the *Moderation*; she could not afford to alienate them now. She therefore persuaded Orange, Egmont and Hornes to remain at their posts for two months in return for yet more concessions: first, she would ask the king to show the noblemen 'more favour' (sc. to make them more grants of lands, titles and money) and, secondly, she agreed to ask the king that 'everything should be done by the Council of State, morning, noon and night'. After some discussion – for all feared the king's wrath at being asked to give way again – it was decided that Berghes (who had played a large part in engineering the confrontation between Orange and the Regent) and Montigny (who had been to Spain before) should go to the Court to explain the situation and secure royal approval for the proposed changes in the religious policy and in the structure of political power.[1]

Even before the messengers left, however, the situation was fast getting out of hand. On the political front the Beggars began wearing liveries of grey and badges and medals showing a beggar's scrip, and they even began to trim their beards in a common style. On the religious front the government noted with alarm the influx of many of those outlawed for heresy; before long these exiles began to organize open-air Calvinist services, similar to the ones which had been legalized in France by the Edict of January 1562. There were services in Flanders and Hainaut in May, in Brabant from early June. The first public service in Zealand took place on 30 June, the first in Holland on 14 July. Within two months, therefore, organized Calvinist worship had spread throughout the western Netherlands and, with the lengthening summer evenings and the widespread unemployment which left many men and women with nothing better to do, it was not long before the clandestine Calvinist preachers were drawing crowds first of hundreds and then of thousands to their open-air services beside the woods and hedges of the countryside outside the city walls. These sites were normally selected with a careful regard for legal niceties. It was safest to meet on land outside the jurisdiction of a town (and its law officers) and so conventicles were held for preference on the lands of a sympathetic nobleman, where the government officials could not go, or in a rural area where the local police force did not possess the means of dispersing the faithful and therefore dared not try. Even beneath the walls of some towns of the south, however, the Protestants were in no danger. At Tournai the local militia refused as early as 12 July to act against the open-air services 'seeing that some of their relatives and friends might be there . . . and some of them even declared that they went to the *presches* themselves and took their arms with them'.[2] In such circumstances attendances quickly rose.

Encouraged by their success, the Calvinists took steps to improve their organization. Although a partial Presbyterian organization, with elders, deacons and consistories, had grown up at least in west Flanders, Hainaut and Antwerp before 1566, organization in most other areas was rudimentary. There were few fully trained ministers or lay preachers active and congregations were small and furtive. A major policy meeting was held by the leaders of the consistories at Antwerp late in April 1566, which made improvements to ecclesiastical organization, asked Geneva to send more trained pastors and arranged more preaching in the Netherlands. It was, however, the open-air meetings which made possible the organization of fully fledged Reformed churches, and not vice versa. The size of the meetings actively compelled the Calvinists to create some institutions in order to cope. On 30 June one observer estimated that 30,000 people went to the Calvinist meetings in the Antwerp area alone. On 7 July the same chronicler noted for the first time that the Antwerp people went to their open-air services fully armed. The same alarming phenomenon was observed elsewhere. Breughel's painting, *The Preaching of St John the Baptist*, has captured much of the spirit of such gatherings: women and children, a soothsayer, gentlemen and artisans all crammed together – people drawn from all walks of life coming together to hear the Gospels and sing the Psalms. Everyone carried a copy of Marot's French translation of the Psalms which, according to one chronicler, could be bought in Ghent for just one penny.

On 9 July the Council of State discussed the dangers presented by these armed meetings. The grandees were forced to recognize that they had lost control of the situation and only three courses of action suggested themselves: the first, to instruct the bishops and clergy to make every effort in their sermons to exhort the people to pious works and obedience; the second, to call the States-General; the third, to beseech the confederates to prevent the *presches*. In the end the Council pinned all its hopes on the confederates; although they were only some 200 strong by that time, as Orange observed, 'without the Gueux, all is lost'. Margaret reluctantly deputed the prince and Egmont to meet the confederates, then holding an assembly of their own at St Truiden (St Trond: a town of the neutral bishop of Liège only thirty miles from Brussels).[3] The two grandees met twelve delegates of the confederates – popularly known as 'the twelve apostles' – at Duffel, a town a little south of Antwerp, on 18 July. There they were shown a 'second Request' prepared by the confederates, which demanded full toleration for non-Catholics and a firm promise that the States-General would be summoned immediately. Orange and Egmont offered fair words and took the 'twelve apostles' with them to Brussels where they presented the second Request to the regent on 30 July. Margaret, indignant at this new humiliating confrontation and, according to Count Louis, 'so angry that she seemed about to burst', persuaded the confederates to wait for twenty-four days until the expected letter from Spain arrived, giving the king's decision on the first Request. During this interlunary period the confederates promised to keep the peace, to do nothing further to achieve their ends, and to aid the local authorities to suspend all *presches* for twenty-four days.

By this time, however, the confederates too had lost control. The number of their supporters had fallen sharply and those who remained were caught between the delays of the government and the precipitation of the Calvinists, who had no intention of remaining idle even for three weeks. If any group now controlled the march of events in the Netherlands, it was the *predikanten*, the Calvinist pastors, who seemed to make new converts every day. The Ghent patrician and chronicler, Marcus van Vaernewijck, marvelled that four or five sermons were enough to change the beliefs ordinary people had held for thirty or forty years, but so it was. After decades of neglect from the old church and a mounting tide of anti-clerical criticism, many people appear to have become spiritually disorientated and ready to rally to any authoritative figure who could reassure them about the after-life and salvation. Such figures were to hand in increasing numbers. A steady stream of new preachers arrived in the Netherlands, some from Geneva, more from France, England and Germany, some of them wearing (of all things) blue leggings (*blaye upgherolde slapkauskens*), which appear to have become, at least in Flanders, the insignia of a 'hedge preacher'. Some of the *predikanten* were foreigners, like Johan Scheizhabener (the senior pastor at Maastricht, who was born in the Rhineland), or François du Jon or Junius (from Bourges), but most were born in the Netherlands. Many were returning from several years in exile, determined that they would never be chased out of their homeland again. One such returned exile was Sebastian Matte, a hatmaker by trade, born at Ieper in or about 1533 and forced to flee to England in 1563 on account of his Protestant sympathies. By 26 May 1566 he was back in his native Flanders and preaching at Roesbrugge (north-west of Ieper). On 1 August he appeared before the walled town of Veurne with an entourage of 2,000 armed Calvinists from the Ieper area, hoping to force an entry and make the town a fortified base for further operations. The plan failed. Undaunted, Matte continued to preach and on 10 August he delivered an inflammatory sermon just outside the monastery of St Laurence at Steenvoorde. The exact text of his sermon is unknown, but after he had finished a group of about twenty of his audience went into the convent and smashed all the images there, led by another *predikant*, Jacob de Buzere (a renegade Augustinian monk, also from Ieper and also an exile newly returned from England). On 13 August de Buzere preached a rousing sermon himself and promptly led his hearers to the monastery of St Anthony outside Bailleul, which they proceeded to sack. The following day Matte preached at Poperinghe and this time his sermon was followed by a rather larger iconoclastic outburst, involving about 100 people (over half of them refugees returned from England) and from there Matte's disciples fanned out to break the images in scores of towns and villages all over Flanders. The 'iconoclastic fury' had begun.

In many ways the iconoclasm was not totally unexpected. In the first place Calvin himself, following Karlstadt and several other early reformers, had written with characteristic vehemence against the Catholic practice of having images in churches. He regarded them as idols and urged their forcible destruction. Calvinists everywhere believed that images defiled a church and insulted God: to remove all objects of idolatry was a sacred duty which Calvinist zealots in Scotland and France had proudly accomplished some years before the iconoclasm in the Netherlands. (It also brought the advantage of utility: a 'purged' church was fit to be used for Protestant worship and certainly some iconoclastic outbreaks, particularly those of the autumn, were directly related to the need of the Reformed communities to find a sheltered meeting-place during colder weather.) By itself the 'casting down' of the churches in two neighbouring countries should have been enough to warn the Catholics of the Netherlands what lay in store for them, especially since there were other more immediate portents. In 1562 an open-air service attended by some 200 Calvinists at Boeschepe (between Ieper and Poperinghe) had ended in the sack of some near-by shrines and images, and there were a handful of similar outbreaks later. In 1566 a government agent at Kortrijk was able to report by mid-July that:

'the audacity of the Calvinist preachers in this area has grown so great that in their sermons they admonish the people that it is not enough to remove all idolatry from their hearts; they must also remove it from their sight. Little by little, it seems, they are trying to impress upon their hearers the need to pillage the churches and abolish all images.'

Similar tidings soon flowed in from other quarters. The deputy bailiff of Veurne noted on 22 July that the tone of the Protestant sermons delivered in his locality was becoming more strident and 'it is to be feared that . . . they will soon commit some shameful pillage of the churches, monasteries and abbeys; some of them are already making boasts about it'.[4] On 2 August Viglius wrote to a friend in Spain:

'The town of Ieper, among others, is in turmoil on account of the daring of the populace inside and outside who go to the open-air services in their thousands, armed and defended as if they were off to perform some great exploit of war. It is to be feared that the first blow will fall on the monasteries and clergy and that the fire, once lit, will spread, and that, since trade is beginning to cease on account of these troubles, several working folk – constrained by hunger – will join in, waiting for the opportunity to acquire a share of the property of the rich.'

Viglius's point was a shrewd one: the economic malaise in the Low Countries added an additional element of uncertainty to an already tense situation. He went on to remark in the same letter that a magistrate from Oudenaarde had told him that 'through the cessation of trade and industry, more than 8,000 people about the town who were once maintained by the merchants were now redundant and obliged to find some other means of support'.[5] It was the same elsewhere: the trade war with England had damaged the great cloth trade, the staple of the south-west Netherlands, and at the same time the war in the Baltic closed off another prime area of Low Countries trade. Unfortunately, as noted above, these commercial difficulties coincided with a severe food shortage. In November and December 1565 there were bread riots in Breda, Mechelen, Ghent, Ter Goes and elsewhere, and grain reached its highest price since the famine of 1556 at Diksmuide, Antwerp, Lier and Utrecht. Although prices began to fall in the spring of 1566, as a little grain from the Baltic and elsewhere (notably Spain) began to arrive, the employment situation did not improve and the poor still found the price of daily bread beyond their reach. This continued to be true even when the plentiful harvest of 1566 was brought in. At Ghent at least, prices did not fall as rapidly as expected and on Wednesday, 21 August, a market day, the poor rioted in desperation and placed their own prices on the grain sold. This was just what the Calvinists needed. The very next day, profiting from the chaos caused by the rioting, a

5. *The iconoclastic fury in the Low Countries, 1566*

This map, although incomplete, indicates the broad pattern of the iconoclasm, beginning in west Flanders with an organized itinerant body of image-breakers who came over from England. The same 'gang' of iconoclasts seems to have travelled from Poperinge in west Flanders (14 August) to Antwerp (20 August) and to Breda, Middelburg and 's Hertogenbosch (22 August). After this there were spontaneous outbreaks in the provinces of the north and east which yield no evidence of organization or 'specialists' like the south. Some towns experienced two outbreaks of iconoclasm (Brielle, Amsterdam, Delft and 's Hertogenbosch). Since this map is based only on printed sources, further research will doubtless reveal other towns where iconoclasm occurred.

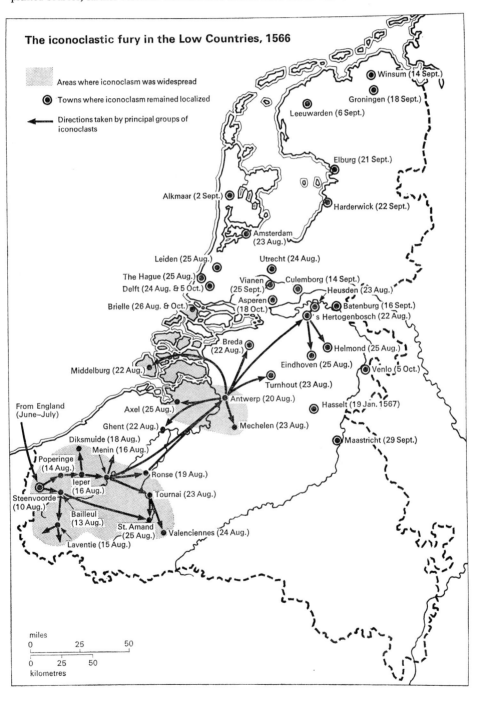

column of Calvinists entered and sacked the churches and convents of the city.[6] All the images, stained glass and other articles associated with the Roman Catholic worship were destroyed.

This outbreak of violence was not idly christened the 'iconoclastic fury' by contemporaries. The events at Ghent were repeated elsewhere: at Antwerp on 20 August; at Middelburg, 's Hertogenbosch and Breda (as well as Ghent) on 22; at Mechelen, Amsterdam, Heusden, Tournai and Turnhout on 23; at Delft, Utrecht and Valenciennes on 24; and at The Hague, Leiden, Eindhoven, Helmond and St Amand on 25 (cf. map on p. 77). And these were only the larger towns to be affected: countless rural churches and wayside shrines were smashed (often by gangs from the neighbouring towns). In west Flanders alone at least 400 individual churches and convents were sacked.

Yet the fury was carried out, at least in the southern provinces, in a remarkably orderly way. In contrast to the 'casting down' of the Catholic churches in Scotland and France, the destruction in the south Netherlands was the work of a very small band of determined men. There appears to have been a hard core of iconoclasts, between fifty and a hundred strong, many of them newly returned from exile abroad, recruited and paid by the Calvinist consistories of Antwerp and the other great towns. The rate of pay ranged from three to seven stuivers a day, the wage of an unskilled labourer, and the band thus recruited included – besides the exiles – unemployed manual workers, habitual drunkards, whores and boys in their early teens. They may or may not have been motivated by religious zeal as well as by the offer of a daily reward.[7] The iconoclasm in the northern provinces was accompanied by more tumultuous scenes and involved more popular participation. In Amsterdam and Delft, for example, the 'casting down' was carried out entirely by the local Calvinists and appears to have been a spontaneous reaction sparked off by news of the events at Antwerp. In smaller communities, however, the destruction was again perpetrated by a small number of committed Protestants led either by the local pastor, or by local merchants, or (on aristocratic estates) by the local lord. Sometimes, in order to avoid unnecessary violence, the iconoclasts attacked at dawn (at Turnhout they waited until the sexton had climbed up the church-tower to ring the day-bell) or at lunchtime (at Garsthuizen near Groningen they waited until the vigilant sexton had gone off to have his lunch). But on other occasions the destruction was done openly, in full view of great crowds who watched in silence and lifted not a finger. 'When they entered into some . . . churches [there were not] above ten or twelve that spoyled . . . but there were many in the church lookers-on,' wrote an English eye-witness from Antwerp. The burgher guard, he continued, stood ready for action: 'standing before their dores in harness, lookyng upon these fellows passing from church to church' but doing nothing. They were clearly indifferent to the fate of clerical property. The burgher guard (*schutters*) of Middelburg seem to have spoken for most of their fellows elsewhere when they informed their magistrates: 'We will not fight for church, pope and monks.' At Ghent an inquiry held by the magistrates shortly before the iconoclasm revealed that of 1,767 well-to-do citizens questioned, only 332 (18 per cent) were willing to defend the Catholic churches against possible attack.[8] At Leiden and Amsterdam likewise the *schutters* refused to hinder the iconoclasm just as they had, in previous weeks, refused to hinder people going to the open-air Protestant services. At 's Hertogen-bosch 400 of the *schutters* actively supported the Calvinists and were eventually obliged to flee for their pains.

In August and September 1566 everything hinged upon the attitude of the *schutters*. Where they obeyed orders and moved to defend the churches, as at Lille or Leuven or Bruges, there was no iconoclasm. Where they refused to act, the magistrates were completely powerless. At such short notice there was no chance of receiving military aid from Brussels (the normal source of support in time of trouble), and appeals to local noblemen and provincial governors were equally fruitless: Orange, Egmont and Hornes (between them governing all the provinces of the western Netherlands) refused to act against the Calvinists at this stage, while lesser men like Brederode and Culemborg actively favoured iconoclasm in the towns near to their estates and actually led the 'casting down' on their own lands. The magistrates were thus left on their own to puzzle out the correct course of action, a task which was complicated by the government's circular of 9 April, following the Request, which had ordered circumspection and restraint in all dealings with heretics. The plight of magistrates everywhere emerges from the confessions of the burgomasters of Middelburg, made in 1567 when the government sought to discover how the iconoclasm had been allowed to occur. One after another they complained of the speed with which it had all happened: news of the Antwerp outburst arrived at 4 p.m. on

21 August and the iconoclasm in Middelburg began at 6 a.m. the next day. It was all over within four hours: three churches, five convents and a *begijnhof* had been sacked, and the iconoclasts left at once for other towns. 'I found myself in such great perplexity that I scarcely knew what was to be done,' Burgomaster Schijs confessed. Burgomaster Claesz 'became frightened by the changes and novelties of that time . . . so that he scarcely knew what he had to do'. In Antwerp the magistrates knew just what to do: they took refuge to a man in the town hall when the 'casting down' began, and there they stayed until it was over. A lone sheriff who came into a church where the iconoclasts were at work 'being willed to leave, stayed not'. In The Hague the magistrates actually paid for the images to be removed from the churches as soon as they heard of the events in Antwerp, in order to avoid any unseemly tumult which might excite the mob; while at the Brill four magistrates were Protestant sympathizers and paralysed all efforts to persecute the reformers while the sheriff (*schout*) turned out to be a crypto-Calvinist and he led the iconoclasm in person![9]

It was hard, amid this collapse of authority, for the government to assess the precise extent of the support enjoyed by the iconoclasts. Few hands had been raised against them anywhere, and in some areas encouragement had even come from schoolchildren and street urchins. In Ghent, for instance, the children placed saints' statues in the street, issued the ultimatum: 'Say "Long live the Beggars" or we'll cut your head off' and then decapitated them.[10] Ghent, however, was exceptional in its hostility to the established church. Elsewhere, active support for the 'casting down' seems to have been slight. It would seem that there were few, if any, cases where more than 200 iconoclasts were involved at any one time. There can be no doubt, however, of the widespread, passive support for the attack on clerical property. Many people only saw the established church in its secular roles of landlord, tithe-collector and savage judge in its own suits; its role as haven of charity and ladder to salvation were, in some areas, less evident. And the latent anti-clericalism of the Netherlands political élite had been intensified, as noted above, by the schemes to introduce new bishoprics and to increase the activity of the inquisition – two proposals which made the church (through no fault of its own) into an aggressor against traditional privileges and local independence. Those who had come to see the Catholic church in this light were certainly not all Calvinists, but they were likely to see the iconoclasts as valuable allies in August 1566, albeit as disreputable allies to be disowned after the event.

All this was far from clear at the time of the crisis, however. The outstanding fact, as far as the government was concerned, was the complete collapse of public authority in most areas: provincial governors, magistrates, urban militias and ordinary subjects were all openly refusing to obey orders. The sequence of disasters in one town after another compelled Margaret of Parma to surrender to the demands for full toleration made in the confederates' second Request. In fact she received a letter from the king, dated 31 July, which agreed to several concessions, but she recognized that it was too little and too late. 'Eating her heart out' (as she informed the king), on 23 August Margaret reluctantly conceded freedom of Protestant worship in all areas where it was already taking place (but prohibiting it elsewhere). She also required the Court grandees, who had advised her to make this compromise, to enforce the Accord in each area where disorders had taken place. In this they were to be assisted by the confederates even though, on 25 August, the 'twelve apostles' signed an act dissolving their confederation.

The Accord of 23 August, with its apparent harmony between the regent, the grandees, the confederates and the Calvinists, deceived no one. Calvinist groups in the north continued to smash images – as at Groningen (17 September) and Culemborg (14 September, at the command of the count) – or to cause the images to be removed so that the churches could be used for Protestant worship – as at Leeuwarden (6 September) and Vianen (25 September, at Brederode's command). Calvinists in all areas refused to accept that the religious situation was to be frozen as it was on 22 August, and their defiance was encouraged, more or less openly, by the confederates and grandees who arrived in each province to implement the new *'religionsvrede'* ('religious peace' – people began to call it this in imitation of the Augsburg settlement of 1555). The first local compromise was made by the prince of Orange at Antwerp on 4 September, and it allowed full Protestant worship both inside and outside the city: both Calvinists and Lutherans were to be permitted to build churches of their own; only the Anabaptists remained proscribed. On 7 September Hornes arranged a similar Accord with the Calvinists at Tournai and on 10 September Egmont followed suit at Ghent. These agreements provided an example for others and similar local compromises were implemented in the towns of Flanders, Brabant, Hainaut and Holland.

Naturally the regent was appalled by the concessions made in her name. At all costs she had wished to avoid allowing open Calvinist worship inside the towns, and here were her three leading advisers blatantly flouting her wishes. The Council of State, in Orange's absence, denounced the Antwerp Accord, and Margaret disowned all the agreements mentioned above in her letters to the king dated 13 September. Her letters to the king during August and September painted the situation in the blackest colours she could manage: on 29 August, misled by the ease with which the iconoclasm had been carried out, she even asserted that half the entire population was infected with heresy, with over 200,000 people up in arms against her authority, while the grandees sat back and waited to carve up the provinces between them once the king's government was at an end.[11]

The grandees were scarcely more popular with the Calvinists. In the weeks following the iconoclasm, a number of the leaders of the disorders were arrested and executed by the town magistrates or by the nobles themselves (especially by Egmont) and this alienated many of the Reformed leaders. At the same time, once the Calvinists gained a measure of official recognition they became bolder, asking for more than one church, appointing elders, deacons and almoners, arranging baptisms, marriages, burials and communions as well as simple acts of worship. Consistories sprang up in Holland and Limburg as well as in Hainaut and Flanders, with congregations in some towns numbering over 1,000.

The grandees were being driven into an impossible position. They were not in favour of enforcing the heresy laws too hard, but they were reluctant to advocate their abolition. They wished to preserve the 'uncertainties' of the faith; they wanted a church which taught morals rather than doctrine. They stood for the 'magnificent religious anarchy' of the days before the Tridentine, Genevan and Augsburg confessions defined what a Christian must and must not believe. Theirs was a middle-of-the-road position, both in religion and in politics, and it was rapidly becoming untenable – and they knew it. On 3 October 1566 Orange, Egmont, Hornes, Hoogstraten and Count Louis of Nassau met at Dendermonde to discuss the situation. They were worried that the regent had so obviously taken exception to the agreements negotiated by them with the Calvinists, and they were alarmed by the growing body of evidence that the king, extremely dissatisfied with their conduct, was preparing an army in Spain with which to restore order in the Netherlands. The meeting was convened by Orange and each member present gave his view of the situation. Hornes was particularly well informed since his brother and his secretary were both at the Court of Spain. From the latter, Alonso de Laloo, he had a letter dated 31 August which mentioned a growing feeling among Philip II's advisers that strong measures would be required and that the king was beginning to make military preparations in Germany (3,000 horse and 10,000 foot were to be levied). Laloo also mentioned that the decision of the three grandees to act as guarantors of the second Request 'has done you much harm because it puts you under suspicion of having some sort of arrangement with the confederates, or of having the same religious sympathies, and of wishing to create a triumvirate [as in France]'. No one at Court now put any trust in the grandees, warned Laloo. Hornes also had a letter from his brother Montigny which likewise mentioned the king's disgust at the nobles' failure to prevent the iconoclasm. These tidings were disturbing, but the prize exhibit was provided by Orange: an intercepted letter to Margaret of Parma from Don Francés de Alava, the Spanish ambassador in Paris and a man known to favour a strong line in the Netherlands. The letter, dated 29 August 1566, stated in no uncertain terms that the three leading nobles were already marked men and that as soon as the king came to the Netherlands they would be punished for their part in the troubles; but he advised Margaret that until then she should continue to show them all favour and keep them within easy reach. The letter further assured her that Montigny and Berghes would never be allowed to leave Spain.[12]

Although subsequent events lent greater authenticity to this letter, there seems little doubt that it was a forgery. Perhaps Orange himself was responsible (it was later printed as an annexe to his *Apologie*), perhaps his brother Louis did it; but in any case it failed to convince Egmont, who took a copy of Alava's supposititious letter to Brussels and showed it to the regent. Egmont refused to believe that he and his peers were in any danger; he could not admit the possibility that the king was displeased with them. Margaret of course welcomed this rift in the ranks of the grandees and reassured Egmont that his signal services would be duly rewarded. Shortly afterwards, however, news of unquestionable authenticity arrived from Spain warning the grandees of their perilous position. On 9 October Hornes received another letter from Laloo in Spain, dated 20 September, informing him that the king was gravely offended by the failure of the grandees to stop the iconoclasm, especially since it was perpetrated by so few people; and that it now seemed inevitable that the king would take firm action. A further letter dated 26 September confirmed the intense ill-feeling which Philip II's entourage felt for those who had failed to prevent the troubles. Indeed, wrote Laloo, the Netherlanders at the court did not dare to show their faces for some days, and 'Sooner or later, His Majesty cannot fail to exact vengeance for such great disrespect and if he does leave Spain it will be with more strength and power than any king ever took to the Low Countries'. Montigny too furnished evidence about the winds of change blowing through the Spanish Court. Writing to the prince of Orange on 4 October, he reported that the king had ordered his veteran troops in Italy to move up to Genoa where they would be joined by more men to be raised in Spain.

'The army His Majesty is raising with which to visit us is thought certain to consist of ten thousand Spaniards (eight thousand veterans from Italy and two thousand recruits . . .), six thousand Italians, twenty-four thousand Germans, two thousand light cavalry, one thousand men-at-arms and five thousand heavy cavalry. As for money, I can assure you that it is a long time since a Christian prince was better supplied, even for a greater enterprise.'

Montigny's news was absolutely right: major policy decisions had been taken in Spain which were to transform the situation in the Netherlands.[13]

Spain, 1566: the time of decisions

Philip II's fateful decision to send the duke of Alva with a large force of Spanish troops to the Netherlands was a turning-point in European history. It was a Rubicon for Spanish imperialism: a threshold which, once crossed, transformed the political situation in northern Europe and, with it, the prospects of Habsburg hegemony there. But unfortunately it is almost impossible to penetrate with assurance the mysterious processes by which the king and his council decided to send Alva – although men have been trying to do so for 400 years! Late in 1576 several of the duke of Alva's former ministers were captured by the prince of Orange and his allies. The most important of these was Dr Luis del Rio, a Spaniard born in Bruges who had become a distinguished lawyer and a member of the 'Council of Troubles'. Del Rio had actually been in Spain in 1566–7 and had even been at Court. It was natural for Orange, his captor, to ask him: 'At whose instigation did the king of Spain send the duke of Alva here?' and 'What arguments and reasons were used to persuade the king to send the duke?' Sadly for posterity, Dr del Rio did not know the answers. Neither he nor any other Netherlander had been permitted to attend the meetings of the royal Council at which the fate of the Low Countries was determined. The prince of Orange, like every one else since, still did not know who to 'blame'.[14]

The first steps which eventually led to the duke of Alva being sent were taken in the spring of 1566. Long before news of the revolt in the Netherlands arrived at the Spanish Court Philip II decided that strong measures were required there. Plans had been laid for a personal visit by the king in 1565, but the siege of Malta made it necessary to suspend them. The situation early in 1566 seemed rather more promising, since reliable information arrived in Spain that the Turks' main effort for the year would be directed against Hungary, leaving the west Mediterranean relatively safe and the king free at last to deal with some of his other problems. Accordingly on 6 May 1566 he informed his Netherlands subjects that he was making serious preparations to send financial and military assistance to the government in Brussels and that he would go to the Low Countries himself later in the year.[15] But these plans too had to be shelved when news arrived of the confederation of the nobles and the presentation of the Request, twin developments which were taken extremely seriously by the king: any league or association of vassals without the consent of the sovereign was, after all, treason. In July, while the king was still undecided on the correct policy for the Netherlands, Montigny arrived at Court with demands from the Brussels government to ratify the *Moderation* and to give the Council of State supreme authority. On 26 July, after much discussion, the king and his Spanish advisers decided not to give in to pressure: the *Moderation* was to be repudiated. Instead Philip II stated his determination to make a personal visit to the Netherlands, accompanied by troops, in the spring of 1567. Montigny, however, who had not been called to the council, was outraged by this decision. In a tempestuous scene, somewhat uncommon in the elaborately formal court of Spain, Montigny stormed up to the king and roundly condemned his decision as ill advised, unwise and unchristian. The king's normally pale face coloured as the baron, beside himself with rage, told him that the rejection of the *Moderation* proved that Philip cared nothing for the well-being of the Netherlands, nothing for the counsel of the nobles (as they had always suspected) and nothing for the maintenance of the Catholic religion. Unless Margaret of Parma's concessions were confirmed forthwith, Montigny warned, and unless the king made plans to leave for the Netherlands at once and without troops, it would be too late.

Shortly after this outrageous display, disturbing new information arrived from the Netherlands which fully justified Montigny's alarmist tone. In a near-hysterical letter, dated 19 July, Margaret of Parma reported that the Calvinists were meeting in ever greater numbers, their emotions stirred up by ever more inflammatory sermons, while she had neither the troops, the money nor the supporters necessary to preserve order. She begged the king to appreciate the true situation of the Netherlands. The provinces were on the brink of rebellion and there were only two possible courses of action left: either the immediate despatch of troops to restore order or the immediate confirmation of the *Moderation;* 'either to take up arms . . . or to make concessions in certain matters'. Again the presence of the Turkish fleet off Italy led the king to delay a decision on this crucial issue. Until the Turks' objective was known for certain, Spain had to be ready to defend any part of the Mediterranean littoral against sudden attack and all available forces had to be aboard the navy. Under the circumstances the king could only try and buy time. On 31 July therefore, only five days after his resolution to refuse all further concessions, Philip signed a letter which abolished the inquisition and offered a pardon to all. Of course the king signed with great reluctance (duly recorded before a notary!): he had not changed his aim of ending the troubles in the Netherlands by force of arms. At the same time as his letter conceding partial toleration, he dispatched orders to recruit 13,000 German troops for service in the Netherlands and a bill of exchange for 300,000 crowns to pay for them.

Yet again, however, these contingency plans were shattered by the rapid march of events in the Netherlands. On 3 September a courier arrived at Court bearing Margaret of Parma's letters of 17 and 18 August which described in detail the desecration of the churches in west Flanders and other areas and repeated the warning that there were only two courses of action still available: to send an army and restore order by force, or to abandon the Low Countries altogether. The same evening, before he had read the letters in full, the king went down with a fever. He had seven seizures in the following fortnight; no important business of state could be transacted. It was not until 22 September that the royal council met to discuss the Netherlands problem.

Everyone in the council agreed that only force could now restore royal authority. Accordingly they reviewed the current position of the Spanish monarchy. It was noted that the financial position was encouraging: the Indies fleet had arrived at Seville with over four million ducats (one and a half million of them for the king) and the *cortes* of Castile and the Castilian church could be relied on to make new grants in case of need. On the political front too there was room for optimism. The Turkish fleet was fully occupied in the Adriatic and there was little risk of its coming west against Spain before the winter. The Emperor Maximilian, Philip II's cousin, had received considerable financial help during the year to aid his defence of Hungary, and it was hoped that in return he might support Spain's policy in the Netherlands. The governments of France and England, which might object to the use of force, were too weak to cause any trouble. It was therefore resolved that troops could and should be used to restore royal authority in the Netherlands and orders were approved directing the galleys of the Mediterranean fleet to carry all the veteran Spanish troops in Italy to Genoa, and then to come to Barcelona to embark thirty companies of new recruits which were to be raised forthwith. It was intended to have 10,000 Spaniards at Milan by November, ready to march overland to the Netherlands where they were to form the nucleus of an army of 60,000 foot and 12,000 horse to be assembled in the loyal province of Luxemburg (or, if even that was occupied by the rebels, in Franche-Comté). The Council recognized that the opponents of royal policy in the Netherlands were in deadly earnest, and that some of them would stop at nothing. They appreciated that it was important to safeguard the king's authority in the Netherlands not only for their own sake but also to discourage discontented elements in other parts of the Spanish empire from organizing a revolt of their own. Already in June Cardinal Granvelle in Rome warned the king that: 'All Italy is plainly saying that if the troubles in the Netherlands continue, Milan and Naples will follow.' The message was received and understood. The Council of State, on 22 September, recorded as its opinion that: 'If the Netherlands situation is not remedied, it will bring about the loss of Spain and of all the rest.'[16]

After this initial decision on basic policy, there was nothing for the king and his advisers to do but wait for their orders to be carried out. Depressing news continued to arrive almost daily: the progress of the iconoclastic movement, the concessions to the Calvinists . . . And at the same time a letter arrived from the Emperor Maximilian which advised the king to acknowledge defeat and implement a sort of 'Augsburg settlement' in the Netherlands, granting toleration to the new religion wherever it already existed, but not elsewhere. (This was the solution actually adopted in Margaret of Parma's 'Accord' of 23 August.) The emperor's reply came as a sad blow to the king. Maximilian was known to be a friend of Orange, Egmont and Hornes and a secret sympathizer with Protestantism but, in the face of armed resistance, Philip had expected firm support from his Austrian cousin – especially in view of the considerable sums of money which Spain had provided in 1565 and 1566 for the defence of Hungary against the Turks. At their meeting on 23 October the Council of State rejected Maximilian's proposal out of hand. Instead, the 8,000 Spanish veterans at Milan were ordered to stand by, while ambassadors and commissaries were appointed to arrange a route from Lombardy to the Netherlands via Savoy, Franche-Comté and Lorraine. On 29 October the king summoned his principal advisers to the Escorial to make a final decision on the policy to be adopted in the Netherlands.

The critical discussions which followed were dominated by the long-standing rivalry between Philip II's two principal advisers on policy: Don Fernando Alvarez de Toledo, duke of Alva, and Ruy Gómez da Silva, prince of Eboli. It was taken for granted by all that there could be no question of permitting open Calvinist worship to continue in the Netherlands: Philip II had declared too many times his firm intention never to become the ruler of heretics. It was also assumed from the

outset that the disturbances and rebellion in the Low Countries would
have to be ended by force: to permit the troubles to continue would
'hazard Spain's prestige' and would be 'an example of weakness and an
encouragement to other provinces to rebel'. The debate of the council
centred on the question of how much force was to be used and who
should control it. Ruy Gómez and others argued that only a small
number of troops would be required, provided that the king went to
the Netherlands in person to supervise the repression. No one else, he
insisted, could command sufficient respect to make the right concessions
from a position of natural strength. To this, however, an ancient
councillor (Don Juan Manrique de Lara) raised an unanswerable
objection: it was simply not safe for the king to go. The maritime
provinces of the Netherlands were in ferment and under the control of
the most suspect noblemen – Orange (Holland and Zealand) and Egmont
(Flanders). The sea route to the Netherlands was thus totally imprac-
tical. On the other hand a passage through France, similar to Charles
V's journey in 1540, ran the risk of an assassination attempt by the
French Huguenots, while neither the duke of Savoy nor the emperor
could guarantee the king's safety should he pass through their domains
on his way to the Netherlands. In these unfortunate circumstances,
argued Don Juan Manrique, it was impossible for the king to go. It
would be better to arrange for an army to be sent to the Low Countries
at once under some reliable minister who could suppress all sedition.
When this was achieved, the king could follow safely by sea. Manrique
also urged that the operation should be represented to the world as
merely a 'police action', a measure against civil rebels, and not as a
crusade against heresy. In this way foreign support for the Netherlands
rebellion would be minimized. The duke of Alva spoke next, agreeing
(predictably) with all that Don Juan Manrique had proposed. He insisted
on the need for firm, speedy and drastic action against those who had
placed the authority of king and church in jeopardy, to ensure that
they would never be able to do the same again.

   Other councillors spoke, but at the end of the debate the king was
persuaded by Manrique and Alva. Letters were sent to the duke of
Savoy asking permission for 8,000 Spanish foot and 1,200 horse to pass
through his territories on the way to the Netherlands. The governor
of Spanish Lombardy was ordered to send surveyors and engineers
into the Alps in order to chart and construct a route for the Spaniards,

and an experienced engineer, Don Juan de Acuña Vela, left Madrid on 2 November 1566 to arrange the details of the great expedition. At this point there was still no agreement on who should command the army, which might eventually number 70,000 men. The duke of Alva, who was in some ways the obvious candidate, was not seriously considered at first because of his advanced age (he was sixty in 1566) and his indifferent health (gout had kept him immobilized for much of the autumn). The dukes of Parma and Savoy, both of whom had commanded impressive armies for Spain in the 1550s, were therefore in turn offered the command of the new army. Neither of them showed the least enthusiasm. At the same time Alva's gout abated. Accordingly on 29 November 1566 he accepted the post of captain-general of the army to be formed in the Low Countries and his patent was drawn up two days later.

The next urgent problem concerned timing. It had originally been intended to assemble the king's forces in Franche-Comté or Luxemburg in December. The Spanish troops, who were to form the nucleus of the army, had therefore to cross the Alps from Lombardy before the winter snows closed the passes. Unfortunately the delay over choosing a commander made this impossible. The Spaniards from Sicily only reached Milan on 11 December; those from Naples and Sardinia were later still. A last-minute attempt to persuade the king of France to allow Alva's expeditionary force to sail to Marseilles and then march direct to Franche-Comté failed, and it was therefore decided to postpone the whole operation until the spring of 1567. The Spaniards wintered in Lombardy and the duke of Alva wintered in Spain.

The failure of the first revolt

While the king's master plan was in this state of suspended animation, events in the Netherlands moved faster than ever. The government's determination to use force to restore its authority soon became generally known and some of those who had reason to fear reprisals took steps to defend themselves. Brederode began to put his castle of Vianen in a state of readiness – aided by three cannons loaned for the purpose by William of Orange. The confederates also made serious efforts to raise troops in the empire. Gilles Le Clercq, secretary to Count

Louis of Nassau resided in Germany from December 1565 to May 1566, dividing his time between the Calvinist Elector Palatine and the Imperial Diet at Augsburg and trying to solicit promises of support from all princes of the empire who favoured the Protestant cause. The grandees also did their best: Orange and Egmont corresponded with their German relatives, and Count Hoogstraten pleaded the confederates' cause with the emperor in person at the Augsburg Diet. However the grandees hesitated to pass beyond petitions to troop-raising: Egmont had declared his unwillingness to raise troops for service against the king at the Dendermonde meeting in October 1566; Hornes retired disconsolate to his country house in November; Orange, although in January 1566 he had instructed his brother Louis to sound out some German military entrepreneurs on whether they were prepared to fight against the government in the Netherlands, remained undecided after the iconoclastic fury.[17] Others, however, were more determined. On 30 August Louis of Nassau signed an agreement with Colonel Herman von Westerholdt to raise 1,000 horsemen for the confederate cause, but this arrangement (and no doubt others like it) was invalidated by an outbreak of rebellion in Saxony which resulted in the mobilization of an imperial army numbering around 20,000 foot and 8,000 horse. By December 1566 the rebels were cornered in the town of Gotha, only about 200 miles from the Netherlands border, and it was not long before Louis and Nassau and the confederates were in the imperial camp looking for volunteers to fight in the Netherlands after Gotha fell. Unfortunately for them, however, the Saxon rebels held out until 13 April, and even then many of the besieging troops were retained in imperial service for another six weeks specifically to prevent them from serving in the Netherlands.[18] The confederates, however, had another string to their bow.

Steps had also been taken to secure aid in France from the Huguenot leaders. Montigny's mission to Spain had proved the occasion to cement contracts between Huguenots and Gueux. Montigny left Cambrai on 29 May 1566 and on 1 June he was at Écouen with his cousin, the constable of France, Anne de Montmorency, in whose household he had been brought up. There he held secret discussions for two days, after which he and the constable moved to Paris to be joined by the latter's nephews, Coligny, d'Andelot and Châtillon, the leaders of the French Huguenots. Their every move was noted by the diligent Spanish Ambassador, Don Francés de Alava, who was of the opinion that the Montmorency connection had long been the chief means by which the French Court learnt of developments in the Netherlands. Although it is difficult to establish what was arranged at these furtive meetings, Count Egmont later volunteered the information that Montigny had written a letter after he left Paris which stated that the constable had offered to place money and men at the disposal of his Montmorency nephews in case of need and vice versa.[19]

The government was at first reluctant to believe wild stories like these about military preparations of the opposition, but all remaining doubts were dispelled when on 30 July the 'twelve apostles', while presenting the second Request, openly admitted that (fearing reprisals by the government) they 'had been obliged to find ways of making friends in a certain country to serve and aid us' (namely Germany) and that they also had men standing by in the Netherlands (but they expressly denied any contact with France).[20] Margaret lost no time in telling the king of this extremely serious development and before long the king began to raise troops in Germany himself. He also authorized and financed levies in the Netherlands. The faithful Count Berlaymont ordered the clergy of his province, Namur, to donate 6,000 florins (either in money or in grain) to pay for defensive measures against the Calvinists. The 300,000 crowns dispatched from Spain on 9 August was used to pay the arrears of the 3,000 or so veteran troops who garrisoned the southern frontier and to enlist 5,000 more Netherlands recruits (21 August–11 September, see the figure on p. 95). The government steadily and stealthily built up its strength, using its fragile resources in a series of holding operations: to prevent disorders in Brussels (a guard was mounted on St Goedele and the Kapellekerk night and day), to forestall a Calvinist coup at Maastricht and to restore order in Ghent. As the number of troops at the government's disposal grew, its actions became a little more positive. On 17 October Count Meghen, now a staunch supporter of the regent, told her that in his opinion the time for action had come, since 'Neither admonitions, nor proclamations, nor speech, nor writing can achieve anything more'. Margaret had reached the same conclusion. The first step was to recall Hornes from Tournai, more or less in disgrace, and to send a reliable replacement to restore Catholic worship. In Gelderland, Overijssel and Friesland, the north-eastern provinces which had suffered image-breaking only recently, Governors Meghen and Aremberg were ordered to punish any Calvinists who attempted to hold services in places where no Protestant worship had taken place before the Accord (23 August).

In the face of provocation like this, the Calvinists and the confederates could not wait for the aid promised from France and Germany to materialize. They had to take steps to defend themselves at once. The consistories of Flanders had possessed modest financial reserves for some time – they used them to pay the iconoclasts – but in August 1566 Gilles Le Clercq, a secretary of Count Louis, mooted the idea that all the consistories might pool their resources in order to offer the king a large sum of money if, in return, he should grant them freedom of conscience. The consistory of Ghent drew up a formal petition, offering three million florins in return for this toleration, and presented it to some government representatives on 27 October. Without waiting for their reply, the 'Three million guilders request' was printed within a week and circulated. Before long many prominent persons bound themselves to pay a given sum (Count Louis promised 10,000 florins, Brederode 6,000 and so on). An instruction for the collectors of the donation was drawn up on 10 December and collection began almost at once. One sixth of the money was to be raised within eight days and held in Antwerp in case the king should agree; 'otherwise', the instruction continued ominously, 'the money would be employed in paying the troops which the confederates were holding in readiness in Germany for the country's defence'.[21]

Clearly several groups in the Netherlands were prepared for open revolt. The towns of Tournai and Valenciennes, whose large Protestant populations had given trouble throughout the 1560s, were particularly restless and, in an attempt to forestall greater troubles, at the end of November Margaret decided to send a garrison to each. At Valenciennes the Calvinist preachers Guy de Brès and Pérégrin de Lagrange persuaded the people to close their gates in order to prevent the entry of any troops (14 December). They were encouraged in their defiance by Gilles Le Clercq, Count Louis's man, who announced that his master had some 4,000 horse and thirty or forty companies of infantry prepared in Germany, and by Count Hornes, who was in the vicinity, who told a magistrate of Valenciennes that three weeks' resistance would suffice to break the government's authority anew.[22]

Tournai too closed its gates but the presence of a small citadel containing a royal garrison made its position less tenable.

The regent took a strong line in the face of this defiance. Already on 4 December she had ordered the levy of 1,000 more soldiers and had dispatched letters to the magistrates of what she termed the *'villes mauvaises'* ('bad towns' – Antwerp, Maastricht, Valenciennes and so on), in which she informed them that the Accord of 23 August had permitted only *presches*, i.e. sermons and worship, and that all Calvinist baptisms, communion and collections must stop. To the *'villes bonnes'* (such as Mons, Arras and Arnhem) she sent orders to the magistrates to prevent all further Calvinist worship forthwith. Then on 15 December Margaret declared it to be a capital offence to attend a 'Calvinist service' (i.e. one where a sacrament was involved – ordinary worship was still permitted) and on the 17 December she declared Tournai and Valenciennes to be guilty of treason and rebellion unless they agreed to accept a royal garrison. This ultimatum provoked an unexpected reaction. Sensing danger, the Calvinists of the Westkwartier of Flanders (roughly speaking the area bounded by Gravelines and Nieuwpoort on the North Sea and Aire and Commines on the Lys) began to raise troops. By 10 December they were about 700 strong. About a week later the force was some 1,500 strong (although only 700 were armed), organized in nine companies, and some of the confederate lords arrived in the area from Antwerp. A meeting of the Calvinist ministers of the Westkwartier and elsewhere was immediately held at Nieuwkerke and the assembled pastors ordered each consistory to raise 100 men under its own captain. A central treasury was established under Peter Dathenus (a minister at Antwerp in close contact with Orange) and Herman Modet (a minister at Ghent). An assessment of resources was made: the Bruges Calvinists agreed to contribute 8,000 florins, those of Ieper 3,000, and so on, for military operations. Time was now precious. On 17 December the royalist siege of Valenciennes commenced and the Calvinist relief force began to collect at Tournai. The new levies of the consistories made their way there in bands of about 200 plundering and sacking Catholic property as they went (every party included many ex-iconoclasts), and on 26 December the force reached the village of Wattrelos, nine miles north-east of Lille. Lille, however, had a royal garrison and a loyal governor, Maximilien Vilain, seigneur de Rassenghien, and on 27 December he delivered a

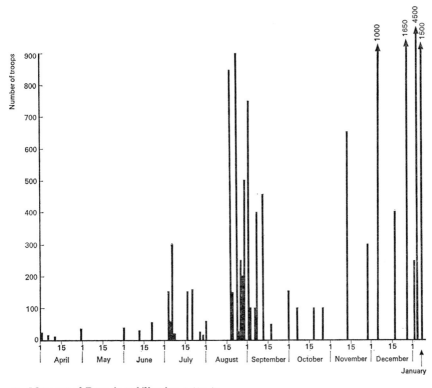

6. *Margaret of Parma's mobilization, 1566–7*
This diagram, compiled from the government's own register of recruiting
commissions signed and dispatched, reveals the impact of the iconoclastic fury
(21 August–11 September: patents for the levy of almost 5,000 men) and the open
rebellion of Valenciennes (17 December–7 January: patents for the levy of over
8,000 men). After December the government also began to recruit troops in Germany
against the rebels while in Spain and Italy troops were beginning to assemble for
the duke of Alva's march.
Source: AGRB *Audience* 2774, unfol., 'Retenues pour lever gens de guerre au service du
Roy nostre Seigneur depeschées dèz le commencement des troubles advenuz par deçà'.

surprise attack and routed the small detachment. News of the defeat
soon spread to the main Calvinist force in Tournai (only about ten
miles away) and the effect was astonishing. All the troops streamed back
towards Wattrelos. The exact reason for this disastrous move is
obscure: perhaps they hoped to catch Rassenghien unawares (he only
had 400 soldiers and 2,000 peasants with him); perhaps they were
gripped by panic and hoped to find a safer refuge. Certainly when they
arrived at the town of Lannoy, just south of Wattrelos, on 28 December

they demanded to be let in. The townsfolk refused. The next day, unexpectedly, the Calvinists found themselves confronted by the greater part of the royal army from the siegeworks around Valenciennes: baron Noircarmes, the government commander, had collected a force of 650 horse and 950 foot and, in conjunction with Rassenghien's troops, he attacked and defeated the Calvinists. Of about 3,000 Calvinists, some 600 were killed outright and the rest fled.

The victories of Lannoy and Wattrelos virtually destroyed the Calvinist movement in west Flanders, despite its deep roots. The pastors and the other leaders fled to Antwerp or Vianen; the rank and file made their way into exile in England or Germany. The royalist cause gained adherents daily and Catholic worship and obedience to the government were re-established in all areas. Noircarmes himself led his victorious army from Lannoy to Tournai where, on 2 January, he compelled the magistrates to open the gates, admit a garrison and lay down their arms. This left only Valenciennes, and Noircarmes's forces returned forthwith to tighten the siege around that last centre of resistance in the south.

The isolated town still had high hopes of being relieved. In the first place there were Brederode and the confederates in the north. The 'Grand Gueux' (Big Beggar) had mobilized eight companies of infantry to defend his castle of Vianen against attack (financed in part by melting down the family plate to strike coins) and since 1566 the castle had harboured a clandestine printing press, provided by Christopher Plantin at his own expense. The press was used to print not only Dutch editions of Calvinist tracts but also seditious literature such as (almost certainly) Dutch copies of the 'Three million guilders request'. It was also used to print propaganda in favour of Valenciennes's resistance. Brederode, with his troops and his printing press, had become in effect the head of the opposition and in January 1567 this situation was regularized, with the consent of the Calvinist communities: Brederode was elected leader of the Gueux and a committee of twelve (six delegates from the consistories and six from the Calvinist merchants) was chosen to advise him. Brederode's position now resembled that of the prince of Condé in France: he was official 'Protector' of the Calvinist movement and medals and portraits of him were sold all over 'as if they were pictures of Scipio', according to one outraged Spaniard.[23] Arrangements were made by the Big Beggar and his supporters to finance the levy of more troops (still under the guise of the 'three million guilders request') and a new, third request for the freedom of worship was composed. The grandees met Brederode and the other confederates at Breda (Orange's home) to discuss the new document on 29 January 1567 – the last in the series of such assemblies – but Orange and his compeers offered no open support. Brederode therefore went to Antwerp alone on 2 February and asked the regent for a safe-conduct to enable him to come to Brussels and present his new Request, essentially a demand that the Accord of 23 August be observed, but Margaret angrily refused and advised le Grand Gueux to go home and keep out of public affairs.

This was somewhat humiliating, but Brederode's position was still strong. Calvinist worship was still taking place in many parts of north Brabant, Limburg, Holland, Zealand and Utrecht. Many towns still openly defied the government. Moreover on 16 February Brederode's lieutenant, Antoon van Bomberghen, entered the town of 's Hertogen-bosch in north Brabant, controlled by the Calvinists since the previous October, and took command in the name of the Gueux. Next Brederode raised troops in Antwerp, paid by the consistories, and sent them to a small, specially prepared fortified camp at Oosterweel, a village just outside the walls of Antwerp. When around 3,000 men had assembled there in mid-February Brederode went back to Holland to raise yet more troops for the relief of Valenciennes.

The government was fully aware of these developments and it was thoroughly alarmed. The assembly of troops at Oosterweel was particularly disturbing because of the proximity to Antwerp, with its impregnable fortifications and its strong Protestant sympathies, and because of the rumours that the rebels intended to use their troops to capture the island of Walcheren and prevent the king from sending an army from Spain by sea. To forestall such a disaster, a desperate gamble was taken. On 13 March a picked force of 800 government troops, about half of them supplied by Count Egmont, mounted a surprise attack upon the camp of Oosterweel. The rebels were routed. Most, like their leader Jean Marnix, were killed outright; a few were taken prisoner and later executed; hardly any escaped. Orange, like Egmont, now sided openly with the government: he intervened in person to prevent the Calvinists of Antwerp from leaving the city to rescue their co-religionists at Oosterweel. The grandees could no

4

longer afford to challenge the government. Egmont even went to Valenciennes to direct the siege in person.

The rebellion was collapsing on all fronts. The count of Aremburg restored royal authority in Friesland and Groningen in January (the first Catholic services – upheld by a new royal garrison – took place in Leeuwarden on the 25 January) and Count Meghen arrived in Utrecht, the gateway to Holland, on 28 February. It was clear that the troops at Vianen could no longer march south to relieve Valenciennes.

The beleaguered town's only hope thus lay in foreign aid. Still no help came from Germany, but there was always France, and until the bitter end the hard-pressed citizens of Valenciennes imagined that relief would be sent from that quarter. For several months the confederates had maintained an agent in Paris full-time (the seigneur d'Andelot) and there was a constant exchange of envoys between the Huguenots and the Gueux. At the end of October 1566 a *grand consistoire* was held at Laventie (twelve miles west of Lille), attended (it was said) by Coligny and other Huguenot leaders. Another meeting with confederate leaders followed, after which Coligny returned to the court of Charles IX and the confederates returned to a general assembly in Antwerp. Nothing concrete appears to have resulted from these secret contacts, but on 14 March Margaret of Parma reported with some alarm that certain agents sent by Montmorency and the Châtillon brothers had been to Antwerp to negotiate with Hornes and offer him military and financial assistance. At the same time the Spanish ambassador in Paris, Don Francés de Alava, reported that two envoys from Valenciennes had been to see Condé, leader and protector of the French Huguenots, begging him to send help to the town. But they had returned empty-handed, 'saying that in the end they would have to tell the town to surrender unconditionally because all the help that had been promised in France and elsewhere had proved false'. As usual, Alava was right: on 24 March, while the Huguenots were still discussing whether or not to organize relief for Valenciennes the despairing town surrendered to Noircarmes and his besieging army.

The surrender of Valenciennes, which freed the government's veteran troops for new operations, was soon followed by other successes. As Noircarmes wrote to Granvelle: 'The capture of Valenciennes has worked a miracle. The other towns are all coming out to meet me, putting the rope around their own necks.' Maastricht expelled its

Calvinist preachers on 31 March and admitted a royal garrison soon afterwards. On 11 April the Calvinist dictator of 's Hertogenbosch, Antoon van Bomberghen, abandoned the city, followed by the *predikanten* three days later. Again government troops were soon admitted. Even Antwerp agreed to accept a garrison on 13 April and 3,000 troops entered the city on the 26 April. Finally, on 3 May, Vianen fell and, with this, the rebellion was over. Orange had resigned all his offices on 10 April and left Antwerp; on 21 April he fled to Germany. On 27 April Brederode, having made a desperate but unsuccessful bid to win Amsterdam over to his cause, admitted defeat too and fled ignominiously to Emden. He left his surviving supporters from Oosterweel, Antwerp and den Bosch behind him – perhaps 4,000 men in all – many of whom fell into government hands as they tried to follow their late leader by sea to Emden.

The government had thus won a signal victory. By the middle of May 1567 the revolt was over and open Calvinist worship at an end. It was true that, as Meghen put it, 'the fat birds have flown . . . leaving only the thin ones', but there still was a very impressive catch: Valenciennes, Tournai, Antwerp and Vianen had all yielded their share of iconoclasts and leaders of the rebellion. The transformation since January was scarcely credible, even for loyalists like Berlaymont. Yet much of the credit for this state of affairs, it must be admitted, did not lie with the government in Brussels at all. Although as late as November 1566 wealthy Netherlanders were still laying bets of 16,000 florins that the king would not come to the Netherlands the following year, by the spring of 1567 no one in the Low Countries could be unaware of the preparations which the king was making in Spain for his own voyage and for the military expedition of the duke of Alva. The knowledge that the king was at last about to take the Netherlands situation in hand was a major factor in persuading some reckless politicians – Meghen, Mansfelt and eventually even Egmont – to rally behind the regent.[24] And yet, for all that, Alva's expedition was nearly called off more than once.

The sending of the duke of Alva

Even before the king signed Alva's patent to command the future army of Flanders on 29 November 1566, attempts were made to sabotage his mission. On 15 November Montigny and Berghes, still vainly labouring in Madrid to have the *Moderation* endorsed, presented a memorial to the king begging that Ruy Gómez should be sent to the Netherlands as Philip's personal representative with full powers but no troops. Since (unknown to them, no doubt) the king had rejected precisely this argument from Ruy Gómez himself on 29 October, it is scarcely surprising that he rejected it again a fortnight later. However, having failed with the king, the ambassadors turned their attention to the crown prince, Don Carlos. In this they were embarking upon a very dangerous course, because the prince was already a source of very grave concern, embarrassment and sorrow to his father. For some years it had been fairly common knowledge that Don Carlos was mentally unstable (like Joanna the Mad, his great-grandmother both on his mother's and his father's side). He was often ill, sometimes suffering fits, and he regularly quarrelled with his father and others. In September 1566 Don Carlos all but murdered a man who caught him eavesdropping outside the room in which the Council of State was discussing the affairs of the Netherlands in the presence of Philip II. In view of these and many other incidents which kept Madrid humming with gossip, it was clearly both difficult and dangerous to involve the unpredictable and unbalanced Don Carlos in politics. And yet, on the other hand, the prince of Spain possessed an inherent authority which could not be discounted, especially since Don Carlos was the only son of Philip II, a monarch who was himself often ill, and not least in the autumn of 1566. However, Don Carlos's chief recommendation to the Netherlands' ambassadors was not his malleable personality nor his high position but the master of his household: Ruy Gómez da Silva. If the crown prince went to the Netherlands as the figurehead for a new administration, he would be accompanied by Ruy Gómez, reputedly the friend of Hornes and Egmont and certainly the apostle of relatively mild measures to appease the discontented Netherlanders. And if Ruy Gómez went, Alva and his troops would not.[25]

The stratagam was subtle, and it almost worked. In mid-December almost every foreign ambassador at the Spanish Court reported that the king had adopted a new policy for the Netherlands. It was thought that Ruy Gómez would go straight to Brussels, perhaps to occupy a position analogous to that of Cardinal Granvelle a few years before, and there direct the government's efforts to pacify the troubles, while Alva would go to Milan and wait there to see if his forces were needed. If not, they could be used to mount a new attack on the pirate stronghold of Algiers.

Once again, however, the proposals of the Gómez faction were rejected by the king. Alva was still at Court to defend his point of view, harping on the pessimistic letters of Margaret of Parma which had asserted even before the rebellion that a good half of the population of the Low Countries was infected with heresy, with perhaps 200,000 people under arms, while her letters of September warned that the Calvinists aimed at deposing the king in favour of a Protestant ruler. As late as 29 February 1567 Margaret was warning that a long civil war seemed inevitable since Brederode's forces were as strong as her own, while reinforcements were promised from the Protestants of France and Germany. Under the circumstances Philip II could only continue to believe that the dispatch of a large army was the sole effective solution to the Netherlands problem.

Preparations for Alva's expedition therefore continued at a steady pace and on 18 February 1567 Francisco de Ibarra, appointed to be commissary-general of the new army, left the court with instructions to prepare food, munitions and transport along a predetermined route from Milan to Franche-Comté for the duke and his Spanish veterans. All observers at the Court regarded this as an indisputable sign that Alva would definitely go to Italy in the spring to take command of the forces assembled there and, sure enough, on 17 April the duke took his leave of the king at Aranjuez. Ten days later he set sail from Cartagena.

Ironically, on the very day that Alva left Spain for Italy, a special emissary from Margaret of Parma arrived at Court with orders to persuade the king that Spanish troops were no longer needed in the Netherlands and, indeed, could now only do harm to the settlement which had already been secured. The envoy was Gaspar de Robles, a Portuguese whose family had settled in the Low Countries. The son of Philip II's childhood nurse and a man who had taken part in restoring order in the Netherlands, Robles was as likely as anyone to gain the king's ear and he eventually managed to persuade Philip to allow the Council of State to debate once more the basic question of whether or not to send a Spanish army to the Netherlands now that Margaret of Parma had defeated and driven out most of the rebels. Again the council was divided: four ministers remained convinced that the existing arrangements were still best, while an equal number argued that Alva and his troops should wait in Lombardy while Ruy Gómez went alone to the Low Countries. And again the king stood firm and confirmed his earlier policy decisions, although he did agree that the 60,000 foot and 10,000 horse originally projected for the royal army was now clearly excessive. It was therefore resolved that only the Spaniards (about 10,000 men in all) and a single regiment of German infantry (under Count Alberic de Lodron) would be required to supplement the efforts of the 10,000 or so Walloon and German troops already serving Margaret of Parma in the Netherlands.

The duke of Alva, who joined his Spanish veterans on 31 May after a long sea-crossing and another attack of gout, therefore continued to prepare for the long march from Lombardy to the Low Countries. The news from the east was encouraging: the death of the aged Suleiman the Magnificent the previous September had provoked mutinies in the Ottoman army and revolts in some outlying provinces against his successor, and these restrained the new Sultan from aggression against the west in 1567. Italy could be denuded of its veteran defenders without serious risk. On 18 June 1567 the duke set out with his men from Asti on the borders of Lombardy to cross the Alps and the 700 miles which separated them from the Netherlands.

Given the political and geographical configuration of Europe, the route chosen by Philip II was probably the safest available. Politically speaking it ran through his own dominions of Lombardy and Franche-Comté and through those of his close allies, the dukes of Savoy and Lorraine. Geographically, although the Mt Cenis pass through the Alps was fairly difficult, from there onwards wide valleys and long plateaux made the going relatively easy. The first contingents crossed the Mt Cenis on 24 June:

'[the crossing] is four and a half long leagues of very bad road, because there are two and a half leagues ascent to the top of the mountain – a narrow and very stony road – and after reaching the top we marched another league along a ridge of the mountain, and on this level space there are four huts in which the post-horses are kept. After crossing the top of the mountain there is a very bad descent which lasts another league, the same kind of road as the ascent, and it leads down to Lanslebourg [a village] which is at the foot of the mountain on the other side, and there the army was billeted. It is a miserable hamlet with a hundred small houses. While we crossed the mountain it snowed and the weather was awful.'[26]

The army survived this ordeal with few losses – even Alva's gouty legs were unaffected – and on 29 June, clear of the Alps at last, the duke and his men arrived outside Chambéry, the capital of Savoy. There was now no other physical obstacle between them and the Netherlands, but the duke could not discount the possibility of an ambush, either by the rebels or by the French Huguenots, and so the troops were regrouped into a single column for the rest of the journey and their progress became slower, more hesitant, more cautious. Scouting parties were sent ahead to reconnoitre the road and to make sure all was safe, but apart from a fire in the camp on 16 July, which destroyed some baggage, there was no cause for alarm and the morale of the troops was high. On 24 July, the eve of St James's day, the army reached the little town of Ville-sur-Illon in Lorraine and the duke and all the other knights of Santiago (St James) with the expedition donned the cloaks and hoods of their Order and went to the local chapel to hear vespers sung by the army's chaplains. At midnight, and again on the following day (the Feast of St James – Spain's national day), all the soldiers fired a salvo in honour of *el señor Santiago*. Brantôme, who saw Alva's army on the march at about this time, compared the ordinary soldiers to captains, so impressive were their clothes and their gilded and engraved breastplates, and the musketeers he compared to princes.

Alva and his refulgent troops crossed the border into the Netherlands on 3 August and at Thionville, just beyond the frontier, the duke was greeted by most of the prominent nobles and officials of the Low Countries. They had flocked down from Brussels – to the fury of Margaret of Parma, who suddenly found herself almost alone in a deserted palace – in order to ingratiate (or exculpate) themselves with the new captain-general. Alva spent some time in consultation trying to ascertain the true state of the Low Countries and whether it was safe to proceed further. In the end he was convinced and after a leisurely progress from Luxemburg the duke and his entourage rode into Brussels on 22 August, just four months after he had taken leave of the king at Aranjuez. After all the hesitations and delays, the duke had made good time.

Once in Brussels, Alva took immediate steps to consolidate his position. He presented his credentials to Margaret of Parma and explained his mission: he had come to pacify the Netherlands thoroughly so that the king would be able to come by sea at once. To achieve this, Alva proposed that the 10,000 Spaniards who had accompanied him should be garrisoned close to the capital: the infantry at Ghent, Lier, Enghien and Brussels itself, the cavalry in the area around Diest. The duke would admit no objection to this plan. He informed Margaret of Parma:

'I fail to understand how any person of sound mind can be of the opinion that His Majesty should come here with only the mediocre forces at present mobilized. If any moves were made against him from outside or inside the country (where His Majesty has been told that there are more than 200,000 heretics), he would run the dangers and the risks which one can easily imagine.'

Alva was deaf to Margaret's complaint that he was planning to billet his unpopular *tercios* on towns like Brussels and Lier which had remained loyal instead of on those like Maastricht and s' Hertogenbosch which had rebelled; he insisted that it was the king's command that his troops should be kept together so that they could unite rapidly to protect him the moment he arrived from Spain.[27] Margaret was firmly and rather gracelessly overruled and the Spanish troops proceeded to their scheduled quarters at once. The nineteen companies of the *tercio* of Naples, for example, entered Ghent on 30 August, marching into the city in ranks of five followed by a large number of prostitutes decked in flounced Spanish dresses and perched on small nags. A horde of camp-followers brought up the rear, with bare feet and bare heads, escorting the regiment's horses, carts and baggage. After performing a few manoeuvres in the city square and firing a salvo to impress the natives, the Spaniards marched off to their lodgings.

Almost immediately disorders and outrages began. The troops were unruly and insolent, regarding the Netherlanders as heretics and traitors to a man. They mobbed Count Egmont when he came to pay his respects to Alva in Thionville; they beat up local merchants as they marched from Luxemburg to Brussels; and they habitually referred to the population of the Low Countries as 'Lutherans'. The Spaniards were insufferable; but they were also indispensable. Expertly trained and absolutely reliable, they were essential to the 'new order' which

Philip II had resolved to establish in the Netherlands. The duke of Alva was determined to lose no time in implementing it.

The duke of Alva's new order

In spite of the indecision which had surrounded his departure, the duke of Alva's programme when he eventually reached the Low Countries was essentially the same as the one he had proposed at the Council of State in Madrid on 29 October 1566. He came prepared to take all the necessary military steps to ensure that the Netherlands would not make trouble again. The duke was to act simply as captain-general of the king's forces in the Low Countries; all executive civil power was to remain with Margaret of Parma until the king could come in person to sort the situation out.

As far as one can see, Philip II had every intention of leaving Spain for the Low Countries in the autumn of 1567. A fleet was collected at Corunna and troops and provisions were even embarked in readiness. At court Antonio Pérez was instructed to go through the state papers in his possession (his own and his father's) and those in the government's archive at Simancas in order to collect any 'which it might be useful to take to Flanders'. It was reported that a corps of fifty theologians had been detailed to accompany the king, either to advise him on religious issues or to man a new super-inquisition in the Netherlands. The preparations were delayed, however, by the arrival of discouraging news from the duke of Alva describing the situation he found when at last he arrived in the north.

He warned the king that the Netherlands were still dangerously restive, that a large number of the trouble-makers had fled to England and Germany and might be expected to organize resistance to the king's voyage from there. In the duke's opinion, Philip should delay his departure for a few more months until all could be made safe. Subsequent letters from Brussels only repeated this cautious advice and therefore on 23 September the king announced that he would delay his voyage to the Netherlands until the following spring.[28]

Although his own advice had prompted this decision, the duke of Alva did not welcome the postponement of the king's plans. Expecting to be in command for only six months, the duke had taken few detailed political instructions with him and even fewer non-military personnel. In addition the Netherlands climate aggravated his gout, the distance from the Court weakened his hold on royal patronage, and his style of life in Brussels, with so many retainers to support, was beyond his means. Finally, he antagonized Margaret of Parma. The duchess had never wanted Alva to come to the Netherlands, and his actions once in Brussels only confirmed her hostility. In the first place, the duke ordered all the troops raised by Margaret in 1566–7 to be demobilized. It was true that some of the German regiments were openly Lutheran, but all had served well and deserved better treatment from their employer.[29] Their summary dismissal was an open humiliation for Margaret; but worse was to come. The duke arrived with the intention of creating a special judicial court which would try all those accused of heresy or rebellion. The first steps were taken only five days after Alva entered Brussels, and on 5 September a patent was issued creating the 'Council of Troubles'. At first the existence of the new tribunal was kept secret because Hornes, Hoogstraten and Orange, all of whom were clearly implicated in the troubles, were for various reasons in Germany. They were summoned to come to Brussels, and Hornes arrived on 8 September (Hoogstraten and Orange, more prudent, remained in Germany). On 9 September Hornes, Egmont and their secretaries were arrested by a detachment of Spanish troops and all their papers were seized. At the same time Antoon van Stralen, former burgomaster of Antwerp, was arrested.[30]

These events put Margaret of Parma in an impossible position. She had, at Alva's request, unsuspectingly invited van Stralen and, possibly, Hornes to return to Brussels. Their arrest upon arrival made Margaret appear to be Alva's accomplice and, under the circumstances, she felt compelled to resign. She left for Italy on 30 December, having sworn in the duke of Alva, captain-general of the armed forces, to succeed her as governor-general as well.

Alva was ill prepared for such an accretion of power. Margaret had been expected to remain in office until the king came, and therefore Alva had no political advisers with him. The 'iron duke', however, was not the man to be daunted by such difficulties. 'There is', he told the king optimistically, 'a new world to be created here' and he set about creating it with the aid of the handful of reliable ministers to hand. He employed to the full the few native administrators whom he could trust (many of them half-Spanish like Esteban Prats or Luis del Rio), supplementing their efforts by using the officers of his military staff as political overseers. Executive power was transferred from the native administration to the Spanish and Italian ministers attached to the duke's household. He had his own 'cabinet council' (*consejo de Cámara*) of Spaniards which dealt with all petitions and distributed administrative tasks to the various central government bodies. He used Spanish and Italian lawyers to handle foreign relations (under the overall control of his personal secretary, Juan de Albornoz), to redraft and unify the legal codes of the provinces, and even to run the chief towns as a sort of *corregidor*.[31] As a standard part of the new policy, whenever a Netherlands official died or resigned, the duke left the post vacant. 'Putting in new men one by one is like throwing a bottle of good wine into a vat of vinegar,' he warned the king. 'The wine will instantly turn to vinegar too.' Alva believed that only when all the old ministers were gone should the vacancies be filled by a completely new team of administrators; men who 'possess a spotless character without looking for aptitude for business'. Reliability, the duke believed, counted for more than capacity. After all, when every decision of importance was to be taken in Spain, the calibre of the civil service in the Netherlands was of little moment. As Alva once informed the king: the Low Countries 'must be governed from there and not from here'.[32]

The first objective of the new governor was to eliminate the discomforted remnants of the Netherlands opposition. Although he made one or two attempts to capture Orange and others abroad by stealth, the duke's main counter-insurgency device was the Council of Troubles. There was a central tribunal, sitting in Brussels, and subordinate courts in each province, but in fact executive power was monopolized by Alva, whose signature alone authenticated the acts of the Council. The Council was extremely active over the winter of 1567–8, seeking out and sifting evidence, making new arrests, executing sentences. At the beginning of Lent 1568 a large number of people suspected of complicity in the troubles were arrested on the same day all over the Netherlands. The following year it was the turn of books. On 26 March 1569 there was a simultaneous swoop on all the bookshops of the Netherlands. The booksellers of Tournai, once a Calvinist stronghold, were made to disgorge over 500 heretical books which were publicly burned on 16 June.[33]

The secrecy, the omnicompetence and the efficiency of the new courts impressed and terrified everyone, even the innocent. Albert van Loo, a revenue collector of irreproachable probity, tried to commit suicide for fear that he would be blamed for not stopping the disorders of 1566 single-handed. Even Count Meghen began to tremble lest he too should be punished for his part in the anti-Granvelle league.[34] In all the Council tried over 12,000 people in connection with the rebellion of 1566–7, and almost 9,000 were condemned to lose some or all of their goods. Over 1,000 were executed. Many offenders were tried in their absence, including most of the nobles: Orange, Culemborg, Hoogstraten, Montigny and many others were summoned to appear before the court on 19 January 1568, but they stayed in Germany where they had taken sanctuary (all except Montigny who was still in Spain, under house arrest, and there he was secretly strangled in October 1570). All were judged guilty of treason *in absentia* and condemned to forfeit all their possessions and property in the Netherlands.[35]

This was an important development since, after their sentence, the sole way for the exiles to recover their inheritances was to regain control of the Brussels government. This, of course, could only be done by an armed invasion which would overthrow the military basis of Alva's power. The exiles therefore opened a campaign fund, to which many individuals in the Netherlands, France and Germany secretly subscribed, and on 6 April 1568 the prince of Orange issued official commissions to Count Louis, van den Berg, Hoogstraten and others authorizing them to levy troops to make war on the duke of Alva.

William of Orange was now the undisputed leader of the opposition. The death of Brederode (in February 1568) and Berghes (in August 1567) and the imprisonment of Egmont, Hornes and Montigny removed all the other leaders of the earlier movement, and in any case William possessed a decisive constitutional advantage in his position as ruler of the principality of Orange. As a sovereign ruler he was technically entitled to make war on his enemies – and Alva, who had confiscated the prince's estates and kidnapped his eldest son Philip William, then a student at Leuven, was clearly an enemy. Orange's campaign strategy in 1568, like the later plans of 1571 and 1572, was to send four armies into the Netherlands from different quarters at the same time. An army of French Huguenots was to march into the south Netherlands while a force from England invaded Flanders and troops from Germany entered Limburg in the south-east and Friesland in the north-east. Orange himself would remain in Cleves with a reserve force. The plan was sound in theory but, as in 1572, the difficulties of synchronizing the four attacks proved insurmountable.

The first setback occurred in February 1568 when the lord of Hannecamp, who was to lead the invasion from France, was captured in west Flanders where he had come to lay plans with a group of Calvinist partisans, about 100 strong: the 'Beggars of the Woods' ('Bosgeuzen', specialists in the murder of Catholic priests) who were to assist the invaders from France. Next came the defeat of the Limburg army, about 3,000 men under the seigneur de Villers, which crossed into the Netherlands on 20 April. Not a single town declared for them. A column of Spanish veterans arrived swiftly and defeated the invaders in a brief but decisive encounter before Dalheim on 25 April. Villers and most of his lieutenants were captured or killed. Under interrogation the survivors incriminated many of Orange's supporters, both in exile and in the Netherlands, and they gave details of the prince's contacts with the Protestants of Germany and France.[36] Before Alva could act on this information, however, on 24 April another more powerful army entered Friesland under Count Louis of Nassau. Because of the greater number involved in the invasion, it took Alva rather longer to prepare a counter-attack, but in fact Count Louis was unable to profit from the delay because, as in Limburg, not one town embraced his cause. The 'rebels' stayed close to the German frontier. On 23 May their fortunes changed. A mixed force of Spanish and Netherlands troops came up and gave battle to Count Louis's troops at the monastery of Heiligerlee, just outside Winschoten. The government's forces were repulsed with heavy losses. Count Louis now established a headquarters at Delfzijl on the Eems and organized a fleet to open the sea lanes to England, where the Calvinist churches-in-exile had been actively engaged in raising men and money for Orange's cause. On 15 July a royal fleet which tried to attack Delfzijl was decisively defeated by Count Louis's Sea Beggars, as his men soon came to be called. But already the situation of the Orangists was deteriorating. Late in June a French Huguenot army of some 3,000 men crossed into Artois, commanded by the seignuer de Coqueville.

Yet again the invaders found no supporters within the Netherlands and before long they were driven back into France by superior government forces. There, at St Valéry on 18 July, the Huguenots were surrounded by an army sent by Charles IX and cut to pieces. The Franco–Spanish entente, cemented at Bayonne in 1565, was bearing fruit at last. Next, on 18 September, a new group of Bosgeuzen arrived in Flanders by sea from England. They had been organized by the consistories of the refugee Dutch churches in London, Norwich and Sandwich, and were paid three or four stuivers a day by the same. They were, however, captured within a few days, tortured to reveal their accomplices (which they did) and then executed. Meanwhile the duke of Alva had decided to move against Count Louis in person and he led his Spanish veterans into Friesland to avenge the defeat of Heiligerlee. The rebels made a stand on the peninsula of Jemmigen, which projected into the Eems, and there on 21 July the Spaniards attacked and carried the day. As in previous engagements, no quarter was given and the rebels had to choose between being butchered where they stood or trying their luck swimming the Eems, which was two miles wide at that point. Few of them survived, but news of the disaster nevertheless arrived rapidly at Emden: the incoming tide swept the broad-brimmed hats of the drowned Orangists to the head of the estuary.

The defeat at Jemmigen effectively ruined the whole campaign of opposition against Alva. After such a signal defeat, neither Elizabeth of England nor the German princes were prepared to provide further support for Orange's cause when, in October 1568, he invaded Brabant with 30,000 men. He also found that no one in the Netherlands dared or wished to support him. Alva simply blocked the road to Brussels with his army and waited until the invading host melted away, so forcing Orange to retreat. Late in November, after twenty-nine days of continuous skirmishing, the prince led his troops back to France, disconsolate and defeated. He paid them off, as best he could, in February 1569.

The campaign of 1568 thus proved a total failure for the prince of Orange and his supporters. There had been four invasion-attempts; every one of them had failed. Many trusted commanders and many faithful followers and colleagues had been lost – including Egmont and Hornes, who were executed in Brussels on 5 June. Foreign supporters who had helped the prince since his flight in April 1567 were now discredited and compromised, and they lost no time in disowning him. Worst of all, the prince was bankrupt. All his available financial resources had been thrown into the campaign of 1568: Orange calculated that he had paid out of his own pocket some 500,000 florins, and he probably owed as much again. And it had all been for nothing. Financially, militarily and politically, the 1568 campaign had proved a disaster. At their wits' end, Orange and his brothers decided to throw in their lot with the only friends they had left: the French Huguenots. Together with some 1,200 survivors of the various Netherlands invasions, they set off early in 1569 to join the army of Condé and Coligny fighting in France. Even there they were defeated – twice! – at Jarnac and Moncontour by the French Catholics supported by Alva's veterans. Events appeared to justify the duke of Alva's arrogant presumption in having a massive bronze statue erected in his own honour at Antwerp, cast from the cannon captured at Jemmigen and showing the duke trampling on a two-headed, four-armed figure, with the motto: 'To the duke of Alva . . . who extirpated sedition, reduced rebellion, restored religion, secured justice and established peace'.

The duke had many causes for self-congratulation. He had been sent to the Netherlands to make the way straight and safe for his master. This he had triumphantly accomplished. The rebels in exile had been defeated; a large number of the former rebels in captivity had been executed; the invasions of the exiled opposition had failed to kindle the least spark of sympathy from the population at large. The Netherlands were now ready for the king, and Alva looked forward to a hero's return to Spain, his estates and the Court. But unfortunately for the duke, the king was no longer free to come. A series of personal and political problems now made it impossible for him to leave Spain. The first difficulty concerned the crown prince, Don Carlos. Even the king came to recognize the possibility that his son might be insane and therefore unfit and unable to succeed him, for by the end of 1567 the prince's behaviour had become dangerous. He took to carrying a loaded pistol about with him and he told his confessor at the New Year that he intended to kill a man before long. In view of the rapidly worsening relations between the prince and his father, Philip II feared that the 'man' might be himself. In January 1568 therefore the prince was placed under house arrest. A small committee met at the king's command to discuss the sensitive question of what to do with him. The archives of the crown of Aragon were searched for documents relating to the parallel case of Charles of Viana, the crown prince of Aragon who was disinherited and imprisoned by his father in 1461. It was found that he had died in prison before a final solution could be determined. By an odd coincidence Don Carlos too solved the dilemma of his future status himself: he died suddenly, in custody, on 24 July 1568.

This left Philip II, already forty years old, without an heir to succeed him. His only other surviving children were two infant daughters, Isabella Clara Eugenia and Catalina Michaela. In October 1568 the Queen died giving birth to another daughter and the succession problem became acute. It was imperative for the king to safeguard his life and health: a difficult and possibly dangerous sea-voyage to the Netherlands was clearly a risk which he could no longer take. Any remaining doubts about this were quickly dispelled when a new revolt broke out in Spain itself. At Christmas 1568 the *moriscos* of the mountains around Granada rebelled against the policy of forcible 'Christianization' decreed by the central government. Their dogged resistance continued to tie down a large royal army until the summer of 1571; and in the end it was starvation caused by a harvest failure, and not the king's soldiers, which forced the *moriscos* to surrender. The picture was not entirely black, however. At least the Turkish sultan did not send any support to his co-religionists in the *sierras* of Granada. In 1568, indeed, there were rebellions in the Ottoman empire and then in 1569 the Sultan sent his forces north against the Muscovites and south to the Yemen rather than west against Philip II. The king was therefore able to make considerable sums of money available for the duke of Alva's operations against the Orangists: over seven million florins were received by the Netherlands from Spain in 1568 and 1569. Also in 1568 some 2,400 Spanish troops were sent by sea from the peninsula to reinforce the veteran units in the army of Flanders. There was even a promise from the king that, since he was no longer able to visit the Low Countries in person, he would appoint a new governor-general to take over, allowing the victorious duke to return to Spain for his Triumph. But, until a successor was chosen, Alva was instructed to continue the work of pacification.

The duke's position at the end of 1568 strongly resembled that of Charles V in Germany twenty years before, after the battle of Mühlberg. In both cases a striking military victory over all opponents had been achieved; in both cases the victors were encouraged by their success to impose conditions on the vanquished which, experience was to show, were too harsh. It was argued in favour of the new order of 1548 and that of 1568 that they merely restored a situation which had existed before the troubles, before the growth of Protestantism. But the clock could not be turned back unilaterally in this way. In the new religious climate, renovation seemed to many people like innovation, and was therefore resisted. In both Germany and the Netherlands it took about four years for widespread resistance to materialize and in both cases opposition crystalized around the implementation of the new religious policies and the presence of Spanish troops.

One of the duke of Alva's foremost aims in the Netherlands was to put into effect the religious reforms planned by the king in 1559 which had been shelved because of the obstructionist tactics of the provincial estates. Although the Netherlands inquisition, suspended in 1566, was not revived, the Council of Troubles and its subordinate tribunals in the provinces proved a far more effective weapon in the fight against heresy and they continued to persecute those accused of heresy until 1576 (although their activities were severely curtailed after 1573). Firm action was taken to establish the 'new bishoprics', however. When Alva arrived in the Netherlands in 1567 only four of the fourteen new bishoprics (St Omer, Bruges, Middelburg and Ieper) had actually been admitted to full jurisdiction in their dioceses. Four more (including Granvelle, the archbishop of Mechelen) had been admitted to a part of their functions, and the remaining six had not been installed at all. As might have been expected, the duke insisted on the full and immediate implementation of the 'new bishoprics' scheme and by 1570 it was all working smoothly. The duke also took a keen interest in the appointment of suitable candidates to the bishoprics. He seems to have realized that the Protestant challenge had to be met with sound pastoral care and effective teaching of the articles of the Roman Catholic faith and he persistently recommended to the king men who were distinguished for their preaching of the faith as well as for their integrity and organizing ability.

The duke also sponsored a number of other, less controversial changes, for instance in the field of law. Legislation was enacted to unify the criminal law and the procedure in criminal trials in the various Netherlands provinces (July 1570); much customary law was codified, for instance the complex 'Customs of Antwerp', the bane of all merchants there (1570–71); and the laws regulating marine insurance were revised and codified in a series of ordinances (March 1569, October 1570 and January 1571). These measures were important and useful (although they sometimes overrode local privileges) but, like all the duke's other initiatives, however laudable, they were still only pushed through at sword-point. Alva succeeded in his policies where Margaret had failed largely because he had a trained army at his back.

The duke had brought 10,000 men with him to the Netherlands from Italy and in addition there were the numerous Walloon and German troops mobilized for the invasion of 1568. After the defeat of Orange, the duke of Alva gave serious thought to the problem of financing this large military establishment. He decided upon a standing army of 3,200 Walloon and 4,000 Spanish infantry scattered in garrisons, castles and citadels along the frontiers, with a further 4,000 Spanish infantry and 500 light cavalry stationed near Brussels as a strategic reserve. The cost of this force, together with other defensive arrangements (such as the citadels which he ordered to be built at Antwerp, Groningen and Maastricht), was considerable. Alva himself put the total budget at 1,873,000 florins for defence and 2,312,000 for administration every year. The king had already made it clear that he wanted no part of this sum to come from Spain. In May 1568, before news of Count Louis's invasion reached him, the king informed Alva:

'It is more than necessary to arrange for there to be a fixed, certain and permanent revenue from those provinces for their own maintenance and defence, because clearly the money for that cannot – and will not – continue to come from here.'

After the invaders had been successfully (if expensively) repulsed, the Madrid government returned to the same theme. Cardinal Espinosa, Philip II's chief minister, warned the duke in March 1569:

'The amount of money which the Castilian Exchequer has had to provide for the Netherlands does not cease to cause grave concern. And, indeed, if you do not arrange things so that the outlay stops, I am concerned that it will be impossible to go on any longer.'[37]

In accordance with instructions from the king, in March 1569 Alva convened the estates of all the Netherlands provinces and asked them to consent to the collection of three new taxes devised by his financial advisers: the Tenth, Twentieth and Hundredth Pennies. The last tax was the least controversial and the only one actually to be put into effect. It was a single, once-for-all tax of 1 per cent on all capital. The value of the capital was to be calculated from its yield: those who owned houses were required to pay 16 per cent of the return received from their investment in the year 1569-70; those with other forms of capital asset were to pay 22 per cent of their year's profit. This was taken as equivalent to a tax of 1 per cent on the value of the capital itself.[38] The estates agreed to this tax (the 'Hundredth Penny') and collection was organized immediately. The tax was not farmed out – the usual arrangement in the Netherlands – but entrusted to an army of collectors and inspectors recruited specially and responsible to the central government alone, not to the estates. New registers were opened to record the incomes and investments of all liable to pay the tax and by February 1571 3,300,000 florins had been received. In all, the Hundredth Penny produced 3,628,507 florins of revenue (suggesting a total capital investment in the Netherlands of at least 362 million florins). It proved a major success for the government. However the two other taxes proposed by Alva in March 1569 were different in almost every way. In the first place, unlike the Hundredth Penny, they were to be permanent. The Twentieth Penny was to be a 5-per-cent levy on all future sales of landed property and the Tenth Penny a tax of 10 per cent on all other sales; like the Hundredth Penny they were to be collected and administered by a special staff of officials quite independently of the provincial estates. The duke estimated that they would yield 13,600,000 florins every year, and perhaps more. The estates, whose consent was necessary before the taxes could be raised legally, naturally refused to sign away their power but, intimidated by threats from Alva's Spanish troops (an entire regiment was billeted in Leuven in August 1569 to encourage the town's deputies to approve the new taxes), they offered instead an *aide* of 4,000,000 florins to be collected in the traditional way under their scrutiny over a period of two years (August 1569–August 1571).[39] Alva accepted this offer as a temporary means of financing his army, but he continued to cajole and bluster in order to gain the estates' consent to the perpetual Tenth and Twentieth Pennies. First he made concessions: the Tenth Penny was restricted to only the first and the last sale of movable goods; and transport, carriage charges and the first sale of primary produce and raw materials were exempted altogether. This brought the estimated yield of the taxes down to 4,000,000 florins annually, which would not cripple trade (especially since existing purchase tax and excise duties were to be reduced) yet would provide enough revenue to support all the troops stationed in the Netherlands. Nevertheless the estates' basic objection remained: it was to be a permanent imposition, voted once and for all. The estates offered to vote another *aide* in 1571, but they would never consent to the Tenth Penny.

Exasperated, the duke of Alva overstepped the bounds of constitutional propriety. On 31 July 1571 he declared that he would proceed to collect the new taxes whether or not the estates consented, starting the following day (when the *aide* of 1569 ran out), and tax collectors were appointed. Every transaction was to be recorded in a special register, under the scrutiny of special assessors, to determine liability for tax. Until this had been done no money could be collected and so, towards the end of 1571, with the yield of the Hundredth Penny and the *aide* of 1569 mostly spent, Alva began to experience difficulty in meeting all the government's obligations. He wrote to the king to ask for some help from the Spanish treasury until the money from the Tenth Penny began to come in. The king was not sympathetic: in February 1572 he drafted a letter which reproached the duke (rather unjustly) 'for the scant attention which you have devoted to putting the Tenth Penny into effect'. The revolt of the *moriscos* and the new offensive of the Turks in the Mediterranean were placing an intolerable strain on Spain's resources, he complained, and 'with the Holy League [against the Turks] and so many other things which must be paid for from here it is impossible to meet the needs of the Netherlands to the same extent that we have been doing up to now'.[40] Alva was peremptorily instructed to see to the collection of the new tax, whatever the opposition. The duke lost no time. In March he moved detachments of troops into the premises of the shopkeepers and merchants in Brussels who had ceased business in protest against the new tax, but it did no good: the taxpayers continued their obstructionist tactics and scarcely a penny was collected. The tax strike was strongly supported by the local institutions. The provincial estates of Hainaut, Artois, Flanders and Brabant sent deputies to Spain to protest in person to the king against the imposition of new taxes without their consent and against the use of troops to support the tax collectors. Trade and industry ceased, unemployment grew and discontent mounted. The government was clearly risking a general rebellion. 'If the prince of Orange had conserved his forces until a time like this,' wrote one shrewd observer on 24 March 1572, 'his enterprise would have succeeded.'[41] Little did the writer know that the prince too could read the signs of the times and was preparing a massive invasion of the Low Countries. Just one week later, on 1 April, the first blow in the second revolt of the Netherlands was struck: the small seaport of the Brill in south Holland was captured by a fleet acting in the name of Orange and Liberty.[42]

[3]

THE SECOND REVOLT

(1569–76)

The gathering storm

The flight of the leaders of the Netherlands opposition in 1567 determined to a large degree the methods and character of future resistance
to Philip II and his policies. Above all it ensured that only an invasion
could effectively challenge the duke of Alva's authority; the leadership
of the opposition would therefore inevitably rest with those in exile.
This in turn meant that the Calvinists would play a far greater role
in the movement than before, since they constituted the majority
of the exiles.

Ever since the severe persecution which followed the peace of
Crépy in 1544, groups of Protestant fugitives from the Low Countries
had sought refuge in the Lutheran and Calvinist states of Germany,
especially in those close to the Netherlands border and in south-east
England. At first the exiles worshipped with the town congregations,
but before long their numbers had grown large enough to justify the
creation of separate churches. At Emden and Norwich the Netherlands
refugees made up almost 40 per cent of the total population by 1570.

Approximate strength of the principal Dutch exile communities

	In Germany			In England	
	c. 1560	*c.* 1570		*c.* 1560	*c.* 1570
Aachen	1,000	3,000	Canterbury	—	800
Emden	2,000	5,000	Colchester	—	200
Frankfurt	2,000	1,500	London	1,000	3,500
Hamburg	—	2,000	Norwich	—	4,000
Wesel	10,00	7,000	Sandwich	400	1,200

By 1572 there were probably seventeen communities of Dutch Calvinist refugees in south-eastern England, and as many again or more in Germany. Each of the larger communities had its own pastor, deacons, elders and consistory. They had their own literature too: a Dutch version of the Psalms was composed during the 1550s, then came the first Dutch edition of Calvin's *Institutes* (printed at Emden in 1560) and a special Netherlands Confession of Faith (the *Confessio Belgica* printed at Rouen in 1561). Each separate church of the exiles was independent and equal, according to Calvinist precept, and although the churches in London and Emden were recognized as senior and in certain circumstances entitled to speak for the entire Dutch Reformed community in each country, they could seldom exert any control over the other churches.

Although between 1564 and 1567, when the persecution in the Netherlands was less effective, the size of the congregations in exile declined somewhat, they rose again rapidly after 1567 as the activities of the Council of Troubles and economic hardship drove increasing numbers of Netherlanders abroad. In all perhaps 60,000 fled into exile during the duke of Alva's governorship. Sometimes whole cells of Protestants fled: of 190 members of the Reformed community at Ieper who signed the Accord with Egmont on 30 September 1566, no less than 109 are known to have come to England after 1567.[1] Almost all the new refugees fled to existing communities of exiles, strengthening their connections with the 'churches under the cross' (sc. in hiding) which remained in the Netherlands. Gradually an elaborate underground communications system grew up, linking all the Protestant cells together. The extent and efficiency of the labyrinthine network is revealed by the voluminous surviving correspondence

both in Emden and in London, and by the well-attended con-
ferences which the Reformed church organized from time to time.
A 'general assembly' (or *Konvent*) was held at Wesel in October
1568, attended by sixty-three Calvinist leaders representing twenty
'churches under the cross' and a somewhat smaller number of refugee
churches in Germany and England. A 'provincial synod' for the Lower
Rhineland exiles assembled at Bedburg (a town in the duchy of Cleves
not far from Wesel) in July 1571, attended by delegates from the
various exiled communities in western Germany, and there plans were
laid for a first 'national synod' of the Netherlands Calvinists to be
held in the autumn at Emden. The delegates at Bedburg went straight
to Emden, where they were joined by others from the other exile
communities and from the 'churches under the cross', although no
representatives arrived from England (they were not given enough
notice and therefore failed to arrive in time). The meeting opened on
4 October and lasted for ten days. In the end a protocol of fifty-three
articles was signed by those present which laid down in detail the
organization, the discipline and the theology to which all members
of the Dutch Reformed church were to subscribe. These articles were
of crucial importance. Above all they completed the ecclesiastical
organization of the Calvinist church of the Netherlands, creating three
'provinces' (England; Germany, with four 'classes'; and the Netherlands, also with four 'classes'). Each was given its own administration
and was enjoined to correspond with the others on 'anything concerning
the advancement and conservation of the churches in general and of
each in particular'. It was the tightly knit organization of the Reformed
church, to which the synod of Emden put the finishing touches, which
enabled the Calvinists to exploit the unexpected successes of the Sea
Beggars in 1572. After Emden the Calvinists were ready for another
revolt – whenever and wherever it might occur.

After the abortive campaign of 1568 William of Orange and the
other leaders of the political opposition to Philip II strengthened
their ties with the Calvinists. The 'churches under the cross' were
regarded as a Fifth Column in the heart of the Netherlands, and
Orange's agents regularly visited their leaders to sound out opinions
and pass on information about the prince's plans. Orange also corresponded with the churches in exile, especially with the 'mother churches'
at Emden and London, and he was represented at both the synods

of 1571 by his political adviser (who was also an elder of the Dutch church at Heidelberg), Philip Marnix, lord of St Aldegond. Although Marnix failed to persuade the synod of Emden to give full and open support to Orange's cause (as the French synod of La Rochelle, held in April 1571, had endorsed the cause of Coligny), he did persuade the delegates at Emden to sign the 'Confession of Faith' of the French synod as an act of solidarity. It was also a fact that for some years the exiled communities in several English and German ports had been providing aid, men and money for the prince's fleet created to attack the ships and supporters of the duke of Alva: the 'Sea Beggars'.

The Watergeuzen or Gueux de Mer were born in May 1568, when Count Louis needed some ships to protect his supply-route for men and munitions into the Eems estuary after his invasion of Friesland. Some ships were hired and equipped by the count in Emden, others were supplied under contract fully equipped by a local pirate, Jan Abels. By July 1568 there were about fifteen ships in Count Louis's fleet, but his resounding defeat at Jemmigen (21 July) deprived them of a port and Abels and the rest were forced to resort to indiscriminate privateering (although still claiming to operate under the 'letters of marque' issued by Orange). In the summer of 1569 Orange hired some new ships in England in order to form a new war-fleet, but again after a short time the captains he appointed turned to piracy – since Orange was unable to pay them an adequate wage, they had no alternative other than to support themselves by plundering merchant shipping. It was here that the consistories came in. The Dutch colonies of refugees in England provided an ideal market for the prizes taken by the Beggars, and they soon became the centres of a highly efficient distribution network. They also worked hard to recruit seamen for the fleet, which by the spring of 1570 numbered about thirty vessels. However, the prince of Orange was not satisfied. He wanted the fleet to be in reliable hands so that it could be used in his various schemes to invade the Netherlands. Although in December 1570 a detachment of Beggars captured the fort of Loevestein on the island of Bommel in Gelderland, other invasions and uprisings planned to coincide with the Loevestein coup did not take place and the Beggars were driven off with heavy losses. Undaunted, in 1571 Orange sent the sea-rovers against the coastal towns and villages of Holland and Zealand, where they plundered property, murdered clergymen and harassed local troops. In between their coastal raids they scoured the Channel, attacking and robbing shipping of all nations, even neutrals.

It could not last. Emden, alienated at last by the Beggars' damage to her shipping, sent an ambassador to England and France in November 1571, begging them to offer no further support to the pirates. Queen Elizabeth was already besieged by Hanseatic merchants who complained of the substantial losses which had been inflicted on their trade by the privateers who frequented her ports. Although the English Privy Council recognized that the prince of Orange, as a sovereign ruler, was entitled to issue letters of marque, they also realized that the Sea Beggars had gone too far in attacking neutral shipping. On 1 March 1572 they were expelled. Now the Beggars' position was desperate: they had nowhere to go. Emden and England were closed to them; they dared not go to La Rochelle, where Orange was organizing another fleet, because they had disobeyed his previous commands so often. They therefore sailed aimlessly up and down the Channel, seemingly a spent force. Orange reluctantly discounted them in the elaborate new plans he and his friends were concerting to overthrow the duke of Alva in the summer of 1572.

After his defeat in 1568 Orange had placed all his hopes in securing active military and financial support from England and France for another invasion attempt. To that end he, Louis and many others joined the French Huguenot army for the campaign of 1569; they were present at the battle of La Roche l'Abeille (and Count Louis at Moncontour as well), at sieges and actions all over France, and eventually Louis rose to be second-in-command of the entire Huguenot army. The reward for this loyal service came in the Peace of St Germain, signed by Charles IX and the Huguenot leaders on 8 August 1570, which recognized Orange and his brothers as the 'good relatives and friends' of the French monarch. Count Louis began to receive a royal pension. The peace also brought the friend and ally of the Nassaus, Gaspard de Coligny, back to prominence in the royal council, and he at once began to work with Orange and Louis to forge a Grand Alliance with England and those German and Italian princes opposed to Spain. After some false starts it was decided that Queen Elizabeth was to marry the young duke of Anjou, brother and heir to the king of France (and later to be Henry III); the king's sister Marguerite was to marry Henry of Navarre, titular head of the French Huguenots (and later to be Henry IV); and there was then to be a joint invasion of the Spanish Netherlands by the exiles, France and England.

To a large extent Alva had provoked this formidable hostile coalition by his aggressive policies. Ever since his arrival in the Netherlands he had pursued a dangerously active foreign policy in northern Europe, intervening rather too often in the internal affairs of the Low Countries' neighbours. In November 1567 he sent Count Aremberg with 1,400 cavalry troopers into France to assist the army of Charles IX; they only returned in May 1568 to resist the invasion of Count Louis. In 1569 Alva sent another army to France to fight for the royal cause at Jarnac and Moncontour. In the same year a trade war started with England.

It all began in November 1568 when five ships carrying about 400,000 florins in cash from Spain to the Netherlands were attacked by Huguenot pirates and forced to seek refuge in Southampton and Plymouth. The money was being sent by some Genoese merchants who had agreed to make a loan to the Brussels government and needed the money to finance their credit operation. They were rather surprised when the ships were placed under arrest (19 December) and the treasure transported to the Tower of London. Elizabeth's intention's at this point are unclear, but her hand was forced by the duke of Alva. Acting it seems on the alarmist account of the incident provided by the inexperienced Spanish ambassador in England, Don Guerau de Spes, Alva ordered all English property in the Netherlands to be seized (29 December) and the king, at Alva's request, followed suit and confiscated all English property in Spain in February 1569. Elizabeth retaliated at once, and all trade between England and the Hispanic world ceased, but almost immediately these commercial difficulties were overshadowed by the outbreak of rebellion in the north of England. Spain was not directly involved in these troubles at first (except by offering asylum to the rebels after their defeat) but Philip II was induced by the trade war with England to look with favour upon the plan of Roberto Ridolfi and others to dethrone Elizabeth and replace her with Mary Stuart.

The plot seems to have originated with Mary Stuart herself. At the end of 1570 she wrote directly to Philip II, asking for support, and almost at once the king turned the problem over to the duke of Alva. The duke was well aware that in 1558–9, just after the death of Mary Tudor, a number of plots were hatched to secure Philip II's succession to the throne of his late wife. At that time the king decided to do nothing, although Elizabeth's authority was precarious in the extreme. In 1570, with twelve years' sound government behind her and the Northern Rebellion crushed, the chances of a successful *coup d'état* appeared slim, to Alva at least. In May 1571 the duke declared himself willing to send open support to Mary the moment he heard that Elizabeth was dead (by Ridolfi's hand or otherwise), but he remained convinced that open invasion was imprudent unless Spain were prepared for outright war with Elizabeth and, possibly, with France as well. Philip II, however, was less cautious. His Court (like Alva's) was full of English Catholic exiles and one of his closest advisers, the duke of Feria, was married to an English Catholic (Lady Jane Dormer). It was Feria, himself an ex-ambassador to England, who led the support for the plan proposed by Mary Stuart and Ridolfi. The project, approved by the Spanish Council of State on 7 July 1571, involved the arrest of Elizabeth by a group of English conspirators led by the duke of Norfolk; this was to be the signal for an invasion of 10,000 soldiers from the Netherlands, led by the second-in-command of the Army of Flanders, Chiappino Vitelli (another Florentine). However, the overall control of operations was entrusted to the duke of Alva, and his misgivings led him to put one obstacle after another in the path of the enterprise, particularly when it became clear that Elizabeth knew all about it (she had Norfolk arrested on 7 September). However, the king was adamant. 'I am so keen to achieve the consummation of this enterprise,' he wrote to Alva on 14 September, 'I am so attached to it in my heart, and I am so convinced that God our Saviour must embrace it as his own cause, that I cannot be dissuaded from putting it into operation.'[2] In the face of such rugged and reckless determination, so similar to the king's attitude to the 1588 invasion project, Alva reluctantly ordered much cumbrous siege-artillery to be moved from the great arsenal of Mechelen and even from certain inland towns to the naval arsenal at Veere in Zealand, ready to be shipped across to England should Ridolfi's plot succeed. Of course, it did not; and by November 1571 even the king had given up all hope of an invasion. The damage, however, had been done.

Speaking to his successor, Don Luis de Requesens, in December 1573, the duke of Alva asserted that the abortive invasion plan of

1571 was responsible for Elizabeth's aid to the Dutch rebels, aid which (he considered) had been essential to the success of the revolt in Holland. The duke did not blame Elizabeth; in his eyes, the plots, threats and projected invasion (all of which were made known to the queen either by her own spies or by the indiscretions of the English Catholics and others) amply justified England's hostility to Spain. But for Spain's support of Ridolfi, Alva claimed, Elizabeth might have remained neutral in 1572 and the Dutch revolt would have foundered.[3]

There was as usual much truth in the duke of Alva's perception. Throughout 1571 William of Orange laboured to exploit Elizabeth's fear and resentment of Spain in order to secure a commitment from her to assist his new invasion plans. In these efforts he was ably assisted by the French Huguenot party, who also hoped to engineer Alva's downfall with the aid of Orange and England. Gradually the differences between France and England were eliminated and in the spring of 1572 it became clear that a treaty of friendship would be signed: the final act took place at Blois on 19 April. A few days earlier, on 11 April, the government published the news that the Protestant leader, Henry of Navarre, would marry the king's sister, Marguerite. This event, carefully arranged by count Louis and his Huguenot friends, was intended to heal some of the divisions at the French court and thus pave the way for a powerful invasion of the Netherlands by government forces.

A fivefold invasion was planned. There was to be a small operation in the north-east, commanded by Orange's brother-in-law, count van den Berg, which was to coincide with a major incursion in the south by Netherlands and Huguenot forces led by Count Louis, to be followed after the Navarre marriage by a declaration of war against Spain by the French king and a further invasion under Coligny. Orange was to raise an army in Germany which, as in 1568, would invade Brabant from the east once the other expeditions were under way. Finally, a fleet was to be assembled at La Rochelle under Admiral Philip Strozzi, ready to invade Holland and Zealand in order to complete the confusion of the Spanish forces. It was hoped that the Sea Beggars in the Channel, possibly with English assistance, would join with Strozzi's fleet. Attempts were also made to involve the Ottoman sultan, the grand duke of Tuscany and the king of Sweden in the attack on Spain, but in the event none of them acted. Coligny and Louis decided to put their plan into execution as soon as Navarre's marriage had taken place, but, as the date for this was continually postponed, it became increasingly likely that one or other of the participants would move out of step. Coordination of the various invasions became virtually impossible.

In the event the careful arrangements of Count Louis and his friends were ruined by Queen Elizabeth. On 1 March, at the insistence of the Hanseatic League, she expelled the Sea Beggars from her shores. After some uncertainty they decided to make a landing somewhere in the great river delta in order to secure a town which might serve as a naval base for their ships, as Delfzijl had done in 1568. One of the Beggar captains, Willem Blois van Treslong, came from Brill, a town of about 3,000 inhabitants in south Holland, and he convinced his comrades that it would meet all their requirements and would be easy to capture. With their customary indiscretion the Beggars bragged about their intentions, so that on 25 March 1572 Alva's ambassador in London could inform his master that the pirates were off Dover, 'Broadcasting among themselves that they were awaiting the arrival of some friends so that, all together, they could attack Brill on the island of Voorne'.[4] Fortunately for the Beggars, this letter arrived in Brussels just too late to be acted upon. On 1 April 1572 the Beggars landed on Voorne and took Brill. The second revolt of the Netherlands had begun.

1572

'The exiles have things all their own way and they revel in it,' wrote Maximilian Morillon, vicar-general of the diocese of Mechelen, to his master, Cardinal Granvelle, on 24 March 1572.

'People are so incensed that there is talk of changing our prince for another, irrespective of his religion, an act which would plunge the country into a long war which would bring about the death of very many people . . . Poverty is acute in all parts . . . The money-lenders are closing their doors because they have no more money; all their cash has already been lent out to people. In Holland everyone began by pawning their best items of furniture and clothes, then they pawned the anchors and rigging of their boats, something unseen and unheard of before. There used to be several towns and villages [in Holland] where no beggars were to be found; now they have multiplied in some places to six or seven hundred, most of them sailors and fishermen. The magistrates have had to give them a little bread and money over the past few days, otherwise there would have been disorders.'[5]

Morillon's letter, written just one week before the attack on the Brill, goes a long way towards explaining the Sea Beggars' success in Holland and Zealand. Conditions were scarcely better elsewhere. In Brussels the bakers, brewers and butchers ceased trading in order to avoid paying the Tenth Penny, so that after January 1572 the citizens were reduced to a diet of fish washed down with the watery concoction brewed by the magistrates in place of beer. Even the duke of Alva's threat to quarter hordes of rapacious and underpaid Spanish soldiers on the dissentient shopkeepers failed to produce results.

The snow fell in heavy drifts in the winter of 1571–2 and there were exceptionally heavy frosts for five weeks which froze the rivers and killed off most of the fruit trees and vines. Work, like food, became scarce and by mid-March Morillon reported that there were between eight and ten thousand unemployed dependent on poor relief in the capital, 'Dying of hunger because they have no work'. It was the same at Antwerp while at Ghent, on 16 March 1572, people found the streets littered with copies of a parody of the Lord's Prayer, composed 'in the style of the Rhetoricians' in honour of the duke of Alva: the 'Paternoster of Ghent'.[6]

'Hellish father who in Brussels doth dwell
Cursed be thy name in heaven and in hell;
Thy kingdom, which has lasted too long, be gone,
Thy will in heaven and earth be not done.
Thou takest away daily our daily bread
While our wives and our children lie starving or dead.
No man's trespasses thou forgivest;
Revenge is the food on which thou livest.
Thou leadest all men into temptation;
Unto evil hast thou delivered this nation.
Our Father, in heaven which art,
Grant that this Devil may soon depart;
And with him his Council, false and bloody,
Who make murder and plunder their daily study;
And all his savage war-dogs of Spain,
O send them all back to the Devil again. Amen.'

There was more to such intense distress and discontent than new taxes and a hard winter. The effect of both was intensified because they came at a time when many families normally employed in weaving or in processing English cloth were thrown out of work by the trade war which followed Queen Elizabeth's seizure of the duke of Alva's payships in December 1568. In Antwerp alone some 1,600 families normally employed in cloth-making were unemployed, while the number of cloths produced by the important centre of Hondschoote fell from almost 98,000 in 1568 to 83,000 in 1572 (a fall of over 15 per cent). At the same time those whose living depended on trade with the Baltic suffered in 1571. No sooner did the war between Denmark and Sweden come to an end (November 1570) than the harvest in eastern Europe failed. There was no grain for export to the west and no market for the salt from Spain and Portugal; very few Dutch ships sailed to the Baltic.

Very few Dutch ships, indeed, dared to put to sea at all in 1571. The Sea Beggars' fleet, well organized and merciless, at last began to have a serious effect on the seaborne commerce of the Netherlands. The trade of Holland and Antwerp in particular was disrupted, keeping both fishermen and seamen unemployed in port. Moreover, without the customary supplies of grain from the Baltic to augment local production, the spectre of famine began to haunt the magistrates of many towns of the Low Countries. Steps were taken to ration the stock of grain for the winter of 1571–2. The magistrates of Amsterdam, for example, prohibited the export of grain from the city on 26 October 1571. They had not had to do that since November 1565. At Ghent on 15 November so little corn was brought to market that the sheriff and his men had to be called in to prevent a riot. Other towns also experienced disorders over the winter months due to the dearth of corn. The bleak economic situation seemed to cast a blight on everything. Jan de Pottre, a Brussels (Catholic) merchant whose diary has survived, noted both in 1570 and in 1571 that the Ommegang (the city's annual festival held every May) was the most miserable he had ever seen. Nobody smiled and nobody sang. In Ghent the magistrates forbade dancing in the streets and the public performance of dance music from July 1571 onwards 'on account of these oppressive times'. Then on 1 November 1571 great storms and high tides destroyed several sea-dikes around the coasts of the Netherlands and flooded a good deal of farmland. On top of everything else plague struck the Low Countries during the summer of 1571 with greater severity than at any other time during the sixteenth century. Material conditions were the worst since the *wonderjaar* of 1566.

The general position of the Spanish monarchy too was the worst since 1566. The revolt of the *moriscos* of Granada, which broke out on Christmas night 1568, continued throughout 1569 and 1570. Then, just as it seemed about to be crushed, war broke out again in the Mediterranean. After three summers of relative inaction, in January 1570 the Barbary corsairs captured Tunis (a Spanish fief since 1535) and in July the Turkish Grand Fleet attacked Cyprus (a Venetian possession since 1489). The pope at once proposed an alliance of the Christian states involved and, after much hard bargaining, the Holy League was signed by Venice, Spain, Genoa, Savoy and other lesser Italian states, and a fleet was immediately sent east to relieve Cyprus. It failed. The next year, 1571, a much larger fleet (over 200 galleys) was assembled and, although Cyprus was still overrun, the Turkish navy was cornered and heavily defeated in the gulf of Lepanto (7 October). Encouraged by this success, the Christian allies decided to mount an even larger operation in 1572 and Philip II determined to mobilize every available revenue for the new campaign. Small wonder that he renewed his injunctions for the duke of Alva to make the Low Countries pay for themselves (cf. p. 116).

All these factors made the Tenth Penny tax of crucial importance in the early months of 1572. The duke of Alva's troops stood in urgent need of it; the king could brook no further delay in collecting it; and the Netherlanders, their standard of living and their trade seriously reduced, were desperately opposed to it. However, the significance of the tax was by no means purely economic. The Tenth Penny had become a symbol: it epitomized all the disagreeable characteristics of Alva's rule. It was unconstitutional; it weighed heavily on the people; it was needed to pay the foreign troops and it was Spanish in inspiration. The Sea Beggars knew what they were about when they flew flags showing ten coins at their mastheads; of 108 Sea Beggar songs composed between 1569 and 1584, twenty-nine mentioned the Tenth Penny by name, and some of them went on about it at length. Because it came to be the touchstone of the whole Spanish regime in the Netherlands, the Tenth Penny assumed a political significance out

5

of all proportion to its economic importance. In Brussels about 400 children testified to this strength of popular feeling by gathering outside Alva's palace one morning in December 1571 and starting to play a new game called 'the Tenth Penny': they appointed collectors who counted off the children into tens, saying 'the tenth child is for the duke of Alva', but the rest of the children then closed in on the collectors and pretended to beat them to death. Any political figure who had anything to do with the new tax was immediately discredited among the people. Those magistrates, for example, who failed to put up a convincing opposition to the collection of the tax thereby forfeited all authority in their towns. 'Since the magistrates were appointed to put the Tenth Penny into effect', observed Maximilian Morillon, 'their authority has entirely collapsed.' Popular bitterness and disenchantment is reflected in almost every diary of the period which has come down to us. The Frisian farmer, Rienck Hemmema, who saw his annual tax bill rise from 334 stuivers in 1569 to 1,345 stuivers in 1571, referred to the new taxes (which were largely responsible for the increase) as 'the duke of Alva's pennies' with evident disapproval. Neither Jan de Pottre from Brussels nor Godevaert van Haecht from Antwerp, in the secrecy of their diaries, could forgive the magistrates who had accepted the new taxes with scarcely a fight. They realized that even the magistrates who, early in 1572, sent deputations to protest to the king about the Tenth Penny, did so more as a face-saving exercise. 'If they achieve nothing,' the States of Hainaut noted, 'they will nevertheless help to restrain the people and show that everyone has done what was required for the discharge of their conscience.'[7]

The fact was that the town corporations could not afford a confrontation with the central government. Throughout the sixteenth century, the municipal governments of the Netherlands, and particularly those of the trading towns of Holland and Zealand, became more oligarchic. The central administration, for its part, did everything in its power to further this development. Inevitably an increasing number of prosperous citizens found themselves deprived of a voice in urban affairs as a small number of closely allied families in each town extended their monopoly over all important offices; equally inevitably the excluded citizens agitated and intrigued to undermine the power of the oligarchs. The magistrates thus became isolated from the rest of the community and were compelled to look to the central government for support. In effect this meant that either the oligarchs carried out the policies decreed by the central government – the new bishoprics, the Tenth Penny and so on – or they forfeited their only support in the face of popular hostility. With few exceptions the local authorities in Holland accepted the duke of Alva's 'novelties' with scarcely a protest, and they were therefore unable to control their fellow-citizens when the Sea Beggars approached.[8]

A seaborne attack by the Beggars on some part of the north-west Netherlands in the spring of 1572 was by no means unexpected. The previous year, as in 1569, they had carried out numerous raids on the coast of Holland and Zealand which led the government to send some 1,500 Spanish soldiers to garrison and protect the main towns and villages of the provinces during the vulnerable summer season. Two hundred and fifty men were sent to Brill in south Holland, despite the fact that 'it is a terribly impoverished town and declines from year to year', and they only retired on 7 November 1571 because a further attack before the winter was considered unlikely. It was intended that the Spaniards should return for the summer of 1572, but over the winter responsibility for defending the sea coast devolved upon the provinces themselves. This was a crucial development, for it prevented the government from exploiting an accident which temporarily crippled a part of the Sea Beggar fleet. In January 1572 about ten pirate ships, with ten prizes in tow, were driven by storms on to the island of Vlie, just north of Holland. There they took steps to repair their damaged vessels and take on fresh supplies, but it was of necessity a prolonged operation. The royal governors of Holland and Friesland at once asked the duke of Alva to send money and a detachment of Spaniards to flush them out, but Alva pleaded poverty and argued that the provincial estates should finance the operation. It was consequently not until 7 March that a government force of about 150 men crossed from Friesland to Vlie, carefully avoiding the ice-floes which littered their path, and captured the pirates' artillery and about thirty prisoners (who were later executed).[9] The rest of the Sea Beggars escaped in their repaired vessels, however, and sailed south to join their colleagues in the Channel for the attack on Brill. Had they been attacked sooner, all might have been captured.

Despite his somewhat short-sighted reaction to the landing at Vlie, the duke of Alva was certainly not unaware of the need to take more active steps against the Sea Beggars. He appreciated that Holland and Zealand would again need garrisons and that the defensive preparations would have to be on a far larger scale than in the previous year. In February 1572 he agreed to a proposal from Count Bossu, the governor of Holland, that as many as forty or fifty villages would have to be garrisoned, involving up to 4,000 Spaniards. He also agreed to strengthen the fortifications of the island of Walcheren, 'because it is the key to all the provinces', and on 29 March a military engineer was dispatched from Brussels to supervise the construction of a citadel in Flushing. On 1 April a special council of war met in Alva's presence to discuss the general problem of the defence of Zealand. It was decided that a garrison of 1,000 Walloons should be raised immediately.[10] The government was worried by reports that the prince of Orange was assembling a fleet at La Rochelle to attack Zealand. It therefore acted with unwonted promptitude . . . but just a little too late. When the discredited Sea Beggars arrived off the Brill in the afternoon of 1 April they found that most of the men of the town were away fishing and that there were no troops. Had the pirates obeyed orders and awaited Orange's command before attacking, they would have met with a very different reception. As it was, although only 600 strong, they quickly gained control of the town, sacked the churches and issued a characteristically flamboyant proclamation assuring the inhabitants that everyone would be well treated 'except priests, monks and papists'.

Nevertheless, for all their apparent confidence, the Beggars' situation was precarious. The vigilant Bossu happened to be at Maassluis (only twenty miles from Brill) when the Beggars struck and, although unprepared, he immediately marched all night with the 200 soldiers who were with him and summoned the Spaniards from Utrecht, fifty miles away, to join him at once. They arrived on 4 April at Vlaardingen, just across the river from Brill, but they arrived without ships and without artillery. A strong wind from the south-east sprang up and prevented them from crossing the Maas to attack the Beggars. The 'Protestant Wind' only relented on 6 April and when Bossu and his troops at last crossed over they found the Beggars had received reinforcements, 'some of them very fine soldiers' as Bossu was forced to admit, and his forces were driven back. Moreover, while the Spaniards crossed from the mainland to Voorne, the Beggars sent an expeditionary force to the mainland which captured Delfshaven, just west of Rotterdam. This proved a shrewd manoeuvre since Bossu, outnumbered on Voorne, felt it imperative to drive the Beggars from their foothold on the mainland and he retreated via Dordrecht to Rotterdam (lacking command of the waterways, he had to travel the long way round). It was not until 11 April that the pirates were forced to abandon Delfshaven and retire to the Brill, bringing the total number of fighting men there to about 2,000.

Bossu had another reason for marching via Dordrecht, however. The magistrates of the town reported to him their fears of a popular uprising which, thanks to their enforcement of the Tenth Penny, they would be powerless to suppress. On 8 April rioting against the Spanish regime did indeed break out in Rotterdam, followed by similar troubles in Gouda, but Bossu and his troops were at hand and the situation was quickly brought under control. But things were different at Flushing. On 6 April, Easter Day, as the local people poured out of the Great Church after Easter Mass, they caught sight of the quartermasters of three Spanish infantry companies approaching the town hall to arrange billets for their men. After their bitter experience of Spanish troops in garrison in 1569 and 1571 the people of Flushing were in no mood for more. They pledged that they were the loyal subjects of the king and that they would accept a garrison of Netherlands troops, but they swore that not one Spaniard should set foot within their walls. Two days later, while the town was still in ferment, a Spanish gentleman landed on the quay. It was the duke of Alva's engineer, Hernando Pacheco, bearing not just plans to build a new citadel but also a commission to arrest the magistrates and to start collecting the Tenth Penny. That commission was to cost him his life: Pacheco was seized by the mob and hanged, although for some time Flushing continued to claim that it was loyal. The Walloon garrison of fifty men was only expelled on 14 April; an emissary was sent to Middelburg on 17 April to negotiate with Alva's special representative there about accepting a new garrison; and not until 22 April was a fleet of fourteen Beggar ships allowed into the harbour – although even then the ships flew a banner which bore the arms of the king and the prince of Orange together.

On the whole the government coped well with the emergency throughout April. The trouble was confined to Brill and Flushing, and loyal garrisons were swiftly sent to all the major towns of the south Holland coast – Vlaardingen, Schiedam and Rotterdam – and of the Zealand isles – Zierikzee, Middelburg and Ter Goes. Nevertheless the situation was precarious. Bossu reported that the whole country was against him while the Beggars were receiving reinforcements all the time. Unemployed and destitute fisher folk and seamen from the coastal provinces streamed in to the Brill, some from conviction others doubtless in the hope of earning their daily bread; the consistories in England sent men and money; and ships from Count Louis in La Rochelle carried troops and commanders from France. Flushing and the Brill became an enemy bridgehead which the government could do nothing to eliminate until a fleet could put to sea, and this became increasingly difficult. In late April two useful naval bases in Walcheren, Arnemuiden and Veere, were captured by the men of Flushing. Veere was a particularly rich prize for it contained a large arsenal well stocked with powder, shot, 2,000 bronze naval guns and yet more iron guns (all moved up from Mechelen in 1571 in preparation for the invasion of England). Farther north rioting occurred at Enkhuizen on the Zuider Zee, where the government was preparing a fleet of twenty ships with which to attack the Beggars. The ships were arrested for a time, but order was eventually restored and eleven ships put to sea on 11 May. Almost at once fresh rioting broke out in the town, this time actively encouraged by Orangist sympathizers. The magistrates launched one appeal after another to Bossu for help, but the count's troops were all tied down along the Maas facing the Brill and he could not help them. At last on 21 May the mob asked the Beggars to send help, and a squadron which had been cruising expectantly off Vlie arrived the same night.

The general situation thus still hung in the balance. Enkhuizen and Flushing had not defected to the pirates wholeheartedly; they had only defied the king after a long period of neutrality during which the arrival of government troops could have saved the situation. The attitude of the population in general was apathetic rather than actively hostile. Bossu feared that famine, not the pirates, would eventually undermine the royalist position. He wrote to Alva in mid-May:

'Although people here take their impending ruin on account of the Tenth Penny as the sole pretext for the revolt . . . the real cause is that there are twenty or thirty thousand men in this province [Holland] whose sole livelihood consists of fishing and seafaring, and, since this has now altogether ceased, and since for some time they have been spending all that they have managed to save in the past, they will eventually be so oppressed by poverty that they will no longer care what price they pay for relief.'

A little later he added:

'A general uprising is to be feared here because already the poor people suffer from a shortage of food so that they do not know which way to turn, and the corn from the Baltic, which is the mainstay of this province, no longer arrives.'[11]

However, as long as Bossu still had troops in Holland and believed that more were on the way, he continued to be confident that the situation could be saved and the Beggars expelled from their three or four bases. His optimism only left him when he received a laconic missive from the duke of Alva, dated 15 June: 'This is to warn you that, for urgent reasons, I have resolved to withdraw all the Spanish troops from Holland.'[12] The decision was taken without reference to Bossu, but the situation in the south Netherlands had suddenly become critical. At long last the Grand Strategy prepared for 1572 by the prince of Orange and his allies had been put into effect (see the map on p. 139).

The town of Mons, the capital of Hainaut, had been provided with massive fortifications at the time of Charles V's wars against France. In May 1572, however, it was poorly defended. The town's artillery and munitions had been removed to Veere in preparation for the invasion of England; its guards were lax; and its most vigilant magistrates had gone to Spain in order to lodge their personal protest against the Tenth Penny. All this was well known to the numerous Protestants of the town, and they in turn made it known to Count Louis of Nassau at La Rochelle. Early in May Louis sent his intimate adviser, Antoine Olivier, to survey Mons for himself and to assess the extent of support for his cause. Olivier's report was favourable and on 23 May he returned to Mons with some friends. Early on 24 May, when the town gates were opened, Count Louis and a group of supporters rode in. After a few tense hours the Protestant minority declared their support and reinforcements arrived from France. Count

Louis soon commanded about 1,500 troops (many of them French) and about 1,000 local supporters (most of them Protestant) in the town. A provincial government was set up and Calvinist worship was legalized. At the same time another force of Huguenots and Netherlands exiles commanded by François de la Noue crossed the frontier farther west and captured Valenciennes (although the citadel, garrisoned by Spaniards, held out). Then with amazing audacity, they launched a raid on Brussels in order to capture the duke of Alva himself by surprise.

Shortly after the capture of Mons another army under Count van den Berg invaded the central Netherlands from Germany and on 10 June took the important stronghold of Zutphen with scarcely a struggle. Again the Beggars were aided by Alva's command of mid-June to withdraw all available forces southwards against Mons: within six weeks almost all of Overijssel and Drenthe and much of Friesland was in the hands of the prince of Orange's supporters. The only towns in the north-east which remained under government control by the end of August were Leeuwarden, Staveren, Harlingen, Groningen, Lingen and Deventer (see the map on p. 139).

The Orangists and the Beggars had achieved a great deal in a short time. Although the daring swoop on Brussels had miscarried and even though Valenciennes had been swiftly recaptured (thus discouraging the prince's supporters elsewhere in the south from showing themselves), a large part of the Low Countries had defied the government and was in open rebellion. The duke of Alva was not unduly perturbed, however; given time, he had the resources to reduce each of the revolted towns in turn. What worried him was evidence that Orange and his fellows now enjoyed the full support of Coligny and at least a section of the French Court, and that France was almost certain to declare war on him. In 1552 he had seen his former master, Charles V, surprised by a combination of domestic rebellion and foreign aggression, forced to flee for his life, alone, to Villach; now he realized that the same fate was about to befall him. Immediately he issued a string of patents to recruit troops in Germany and the Netherlands; he ordered his Spanish forces to move south; he rushed reinforcements into the strongpoints along the French frontier and he urged the king and the Governor of Spanish Lombardy to mobilize. But Alva dared not go any further on his own authority:

he could not declare war on France without the consent of the king. He therefore contented himself with throwing a noose of government forces around Mons. Although this meant denuding the northern provinces to a dangerous degree, the duke feared France far more than the Sea Beggars. He had to concentrate his forces in the south in order to meet the threat of a new invasion from France, which he expected to be led by Coligny in person.

Alva's fears were fully justified. Just before Alva's blockade of Mons became total, in mid-June, Count Louis sent a messenger out of the city to beg the French Huguenots to carry out their promise and mount a massive invasion of the Netherlands in the name of Charles IX. The messenger, Jean de Hangest, lord of Genlis and a cousin of Coligny as well as of the late Montigny and Hornes, arrived in Paris on 23 June and he at once set about persuading Coligny and King Charles to send immediate relief to Mons, whether or not there was a decision on a total break with Spain. In this limited objective Genlis was successful and on 12 July he left Paris with about 6,000 men. Five days later he marched straight into a Spanish ambush at St Ghislain, about six miles south of Mons, and almost his entire force was destroyed either by the enemy troops or by the peasants, for whom the French were still the traditional enemy. This was a shattering blow. The prince of Orange had just set off from his family castle at Dillenburg with an army of 20,000 men. He crossed the Rhine and entered the Netherlands on 7 July and in the next fortnight he captured Roermond, Straelen, Geldern and Wachtendonck; but the news of St Ghislain made him hesitate. He resolved to wait at Roermond until France declared war on Spain.

This move was expected by Alva too. The evidence of Charles IX's support for the Netherlands opposition was growing – mainly made up of letters and papers found on the Huguenots captured at Valenciennes and killed at St Ghislain. Charles himself was aware that his plans of the spring were now in the open. On 12 August he wrote to his ambassador in the Netherlands:

'The papers found upon those captured with Genlis [show] . . . everything done by Genlis to have been committed with my consent . . . Nevertheless, [you will tell the duke of Alva] these are lies invented to excite his suspicion against me. He must not attach any credence to them . . . You will also tell him what you know about the enemy's affairs from time to time, by way of information, in order to please him and to make him more disposed to believe in your integrity.'[13]

At the same time, however, the ambassador (Claude de Mondoucet) was instructed to keep in constant contact with the prince of Orange.

Charles IX was in the process of making up his mind. In the spring he had listened to Louis and to Coligny as they urged upon him the need to strike at the might of Spain. Now the expected aid from England was withdrawn – whatever France did, it was clear that Elizabeth was not now going to declare war on Spain – and the débâcle of St Ghislain discredited and debilitated the Huguenots who had pushed the king into his embarrassing predicament. It began to dawn on Charles IX – and on Philip II, the pope and many others – that here was a favourable opportunity to liberate the crown from Huguenot influence. The decision was not easy, however. The Court ardently desired the marriage of the king's sister Marguerite to Henry of Navarre, scheduled to take place on 18 August; nothing could be done against the Huguenots until after that. At about this time Charles therefore gave Coligny leave to invade the Netherlands during the week beginning Monday, 25 August, but he had probably already decided to ensure that the admiral would never go. On the night of 23 August orders were issued for the assassination of Coligny and of some 3,000 prominent Huguenots still in Paris after the Navarre wedding. The massacre continued throughout 24 August, St Bartholomew's Day, and spread rapidly to about twelve other cities of France.

The massacre of St Bartholomew was an event of enormous significance for the Netherlands. Philip II, when he heard the news on 6 September, for once failed to conceal his feelings: he laughed out loud and danced about his chamber – and he had good reason. After St Bartholomew there could be no relief of Mons by the Huguenots, and unless Mons was relieved Orange's cause would lose all credibility. The massacre was a 'stunning blow' to the prince, because 'my only hope lay with France'. But for St Bartholomew, he wrote to his brother John, 'we would have had the better of the duke of Alva and we would have been able to dictate terms to him at our pleasure'.[14] Now he even feared that the Huguenots with his brother Louis in Mons would

This sketch-map is intended to bring out the phases of the Orangist advance in 1572. By the end of May there were still only seven towns in revolt against Philip II; by mid-June the total had only risen to ten. It was during the three months which followed that real progress was made. It is no mere coincidence that on 15 June Alva ordered his forces to withdraw from Holland and on 25 June he ordered them to pull out of the north-east in order to parry the expected invasion from France.

Towns in revolt against Philip II, 1572
(with date of defection)

◉ before 15 June
▣ 16 June – 31 July
▲ 1 August – 10 September

▲ Franeker (28 Aug.)
▲ Bolsward (24 Aug.)
▲ Sneek (18 Aug.)

Medemblik (27 May) ◉
Enkhuizen (21 May) ◉
Hoorn (20 June) ▣
Alkmaar (21 June) ▣
Kampen ▲ (12 Aug.)
Zwolle (13 Aug.) ▲
Hattem (c. 15 July) ▣
Monnikendam (27 June) ▣
Elburg (5 July) ▣
Oldenzaal (c. 15 July) ▣
Haarlem (15 July) ▣
Harderwijk (4 July) ▣
Naarden (13 July) ▣
Amersfoort (c. 20 Aug.) ▲
Zutphen (10 June) ◉
Leiden (23 July) ▣
Doesburg (14 June) ◉
Gouda (21 June) ▣
Oudewater (20 June) ▣
Doetinchem (14 June) ◉
Delft (26 July) ▣
Schoonhoven (8 July) ▣
Rotterdam (25 July) ▣
Buren (11 July) ▣
Brielle (1 April) ◉
Bommel (14 July) ▣
Dordrecht (25 June) ▣
Worcum (27 June) ▣
Zierikzee (10 Aug.) ▲
Geldern (17 July) ▣
Gorinchem (28 June)
Straelen (19 July) ▣
Wachtendonck (19 July) ▣
Veere (4 May) ◉
Flushing (22 April) ◉
Arnemuiden (29 April)
Weert (27 Aug.) ▲
Roermond (23 July) ▣
Dendermonde (6 Sept.) ▲
Mechelen (30 Aug.) ▲
Diest (20 Aug.) ▲
Leuven (3 Sept.) ▲
Tienen (2 Sept.) ▲
Oudenaarde (7 Sept.) ▲
Nivelles (5 Sept.) ▲
Mons (24 May) ◉
Valenciennes (24-9 May) ◉

miles
0   25   50

0   25   50
kilometres

surrender at once in desperation. But it was too late for him to draw back. Still believing that Coligny's invasion was imminent, and fortified with money from Holland and England, the prince had crossed the Maas and invaded Brabant on 27 August, intending to relieve Mons and break the duke of Alva's siege. His campaign began well. One town after another opened its gates to him – Weert and Diest in late August, Tienen, Leuven, Nivelle and Dendermonde in early September. Mechelen and Oudenaarde revolted spontaneously and then asked the prince for a garrison. These successes, coupled with the rebellion of most of Holland and Zealand, created problems for the loyal towns. 'Brussels is more or less under siege,' wrote the French agent, Mondoucet, 'with the garrisons [of Orange] at Mechelen, Leuven, Dendermonde and elsewhere in control of the countryside and able to ensure that no victuals get through.' Morillon, in Brussels, feared that the city would fall if the prince's forces approached, because its fortifications were in disrepair and the magistrates could not find anyone to rebuild them. Even the unemployed refused the wages offered, saying 'they do not wish to fortify the city for the Spaniards'.[15] However, in spite of all this support, the key to the situation remained the outcome of the siege of Mons. Unless Orange could defeat or drive off Alva's main army, his cause and all the towns which had declared their support for it were lost.

On 9 September Orange arrived outside Alva's encampment, hoping to provoke the duke to fight a pitched battle. As in 1568, however, the duke had no intention of risking a major engagement. His siege-works were impregnable, and he knew it. He would wait for Orange's army to melt away through lack of pay, as it had done four years before, and sure enough on 12 September, after a brief skirmish in which the prince's forces were worsted, Orange withdrew. It was recognized by everyone that Mons was now doomed and Count Louis surrendered on terms on 19 September. After the count and his regular troops had departed unmolested, Alva entered the town on 22 September and organized a special court to try and sentence all those who had collaborated with the invaders.

With Mons regained and the danger of French aggression abated, the duke of Alva was at last free to move against the other towns captured by Orange and his adherents in the course of the summer. Until the fall of Mons the revolt had made little impact on the population at large. Most people had, in Morillon's phrase, 'kept their arms folded and let the activists get on with their work', just as in 1566. The Frisian farmer Rienck Hemmema bought and sold goods without hindrance both at royalist Leeuwarden and at Orangist Franeker during the late summer of 1572. He was even in Franeker on the day when it defected to the Beggars (28 August) but still managed to sell his two rams to the butcher for a good price![16] This 'business as usual' situation stopped abruptly at the end of September, as the duke of Alva moved on Mechelen, one of the few towns in the south which had spontaneously rebelled in favour of Orange. After his failure before Mons, the prince had withdrawn to the city, but as Alva approached he retreated to the north. The town therefore opened its gates and offered no resistance when the Spaniards marched up but, despite this, the troops – cheated of their spoil at Mons and long unpaid – were allowed to sack and plunder the town for three full days 'in order to refresh them a little' (1–4 October). Four years later Jean Richardot, who had witnessed everything, was still unable to describe all that he had seen: 'One could say a lot more about it if the horror of it did not make one's hair stand on end – not at recounting it but just at remembering it!' The effect of the atrocity at the time however, was more positive: within a few days representatives from Oudenaarde, Dendermonde, Diest, Tongeren and other towns in Brabant which had declared for Orange hastened to Mechelen to make their peace with the duke and thus avert a similar vengeance. Alva had expected this and he graciously accepted their surrender, thus regaining control of all territory south of the Maas at a stroke.[17]

After Mechelen Alva kept the bulk of his forces in pursuit of Orange and his field army, still intact, which had withdrawn into Gelderland. The duke crossed over to Maastricht and then to Nijmegen (which he reached early in November). Orange, hemmed in on all sides, decided to flee to Holland rather than to Germany (as he had in 1567 and 1568). Defeated for a third time, there seemed little point in living to fight another day. He took refuge in Holland as a last resort, 'to maintain my affairs over here as well as maybe, having decided to make that province my tomb'.[18]

Alva decided to mop up the Orangist outposts in the north-east before following the prince to Holland. His army moved against Zutphen, which had defected to van den Berg without a blow in June.

After a few days' siege, on 14 November, the Orangists offered to parley but there was panic at the last moment, before terms were actually agreed, which the Spaniards exploited to gain access to the town. Like Mechelen it was promptly put to the sack. The screams and shrieks of the victims could be heard many miles away, according to the nearest Orangist commander.[19] For some days the full extent of the massacre and devastation was not known, but once the truth was out 'beastliness' again paid dividends. The terrible fate of Zutphen expedited the royalist triumph since the few towns in the north-east which remained loyal to Orange hastened to save themselves and come to terms with the invincible Spaniards.

Now only Holland and Zealand were left. Even the French ambassador in the Netherlands thought they were an easy target: 'Since the people of Holland are not warlike and lack spirit, there is not a town there which will not ask to surrender when the duke's army approaches.'[20] Just to make sure of a speedy conclusion, the duke decided to make an example of another town in rebellion. Naarden on the Zuider Zee, just within the province of Holland, refused to surrender when asked to do so. The Spaniards closed in and the town belatedly offered to capitulate on terms. Again there was a panic among the defenders when the surrender was almost signed, which the Spaniards exploited to force an entry. On 2 December 1572 the inhabitants were murdered *en masse*, their property was plundered and finally their town was razed to the ground. According to Alva's smug report to the king, 'not a mother's son escaped'.[21] Confident and victorious, the Spanish army repaired to Amsterdam (which had remained loyal to the king throughout) to await the surrender of the rest of Holland and Zealand, the only areas of the Low Countries still in revolt.

The prince of Orange's new order

By the beginning of August 1572 a large part of Holland and Zealand was controlled by the agents and friends of the prince of Orange. The Spanish garrisons along the Maas (at Delft, Rotterdam and Schiedam) withdrew with about 4,000 refugees in mid-July, leaving only Amsterdam (which refused to accept a government garrison)

8. *Areas of the Netherlands in revolt, December 1572*

The position of the rebels in December 1572 was in strong contrast with their successful situation three months earlier: all the gains in the south and north-east had been lost. The duke of Alva's victorious army appeared to be poised for a reconquest of the maritime provinces.

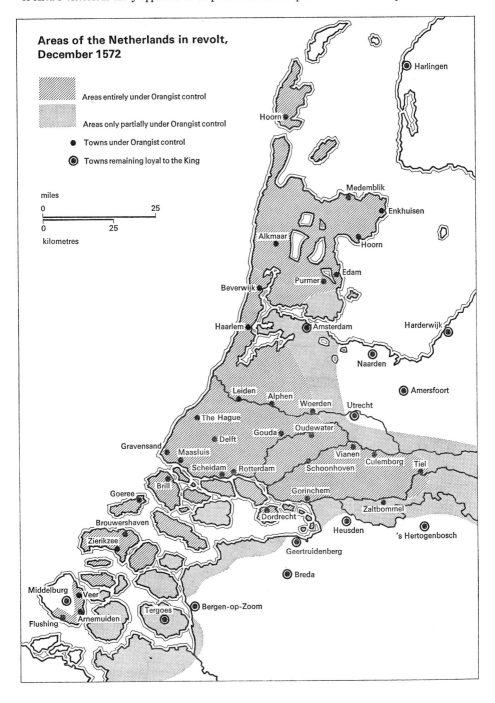

Areas of the Netherlands in revolt, December 1572

Areas entirely under Orangist control

Areas only partially under Orangist control

● Towns under Orangist control

◉ Towns remaining loyal to the King

miles
0 — 25
0 — 25
kilometres

Harlingen

Hoorn

Medemblik

Enkhuisen

Alkmaar

Hoorn

Edam

Purmer

Beverwijk

Haarlem

Amsterdam

Harderwijk

Naarden

Leiden

Alphen

Woerden

Amersfoort

The Hague

Gouda

Oudewater

Utrecht

Gravensand

Delft

Maasluis

Scheidam

Rotterdam

Schoonhoven

Vianen

Culemborg

Tiel

Brill

Goeree

Gorinchem

Zaltbommel

Brouwershaven

Dordrecht

Heusden

's Hertogenbosch

Zierikzee

Geertruidenberg

Breda

Middelburg

Veer

Bergen-op-Zoom

Flushing

Arnemuiden

Tergoes

and Utrecht loyal to the king. The royalist position was slightly better in Zealand where Middelburg, Arnemuiden, Rammekens, Ter Goes and Zierikzee held out, although all five were under siege (and Zierikzee, with its royal fleet in the harbour, fell on 10 August).

In an attempt to save the situation, on 24 June the duke of Alva wrote to the principal towns of Holland requiring them to send deputies to a meeting of the provincial States to be held at The Hague on 15 July. This initiative was welcomed and exploited by the rebellious towns. Dordrecht, traditionally the senior town of the province, wrote to the rest asking that the meeting should be held there and not in The Hague 'on account of the disorders of these days'. Delegates of the province's nobility and of twelve of the eighteen towns habitually represented in the States of Holland repaired to Dordrecht on the appointed day and on 19 July they were addressed by Philip Marnix, Orange's special representative, who invited them to regularize their position by doing three things. In the first place, he asked the States to recognize Orange as the king's stadholder for Holland, Zealand and Utrecht, to fight with the prince in the king's name to recover the rights and liberties of the province removed by Alva and to swear not to make a separate agreement with the king without Orange's consent (Orange made a reciprocal undertaking). Secondly, Marnix demanded that the States should arrange to pay for the ships, soldiers and sailors fighting in the prince's name in the province. (In return the prince agreed that all military and naval commands in the province should be held in the joint names of Orange and the States.) Thirdly, the States were to stand by Orange's professed aim of freedom of worship for all the province: 'the free exercise of religion should be allowed as well to Papists as Protestants, without any molestation or impediment'. Each of these points was of crucial importance if the rebellion in Holland were to succeed. There had to be a provisional government with the constitutional position and powers of each major participant defined; there had to be a financial organization to support the war effort against Alva; there had to be a broad-based religious policy which would appeal to the maximum number of people. In the event the States of Holland endorsed and enacted each of Orange's propositions and on 22 July Count Lumey van der Mark, the victor of the Brill, appeared before the provincial assembly with the prince's commission to be lieutenant-governor of south Holland. The States accepted him, thus officially inaugurating the new order in the north, and on 23 July they voted taxes for Orange worth 500,000 florins.[22]

At the head of the province was the prince, as stadholder. His powers, executive and military, were modelled on those of royal provincial governors with the important exception that he had no supervision from Brussels. The other existing provincial institutions, the Reken-kamer (Audit Office) and the Hof (Law Court), were retained – albeit with a new personnel and subordinated to the States – and the States set up some new committees to assist Orange with his executive and administrative decisions: the Admiralty College, the Financial College and most important, the Standing Committee of the States as a whole (the Gecommitteerde Raad) created on 28 July 1572 to act as advisory council to the prince or his representative. The position was slightly different in Zealand, since so much was still in royal hands, but Orange's authority was accepted by the towns controlled by the Sea Beggars, and in March 1574 a system of government similar to Holland's, in which Orange and the States ruled conjointly, was set up in the province. As time passed and the war continued, it naturally became necessary to make minor changes to this provincial structure of government. In 1573, when the Spanish capture of Haarlem split Holland in two, the Gecommitteerde Raad was also perforce divided: one for the north to advise the lieutenant-governor there (Sonoy) and one for the south to advise Orange. Adjustments were made to the other committees in December 1574 and special financial officers were established to deal with certain sources of revenue (e.g., the *commies general der licenten*). Another important change was the estab-lishment of a university at Leiden on 5 February 1575 (modelled on the Geneva Academy of 1559 albeit with mainly Catholic students and some non-Calvinist teachers) which was founded to produce men of humanist outlook to become the administrators, governors and reformed clergy of the rebellious provinces.

The Dutch decision to create their own university reflects a new attitude towards their constitutional position. They had long recognized that they were independent *de facto*; now they began to consider whether they should not become independent *de jure* as well. The States of Holland discussed the question in June 1575. As a preliminary step they proposed a formal union between themselves and the States of Zealand, now fully functional, and an act of union was signed on 4

June. On 11 July Orange agreed to serve as chief executive of the
new union and on 13 October 1575 the States decided unanimously
'that we should forsake the king and seek foreign assistance'. The
prince of Orange was empowered to negotiate for this with foreign
powers and in November 1575 a deputation approached Queen Elizabeth
with an offer of sovereignty. She refused. The two provincial estates
therefore looked again at their position and decided upon a new
defensive pact or union, which was signed on 25 April 1576. This
ordained that taxes and other charges were to be apportioned among
the provinces, towns and villages 'as if the provinces and towns in
the Republic were counted and included as parts of the same city'.
Tolls within the provinces were abolished and cooperation in law-
enforcement was enjoined. The prince was again recognized as chief
executive, but this time he was accorded sovereign power (he was vested
with *hoog overicheyt*, or high authority) until some other body or person
should take up the sovereignty previously held by Philip II, and he
was to be advised by a permanent committee of nine (the Landraad)
appointed by him from a list of candidates proposed by the joint
estates.

Despite the apparent democracy, however, and despite Orange's
anxiety to involve more people in the governmental processes, most
power in the internal administration of the new Republic remained
with the politicians of the various towns in the union. The town
councillors, or *vroedschappen*, gained power at the expense of the
central and provincial authorities; they never lost their monopoly of
municipal government, not even in the crisis of 1572. After the capture
of the Brill the corporations of almost all the towns of Holland and
Zealand which went over to the rebels made a formal capitulation
with the Sea Beggars which safeguarded their power. As a result
the same class of people tended to keep control of the towns of Holland:
either the same magistrates remained in power throughout or else
the politicians banished in 1567 returned to the offices they had abandoned. This 'palace revolution' character may be observed in the *overgang* (defection) of most of the towns of Holland during the summer
of 1572. Time and again a town's capitulation was negotiated with
exiles from the town itself who were with the Beggars: Marten
Ruyschaver at Haarlem, Pieter van der Werff at Leiden and so on.
Even the surprise captures were normally effected by local people:

of the sixty-nine men who surprised Oudewater on 21 June, all but fourteen were natives either of Oudewater or of nearby Gouda. They then purged the *vroedschap* to produce a city government favourable to Orange and to the Calvinist cause, but always replacing Alva's nominees with other men from the same social class. There was a more radical change in some towns later on – in Gouda in July 1573 the *vroedschap* was purged and of the forty new 'regents' twenty-four had never before held office and fifteen came from new families; in Dordrecht sixteen men were appointed in place of defectors, eight of whom came from non-patrician families – but even then the change was once and for all. Office remained with the men of 1572 for over thirty years.[23] Although the urban militias, the *schutterijen* abolished by Alva, were restored, neither they nor the common people secured any lasting share of power.

Thus the new magistrates were just as dependent on outside support to maintain their position as their royalist predecessors had been. They had no power of their own. When Bossu and the Spaniards departed in July 1572, the magistrates of Delft simply did not know what to do. They sent a deputation to the law-courts at The Hague 'to explain the perplexity in which they, the governing body of this town, find themselves through the sudden departure of the Spanish garrison'.[24] That was on 23 July; three days later, with no great enthusiasm, the magistrates negotiated their surrender to the Sea Beggars and waited for the prince of Orange to arrive in person, which he did in November.

At first the prince's personal position was not strong. His military record was distinctly uninspiring and many criticized his failure to relieve Mons and his rash promise to keep Mechelen out of Alva's hands. His diplomatic achievements were also slender: he had failed to produce the massive foreign support of which he had spoken so confidently when urging the Dutch to rebel. He arrived in Holland with only eighty horsemen, none of them men of note. Before long his prestige was further eroded by his inability to relieve beleaguered Haarlem, a failure which involved the massacre of a relief column composed largely of untrained burgesses (9 July 1573). Orange was like a fish out of water: no soldier, he was forced to direct a life-and-death struggle; a Lutheran, he was forced to depend on Calvinists and Catholics; a great nobleman, he was forced to rub shoulders only with merchants, artisans and outlaws. Even some of the Calvinists, who still remembered Orange's betrayal at Antwerp in 1567, felt sorry for him and criticized those who, like the Dutch Church at London, deliberately withheld funds because they did not trust the prince.[25] Orange was to make many sacrifices and many compromises in order to earn the confidence of the Dutch (in October 1573 he even became a Calvinist), but it all took time.

It took time too before his armed forces were able to command the respect of those they were meant to protect (or of those they were meant to fight). These forces were of three types: the Sea Beggars, the foreign volunteers and the native levies. The Sea Beggars themselves were mainly Netherlanders. Of the captains, 108 out of 170 are known to have come from the northern provinces (and thirty-three from the south) while 50 per cent of the crews came from Holland and Friesland. About 40 per cent were exiles, the rest drawn mainly from the reservoir of unemployed fishermen in the seaward provinces, (estimated at twenty to thirty thousand in spring 1572). Following Lumey's initial landing at the Brill with some 600 men, reinforcements quickly flowed in from France and England. Many of them were recruited from the exiled communities in eastern England; more still were recruited elsewhere at the expense of the Calvinist consistories there. There were also the units recruited abroad by sympathizers with the rebels' cause: the French from La Rochelle under Strozzi (part of the Nassau brothers' plan for 1572) and later the English under Sir Humphrey Gilbert (sent by Elizabeth to prevent the French gaining control of Flushing). Elizabeth, however, was lukewarm in her support. Characteristically she instructed Gilbert to behave 'as thoughe he and his companies departed out of England thether without Her Majesties assent'. She sent Orange some money (about 300,000 florins) in August, and she allowed the exile churches in England and other well-wishers to send money, men and munitions, but as the year wore on she forbade further official assistance to the rebellious provinces. The Calvinist government of Scotland was more open-handed. On 20 June 1572 the Scots Privy Council issued a proclamation which, in view of 'the present hunger, derth and scarcitie of viveris' called upon all able-bodied but unemployed men to fight in Holland 'quhair they may haif sufficient interteniment'.[26] Whether or not this proved to be the case, by 1576 there were perhaps 2,000 Scots fighting for the prince of Orange and the States, fighting alongside other volunteers from England, France and Germany, most of them convinced Calvinists. They also fought with the 'Holland regiment', eventually a force of some 3,000 men raised in the province with just a smattering of foreign volunteers. The first company of these local troops was mustered on 9 July 1572, and most of them were used for garrison duties.

All these troops required wages, and required them urgently if the rebels' cause was to be sustained. Fortunately for them, the Dutch could count upon a certain amount in windfall revenue and foreign subsidies to finance their war effort. In the first place there were the treasures of the Catholic church – vestments, chalices, even bells – which could be sold for cash. Then there were the ships and merchandise captured by the Sea Beggars. Apart from the major successes, like the seizure of a rich Portuguese merchant fleet off Flushing in May 1572 or the capture of Catholic merchandise worth 75,000 florins at the fall of Middelburg in February 1574, a steady stream of smaller prizes was taken. In the two years from April 1575 to April 1577 the pirates of Flushing alone took 258 prizes, valued at 72,000 florins. Over the same period 85,000 florins were also received in payments for licences to sail up the Scheldt to Antwerp.[27] This was useful, but it was not enough to win a war. Rather more substantial was the contribution received from outside sources. Orange himself had spent all his assets in the 1568 campaign, but his brothers somehow managed to raise more in their own names and transmit it to Holland. The patrimonial Nassau estates contributed perhaps 600,000 florins to the Dutch cause between 1568 and 1573. The total support from England, official and otherwise, probably provided about as much again over the same period. Rather more important as a source of foreign aid in these years, however, was Charles IX of France, the butcher of St Bartholomew. It seems clear that substantial sums – possibly as much as 200,000 florins a month – were reaching Orange from France throughout 1573 and the early months of 1574. But it seems likely that these payments ceased with the death of Charles in May 1574.[28]

In the end, the success of the revolt depended on the taxes voted by the provinces themselves. Zealand was poor (and still partially under royalist control) and provided little: only 6,571 florins were received by Orange's receiver-general in the province between April 1572 and February 1574; only a little over 350,000 florins between then and April 1576. Since it was estimated that the army of the States cost 8,000 florins a day to maintain, the lion's share of the troops' wages necessarily came from Holland. To meet the heavy burden, the States enacted a series of new fiscal measures. They placed heavy excise duties on salt, herrings, butter, cheese and beer; they imposed new surcharges on exports; and they levied a 1 per cent tax on everyone owning over 100 florins of capital. In this way they hoped to raise 500,000 florins within a year. Needless to say, the target could not be reached; no war can be fought on current revenue alone. The States of Holland as a body, and each town for itself, therefore had to raise more money by selling annuities. The problem was that, due to the troubles, municipal revenues had fallen, making it more difficult to raise public loans. The town of Delft, for example, which was never directly involved in the fighting after July 1572, had an income of around 50,000 florins in the 1560s, but this had been more than halved by 1575–6. The principal tax, the beer excise, produced 28,565 florins in 1571–2 but only 5,670 in 1574–5 and 4,888 in 1575–6, no doubt through the loss of the traditional markets for Delft beer in the south Netherlands. The town had to sell annuities worth almost 200,000 florins during these early war years in order to pay the taxes decreed by the States. Other areas also experienced difficulties in meeting their fiscal obligations.[29] Edam, in north Holland, which had 898 houses in 1569, had only 613 in 1579, a fall of 32 per cent; in 1588 it still had only 717. Nearby Monnikendam had 642 occupied houses in 1572, and 636 in 1588; like Edam, its population no doubt fell much farther between the two dates. Demographic losses like this were bound to increase the fiscal burden on those who remained, and the fall may have been even greater in south Holland and Zealand which were more directly involved in military operations than Edam and the other towns farther north. Leiden, once a thriving cloth town, lost perhaps one third of its population during the siege of 1574: a census of 1581 revealed a population of 12,000 – slightly less than on the eve of the siege – of whom roughly 35 per cent were recent immigrants.[30]

In the face of a reduced capacity to pay, the States of Holland found that tax revenue constantly fell short of their expectations. On 4 March

1575 they found it necessary to suspend all payments on annuities sold during the previous three years, in order to concentrate their full income on paying the troops. This device was little different from the Decree of Bankruptcy issued by Philip II later in the same year, but, whereas Spain resumed payments in 1577, the States of Holland could only begin to honour their annuity debts again in 1586. Although historians, like contemporaries, tend to stress the financial problems of Spain in 1575–6, it must be remembered that the insolvency of the 'rebels' was just as acute and was, if anything, more dangerous, for the Dutch had no Genoese or German bankers to back them. Their deficit could not continue for long without bringing disaster. Already in May 1574 Orange was concerned that bankruptcy would bring the revolt to an end. He told his brother:

'The ordinary expenses which we have to bear if we want to defend the country are so enormous that I see very little chance of providing for extraordinary wants, if we do not find some one to come to our aid. In this connexion I recollect that I told you some time ago that we could defend this country against all the forces of the king of Spain for two years, but that then we would inevitably need help, unless God can defend the country without any help, as He has done so far.'[31]

To the eyes of many besides Orange, God played an important role in the outcome of the Dutch struggle. In the declaration of 20 July 1572, the States of Holland had taken up the prince's invitation to promise freedom of religious worship to all the 'Reformed and Roman Catholic, in public or in private, in church or in chapel'. Although not specifically mentioned, it seems to have been Orange's intention that other dissenters, such as Lutherans and Anabaptists (both quite numerous in Holland), should be likewise free from persecution. Even Catholic priests were to be left unmolested. This 'religious peace', safeguarding explicitly the practice of the two main religions in Holland, was expressly reiterated in several of the capitulations by which the individual towns of Holland joined the revolt. Although public Catholic worship was forbidden by the States of Holland in February 1573 (an edict which contravened the capitulations but which could be justified by the troubled situation), the Catholics were free to practise in private, while Lutherans, Anabaptists and sectaries were left alone.[32]

The 'established church' of the new order was definitely that of the Calvinists, however. From August 1572 onwards they gradually gained control of the buildings and the ecclesiastical property of the Roman church; from March 1573 they were given control of state education in the province of Holland. The many Calvinist exiles who flooded back to Holland and Zealand, together with the probably smaller but still considerable number of Calvinists and crypto-Calvinists who had survived Alva's purges undetected, lost no time in organizing a formal Reformed church to serve each community. In some areas an embryonic church order (a 'church under the cross') was already in existence, but in most places one had to be created from the foundations, according to the guide-lines laid down by the Synod of Emden, with elders and deacons elected by the congregation and the ministers chosen by the elders or, in some towns, by the magistrates. The magistrates kept a tight rein on the new church, though. They often paid the stipend of the minister, either from municipal funds or out of the confiscated goods of the Roman church. While the distribution of poor relief and the staffing of schools were entrusted to the ministers, elders and deacons (financed by the former possessions of the Catholic church), the magistrates still kept an eye on things, since many of them served as elders and deacons of the Reformed communities. Thus the poor-relief books of the church of Tiel in Gelderland were kept by magistrates (in their capacity as deacons) and were inscribed 'The deaconry of the town of Tiel' and not 'of the Reformed church of Tiel'. To some extent, however, at Tiel and elsewhere, benefits were restricted to members of the church, and the orphanages and poor-houses tended to serve as centres for the encouragement of Calvinism.[33]

Above this 'parish organization' the leaders of the Reformed church created three important institutions. First came the consistory (*kerkeraad*, similar to the Scottish 'kirk-session') which brought together the minister and the elders of each established church; between them they scrutinized and controlled the behaviour, the morals and the beliefs of their congregation. Above them was the classis (equivalent to the Scottish presbytery), consisting of all the ministers serving a certain area (normally a town and the surrounding rural parishes) together with one elder from each kirk-session. The classis supervised the ecclesiastical affairs of all its constituent communities and was particularly important in checking any Romish or Anabaptist tendencies among its clergy and in ensuring that all ministers preached the 'true word'. At the top of this new hierarchy came the synods of each province of the Reformed church (held bi-annually in north Holland from August 1572 and in south Holland from June 1574) and the irregular but important national synods held for the entire Netherlands (the first after Emden was held at Dordrecht in June 1578).

This edifice was an impressive achievement for a church only a few years old, but the façade covered some important defects. At first, ecclesiastical arrangements were often disrupted by the war: thus the second synod of north Holland, held at Hoorn in the summer of 1572, left no resolutions or minutes 'because the times were then so troubled'; no one from Leiden was able to attend the first south Holland synod, held at Dordrecht in June 1574, because of the siege. There could be no classical organization around Haarlem or Amsterdam until after the end of hostilities in mid-1576, while churches in the areas about The Hague, Leiden and Oudewater were frequently abandoned as royalist troops approached. There was no formal synod at all in Zealand until 1579. More serious, the numerical base upon which the impressive superstructure rested was surprisingly small. In the spring of 1573, after a year of full toleration for the Calvinists, there were still only thirty-three Reformed communities in the whole of north Holland; on the island of Walcheren, in Zealand, there were only six communities with their own pastor as late as 1580. Although the position was substantially better in south Holland, everywhere the Calvinists were few in number. Most pastors in the early years were, in the acid phrase of L. J. Rogier (a Catholic historian), 'generals without troops'. In Dordrecht, a town of perhaps 13,000 people, there were only two Calvinist ministers with a flock of 368 communicants in July 1573; in Delft, with 14,000 people, at the same time there were three pastors and 200 communicants. In north Holland, in Alkmaar (which heroically withstood a Spanish siege in the autumn of 1573) there were only 176 full members of the Reformed church in January 1576 (in a population of around 5,000); Enkhuizen (also 5,000 people) had 340 communicants, and Enkhuizen was a town where the Calvinists enjoyed special advantages: there was a long tradition of crypto-Protestant priests, stretching back to the 1550s, and after 1572 the magistrates gave full-hearted support to the Reformed community. Moreover, where we know the identity of the Calvinist congregations, they appear not to have included many influential citizens. In 1587 only ten of the twenty-seven members of the *vroedschap* of Alkmaar were professed Calvinists (the congregation now numbered 440); at Delft in 1573 two thirds of the communicants were women; the faithful in Walcheren were all said to be 'fishermen and sailors', wilful and turbulent.[34] Comparison with the Catholic church's flock earlier in the century may be misleading, but there is no mistaking the sense of the figures from Nieuwe Niedorp, a village in west Friesland north of Amsterdam: there had been about 700 Catholic communicants there in 1514, but there were only thirty-eight Calvinist communicants in Lent 1574 and only eighty-eight by the end of the year. There can be no doubt that the professed Calvinists formed only a small minority of the people in revolt against Spain throughout the sixteenth century. When in 1587 it was suggested that only one tenth of the population were Calvinists, the Reformed ministers did not dispute this figure.[35]

There are many reasons for the small size of the Reformed communities in the rebellious provinces after 1572. In the first place, until 1578 royalist forces were never far away and it was dangerous to belong to the Reformed church. The ministers of Haarlem, Leerdam and Oudewater were hanged out of hand when their towns fell to the Spaniards, and several of their flocks soon followed. Everyone knew what had happened to those who declared their support for Protestantism in 1566: the Council of Troubles had acted against them then, and it was still in existence (until 1576). Reluctance to join the Protestants openly after 1572 on the grounds of prudence was reinforced, for many, by a sense of pride and a fear of humiliation. In the Netherlands Reformed church no one was allowed to attend communion unless he had undergone a rigorous examination of their beliefs, habits and deeds; even after that initiation their private lives were subject to regulation and condemnation by the consistorial organization. Even a burgomaster, if he misbehaved, could be hauled before the kirk-session and reprimanded by (probably) his social inferiors. This discipline, however, only extended over church members, not over the *liefhebbers* (sympathizers or fellow-travellers) who attended: the minister at Leiden who noted in 1579 that twenty-three of the twenty-eight magistrates came to church every Sunday but left before the communion service began was merely testifying to the daunting character of the Calvinist discipline. The point was important, because ultimately the attitude of the magistrates determined the place of the new church in Dutch society. Although they were prepared to provide protection, a place of worship and funds to the Reformed church, the 'regents' were not prepared to compel anyone to attend Calvinist services. They prohibited Catholic worship, but they allowed men to believe what they chose, provided it did not cause 'scandal' or endanger public order. People were even allowed to believe in nothing at all. It seems likely that, for many people, de-Catholicization also meant de-Christianization. The Catholic church may have been corrupt and inefficient, but it had at least provided a 'service' which it was not in the power of the new Reformed church to provide for many decades after 1572. There were simply not enough suitable trained pastors to go round: some of the early ministers displayed Romish tendencies after a while, or else spoke with a thick Frisian or 'Oosters' accent which made them incomprehensible to their congregations.[36] The almost complete breakdown in 'Christian order' is illustrated by the situation at Leiden where, in November 1575, the magistrates became aware that due to the troubled times a considerable number of people were living together as man and wife without having had their union solemnized by any church. The corporation therefore deputed two of their number to act as 'commissioners for matrimonial affairs' and ordered all persons who had lived together since 24 June 1572 to register themselves within fourteen days. It took some time before the matrimonial irregularities occasioned by the troubles could be dealt with.[37]

Although the degree to which the North Netherlands were 'Protestantized' in the early years of the revolt has been (and will doubtless continue to be) bitterly disputed, there can be no doubt that Calvinism alone did not and could not provide a broad enough base to unite the Dutch behind William of Orange in his struggle against Spanish tyranny. Although the Reformed faith was crucial in providing an ideology for the exiles in their hours of defeat and in sustaining them in times of trouble after 1572, the role of religion in the revolt of the Netherlands diminished almost as soon as an independent state had been created. The Republic stood in need of help from other quarters if it were to survive.

The failure of repression (1573–6)

Fortunately for the Dutch cause, Orange and the Calvinists had another ally in their war against the king of Spain: geography was on their side. First and foremost there was physical geography. The rebellious provinces were intersected by rivers, canals, drainage channels and streams, all of them flanked by high dikes to guard against the danger of flooding. They were also studded, to a far greater extent than today, with lakes and wide estuaries. In north Holland, the Schermer, Beemster, Purmer, Wormer and Wogmeer, together with the Heerhugowaard, formed a vast complex of lakes sealed off from the sea by just two great dikes. Farther south, the Haarlemmer, Leidse, Oude and Spieringer lakes were all joined together and virtually cut south Holland in two, while the great estuaries which separated the isles of Zealand from each other constituted a formidable barrier to communication (these features appear clearly on every map drawn at the time). The two provinces were, in the words of an English commentator, 'The great Bog of *Europe*. There is not such another Marsh in the World, that's flat. They are an universall Quag-mire, Epitomiz'd . . . Indeed it is the buttock of the World, full of veines and bloud, but no bones in't.'[38] The Dutch turned this fact to their advantage: on a number of occasions, and most notably for the relief of Alkmaar in 1573 and Leiden in 1574 they broke the dikes in order to flood the surrounding countryside hoping, by this means, both to deprive the besiegers of their food supply and to enable a seaborne relief expedition to sail up to the beleaguered town. In 1576, with the Spaniards at last making real progress in the reconquest of Zealand, Orange may even have contemplated flooding the whole of the two provinces and sailing away with their loyal inhabitants to some new land in order to keep them out of the clutches of the king and the Catholics. Such an 'ultimate solution' was certainly within his power.

These natural strengths were reinforced by others. Holland and Zealand were difficult to attack from the south by land by reason of the four great rivers which reached the sea at the same delta: the Lek, Linge, Maas and Waal. In early modern times it was not possible to cross them comfortably west of the Biesbos (the vast lake created by the St Elizabeth's Day flood of 1421 and never reclaimed). The

Dutch added to this natural advantage by capturing the towns of Gorinchem (Gorcum) and Zaltbommel in July 1572 and St Geertruidenberg in August 1573 – the towns which commanded the most westerly crossings of the Maas and Waal. Without these three towns it was necessary for government forces to march far inland, sometimes as far as Nijmegen, in order to cross the river delta and enter Holland. Although not the impregnable 'barrier' which Pieter Geyl made them out to be – especially not until after 1578, when the last royalist strongholds in Holland surrendered – the 'great rivers', together with the heath, lakes and marshes on either side of them, did present a serious obstacle to military movement and supply.

The Dutch were greatly aided by the military as well as by the physical geography of the Low Countries. During the wars against France Charles V had taken steps to improve the fortifications of the towns along the North Sea coast of the Netherlands, lest there should be an attack on them by sea. Antwerp was given a completely new set of defences in 1540, Utrecht shortly afterwards. Other towns were improved piecemeal. The drawings of the sieges and battles of the Low Countries' Wars made in the 1570s by Walter Morgan, an English captain in Dutch service, clearly show the impressive new fortifications of several towns. Morgan's sketch of the Spanish siege of Alkmaar in 1573, for example, shows eight great bastions keeping the besiegers at bay.[39]

The bastion was part of an entirely new concept in military architecture. In the course of the fifteenth century improvements in the art of gun-founding and the casting of artillery rendered the high thin walls of medieval fortifications quite indefensible. A brief cannonade from the new 'bombards' brought them crashing down. The initiative in warfare, from about 1440 onwards, lay with the aggressor and, not surprisingly, military architects began urgently to experiment with new techniques of fortification which might withstand shelling. They eventually devised the 'Italian system', which combined low, extremely thick walls built of brick (which absorbed the impact of shot better than stone) with quadrilateral bastions projecting towards the enemy's trenches and defended by heavy artillery. It soon became clear that a town defended by the 'Italian system' could not be captured by the traditional methods of heavy artillery battery followed by massed assault. Instead it had to be encircled, blockaded and starved into surrender. 'We must confesse', wrote Sir Roger Williams (a veteran of the Low Countries' Wars) in 1590, '*Alexander, Caesar, Scipio*, and *Haniball*, to be the worthiest and famoust warriers that euer were; notwithstanding, assure your selfe . . . they would neuer haue . . . conquered Countries so easilie, had they been fortified as Germanie, France, and the Low Countries, with others, haue been since their daies.'[40]

One must not, however, overemphasize the importance of the bastion in the early years of the revolt. It took many years before every major town in the Netherlands had the new defences. Although Alkmaar had eight bastions in 1573, Leiden had only one and Haarlem, which resisted the Spaniards with the same dogged courage as the other two, apparently had none at all. Fortifications were not everything. They alone could not keep determined enemies out. The fall of Mons, which had a complete set of new bastions, to Count Louis of Nassau proved the point in May 1572. Although the unrestrained paeans of praise heaped by Motley on the courage and steadfastness of the Dutch are somewhat unfashionable today, it must be recognized that the fate of many sieges hinged upon the heroism of the defenders, or a dedicated group of them, who risked everything when they refused to surrender to the forces of the king. The manner in which Alkmaar decided to endure a siege in 1573 is characteristic. The magistrates were divided (several magistrates defected to the royalists between 1572 and 1574) and as the Spaniards demanded entry to the city by the Kennemer gate there were Orangist reinforcements at the Friesland gate. The magistrates could not decide which side to choose, which gate to open.

'A great crowd of citizens had assembled in front of the town hall, waiting for the resolution of the magistrates. When this had gone on for a long time, Ruyschaver [the Orangists' leader] said with anger in his heart: "This is not the time to deliberate any longer. Tell us briefly what you will do or not do." Upon which Floris van Teylingen, one of the burgomasters, said: "With Prince and citizens I live and die," and immediately he went with Captain Ruyschaver out of the town hall. Many citizens crowded in front and behind, Meerten Pietersen van de Mey, the town carpenter, among them, with axes and sledge hammers, and they hacked the Friesland gate open and let in the men of the prince of Orange, and the next moment the Kennemer gate was opened so that these soldiers could make a sally against the Spaniards.'[41]

It was the determination of men like Ruyschaver, an exiled nobleman, and the handful of devoted citizens, probably but not necessarily Calvinists, which made the difference between resistance and submission in the initial stages of the Spanish counter-offensive. The three main towns besieged in Holland – Haarlem, Alkmaar and Leiden – surrendered to Orange almost without a blow. There were many in every town who had never wished to admit the Beggars; there were others who were disillusioned with the excesses of Lumey and his companions; there were others who still feared the horrors which a siege (and possibly a sack) would bring. Such people always counselled surrender, and some of them stooped to 'betrayal'. It was for their benefit that Alva staged the massacres of Mechelen, Zutphen and Naarden.

It may seem strange, at first glance, that the citizens of Alkmaar and the other towns which came under siege should have been so irresolute as the Spaniards approached yet so determined once they were blockaded – for it was often the ordinary citizens, male and female, young and old, who drove the besiegers back from the walls. The explanation of their conduct lies partly in the military customs prevailing in the sixteenth century, and partly in the way the Spaniards abused them. The 'law of war' around 1570 recognized that, if a town agreed to surrender before the besiegers brought up their artillery, it would not be sacked. Everyone knew that – hence the anxiety to capitulate before the siege started. Once under way, however, the besiegers had the right to plunder a town if they took it. Everyone knew that too, especially after the sack of Mechelen, Zutphen and Naarden in 1572. Only Zutphen had actually resisted the Spanish army; Mechelen had not even attempted to close its gates (it was punished for having opened its gates to Orange's forces a month before) and Naarden surrendered when the Spanish artillery actually arrived. But all three were sacked. The fate of Haarlem, which was the Spaniards' next objective after Naarden, was scarcely better. The town was under siege from early December 1572 until 12 July 1573. It surrendered in the end only because the royal commander offered assurances that no one within the town should be harmed; otherwise the inhabitants were prepared to set fire to the town. After the surrender, however, the entire garrison, with the exception of some English and German troops, was executed, together with a few magistrates.

Many other citizens were imprisoned and an indemnity of 200,000 florins was imposed upon the town. All this was seen by Alva as an act of extraordinary clemency, intended to encourage the other towns of Holland to surrender; but the Netherlanders, and particularly the garrisons of other towns, saw it in a rather different light. After all, some 2,000 persons who had trusted in the Spaniards' promise of pardon had been executed in cold blood. Handbills and prints soon began to circulate, describing and illustrating all the gory details. Cardinal Granvelle in Naples was horrified when he heard the news. What was the point, he wondered, 'of executing the soldiers in cold blood . . . The duke of Alva now complains that other areas have not surrendered spontaneously, but he should remember that there are soldiers defending the [other] towns who, fearing the same treatment as the garrison of Haarlem, will fight on until they die of hunger'. Granvelle thus saw the capture of Haarlem as a possible turning-point; so did Alva's successor-designate, the duke of Medina Celi. When he heard of Haarlem's surrender he wrote to Philip II's secretary: 'Affairs here are now at the point where either they will be brought to a speedy conclusion or else they will drag on for a very long time. Everything depends, in my opinion, on the decision to be taken on how to proceed in Holland, because there are many towns there to be forced into submission . . .'[42] Granvelle and Medina Celi were right: Haarlem was a turning-point. After the reprisals there, no more towns surrendered to the Spaniards without a struggle. The legendary reply of the people of Leiden when, after some months of privation, they were called upon to surrender, gives an indication of the general feeling of at least some of those in opposition to Spain:

'You heare that in our Toune are both dogges, kine and horses. And if wee should in the end want these, yet hath every one of vs a left arme to eate, and reserve the righte arme to beat the tyrant and the rest of you which are his blooddy ministers from our walles: but if at the last, our force shall not bee strong enough . . . we will never . . . giue over the defense of the libertie of our countrie, choosing rather when wee are at the verie word [sc. end] to set our Towne in fier, then that it shold [in] any way be gainefull vnto you and we become your slaves.'[43]

Spain, however, was not impressed by such rhetoric. From the moment when he heard the news of the fall of Brill (on 22 April) and Mons (on 8 June), the king appears to have set his face against compromise. Although he did suspend the Tenth Penny (on 26 June), at no stage in 1572 and 1573 does Philip II appear to have considered ending the rebellion other than by force of arms. In this he was supported by the duke of Alva, ever the implacable enemy of compromise, who represented the revolt as the work of Protestants with whom a Catholic monarch could not decently deal. In August 1573, having decided to besiege Alkmaar, he admonished the king:

'I cannot refrain from beseeching Your Majesty . . . to disabuse yourself of the notion that anything will ever be accomplished in these provinces by the use of clemency. Things have now reached the stage where many Netherlanders who until now have been begging for clemency now see and admit their mistake. They are of the opinion that not a living soul should be left in Alkmaar.'

In December of the same year he informed his successor (Don Luis de Requesens):

'These troubles must be ended by force of arms without any use of pardon, mildness, negotiations or talks until everything has been flattened. That will be the right time for negotiation.'

Spain deprecated every attempt made by third parties to start talks with the rebels: the king and Alva refused the efforts to reconcile the two sides made by the emperor in 1568, by the French in 1572, by the English and by the elector of Cologne in 1573. 'Let this rebel lay down his arms and beg for mercy, then we can see what is to be done' was the duke of Alva's icy rebuke to one would-be mediator. On a later occasion the Spanish government seriously debated whether to open the sea dikes and flood the rebel provinces, or merely to burn everything above ground.[44]

Yet for all Alva's lapidary declarations, Spain simply could not afford to go on fighting for ever. In large measure the revolt of 1572 had been provoked by Philip II's anxiety to put an end to the drain of Spanish resources to the Netherlands, via the Tenth Penny, at a time when he needed all his revenues to finance the war in the Mediterranean. The outcome was exactly the reverse of his expectations. Once war broke out in the Netherlands, Alva was totally dependent on subsidies from Spain. Whereas almost nine million florins

6

raised in the Low Countries reached the central treasury in 1570–71, less than two million did so in 1572–3. The shortfall had to be made good by Castile. Yet the fact remains that the central treasury's *total* receipts in the peaceful years, 1570–71, were considerably higher than in the first two years of war, 1572–3.[45]

Receipts of the Netherlands central treasury

Years	From local taxation	From Castile	Total
1570–71	8,809,792 f.	1,111,378 f.	9,921,170 f.
1572–3	1,815,595 f.	6,910,238 f.	8,725,833 f.

All in florins of 20 pattards

The king could not bring himself to abandon the offensive against the Turks, despite all Alva's pleas to do so, and this spelled disaster for the army of Flanders. Already starved of funds when the war began (the Spanish units were owed eighteen months' wages in April 1572), the troops were ill disposed to endure the cold, privations and heavy losses of the war without being paid. In July 1573, shortly after the capture of Haarlem (which they were not allowed to sack), the Spanish regiments mutinied for their arrears. It took a fortnight (and sixty florins per man) to restore order in the army, but the troops remained restless for a long time afterwards. On 18 September the *tercios* refused the order to assault the beleaguered town of Alkmaar; early in October they refused again, indirectly obliging the Spanish commander to raise the siege on 8 October.

These failures were extremely embarrassing for the duke of Alva. Haarlem had been a Pyrrhic vistory (the besiegers may have lost as many as 10,000 men); Alkmaar had not been taken; Rammekens and St Geertruidenberg had been lost. To crown it all, on 11 October 1573 the royal fleet suffered a crushing defeat on the Zuider Zee and its able commander, Count Bossu, was taken prisoner.

After so many military failures, and with the growing perception at the Spanish Court that it was Alva's policies (rather than religion) which had provided Orange with most of his support in 1572, it became increasingly clear that Alva would have to go. Curiously enough the king had long had the matter in hand: as early as 1570

Philip assured his then successful lieutenant in the Netherlands that he would soon be allowed to return to Spain. After considerable reflection the king appointed Don Juan de la Cerda, duke of Medina Celi, to take over the government of the Low Countries. At that stage, Alva's policies were still to remain in force: the new governor's instructions, signed by the king on 25 September 1571, enjoined him to follow the duke of Alva's guidance in all things. The new governor, as it happened, had no choice: he only arrived on Flemish soil in May 1572, after the outbreak of open war in the Low Countries. The king was convinced that Alva's military skill was indispensable to victory and Medina Celi was ordered to wait in the wings. This situation was manifestly unsatisfactory. As heir apparent, Medina Celi now became the target for fervent lobbying by the Netherlands politicians. Aerschot and Champagney, the leaders of the southern Catholic nobility, bombarded him with memoranda, advice and infor- mation about Alva's excesses and their role in provoking the revolt; they also pleaded the cause of moderation and clemency as the only way to end the rebellion. Much to Alva's disgust, Medina Celi appeared to accept the Netherlanders' view, sending back to Court adverse reports of Alva's attitudes and policies and advocating concessions to the rebels. Champagney and his clique, according to one observer, 'gained control of Medina Celi and controlled him as their puppet'.[46] The king was not impressed. Early in 1573 he decided that Alva would have to be replaced with someone made of sterner stuff than Medina Celi and on 30 January 1573 he wrote to Don Luis de Requesens, then governor of Lombardy, appointing him governor and captain-general of the Netherlands in succession to Alva. Both the duke and Medina Celi would be recalled. Requesens, prematurely aged and looking forward to peaceful retirement, was horrified. He did his best to make the king think again, but without success. On 17 November 1573 the new governor made his reluctant entry to Brussels and on 29 November he was sworn in as Alva's successor.

Although reputed to be a man of moderate views, during his first few weeks in the Netherlands Requesens was forced to rely on Alva for advice and information about the needs and problems of the Low Countries. The duke, unrepentant even though defeated, remained in Brussels until 18 December and even after his departure he sent Requesens letters of counsel. The new governor therefore found it difficult to break away from the policies implemented and ably advocated by his predecessor. Above all Alva convinced him of the need to keep on fighting the war. He began his period of office by accepting the duke's advice not to seek any talks with the rebels. He disowned two of his commanders in Holland – Julián Romero and Baron Noircarmes – who had been attempting to discover on what terms the prince of Orange would agree to talk. Only the disastrous events of 1574 changed his mind.

The year began with the defeat of another royal fleet in the Scheldt estuary (29 January) and the fall of Middelburg (18 February), the last royalist stronghold in Walcheren. Then on 21 March the siege of Leiden had to be raised in order to defeat a large-scale invasion of the eastern Netherlands by Count Louis of Nassau and a large army from Germany. Although the count was killed and his army annihilated at the battle of Mook (14 April), on the morrow of their triumph the Spanish victors mutinied and marched on Antwerp, holding the great city to ransom until they were paid their wage arrears (one million florins) on 30 May. With the Spanish veterans thus pacified, Requesens decided to resume the siege of Leiden, but here again he proved unsuccessful. By dint of flooding all the land between the Lek and the town, Leiden was relieved on 3 October and the Spaniards withdrew in panic and disorder. A month later the Spanish troops left in garrisons elsewhere in Holland decided to mutiny rather than spend another winter amid the frozen wastes and waters and they abandoned all the small towns and villages which they held, delivering an armed attack on the Spanish garrison of Utrecht as they went (17 December). The vacated strongpoints were swiftly reoccupied by the Orangists.

The three mutinies of the Spanish veterans, the 'sinews of the army', in 1573–4 were a devastating blow to the royal cause and a deliverance to the Dutch. It was hard not to see the hand of God in it all. 'Surely, gentle reader,' wrote a chronicler of Alkmaar, 'it cannot be otherwise thought but that this dissention and disorder was even the verye mightie work of God, considering the great commoditie, benefit and gaine that redounded to these countries hereby.'[47] On the Spanish side Don Luis de Requesens was moved to the same conclusion: 'When I recall the circumstances in which these mutinies broke out ... I cannot but conclude that God, for some secret reason, wishes to punish us by our own hands because we deserve it.' Some months later he returned to the same melancholy theme:

'Many towns and a battle have been won [he announced to one of the king's councillors], each of them a success enough in itself to bring peace, and even to win an entire new kingdom elsewhere; but here they have been to no avail because after each victory came the mutinies . . . I believe that God for my sins has chosen to show me so many times the Promised Land here, as he did to Moses, but that someone else is to be the Joshua who will enter therein.'

Requesens's despairing presumption that God had abandoned Spain's cause was increased by the knowledge that the king had sent more than twice as much money from Castile to the Netherlands in 1574 as in the two previous years, and all to no avail.

'There would not be time or money enough in the world [he warned the king in October 1574] to reduce by force the twenty-four towns which have rebelled in Holland, if we are to spend as long in reducing each one of them as we have taken over similar ones so far.'[48]

Spain, he realized, simply could not afford to keep on fighting in the Netherlands. In March 1574 the army of Flanders, considerably increased to defeat Count Louis's invasion, numbered over 86,000 men, at least on paper; its running costs were estimated at 1,200,000 florins a month, leaving aside the expense of paying off arrears, debts and other capital charges. This sum was far more than the income of the king from Castile and the Indies combined, and Philip II had other pressing matters on which to spend his money – especially the defence of the Mediterranean. In September 1574 the Turkish fleet, possibly prompted by Orange's diplomacy, came west in force and captured not only Tunis (taken by Don John of Austria the previous year) but also the important Spanish fortress of La Goletta, sited on a promontory overlooking Tunis. It was a stunning blow to Philip's pride. The French agent in Brussels was swift to recognize its implications:

'This disaster of the loss of La Goletta may make Philip II more anxious to seek . . . [peace here] so that he will be able to turn all his forces and resources against the Turks in order to put up a better resistance to them, the war [in the Mediterranean] being of greater importance to him.'[49]

The Dutch, who had heard of the loss of La Goletta by mid-November, also concluded (correctly) that it would lead to a reduction in Spain's military effort against them. They did not know, however, that the king had come to see the futility of fighting on in the Netherlands. On 31 May 1574 Philip II confided to his private secretary, Mateo Vázquez, that he considered 'the loss of the Netherlands and the rest [of his monarchy] to be as certain as, in this situation, anything can be . . . It is a terrible situation and it is getting worse every day.' On 20 June he returned to his despondent refrain: 'I believe that everything is a waste of time, judging by what is happening in the Low Countries, and if they are lost the rest [of the monarchy] will not last long, even if we have enough money.' The financial situation of the Castilian treasury had become the key to the situation. 'We must do everything we can to succour the Netherlands,' he wrote on 4 July, '. . . because if we have no money, our position at the conference table will prove even more difficult.' On 14 July the king's financial advisers warned him that the coffers were empty and that the only way to avoid bankruptcy was to repudiate all public debts and abandon the war in the Netherlands. Four days later Philip lamented: 'I think that the Netherlands will be lost for lack of money, as I have always feared . . . We are in great need and our enemies know it well, so that they will not wish to make a settlement . . .' 'We are running out of everything so fast', the king concluded, 'that words fail me.'[50]

As it happened the king was able to stave off a decree of bankruptcy for over a year, but he raised no objections when his desperate lieutenant in the Netherlands took steps to organize formal peace talks with the 'rebels'. Following some casual feelers, on 30 November Requesens issued formal instructions to Dr Elbertus Leoninus, a former friend and lawyer of Orange who had remained loyal to the king, to seek out the prince and arrange a conference at Breda. Talks began there on 3 March 1575.

Despite Spain's parlous financial state, of which (as Philip II had noted) the Dutch were fully aware, the chances of a negotiated settlement in 1575 were slight. The demands of the two sides were fundamentally incompatible. Ultimately the dispute was over religious toleration and constitutional guarantees. The 'rebels' were prepared to recognize the king's authority again (in theory they had never rejected the king, only his 'evil councillors'), but they were not willing to give up their Calvinist religion. In addition they required constitutional guarantees that there would be no retribution after they laid down their arms, and they therefore demanded that the Spanish troops should be withdrawn. Philip II was prepared to accept the latter, and agreement might have been reached on the question of guarantees, but Spain would make no concession on the religious issue and neither would the Dutch. Requesens offered the 'rebels' full pardon, restoration of all confiscated property and confirmation of privileges for those who were Catholics or would consent to live as such, while Protestants were promised six months of grace to sell their goods and go. This offer went some way beyond what Philip had authorized his representative to offer, but in any case the 'rebels' refused it. Orange and his allies knew that they had a strong hand: they were well aware of Spain's financial difficulties and of the geographical and military strength of their position. As Orange wrote during the siege of Leiden:

'If the poor inhabitants here, forsaken by everyone, persevere despite everything, as they have done until now . . . it will cost the Spaniards half of Spain in goods as well as in men before they have finished with us.'[51]

Left without guidance from Madrid, and meeting with no desire for compromise from the 'rebels', Requesens had no option but to break off the peace-talks at Breda on 13 July 1575. The negotiations had only served to give the Dutch three months' respite and to bring the Spanish crown three months nearer to bankruptcy.

As soon as the talks were called off, Requesens showed real military skill. The Spanish army launched a new offensive intended to split the rebel provinces in two. One column advanced from Utrecht via Oudewater and Buren to Schoonhoven on the Lek, while a second made a daring crossing of the wide but shallow estuary to the islands of Schouwen and Duiveland. Before long the impetuous attacks of the Spanish veterans had driven all the Dutch troops out of the island, leaving only Zierikzee loyal to Orange. The town was soon under close siege and both Requesens and Orange agreed that the fate of the whole revolt rested upon the outcome of that siege. If Zierikzee fell, the rebellious provinces would be cut in two and Orange's position would be far weaker; if Zierikzee could be saved, Orange's credibility in the eyes of foreign rulers, and particularly in those of Queen Elizabeth, would be decisively strengthened. In the event, however, both men were wrong. The town fell, and it made no difference.

On 1 September 1575 Philip II at last agreed to put into effect the decree suspending interest payments on the Castilian public debt. By this action he automatically deprived himself of the means of sending any more money to his army in the Netherlands by the traditional means of an *asiento* or bill of exchange. The significance of the step was immediately obvious to everyone: the Dutch lit bonfires to celebrate the news, the Spanish governor wept. Only the troops around Zierikzee appeared to be unaffected, staying doggedly at their posts throughout the cold winter months. Even the death of Requesens on 5 March 1576, leaving the divided Council of State in charge of government, seemed to make no difference to the Spanish army. Now it was the prince of Orange's turn to despair. Perhaps he should have accepted the terms proffered at Breda since no foreign power had yet provided him with open, substantial assistance? His cause was, as he said, 'abandoned by the world'.[52] On 2 July 1576 Zierikzee surrendered on terms and the Spaniards marched in. Within a matter of hours, however, they marched out again, crossed back on to the mainland and invaded Brabant. The victorious veterans had decided once again that it was time to require a full settlement of their wage arrears from the government in Brussels.

[4]

THE THIRD REVOLT

(1576–81)

Revolution

The decree of bankruptcy, issued by Philip II in September 1575, dealt

> 'Such a blow to the Exchange here [in Antwerp] that no one in it has any credit . . . I cannot find a single penny, nor can I see how the king could send money here, even if he had it in abundance. Short of a miracle, the whole military machine will fall in ruins so rapidly that it is highly probable that I shall not have time to tell you about it. And all this has to come at a time when, if the king could have delayed for three months, I hold it certain that in that time we could have captured all the rest of Zealand and even the other provinces.'[1]

These despairing lines, written by Governor-General Requesens to his brother in November 1575, exaggerated only slightly the position in which he found himself. Philip II's intransigence over the religious problem had sabotaged the peace initiative of 1575; now the king's decision to break off all dealings with his bankers, who alone could funnel adequate funds from Spain to the Netherlands, had doomed Requesens's promising military offensive into south Holland and the isles of Zealand. In the event, it all proved too much for the governor. Sent to the Netherlands under protest, placed in an impossible position from the start, he often said that the decree had broken his heart. It certainly broke his health. According to a close friend and adviser, he was never well after he learned of the bankruptcy and he died early on the morning of 5 March 1576.

The situation facing the surviving members of the government in Brussels was appalling. In the first place, as one of them said, they were orphans: their leader had departed without naming a successor. He had, it was true, dictated an order that power after his death was to be divided between Count Berlaymont (for internal administration), Count Mansfelt (for war and defence) and Gerónimo de Roda (for Spanish funds and personnel), but Requesens was too weak to sign the draft, and in any case there was some doubt about his competence to name successors. A few hours after the governor-general's death, since it was a Monday, the Council of State met as usual in Brussels to discuss the situation, and in particular the measures required to carry on the king's government until new instructions could arrive from Spain. The Council deliberated for some days and eventually took two crucial decisions: on 8 March, aided by advice from the leading Spanish army commanders and a large map of the area, they resolved to continue with the siege of Zierikzee; on 9 March they determined to set aside the last order of Requesens on the question of succession and to assume supreme power themselves.

The nine members of the Council were ill equipped to govern at a moment of crisis. They were almost all old men: the most senior, Viglius and Berlaymont, were both nearly seventy and Viglius remained in his bed for most of the time until his death in May 1577. Effective direction went by default into the hands of two men: Gerónimo de Roda, the only Spanish member, and the duke of Aerschot. Roda, a lawyer from Valladolid called to the Netherlands in 1570 to work for Alva on the Council of Troubles, had become Requesens's most trusted adviser, partly because he could speak and understand French (which the governor could only do with great difficulty). Roda was an excellent administrator and, as later events were to show, not a bad politician;

but as a Spaniard he lacked any following among the Netherlanders. Aerschot was a contrast in every way. One of the largest landowners in the Netherlands, a councillor since 1565 and head of the powerful Croy family, he had become the leader of the anti-Spanish Catholic nobility in the south Netherlands and the darling of the Brussels populace. The duke himself was rather undistinguished: the Spanish governors and their entourage despised him (and not without reason) as 'a wind-bag' – *tan ayre* – but he had able supporters. A group of lesser nobles who believed passionately that the war with the rebels was being fought for political grievances, not for religion, gathered about Aerschot. They included his Croy relatives like the count of Roeulx, governor of Flanders, some minor Walloon noblemen and also an astute politician, Frédéric Perrenot de Granvelle (the cardinal's brother), baron de Champagney. These men believed that if only the Spanish troops could be sent home and the ancient constitution restored, Holland, Zealand and the prince of Orange would agree to a ceasefire. They had pressed this policy on the duke of Medina Celi in 1572–3 with considerable success, and they helped to persuade Requesens to open negotiations with the rebels at Breda. When the talks broke down, Aerschot and his friends (incorrectly) blamed the failure on the king's presumed unwillingness to recall the Spanish troops and convene the States-General. They refused to believe that it was religion which separated the two sides. The duke was a prominent member of the States of Brabant and in December 1575 he voiced his criticisms of the king's policy towards the Dutch at a meeting of the States in Brussels. He managed to persuade the assembly to refuse to provide any more money for the war until the talks were reopened, and all the other provincial estates, as usual, followed Brabant's lead. As Requesens observed early in his governorship, Aerschot and his friends were not averse to the collapse of the Spanish army 'so that His Majesty will be forced to come to terms with the rebels and grant these provinces all the liberties they are demanding'. Champagney at least, the governor added, 'has the most ardent hatred of our nation I have ever seen'.[2] By the spring of 1576 this feeling was by no means confined to Champagney and his circle.

After five years of arrogant and violent behaviour in peace time, the Spaniards added to their unpopularity by the brutal treatment of the rebellious towns in the war of 1572: Mechelen, Zutphen and Naarden were all sacked with an unprecedented thoroughness and cruelty. Later on there was the chastisement of Haarlem, Oudewater and Bommenede on capture. However, it was undoubtedly the mutinies (*alteraciones*) of the Spanish troops in 1573, 1574, 1575 and 1576 which did most to turn the Netherlands against them. Again it was Requesens who observed that even had the people of the Low Countries loved the Spaniards as sons before, 'the Spanish mutinies would be enough to make us loathed'.[3]

The mutinies of the Spanish troops within the army of Flanders were terrifying events. The soldiers, thousands of them at a time, expelled their officers and elected their own leaders, forming a revolutionary committee not unlike a modern workers' soviet. Their behaviour was unpredictable and, when they decided to act, they were practically irresistible: the Spanish veterans were the most experienced and most highly trained troops in the whole of Europe. The mutineers therefore commanded a strong position in their negotiations with the government over their grievances, chief among which was always the question of wages. The cost of maintaining a military presence in the Netherlands had been a problem even before the outbreak of war in 1572: the duke of Alva's failure to exact the Tenth Penny and the king's refusal to send more money from Spain had caused the pay of the Spanish troops to fall seriously in arrears. By April 1574, when the veterans mutinied at Mook, the Spanish units were owed thirty-seven months' wages. When they mutinied again in July 1576 they could then claim to be owed almost two years' back-pay, and the light cavalry could claim six. The basic problem was that, as noted above (p. 165), the army of Flanders cost far more than the government could afford to provide. The Military Treasury received only about 300,000 florins a month from Spain, while the estimated cost of the armed forces stood at four times this sum. Although a considerable amount was raised from the Low Countries in contributions and taxes, such was the disruption and dislocation caused by the war that it was often impossible to be sure where this money went. At the mutiny of Antwerp in 1574 the government, totally incapable of discovering exactly how much its troops had – or had not – been paid, finally agreed to pay half the total claim of the mutineers in return for an admission by the soldiers that they had received the other half in free lodgings, thefts and plunder.

The mutineers totally discredited the Spanish regime in the Low

Countries: they terrorized the local inhabitants; they sabotaged all offensive action against the enemy; and at the same time they consumed enormous sums of money. The mutineers of Antwerp were paid a total of over one million florins in May 1574, of which 400,000 were grudgingly provided by loans raised among the merchants of the city to save their goods from being plundered by the troops intended to protect them.

Here lay the paradox which enraged the Netherlanders as much as the Spanish government: the mutineers managed simultaneously to beggar the Treasury and to enable Orange's men to recover the towns lost in the previous campaigning season. As one serious mutiny followed another, the Netherlanders were bound to question the government's chances of ever winning the war by military means, especially after the bankruptcy decree of September 1575, which meant that the king was unable to send much money from Spain (while the provincial States persisted in their refusal to vote taxes until negotiations with the rebels were recommenced). In desperation, Requesens had tried to intimidate the mutineers by a show of force. In February 1576, a few days before his death, he ordered letters to be written authorizing the provincial governors of Flanders, Artois and Hainaut to move against mutinous detachments of light cavalry with all the armed forces at their command. By the end of March Count Lalaing, the governor of Hainaut, had driven the mutineers into the neighbouring province of Cambrai. It proved impossible to follow up this success, however, since Lalaing had only a handful of regular troops and the Council of State refused permission to raise further units. Early in August therefore the light cavalry drifted back into Hainaut and started levying contributions from ecclesiastical dignitaries around Valenciennes. The States of Hainaut protested to the Council (9 August) and again began to agitate for powers to raise troops in their own name. Already an unexpected and cataclysmic event had forced the Council to allow the States of Brabant to do this.

On 25 July the Spanish mutineers, who had streamed south into Brabant after the capture of Zierikzee, made a surprise attack on Aalst, just sixteen miles west of Brussels. They took it and sacked it. When the news of this unprovoked atrocity – perpetrated on a town of unquestionable loyalty – became known in Brussels, the populace of the capital took to the streets, swords at the ready, chanting 'Death to the Spaniards'. They murdered a servant of Gerónimo de Roda in cold blood, as he went about his master's business, and they broke into the house of a pro-Spanish councillor, Count Berlaymont. In the countryside, more and more people were carrying arms, some by virtue of earlier government orders enjoining them to defend their own towns and villages, others in anticipation of the coming conflict with the Spaniards. It was to appease this popular fury that, on the day after the sack of Aalst, the Council of State published an edict which declared the mutineers to be rebels against God and the king and authorized all and sundry to kill them on sight as outlaws. On 27 July the Council, after some hesitation, granted the States of Brabant's demand for permission to raise troops in order to protect the province against the mutineers. Ten companies of foot and some cavalry were to be raised in the name of the States under commanders whom they were to appoint. The troops raised thus hurriedly by the provincial estates, however, proved to be no match for the Spanish veterans. The men of Brabant were decisively routed near Tienen on 14 September when they tried to block the advance of the mutineers. All the States could do was to push the Spaniards from one province to another. It was clear that the only way to combat the mutinous hordes was for all the provinces to join their forces together. The Pragmatic Sanction of 1549 specifically permitted one province to go to the aid of another in time of war and the States of Hainaut, still suffering from the attentions of the light cavalry, invoked this right on 27 August and asked the Council for permission to consult with the States of Brabant assembled at Brussels about common defence. This the Council could not allow. Like Don Luis de Requesens, they were under strict orders from the king not to permit the provincial estates to meet together, orders reiterated and reinforced by the marquis of Havré who arrived in Brussels from the Spanish Court on 31 July.

Havré was no ordinary messenger. Since autumn 1575 Philip II had promised the immediate dispatch of the marquis with what he termed the *vrayes remèdes*, the real remedies, for the Netherlands problem. However, first Requesens died and upset the king's calculations and then Don John, chosen by Philip to be the next governor-general, refused to go to the Low Countries until he had consulted the king in person beforehand. In the end the unfortunate Havré had to be dispatched with the message that a final solution for the Netherlands' difficulties was (still) under active consideration. Philip II fully realized that his failure to send any new policies with Havré might prove disastrous. On 21 June he wrote to his secretary that Don John's tardiness in replying to the king's letter appointing him governor-general of the Low Countries was:

'Very dangerous, because I was awaiting it in order to finalize all my decisions, and the delay is therefore extremely inconvenient for the affairs of the Netherlands. This appointment was the principal item that I was hoping to send with the Marquis of Havré, but since the acceptance has not come and since Havré must be sent, I am looking around for something to send him with [ando buscando con qué embiarle]. He will simply have to go with promises and it will be extremely hazardous if we do not fulfil them very soon. I am very fearful that this delay will exacerbate the situation so much that it may defeat all our designs.'[4]

In Brussels Gerónimo de Roda also predicted that unless Havré brought some new nostrums with him, the Netherlanders would find their own. He was right. At 10.30 precisely on Monday, 4 September a detachment of soldiers specially picked from those raised by the States of Brabant and led by Jacques de Glimes, deputy-commander of the States' troops, broke into the chamber in which the Council of State was meeting. The astonished members were informed that they were under arrest and they were taken into confinement and kept under lock and key.

At first no one would admit to responsibility for the deed. One of the ringleaders, the abbot of St Gertrude's monastery at Leuven, asserted that God was responsible; more practically, Glimes claimed that he had orders from his superior officer, the lord of Hèze; and Hèze, anxious not to become a scapegoat, asserted that it was the spontaneous action of the commune of Brussels. There is little doubt, however, that the duke of Aerschot and the prince of Orange were privy to the plot; certainly both made haste to make the most of the forcible removal of the king's representatives, the sole obstacle to a meeting of the States-General and, perhaps, to a negotiated settlement of the civil war. On 6 September, the day after the coup, delegates of the States of Brabant and Hainaut met together in Brussels and decided to summon deputies from all the provincial estates except those of Holland and Zealand to a joint assembly. On 8 September letters were dispatched to all provinces inviting them to assemble in Brussels to renew the union of 1548–9 and take counsel for their mutual defence. On the same day the States of Brabant accepted the duke of Aerschot's proposal that they should vote taxes worth one million florins in order to pay for their troops; shortly afterwards they agreed to reimpose Alva's Hundredth Penny (the 1-per-cent sales tax) for the same purpose. These were the very taxes for which the government had asked the States in vain since April 1574! As late as August 1576 the States had refused, although either tax would have provided enough to appease the mutineers.

It was not long before the leading members of the various States began to receive communications from the prince of Orange. Already in mid-July Roda had described his colleagues on the Council as 'bristling with letters from the prince'. On 13 August Hèze asked the States of Brabant if he could read out certain letters he had received from the prince and, although on that occasion a majority of the deputies voted against this, on 23 August they reversed their decision and heard Orange's appeal for cooperation in bringing the war to an end. After the arrest of the Council a number of former members of the States, proscribed after 1567 for their part in the troubles, began to attend meetings again and a small but active Orangist faction was built up. In the States of Flanders too, which sent its deputies to Brussels on 16 September, Orange had his supporters with whom he corresponded – chief among them Jan van Hembyze, a prominent magistrate of Ghent. On 19 September, despite opposition from some members, letters were sent in the name of the three States already assembled (Brabant, Hainaut and Flanders) to King Henry III of France and his brother, the duke of Alençon, asking them to be ready to provide assistance and advice if need arose. Three days later a few members of the States wrote to ask Orange for immediate military aid and on 26 September some of the prince's troops entered the city of Ghent, while the following day, in Brussels, the States asked Orange to appoint representatives to negotiate with them about bringing the war to an end. No time was lost and talks started at Ghent on 7 October, taking up at the point at which they had been broken off at Breda the previous year.

There were good reasons for such haste. In the first place it was common knowledge that a new royal governor had at last been appointed: Don John of Austria, Philip II's only brother and the victor of Lepanto. The States took it for granted that such a champion of Catholicism would be resolutely set against any compromise with heretics and that therefore an agreement to end the fighting must be reached before he arrived. No one in the Netherlands could guess that Don John had been given full powers by Philip II to send home the Spanish troops, recognize the States-General and make other far-reaching concessions. The king had told his new governor-general:

'If matters are in such a state that the States demand unilateral concessions before they will recognize your authority, it seems that, safeguarding religion and my authority as much as may be ... we shall have to concede everything necessary to bring about a conclusion and save what we can. This is the ultimate solution to a problem like this, and we shall have to trust these people, in spite of all the risks involved.'

Unfortunately, the deputies of the States-General knew nothing of all this. Their information was different. Thanks to the prince of Orange's espionage network, they were given a copy of Philip II's secret letter of 11 September to Roda, which ordered him to destroy the States' troops by force if they refused to disband.[5]

The situation was growing more menacing every day. In late August the disaffected light cavalry moved up from Hainaut to join the mutinous infantry at Aalst. On 22 September the States-General decided to reissue the edict outlawing the mutineers, but this time they extended it to all Spanish troops, whether mutinous or not. All could now be shot on sight. Inevitably this order had the effect of uniting all Spaniards under the authority of Roda and the senior officers. The loyal Spanish units at Ghent, at Maastricht and above all in the new citadel of Antwerp made common cause with their compatriots. All converged on Antwerp. It was to be feared that some desperate stroke would be undertaken which the forces of the States-General, unaided, could not hope to parry. The only hope lay in the experienced veterans of the prince of Orange, who might come south if the States made peace.

The talks at Ghent therefore proceeded rapidly. On 10 October the States-General appointed delegates to negotiate peace and by 30 October agreement had been reached. The fighting between the rebels and the other provinces was to cease, and their forces were to turn instead against the Spanish troops. Both sides promised that, as soon as the Spaniards had been driven out, there would be a meeting of the full States-General which would decide the religious and political organization of the entire Netherlands. Until then the situation was to remain frozen, with a Calvinist regime in Holland and Zealand and a Catholic one elsewhere (although it was agreed that persecution of other religious groups was to cease).

This appeared to be an acceptable compromise, and the delegates of the two sides left Ghent to obtain ratification of the agreement. It came just too late. On 3 November Don John of Austria arrived at Luxemburg; and on the same day the Spanish forces in and around Antwerp, together with some German units, prepared to deliver an all-out attack on the city. Anticipating the assault, the magistrates of Antwerp admitted some detachments of the States-General's forces into the city on 2–3 November and ordered a defensive ditch and rampart to be dug against the citadel. By Saturday 3 November it was almost completed, but a small gap remained and the citizens decided not to work on Sunday. The Spaniards attacked at dawn. The troops of the States, poorly supported by the militia (which, incredibly, was never properly assembled), were powerless to save the metropolis of northern Europe from brutal sack. The 'Spanish Fury' lasted for several days: 1,000 houses were destroyed, 8,000 people perished.

The holocaust at Antwerp was one of the worst atrocities of the sixteenth century. It was immediately seized upon by all enemies of Spain and added to the corpus of anti-Spanish propaganda known as the 'Black Legend'. It was commemorated in prints and engravings, in pamphlets and history books; even a stage play was based on it (*A Larum for London or the Siedge of Antwerpe*, printed in 1602). Yet the Spanish Fury at Antwerp solved the two principal problems facing the States-General. It completely discredited Don John of Austria, who was now isolated in Luxemburg; and it removed the uncertainty about where the Spaniards would strike next – they were now isolated in Antwerp. The States-General were therefore free to ratify their bargain with Orange and his supporters. The 'Pacification of Ghent', bringing to an end the second revolt of the Netherlands, was signed and published on 8 November 1576.

Orange's triumph

The States-General of the Netherlands had come a very long way. in a very short time. In the century before 1576 the States had assembled about 150 times, but with decreasing frequency; they had only been properly convened twice, very briefly, since 1559. Moreover their functions were severely restricted: they ratified each change of ruler and they discussed the business placed before them by their prince – mainly requests for taxes – but they could not legislate and they could not meet on their own authority. Their only real strengths were their monopoly of taxation and the right to demand redress of grievances before consenting to fiscal demands. After 1576, however, the States-General became the central organ of government. They began to legislate (from 14 September 1576 onwards); they fixed the times and frequency of their own meetings; they negotiated with foreign powers; they concluded treaties, declared war and made peace; they sent and received ambassadors; and they raised, controlled and financed an army. Before long they even claimed to be a sovereign power. And yet the composition and procedure of the assembly in 1576–7 was little different from the gatherings of previous years. Certainly rather more provinces were represented than normal (all except Groningen, Limburg and Luxemburg sent deputations in the end – and those three provinces had always tried to avoid attending the States-General in order to avoid paying greater taxes); but all decisions still had to be agreed by every delegation before they were binding (although each delegation decided by majority vote). More serious, the delegations still had to refer many matters back to their masters, the provincial States, before they could commit themselves (although in fact the deputies often had considerable powers to take decisions for themselves so long as money was not concerned). The only significant novelty in the composition of the revolutionary States-General lay in its size – there were 239 deputies by spring 1577 representing seventeen *pays* as against the seventy or eighty who normally came – but even then the members still came from the same social classes as before: noblemen, clergy and town magistrates, the first two categories representing their orders in each provincial States, the last composed of delegates appointed directly by each major town.

It would seem that the States-General of 1576–7 was composed of reluctant revolutionaries. They took over the government of the Low Countries, as they had done almost a century before during the chaos following the death of Duke Charles the Bold, simply to avoid anarchy. In 1576, as in 1477, the States-General was the only public authority left which was capable of controlling the growing disorder caused by the death of the head of government. In 1576, as in 1477, their lack of experience and the absence of a genuine desire to govern sabotaged all efforts to find a workable constitution for over a decade. The deputies of the States were unfit to rule.

Perhaps the greatest initial weakness in the position of the States-General was their illegality. They could in no way claim to have been legitimately convoked by the sovereign. It was in the hope of gaining official recognition from the king that on 6 November the States sent an envoy to Don John of Austria, who had unquestionable royal authority to govern the Netherlands, in the hope of bringing him to Brussels. Alas Don John wasted his opportunity. Fearing to place his person in the hands of potential enemies, he refused to leave Luxemburg and asked instead for delegates to be appointed to discuss with him his future actions. This was bound to be a long process since the States-General were agreed on only one thing: that the Spanish troops in the Netherlands must be withdrawn. After the sack of Antwerp there was not a delegate who did not share that view and to that effect on 9 January 1577 most members of the States-General and several more besides signed the Union of Brussels which called for the implementation of the terms of the Pacification of Ghent, particularly concerning the expulsion of all foreign troops. Beyond that, however, there was confusion. Some deputies were prepared to admit Don John virtually without conditions, once they discovered that he had come with full powers to send the Spaniards home. Others wanted to bargain with the new governor over the long-term political and religious settlement before they recognized his authority. Others still were against admitting Don John at all, preferring a different form of state, even a different sovereign. Naturally there were varying shades of opinion within each of these groups, and the mood of the assembly could change from day to day. As Don John once observed: 'since there are so many people with such diverse opinions to deal with, whatever some arrange, the rest disown, and what many reprove others accept'. An angel's patience was needed to deal with them.[6]

Unfortunately for himself and his cause, Don John did not possess an angel's patience. Overbearing and irritable by nature, he could not bear to be contradicted: 'Nothing offends him more than to hear some one criticize him and exhort him to follow a different course of action from the one he has chosen,' wrote a Venetian observer in 1575.[7] In order to get his own way, Don John would lie, deceive and plot; his word could never be trusted. Events were to prove that these deficiencies of character, subtly exploited by the prince of Orange, were to destroy all Don John's hopes of restoring royal supremacy in the Netherlands. But Orange's hour had not yet come. His supporters were still a small minority in the States, and they proved unable to prevent the consummation of the talks which were under way with Don John. A ceasefire was concluded between the forces of the States and the Spaniards on 15 December; on 27 January 1577 the governor accepted the harsh terms dictated to him by the States; and on 12 February he signed the Perpetual Edict, swearing to accept the Pacification of Ghent as it stood. In return the States promised to maintain the Roman Catholic religion and admit Don John as governor-general as soon as the Spanish troops had departed. The States-General also undertook to pay the arrears of the German and the Netherlands troops in the royal army and agreed that, after all the soldiers had been paid, they would dissolve themselves in order to allow Don John to summon a new assembly 'in the form it had when the Emperor Charles abdicated'.

Don John made haste to complete his side of the bargain. By a combination of ingenuity and unscrupulousness he managed to persuade the Spanish troops to leave their fastness of Antwerp on 20 March. Then, with booty in their bags and wages in their pockets (some in bills of exchange), they left Maastricht for Italy on 28 April. Don John was therefore given a tumultuous welcome to Brussels on 1 May and five days later he took the oath as governor-general, swearing to adhere to the terms of the Perpetual Edict and to observe the customs of the land. Beyond this, in theory at least, he was free to do as he pleased.

Recognized at last as Requesens's successor, Don John was faced with one immediate problem: the States-General had signed the Perpetual Edict without the advice or consent of the prince of Orange – and the prince, supported by the States of Holland and Zealand which withdrew their delegates from the States-General in protest, strongly opposed the settlement. At first Don John made genuine efforts to procure Orange's adhesion. In March he sent the prince's former friend and lawyer, Elbertus Leoninus, to offer personal guarantees for the return of Orange's son (still in Spain), and the restoration of his offices under the crown and his confiscated estates. Then Don John arranged a formal conference between Orange and representatives from Holland and Zealand on one side, and a delegation from himself and the Estates at Brussels on the other. Talks took place at the town of St Geertruidenberg from 13 to 27 May. They did not break the deadlock, but they did establish the principal grounds of Orange's discontent. First, it was clear that the prince did not trust the promises of the king of Spain and his ministers. '*Den coninck van Hispaegnien heb ick altijt gheëert*' ran a famous passage in the rather pretentious *Wilhelmus* song: 'I have always honoured the king of Spain'. It was never less true than in 1577! Even Don John noticed it: 'Orange hates nothing more in this world than Your Majesty' he told Philip II in July, 'and if he could drink your blood he would do it.'[8] Orange could not believe that the Spanish government would keep any promises made to heretics – the fate of the Accord in 1566 and of Egmont and Hoorn in 1568 were a terrible warning – and it seemed improbable to him that Philip II would continue to uphold the Pacification of Ghent for a moment longer than necessary. Above all he was convinced that the king would not allow Holland and Zealand to return to royal obedience without insisting that only Roman Catholic worship would be tolerated. Here Orange and the rebel provincial estates were adamant: under no circumstances would they renounce their Reformed religion. When the royal deputation at St Geertruidenberg pointed out to him that the Pacification of Ghent stipulated that every province should obey the religious settlement to be decreed by the States-General, Orange roundly declared that he and his allies did not intend to submit themselves to a States-General called by Don John. 'We can see that you wish to extirpate us,' Orange told the royalist delegates, 'and we do not wish to be extirpated.' He did not trust the outcome of a 'Spanish' assembly.[9]

Orange's refusal to join the States-General and accept Don John produced an impossible position. As the governor-general put it four days after the conference finished, the prince held the estates in the palm of his hand, 'enchanted. They love him, they fear him and they want him for their lord. They tell him of everything that goes on, and without him they decide nothing.'[10] So at one end of the spectrum there was Don John, at the other the prince of Orange; and the deputies of the provinces lay undecided in the middle. Orange realized that Don John would be unable to govern without his help and that, if he waited, the king would either have to accept his terms or declare war on him again, which the States-General would never agree to support. In the event Orange had only two months to wait. On 24 July Don John, frustrated by the deadlock, fled from Brussels and took refuge in the castle of Namur with the intention of organizing a new campaign against the States-General. He tried to take Antwerp by surprise on 1 August (and failed), and he summoned the Spanish troops back on 10 August (although at first the king overruled him). News of the rupture with Don John brought the deputies from Holland and Zealand back to Brussels on 19 August and on 6 September the States-General asked Orange to come to the capital too as a matter of urgency. On 23 September he arrived in Brussels to an emotional, tumultuous welcome; the people received him, wrote Don John (with evident disdain and not a little envy) 'like the Messiah'.[11] He was returning as a hero to the city he had left, just ten years before, as an outcast. It was a very great personal and political triumph.

Orange was not deluded by the display, however. He knew as well as Don John that so large and diverse an assembly as the States-General was fickle and untrustworthy, that it could reverse a decision as easily as it had approved it and that its right hand often did not know what its left hand was doing. All his suspicions, aroused by the States' decision to make terms with Don John without consulting him, were soon confirmed. On 9 October the duke of Aerschot announced to the assembled deputies that they had a new governor-general: the Archduke Matthias, son of the late Emperor Maximilian II and nephew of Philip II. An envoy had been sent by the Catholic nobles in the estates on 16 August, just before the Holland and Zealand deputies arrived in Brussels, to invite the archduke to govern the Netherlands in the king's name. Matthias left Vienna secretly on 4 October and arrived on Netherlands soil on 20 October.

Here was a challenge which Orange could not overcome simply by waiting. Matthias, unlike Don John, was supported by a prestigious, well-organized and determined caucus within the States-General which included the duke of Aerschot and his brother Havré, the Lalaing family, Count Bossu and many other important figures in the south. These men had broken with Don John, but they were not prepared to trust or defer to Orange. They therefore needed an alternative and they chose Matthias mainly because he applied to them, as it were, for the job. It happened that in October 1576 an envoy from the States-General, M. de Malstède, arrived in Vienna to ask for imperial support in the struggle to eject the Spaniards from the Netherlands. Matthias, barely twenty, asked the envoy if he had come to ask for a prince of the blood to govern the Netherlands. If so, he offered his services. Malstède informed the archduke that he had no authority to deal with such matters, and that in fact Don John of Austria was believed to be on the way to the Netherlands, but, after the States-General became disenchanted with Don John, Matthias's offer was remembered and Malstède was sent to Vienna again to ask if the young archduke was still ready and willing to come. He was only too eager to oblige – so eager, in fact, that he made few inquiries and no stipulations about the conditions upon which he would govern and the powers which he would receive. Inexperienced, of limited intelligence, and anxious only to have a title and some respect, Matthias was easy meat for William of Orange, now at the height of his powers, whom he was soon calling 'Father'. However the archduke's supporters in the States were rather more formidable and, to deal with them, the prince needed help.

As early as October 1576, Marnix recognized that Orange's foremost supporters in the south were the common people: 'Our regime finds most support here in the *gemeente* (the commonalty),' he wrote, 'and it is therefore necessary that we comply with their wishes.'[12] All over the Netherlands the end of the fighting in 1576–7 saw a growth in the power of the people. In Brussels the nine guilds (or 'nations') of the city, each of which normally appointed two councillors (*boet-meesters*) to participate in the municipal government (cf. p. 39 above), took an increasing share in the handling of public affairs. Soon whatever was proposed by 'the Eighteen', as these *boetmeesters* were called, became law: no one dared to oppose them. The people of Brussels also began to intervene directly in the discussions of the States of Brabant sitting in the city: on 19 September and 2 November 1576 the people surged into the Grand' Place, directly in front of the room where the States were in session, shouting slogans to encourage them to take a decision in favour of the Pacification. In 1577 the people of Brussels even began to influence the decisions of the States-General. Following the prince's arrival in the city and the announcement that Matthias was coming, Orange's agents persuaded the Eighteen to propose to the States-General that the prince should be appointed governor (*ruwaard*) of the province of Brabant. When the States of Brabant rejected the idea, the multitude invaded the chamber where they were sitting to force its acceptance (18 October); four days later they threatened to do the same to the States-General. Humiliated, the assembly grudgingly made Orange *ruwaard* until the new governor-general should arrive.[13]

However, many bitterly criticized this decision. The duke of Aerschot, now governor of the province of Flanders, felt particularly aggrieved over Orange's appointment, and on 24 October he went to Ghent and persuaded the leading nobles and clergy of the province to sign a document deploring the election of a Protestant to high office. This was a stupid move. Ghent was a turbulent town and throughout the later Middle Ages it had staged many rebellions against its rulers, culminating in the struggle with Maximilian of Habsburg, Charles V's grandfather, in 1487–92. But, in Charles V, Ghent met its match. Its last rebellion, in 1539–40, ended in the execution of several leading citizens, the building of a powerful citadel and the abolition of all the city's charters. The last was the most serious, because without charters there was no defence against government abuse. On 22 October 1577 therefore, when Orange managed to cajole the States-General into restoring Ghent's privileges, he immediately became the toast of the town. Aerschot and his friends, who arrived two days later, were jeered in the streets for their petty hostility to the hero of the hour. Tension mounted in the city until on 28 October two Calvinist magistrates – Jan van Hembyze and the lord of Ryhove – took advantage of the general situation in Ghent to arrest Aerschot and his entourage. Having removed the head of the provincial govern-ment, the conspirators began to create a new order. On 30 October they organized a new militia, raised mainly from the working classes, not, as was customary, from the well-to-do, and on 1 November a special committee, 'the Eighteen', again drawn partly from the artisans, was created to control all military affairs (including the reconstruction of the city walls).

These dramatic developments greatly strengthened Orange's authority in the States-General. At a stroke many of his leading enemies were removed: although Aerschot was released on 10 November the rest were kept in confinement until the prince had got his way with the States. The unfortunate Matthias arrived at Lier on 30 October and Orange at once began to persuade the States-General to impose conditions and restrictions which would ensure that the new governor could not behave like Don John. On 8 December the archduke had to agree that he would accept the advice of a Council appointed and approved by the States-General and that he would submit all his legal, fiscal and political measures to the assembly before enacting them. Next, Orange made the States-General reaffirm its solidarity: by the second Union of Brussels signed on 10 December (also called the Nadere Unie or Closer Union), the States declared Don John to be an enemy of the people and of the *patrie* and undertook to defend Holland and Zealand should they be attacked by the king's forces. After this success, Orange unexpectedly left Brussels for Ghent. He had one further concession to extort from the States-General: he refused to return to Brussels unless he was given full powers as permanent *ruwaard* of Brabant and lieutenant-governor to Matthias. The States-General were reluctant, but again the menaces of the Brussels population (carefully directed by the prince's adherents) forced the assembly to grant all that was asked of them (8 January 1578). At last, on 20 January, Matthias took the oath to govern the Netherlands in the king's name, with Orange as his deputy and chief adviser. The prince had achieved the status he had coveted at least since 1564: he was effectively the head of government. He had succeeded to the position once occupied by Cardinal Granvelle.

However, Orange's triumph did not last long. On 31 January the army of the States was routed in battle at Gembloux, north of Namur, by the troops of the king's true representative, Don John. On 13 February Spanish troops advanced and took Leuven, only fifteen miles from Brussels, and the following day Matthias, Orange and the entire States-General fled north in haste to the security of Antwerp.

The split

William of Orange's surmise that the king of Spain loathed and resented the terms of the Pacification of Ghent was entirely correct. After so many years of effort and expense, it was indeed humiliating for Philip II to concede recognition to the heretics and rebels of Holland and Zealand. However, as his correspondence in the winter of 1576–7 demonstrates, the king gave way because he had no choice. Deprived by the decree of bankruptcy of the services of his financiers, and faced with an annual trial of strength with the Turks in the Mediterranean, he simply did not have the means to make a stand in the Netherlands. The fall of Tunis and La Goletta in the autumn of 1574, which involved the loss of some 9,000 Spanish troops, was followed by further thrusts west by the Turkish fleet in 1575 and 1576. The entire Spanish empire quaked. Never had the inferiority of Philip II's naval resources been more apparent; his arms race with the sultan had failed. Although Philip's Mediterranean fleet had almost tripled from fifty-five galleys in 1562 to 155 in 1574, the Ottoman navy had increased to 300 galleys. It was now irresistible. As Cardinal Granvelle pointed out:

'Whereas in the past the Turk's greatest fleet was 150 galleys with which he could not carry enough men for grand schemes . . . today he sends 300 ships with so many troops aboard that there is no fortress capable of resisting him.'[14]

As long as this menace persisted, Philip II could not afford to dissipate his scant resources on other projects. The Turkish threat, continuing after the decree of bankruptcy, largely explains the king's uncharacteristic compliance with all the concessions demanded of him by the Dutch. He bombarded Don John with commands that on no account was he to break with the States-General, forcing him from one humiliation to another until on 21 September 1577 Don John was compelled to accept an ultimatum from the States which required him to send home all his troops, to surrender all the towns loyal to him, to abide by the Pacification of Ghent and to retire to Luxemburg and ask the king to recall him![15]

This represented the nadir of royal influence in the Netherlands. The power of Spain never fell so low again. Even as Don John contemplated his disgrace, Philip II's situation improved dramatically.

Early in 1577 a special agent was sent to Constantinople to examine the possibility of concluding a formal truce with the Ottomans similar to those previously arranged between the sultan and the Austrian Habsburgs in 1545 and 1568. The mission was surprisingly successful: on 18 March 1577 the Turkish grand vizier laid down fairly modest conditions on which the sultan would agree to make peace and, meanwhile, he gave an undertaking that the Ottoman fleet would not come west that year. News of this agreement arrived in Spain in June, followed by reports throughout July and August from Philip II's various listening posts in the Mediterranean that the Turkish fleet had not put to sea.

Here was a godsend to the king, and he lost no time in dispatching another envoy to the Porte with instructions to procure a similar understanding for 1578 (signed on 7 March 1578 in Constantinople and renewed for 1579 and 1580). To avoid offending the pope, and others, the Spanish government for some time went to great lengths to deny the existence of an armistice with the sultan, but the change in the king's Netherlands policy was immediate and dramatic. On 31 August he ordered the Flanders veterans who had left for Italy in March, to return to the Low Countries. They were to assist Don John to reduce the States-General to reason.[16] However, at first the king did not wish for total war and a fight to the finish: he could not take it for granted that the truce with the Turks would be renewed, and in any case there was still the problem of how to finance the new military presence in the Netherlands. As he wrote to his principal adviser, Antonio Pérez, in November 1577:

'God grant that things will turn out as best suits His service, and if it is to be war [in the Netherlands] may He give us the means to wage it, for without His very special aid we can do little, especially with the business of the [Mediterranean] fleet. I was thinking that the preparations that have to be made now could serve for either purpose [for the Mediterranean or for the Netherlands].'[17]

As it happened God – and the miners of Peru – obliged with the dispatch of immediate assistance: on 18 August 1577 a fleet of fifty-five ships arrived at Seville from the Indies bearing over two million ducats for the king in bullion, a consignment larger than any previously received. And on 5 December Philip II came to an agreement with his

bankers whereby he agreed to honour his debts in return for a new
loan of ten million florins, payable in Italy by instalments in 1578 and
1579. This improvement in the king's financial position was sufficient
to provide the means to maintain enough troops in the Netherlands
to defeat the army of the States at Gembloux in 1578 and to capture
the stronghold of Maastricht in 1579. However, these and other
royalist gains of that time were the fruit not so much of Spanish
treasure as of the deep divisions which destroyed the unity of the
'patriot' cause.

The seeds of dissension had been sown in the course of 1577. The
Catholic leaders in the States-General, in particular the nobles and
clergy, did not trust William of Orange and his Calvinist supporters.
They were alarmed by the efforts of the Orangists to surprise or starve
into submission the Catholic redoubts in Holland and Zealand – Ter
Goes, Haarlem, Amsterdam and so on; by Orange's declaration at
the St Geertruidenberg conference that the rebel provinces would not
be bound by the States-General's decision on the religious settlement;
and by the arrest of Aerschot and his Catholic friends in Ghent, a
city swarming with Orange's troops. In 1578 outrages against Catholics
by the prince's supporters increased. On 16 February the Calvinists of
Ghent unexpectedly marched upon Oudenaarde, removed its Catholic
magistrates and replaced them with a pro-Calvinist 'Committee of
Eighteen'. On 6 March the same thing happened at Kortrijk, on
15 March at Hulst, on 20 March at Bruges and on 20 July at Ieper.
Each coup was followed, sooner or later, by iconoclasm and the re-
establishment of Calvinist worship, suppressed since 1567. On 17
March there was an Orangist-inspired popular rising at Arras, capital
of Artois, and the magistrates were purged of pro-Spaniards and
subordinated to a 'Committee of Fifteen' drawn from the militia
companies. Calvinism soon reappeared in the town. It was the same
story in the north, starting with Amsterdam. In late April 1578 an
acute observer in the city noticed that the children had begun to play
goos en papen (Sea Beggars and Papists – a game for gangs like
'cowboys and Indians' or 'cops and robbers') with new ferocity, and
he rightly interpreted this as a harbinger of greater disorders.[18] Sure
enough, on 26 May the Calvinists of the city, led by those exiled after
the troubles of 1566–7, suddenly arrested the Catholic magistrates
and clergy and expelled them from the city. A new bout of iconoclasm

followed, then came the election of a new, mainly Calvinist *vroedschap* (town council) and the formal establishment of Calvinist worship in all the city's churches. The next day the same thing happened at Haarlem, then later at Ter Goes, Leeuwarden and in several towns of Gelderland. Everywhere the triumphant Calvinists demanded freedom of worship. They received determined support from the National Synod of the Netherlands Reformed Church, held at Dordrecht, which on 22 June 1578 presented a petition to the States-General demanding freedom of worship for Calvinists wherever 100 families together asked for it.

This new assertiveness of the Calvinists, wholly understandable after so many years of repression, soon alienated the Catholic leaders of the southern provinces. The first to abandon the cause of the States-General was Valentin de Pardieu, seigneur of La Motte, general of artillery in the army of the States and governor of the port of Gravelines: he defected to Don John on 8 April 1578, taking Gravelines and its garrison with him. At first no one followed this initiative, but opposition to Orange and the Calvinists within the States-General grew rapidly. In July the Catholic opposition scored a major success: they prevented the promulgation of an edict of toleration, known as the *Religionsvrede* or Religious Peace, which would have compelled local authorities to allow freedom of worship to all religious minorities of 100 families or more in any one place – just what the Calvinist Synod had asked for. Instead each province, and indeed each major town, was told to regulate the religious question for itself. Thus on 4 September 1578 the city of Antwerp accepted the *Religionsvrede* as it stood, but the edict was only to apply within its boundaries. Other areas had no intention of tolerating heresy (just as Holland and Zealand had no intention of tolerating Catholicism). The States of Hainaut declared on 27 July their invincible opposition to the idea of a Religious Peace and the States of Artois, Walloon Flanders and Valenciennes soon followed suit. In this, of course, the Walloon provinces were only repeating the terms of the Pacification of Ghent which had guaranteed the exclusive exercise of Catholicism in the fifteen loyal provinces; their next actions, however, went far beyond the Pacification. On 15 October the States of Hainaut sent deputies to Artois to propose a union of the two provinces to maintain and defend the Catholic faith against the Calvinist threat from neighbouring Flanders and Brabant (themselves allied since April). On 21 October the Calvinist leaders of Arras were overthrown by a Catholic plot and executed almost immediately. Clearly the two religious parties in the south-western provinces were preparing for open confrontation. It is not surprising to find that both looked urgently for outside help to sustain them in the coming conflict: the Catholics turned to France, the Calvinists to Germany.

As early as 16 September 1576 the deputies of the States-General assembled at Brussels sent an appeal to Francis, duke of Alençon and brother and heir to the king of France, asking him to be ready to send them military and financial aid if need arose. Because of the civil wars in France, the duke was unable to respond to this initial approach but when his services were requested again, this time by the Walloon provincial estates, he began to raise troops. On 10 July 1578, at the invitation of Count Lalaing, the governor, the duke entered Mons. Alençon, now promoted by his brother to be duke of Anjou, was in many ways a good choice to lead the States. He was well born, he was wealthy and he had negotiated the peace which brought to an end the fifth French war of religion in 1576, creating Catholic and Protestant 'spheres of influence' with courts of arbitration (the *chambres mi-parties*) to settle religious differences. These were impressive credentials, which were made the most of in works of propaganda such as the Valois Tapestries woven in honour of Anjou in 1581–2. But there was drawbacks. The duke, although advised by able councillors like Jean Bodin, was a man of limited intellectual grasp and uninspiring appearance. He had little more capacity than Matthias, and his role in 1578 was considerably more difficult because Orange, trying to steer a middle course, did not want him: the prince was not convinced that French aid was either necessary or desirable at that moment. However Lalaing's initiative forced his hand and he therefore laboured to detach Anjou from the Catholic faction and draw him instead into the service of the States-General as a whole. On 13 August, after much bitter wrangling, the States agreed to recognize Anjou as the 'Defender of the Liberties of the Low Countries' and, in return, the duke promised to bring 12,000 troops into the field to fight against Don John.

These developments were unwelcome to Queen Elizabeth. The last thing that England wished to see was the south Netherlands fall to the French. The queen therefore promised to send some aid of her own –

for which the States had been vainly pleading since the autumn of 1576. She arranged for John Casimir, administrator of the Rhine Palatinate, to lead an army into Brabant at her expense to strengthen the forces of the States in their struggle against Don John (and to keep them from overdependence on Anjou). John Casimir arrived at the 'patriot' camp with 12,000 hungry mercenaries on 26 August 1578.

By this time, however, the States-General were experiencing the same acute financial problems as had beset the duke of Alva and Don Luis de Requesens: how was it possible to find enough money to pay for an army of 50,000 men and more? The forces in the service of the States-General were numerous and very expensive. In the first place there were the Netherlands troops who had been in Spanish service since 1572: the States had promised to pay their arrears in full. Then there were the forces raised by the States of Brabant and Hainaut in (and after) September 1576. They too had to be paid, and by the summer of 1578 the cost of the military effectives at the disposal of the States-General was 800,000 florins per month. Needless to say the Brussels government, without the provisions from Spain which had kept the army of Flanders together, was unable to meet this enormous charge and the troops therefore reacted in the accustomed manner: they mutinied.

The first units to mutiny were naturally those with the longest arrears – the regiments raised by the lord of Hèze and others in the autumn of 1576. In September 1578 they decided that they would not obey orders again until they were paid and they began to search, in the Spanish tradition, for a fortified town to protect them while they negotiated a settlement of their wage-claim. Before the end of the month, however, they were joined by their Walloon commanders who, horrified by the excesses of the Calvinists of Ghent and by Orange's domination of the States-General, led their mutinous troops on 1 October in a successful attack on the town of Menen, thirty miles south-west of Ghent. Thus secured from attack, the mutineers and their commanders – who now called themselves the 'Malcontents' – refused to return to obedience until their arrears were paid and until Ghent agreed to accept the authority of the States-General again. To strengthen their position, the Malcontents made approaches both to the Walloon estates meeting at Arras to discuss a Catholic Union and to the duke of Anjou. All this thoroughly alarmed the Ghenters and made them feel dangerously isolated. Accordingly they summoned John Casimir, a staunch Calvinist, to come to defend their cause against the 'paternoster soldiers' based on Menen. He arrived in the city with his troops on 10 October and war between Ghent and the Malcontents began in earnest.

These deep divisions within the ranks of the 'patriots' offered Spain a golden opportunity to recover some of the ground she had lost since 1576 and, fortunately for the royalists, at last Philip II was represented by a governor-general equal to the situation: Alexander Farnese, prince and later duke of Parma. He had been summoned to the Netherlands by Don John in 1577 as a personal aide and, despite the misgivings of some courtiers, Philip II approved when Don John, on his deathbed, named Parma to succeed him (29 September).[19] Able and resourceful, rich and cultivated, subtle and shrewd, Parma excelled in both diplomacy and war. He was soon maintaining the court of a Renaissance prince in the Netherlands with a household of 1,500 people, as befitted the heir of a major Italian dukedom and the nephew of the king of Spain. However, these trappings of office did not all come at once. Parma took command in the Netherlands at an exceptionally difficult moment for the royal cause, with his forces largely confined within the fortified camp constructed by Don John's engineers on the hill of Bouge overlooking Namur. Plague was rampant in the camp and it carried off Don John on 1 October. Had the army of the States-General been able to maintain its blockade of Bouge for long enough, Parma might have been forced to surrender; but in the event the siege was lifted on 23 October.

The reason for the withdrawal of the States' forces from Bouge was the widening rift between the Catholics and the Calvinists in the Netherlands, which intensified the ancient particularism of each of the seventeen provinces. The States-General were disintegrating. In the south most of Flanders (led by Ghent) had effectively seceded from the common cause, and Hainaut and Artois were advancing fast down the same road. By the autumn of 1578 all three provinces refused to contribute further to the general war effort. It was the same in the north. Holland and Zealand had always been staunchly independent: they never agreed to acknowledge the authority of Don John and they also refused to recognize Matthias. Instead they maintained the position of a state-within-a-state, holding to their mutual defence pact of October 1575 and seeking to expand it into a confederation

7

of several provinces, after the Swiss model. Ever since the collapse of royal power in 1576 there had been serious discussion of the advantages of forming the Netherlands into a union of cantons similar to the Swiss *Eidgenossenschaft*, and in July 1578 the States of Gelderland put forward a concrete proposal for such a union between their province and Holland and Zealand, which would provide for mutual defence in case of attack. A working party was set up to formulate an acceptable basis for the union and on 23 January 1579 deputies from Holland, Zealand, Utrecht, Friesland, Gelderland and the Ommelanden (the area around, but not including, the city of Groningen) met in the city of Utrecht and signed an act of alliance and union. It bound the signatories in perpetuity to act 'as if they were a single province' in matters of peace and war and defined certain areas of policy wherein the 'united provinces' were to act in concert; however, in all other matters, including the vexed religious issue, the right of each province to govern itself in its own way was expressly safeguarded. Within a few days a 'director' (John of Nassau), a council, a treasurer and other officers of the new union were appointed.

The Union of Utrecht marked a triumph for the political aims and outlook of Holland and Zealand. Its spirit was contrary to that of the Pacification of Ghent: it made virtually no mention of the king's authority or the maintenance of the Catholic faith, and it did not envisage reconciliation with Spain. The provinces which subscribed to the Union of Utrecht thus endorsed the uncompromising position of the rebels of 1572. Henceforth they were committed to fight for total victory.

For all these reasons the new Union was at first unacceptable to the moderate, Catholic majority in the States-General. They still hoped for an honourable compromise with the king. Even non-Catholic moderates feared that the new Union would divide more than it would unite; Orange refrained from signing for four months; Anjou went home almost at once and further defections followed thick and fast. In January 1579 John Casimir went home, leaving the embattled patriots in Flanders. Although Orange profited from his departure to purge the magistrates of Ghent of extremists and to open talks with the Malcontents about their wage-claim, it was already too late. On 6 January the States of Hainaut and Artois concluded a Union of their own at Arras, soon to be joined by the province of Walloon Flanders, and on 21 February they agreed to open talks with Parma. The Malcontents too began to negotiate and on 6 April they were 'reconciled' to the king by the Treaty of Mont St Eloi; their forces, some 7,000 men, became an integral part of the royal army in return for a cash payment of 250,000 florins. The Walloon provinces now hastened to make their peace too: by the Treaty of Arras (17 May) they recognized the full authority of Philip II and Parma. The unity of the States-General was seriously weakened; the position of the moderates within it was shattered. Under the circumstances their only hope lay in the possibility of negotiating a settlement with Spain which would leave them with some of their gains. They therefore welcomed an invitation which arrived from the Holy Roman Emperor, Rudolf II, to attend the peace conference which he had decided to sponsor in the city of Cologne.

Ever since 1566 the Austrian Habsburgs had endeavoured to bring about a negotiated settlement to the Netherlands war. In April 1578 the emperor made a new effort and sent special emissaries to the various parties in the conflict and, after some hesitation, both Spain and the States-General agreed to begin talks in Cologne in May 1579. Hostilities, however, continued. Above all, the prince of Parma laid siege to the great stronghold of Maastricht and captured it on 29 June. This success, together with the defection of the Walloon provinces from the States-General the previous month, encouraged the royal delegates at the Conference of Cologne to adopt an intransigent position: they demanded the restoration of exclusive Catholic worship in all provinces – with the possible exception of Holland and Zealand, where the king was prepared to consider allowing Calvinism to continue for a limited period (but no more) – and a return to the constitutional position as it had been in 1559 (sc. with no effective checks on monarchical power). This uncompromising stance was fully endorsed by Cardinal Granvelle, who arrived in Madrid on 1 August 1579 to become Philip II's chief minister. The cardinal, virtually exiled from power since 1564, was convinced that the rebels had gone too far and that only a major military defeat would bring them back to their senses. Neither he nor any other royalist really expected the States-General as a whole to accept the harsh demands made at Cologne – after all, they had been rejected so often in the past – but Granvelle was confident that the offer of forgiveness in return for obedience would cause some further defections

from among the States' supporters. He was not disappointed. On
27 July Mechelen was betrayed to Parma for 5,000 florins by its
Walloon governor, the baron de Bours, a man so greedy (according
to one of his friends) that 'If God himself had been changed into gold,
you would have put him in your pocket'. The loss of Mechelen was a
serious blow, and it further discredited the authority of the States-
General, already at a low ebb after the failure to save Maastricht.
In particular the members of the Union of Utrecht decided that it was
now necessary to take measures for their own defence, independent of
the States. First they wrote to the towns of Venlo, Geldern and elsewhere in the forefront of the struggle against the Spaniards, promising
to pay all garrisons from Union funds. Then they looked around for
places where the Calvinists had not succeeded in wresting political
power for themselves. Already in March they had fallen upon Amersfoort, in the province of Utrecht, forced it to surrender (after a five-day
siege) and purged the town council of Catholics. Flushed by this success
the leaders of the Union searched around for other Calvinist 'oppressed
minorities' to help, and their gaze fell upon 's Hertogenbosch and
Groningen. In both places a vociferous Calvinist minority was strugg-
ling to attach the city to the Union against the wishes of the Catholic
majority and it was to be feared that the Catholics might appeal to
Parma for assistance. Therefore in December 1579 the Union sent
troops into north Brabant to aid its adherents in 's Hertogenbosch.
It provoked just the reaction they had hoped to avert: the Catholics
countered by signing a treaty of reconciliation with Parma on 20
December. The same pattern of events was repeated almost immediately
at Groningen, where the Catholic inhabitants compelled their governor,
the Catholic baron of Rennenburg (a Lalaing), to take a stand against
attempts by the small but influential Calvinist minority to seize power.
Late in 1579 the Calvinists asked the Union to send military assistance,
which they promised to do; this forced Rennenburg and the Catholics
to appeal to Parma in order to safeguard their religion and their
position. Groningen was 'reconciled' on 3 March 1580 and the first
Spanish troops arrived on 19 June.

These reverses, together with the king's intransigence at the
Conference of Cologne and his insistence on placing a price on Orange's
head (15 June 1580), stiffened the attitude of the remaining patriots.
Rather as the arrest of the Walloon leaders at Ghent in October 1577

had removed the loyalist wing of the States-General and allowed the extremists there to engineer the break with Don John, so the defection of the various Catholic towns and provinces in 1579–80 fortified the remaining deputies to contemplate the need to break openly and permanently with Philip II. The abortive peace talks at Cologne, which ended in November 1579, revealed clearly that the king was never going to concede permanent toleration for Calvinism or guarantees for the liberties of the provinces. They demonstrated that there was no longer a middle way. The States-General now had to choose between abject surrender on the king's terms and outright rejection of his authority. But, in the latter case, who could be asked to replace Philip II as sovereign of the Netherlands? Little could be expected from Archduke Matthias (he was forced to resign on 15 March 1581) and so the obvious choice was the duke of Anjou, already 'Defender of the Liberties of the Low Countries'. In January 1580 therefore, three months after the end of the Conference of Cologne, Orange proposed that the States-General should take steps to ascertain whether Anjou would accept the sovereignty of the Netherlands and, if so, on what terms. A great deal of hard bargaining ensued between the various factions within the States-General (Calvinist Holland and Zealand did not wish Anjou, a Catholic, to rule over them at all) but in the end agreement was reached and on 11 August a set of conditions was drawn up on which the States were prepared to accept Anjou as their prince. Anjou, advised by Jean Bodin among others, found some of the restrictions on his power irksome, but in the end he accepted them all by the Treaty of Plessis-lès-Tours, signed on 29 September 1580. Oaths were exchanged between the duke and the representatives of the States on 23 January 1581 and Anjou became 'prince and lord of the Netherlands'.[20]

Once the question of a successor had been settled, the States-General turned to the problem of repudiating Philip II. After a long recess (30 January to 23 May) the States appointed a committee of four lawyers to draw up a declaration of deposition. This was presented and approved on 22 July. A Placard was ordered stating that Philip was no longer sovereign, that his head should no longer appear on their coinage, that his name and style should no longer be used in their official acts and so on, and it was published on 26 July 1581. The Act of Abjuration (Placcart van Verlatinge), with its rambling, matter-of-fact rehearsal of the grievances and provocations which made the provinces unwilling to continue under Habsburg rule, brought the Dutch Revolt to its logical culmination: the deposition of Philip of Spain. But, as the next decade was to show, the Act of Abjuration solved nothing except a constitutional tangle. It settled the question of who governed the Netherlands in theory only; it did nothing to clarify the practical issue of who was to exercise supreme authority in Philip's place.

[5]

INDEPENDENCE AND SURVIVAL

(1581–9)

The failure of leadership in the Republic

'Let all men know that, in consideration of the matters considered above and under pressure of utmost necessity . . . we have declared and declare hereby by a common accord, decision and consent the king of Spain, *ipso jure* forfeit of his lordship, principality, jurisdiction and inheritance of these countries, and that we have determined not to recognize him hereafter in any matter concerning the principality, supremacy, jurisdiction or domain of these Low Countries, nor to use or permit others to use his name as Sovereign Lord over them after this time.'

It all sounded so smooth and self-confident in the text of the States-General's 'Declaration of Independence', backed up by the requirement that every citizen of the new Republic was to swear an oath 'not to respect, obey or recognize the king of Spain as my prince and master' and 'to promise my assistance according to my abilities against the king of Spain and his adherents'. But appearances were deceptive. The position of the States-General after the deposition of Philip II was curiously like the position of the Rump Parliament in England after the execution of Charles I. Both bodies managed to achieve a major victory over their former sovereign, but in doing so they ineluctably undermined their own authority and created a crisis of political confidence. The 'Engagement', the oath of allegiance, required by the Rump in 1649–50, was the act of a minority government, conscious of its weakness and assailed on all sides – royalist, Presbyterian and even Leveller (John Lilburne's *England's New Chains Discovered* appeared just one month after the king's execution). In much the same way the oath required by the States-General in 1581 was the reaction of a weak institution, conscious of the general apathy and antipathy of much of the population of the Netherlands.[1]

In the south the six provinces reconciled with the king – Hainaut, Artois, Walloon Flanders, Namur, Luxemburg and Limburg – defended their position with a flood of pamphlets and polemics which poured from the presses of Cologne, with its colony of Netherlands exiles, and Douai, with its seminaries. Within the lands controlled by the States, there were three religious groups hostile to the new oath of allegiance. First there were the Catholics, still in the majority in most areas, many of whom were reluctant to abjure the champion of the Counter-Reformation; then there were the Anabaptists, particularly strong in Holland and Friesland, who were against taking oaths of any kind; and finally there were the Lutherans, who were unhappy at withdrawing their obedience from a power manifestly ordained of God. The Lutheran minister at Woerden in Holland had to be expelled by the States for preaching against the Act of Abjuration. There were even some who, although Calvinists, found it hard to take the new oath: many office-holders, especially lawyers, felt bound to resign their posts rather than swear to fight their former sovereign. The collateral councils created to advise the Archduke Matthias soon found themselves paralysed by defections and the surviving councillors resigned in August 1581. More sinister still for the future, a 'peasant war' broke out in Overijssel and Gelderland during the winter of 1579–80. The rural population formed an army which they called 'The Desperadoes' (*De Desperaten*) and, possibly encouraged by the royalists, they attacked the marauding troops of the States-General and the Union. A proper campaign, and pitched battles, were required to put down the movement.

The government of the States thus presented a sorry picture to the outside world, but it was not entirely their own fault. They had not sought revolution: their every step against the authority of the king had been taken with great reluctance. When at length they decided to break with their sovereign, the States-General only did so after they had secured a replacement. They had no thought of assuming the supreme power for themselves; they merely intended to supervise the transfer of power from the king of Spain to the duke of Anjou, who arrived to assume office, amid riotous festivities, in August 1581. He did not last long: in October Anjou left to court Elizabeth of England (again), a fruitless yet time-consuming exercise. During his absence, authority devolved upon his advisory council, the Landraad der Nadere Geunieerde Provincien (Council of the United Provinces), a body representing both the States-General and the Union of Utrecht and chaired by Orange, but still totally incapable of giving union and purpose to the patriot cause. It was fast becoming doubtful, indeed, whether any central institution could hold the Netherlands together, given the strength of provincial feeling. Holland and Zealand even refused to recognize the sovereignty of Anjou; instead they renewed their own union of 1576, which granted Orange the 'high authority and government . . . and power as sovereign and overlord', and they merely entered into an alliance with the other provinces ruled by Anjou.[2] Although this was the extreme example, provincial particularism was by no means confined to Holland and Zealand. All provinces grudged every penny they voted unless the money was earmarked for local purposes; the states adopted the same suspicious, intransigent attitude they had shown towards the government of the Habsburgs.

The same jealousy for provincial autonomy was displayed in religious matters. After an initial attempt to impose the *Religionsvrede* universally, the States-General agreed to allow the estates of each province to improvise its own religious settlement. The problem was basically one of a small minority trying to gain a monopoly of all religious practice. In Holland and Zealand the number both of ministers and of their congregations was still small (cf. pp. 153–5). In Utrecht only 181 full members of the city's congregation were recorded in 1579, while as late as 1593 it was reported that out of fifty-seven churches in the province, twenty-seven still had their altars, images and other

Catholic objects of worship in place, while six had never had a Calvinist service. At Kampen in Overijssel there were sixty-seven Easter communicants at the Calvinist church in 1579 and over 8,000 at the Catholic churches. The situation did not remain like this for long: the sixty-seven Calvinist communicants grew to 235 by Christmas 1579 and to 580 by 1589. The Roman church steadily lost ground to the government-backed Calvinists. The provincial estates of Utrecht outlawed Catholic services in June, 1580; Catholicism itself was banned outside the city in 1584. In December 1581 Holland proscribed Catholic practices and imposed some censorship on the printing of religious and political works 'which at the present time might lead the unlearned . . . common man to error, disruption and sedition'.[3] Most other northern provinces followed suit, freezing out all other religions than Calvinism by legislation in the course of the 1580s. The same thing was happening farther south. In October 1581 the magistrates of Ghent and the areas it controlled forbade all marriages and baptisms celebrated outside the Reformed church and in November it became illegal for a non-Calvinist to run a school, even a primary school. As in the 1570s, however, the Calvinist church did not possess the resources to fill the religious vacuum which it had created by its exclusive policies. The letters received by the Dutch church at London once again bristled with pleas and demands for the immediate dispatch of more ministers, and with complaints about the inadequate 'service' offered by the Reformed church as it existed. Only in the areas where a 'church under the cross' had survived in the south was there an organization capable of rising to the occasion: Antwerp had six ministers by 1579 and 4,000 regular communicants (albeit in a population of perhaps 80,000). Other areas coped less well. Brussels, a town of 40,000, had only two ministers in 1580 and only six in 1583; Bruges had only one. At Ghent, despite the foundation of a Calvinist university expressly intended to train ministers, the problems were similar.[4]

The only place where we can measure the impact of Calvinism is the place where it was probably strongest: the city of Antwerp. A census was taken in 1584, during the Spanish siege, and returns concerning 10,176 heads of household (probably 60 per cent or rather more of the total number then in the city) have been preserved. All but 3,758 of these declared a religious affiliation and also their tax liability, and their information can be presented as follows:

Religion and social structure in Antwerp, 1584

Number in each religious group	Tax liability of those in the group		
	High tax	Medium tax	Too poor to tax
Catholic 3,011	13 %	16 %	71 %
Calvinist 2,131	21 %	19 %	60 %
Lutheran 940	22 %	19 %	59 %

In addition there were 177 who merely declared that they were 'Protestant' and 159 whose return was dubious, as well as the 3,758 who did not state their religion at all.

The appeal of Protestant doctrines to all social groups is striking, and can be illustrated yet more clearly by arranging the same data in a slightly different way:

Social background of religious groups in Antwerp, 1584

Taxpaying group	Catholics	Calvinists	Lutherans	Total
High tax	23 %	25 %	12 %	60 %
Medium tax	31 %	26 %	11 %	68 %
Too poor to pay tax	31 %	19 %	8 %	58 %

It is an important feature of these figures that, together, they only represent around two thirds of the total in any given social group in the city of Antwerp. Many householders no doubt gave no religion because they no longer practised any religion. If this were the case, it would reduce the total Catholic part of the population to around a third and the total Protestant part to almost exactly the same. The numerical, social and political weight of the two rival religious groups was equal.[5]

Outside Antwerp, however, it would seem that the irreligious were in the majority, not belonging to any church at all. It is true that in Brussels the Catholics jeered and shouted down Calvinist services with chanting and singing (sweet revenge for the Calvinists' ridicule in the 1560s), while in Groningen in 1580 the Catholics forced the magistrates to call in a Spanish garrison. And elsewhere Calvinist ministers complained of the number of Anabaptists (in Holland and

Friesland especially) and Lutherans (in some larger towns). But the most common lament concerned the growth of religious indifference, ranging from the Ghent demagogue, Dathenus, who denounced William of Orange as an 'athiest who changed his religion as he changed his clothes', to the Brussels minister, Daniel de Dieu, who lamented in 1582:

'One finds everywhere lots of atheists and libertines, of whom some openly ridicule all religion, calling it a fable and an ornament, saying that it is nothing but a part of politics, invented by crafty and cunning governors in order to keep the wicked populace in fear and obedience . . . others, in order to disguise their contempt for God, say that so many warring creeds have grown up in our fatherland that they do not know which is the true one, nor which they should believe. Some others hang their coats in the wind, and in their outward conduct accommodate themselves to all religions.'[6]

The Calvinists were learning the lesson of other Christian prophets: it is easier to destroy religious faith than to create it.

The anti-Catholic crusade of the provinces still represented in the States-General was, as it happened, almost their only common policy. The 'United Netherlands' were fast degenerating into anarchy. Ever since Gembloux, Orange's authority in the south had been seriously tarnished. On his visits to Ghent, in an attempt to moderate the behaviour of the Calvinists there, he was a virtual prisoner, denied the right to bring his own men with him and accompanied everywhere by a powerful local escort. And, if Orange was reduced to such impotence, no one else could control the disintegration of government authority. The steady slide into chaos was noted by Queen Elizabeth's agent in the Netherlands, Thomas Stokes. In October 1581 he warned Walsingham that the provinces would be lost 'for want of a good government, for there is a number that commands in the country and few will obey'; in December 1581 he complained that 'there is great disorder here for want of obedience; for there is no man that will obey'; the refrain was the same in January 1582: 'Every man will command and few . . . will be commanded, so there is no order nor good government among them.'[7] Part of the problem was a simple one of uncertainty about whom precisely to obey: the Union of Utrecht, the States-General, the king – all claimed the power to give orders. The behaviour of Rennenburg at Groningen or the Malcontents at Menen can only be understood in the light of the conflicting loyalties which each leader had to reconcile. If these men valued provincial liberties, the defence of private property and the free exercise of Catholic worship above all else in the Netherlands struggle, then there can be no doubt that in 1579–80 the king offered the best guarantees for the achievement of these aims. The 'tyrannical' rule of the duke of Alva was never repeated; the southern provinces, after 1579, achieved many of their aims of 1576. They after all had not rebelled in the cause of freedom of conscience.

The alternative to Spain, at least in 1579, appeared to be anarchy, and this prospect only altered, however briefly, with the return to the Netherlands of the Duke of Anjou on 10 February 1582, bearing the blessings and greeting of Queen Elizabeth of England as well as of King Henry of France. Accompanied by the earl of Leicester, Elizabeth's favourite, Lord Hunsdon, her cousin, Marshal Biron and a host of other French and English nobles, Anjou was solemnly sworn in as duke, count or lord of the various Netherlands provinces (except Holland and Zealand and those controlled by Spain). His coronation as duke of Brabant on 19 February was a particularly magnificent event. In a series of tableaux and symbolic ceremonies, Anjou was presented as the peacemaker between Catholic and Protestant and as the great leader who would restore the splendours of the Burgundian Court – the old dukes of Burgundy, like Anjou, belonged to the family of Valois. The States-General, in a flush of enthusiasm, promised to contribute 2,400,000 florins a year to the war effort, and Anjou, for his part, promised to provide aid from France, respect the liberties of the provinces and tolerate both Catholic and Calvinist worship. The prospect for the United Provinces appeared to become brighter, and a series of vast allegorical tapestries were commissioned in Antwerp to symbolize the union of France and Netherlands, of Valois and Nassau, of Catholic and Protestant.

Those 'Valois Tapestries', which now adorn the main corridor of the Uffizi Gallery in Florence, were to prove practically the only lasting monument to Anjou's rule in the Netherlands. In the course of 1582 all the good intentions faded away. The States, needless to say, did not provide the money which they had promised; the Catholics continued to be molested in Flanders and proscribed in Holland and

Zealand; Anjou was almost assassinated by Spanish hirelings in July and he came under intense diplomatic pressure from other Catholic princes to withdraw from the Netherlands altogether. Most tiresome of all was the continuing pre-eminence of Orange. Despite an assassination attempt on 18 March which left the prince bed-ridden for three months, his mastery and his popularity in the provinces remained unabated. In August 1582 he was offered the dignity of count of Holland by the provincial States and, after some hesitation, he accepted.

Anjou's position was fast becoming intolerable. In his own words the Netherlanders had 'made a Matthias' of him and he resolved on a desperate remedy: as he saw it, the only way to regain his authority was to seize Antwerp and the principal towns of Flanders. On 15 January 1583 therefore French troops acting on Anjou's orders seized control of Dunkirk, Diksmuide and Ostend on the Flemish coast, and of Aalst, Dendermonde and Vilvoorde inland. However, an attempt to take over Bruges on the same day failed and the efforts of Anjou himself to gain Antwerp on 17 January were defeated with heavy losses (perhaps 2,000 of the French invasion force of 3,500 were killed).

Naturally these events further weakened and fragmented the United Provinces. Several towns were controlled directly by Anjou, who now began to negotiate with Spain for a possible reconciliation in the interests of religion. The rest of the provinces refused to admit French troops or Anjou's authority at any price. Orange did his best to bridge the chasm which the 'French Fury' had created, and indeed there was a formal reconciliation between Anjou and the States on 28 March, but the duke was a spent force and at the end of June 1583 he left the Netherlands for good. Although his troops and some of his supporters continued to serve in the Low Countries, they did so only as mercenaries in the service of the States and many of the towns they held fell to Spain in the course of 1583.

There was now no effective central authority left in the United Provinces. Orange departed from Antwerp for Holland in July; the States-General moved to Middelburg in Zealand in August; the Landraad, recognizing its impotence, dissolved itself in October 1583. Holland and Zealand once again served as the focus of all determined resistance to Spain, but even they now started to disagree about the powers to be conferred on their chief executive officer. A powerful group of merchants, based on Amsterdam, waged a vicious personal campaign against the efforts to confer the title of count of Holland on the prince. Cornelis Pieterszoon Hooft, magistrate and historian, voiced his misgivings in acid terms.

'If at the beginning of the war [he told the Amsterdam town council] His Excellency had said or shown that he was working to this end [to become count], it is my belief that he would have achieved little and that the people who everywhere opened the town gates for him would not have been so willing to do this. But people were doing everything at that time with the fine words *Pro Lege, Rege et Grege* and everyone was worked up about the liberties of the provinces without a single mention being made, as far as I remember, of the idea of making His Excellency the hereditary lord of these provinces.'[8]

Although a satisfactory agreement on the sovereignty question was reached by Holland and Zealand in December 1583, this alone was not enough to create an effective government for the Republic, and Orange knew it. One town after another in the south was falling to the Spaniards. At last the prince persuaded the States to reopen talks with Anjou and in April 1584 a new treaty was drawn up which allowed the duke more power. The States even agreed that, in case Anjou died without legitimate offspring, the provinces would be 'perpetually united with and annexed to the crown of France on the conditions which the States agreed with the duke of Anjou in the Treaty of Bordeaux'. In fact Anjou died on 10 June 1584, before he could sign this new agreement. Perhaps Orange might have stepped into his shoes, but on 10 July 1584 he too died, murdered in his own house in Delft by an assassin bribed by Spain.

These two deaths completed the constitutional confusion into which the United Provinces had fallen. Orange, at least, was irreplaceable. Despite all his failures he was the only man who could coax decisions out of the patricians who ruled the Netherlands; although he was a rebel, he was able to secure sympathy and aid from foreign powers; for all his mistakes, he commanded the respect and even the love of the population at large. 'As long as he lived', wrote Motley, quoting a contemporary chronicler, 'he was the guiding star of a whole brave nation, and when he died the little children cried in the streets.'[9]

The Spanish reconquest

With some justification, the treaty of Arras in 1579 between Spain and the three Walloon provinces of Hainaut, Artois and Walloon Flanders has been seen as the foundation-stone of modern Belgium. These wealthy provinces, together with Namur, Limburg and Luxemburg (already controlled by Philip II's forces), included over half the area of the present Belgian state. However, at first the Treaty of Arras nearly delivered the newly reconciled provinces back to the rebels. The Walloon leaders were well aware of how much Philip II needed them and they exploited the strength of their position in several clauses of the Treaty of Arras. First of all, they demanded that all foreign troops in the army of Flanders should be sent home (this was also one of the articles of the Pacification of Ghent) and after much vacillation and with much reluctance the king agreed. A column of 5,500 Spaniards left for Lombardy in April 1580 (they eventually took part in the conquest of Portugal) and most of the German regiments were demobilized in June and July.[10] Parma was left with an army consisting almost entirely of Walloon troops, many of them Malcontents who had been in the service of the States.

Other demands of the Walloons, with which Philip II was obliged to comply, concerned the political settlement of the south Netherlands. In the first place the reconciled provinces demanded that their leaders should be appointed to places on the central councils – State, Finance and the Privy Council – and secondly they demanded that the prince of Parma should be recalled. The king hesitated but, as with the recall of the foreign troops, he had to give way. In November 1579, on the recommendation of Granvelle (who had arrived in Madrid in August of that year), he granted places and power to his new supporters. Only two of the twelve members of the reconstituted Council of State had been royalists throughout the troubles; the rest had all, at some stage, rejected the authority of Don John. At the same time Philip informed his nephew that he was to remain in the Netherlands, but only as military commander; his mother, Margaret of Parma, would return to resume the position of civilian governess-general which she had held twenty years before. She arrived in June 1580 and set up court at Namur while Parma resided in Mons. Despite their close personal tie, mother and son refused to cooperate and the administration of the 'obedient provinces' slowly ground to a halt as the prince of Parma refused to relinquish his authority and Philip II refused to recall Margaret.

The paralysis of government was painfully apparent in the poor military performance of the army of Flanders. After the capture of Maastricht there were few outstanding successes, and such as there were came by treachery rather than by military prowess: Kortrijk and Breda were both betrayed in the course of 1580 and although Tournai was captured after a siege in November 1581 it only surrendered in the end because the States-General gave notice to the defenders that no relief could be sent. Gradually the Walloon leaders came to realize that they had placed so many restrictions on the crown that it could no longer afford them effective protection and that, if ever the States-General coordinated their affairs, the southern provinces would be overrun. Accordingly, towards the end of 1581, the Walloon estates agreed that they would accept Parma as their governor for as long as the king pleased (the king consented on October 1581), and then on 8 February 1582 they asked the king to send back Spanish, Italian and Burgundian troops to defend them and reconquer the rebellious provinces. Parma regarded this change of heart as a miracle, and it brought immediate results. The first of the new foreign troops arrived in June, hastening the surrender of Oudenaarde which had been under siege since March. Then came the Spanish units – 6,300 men – and the Italians – almost 5,000 – until by the end of August 1582 Parma's army numbered 60,000 men.

The military situation in the Netherlands was transformed. The foreign troops included some of the finest soldiers in Christendom. To begin with, many of them had already seen active service: two of the Spanish and one of the Italian *tercios* had served in the conquest of Portugal in 1580 and the first expedition to Terceira in 1581. Many individual soldiers had served before that either in Italy or, in some cases, in the Low Countries; several officers and men had fought for Spain since the 1550s. The Spanish troops who came to the Netherlands therefore were already hardened and disciplined before they arrived, in marked contrast to the units raised locally. In any case the soldiers raised in areas far from the scene of the fighting tended to be more dependable: they did not find it easy to identify with either side in what was essentially a civil war, nor did they find it easy to desert.

9. The Spanish reconquest

These three maps show the changing thrust of the Spanish advance into the territories of the States-General. Already by 1581 two salients had been created to north and east, creating a 'front' which ran from Groningen, through Maastricht to the sea at Gravelines. In 1582 and 1583 Spanish control was extended along the Flemish coast and outposts were established in Brabant. In 1584 and 1585 almost all of Flanders and Brabant were taken, and in the three succeeding years the Spanish frontier was advanced to the Waal and the IJssel.

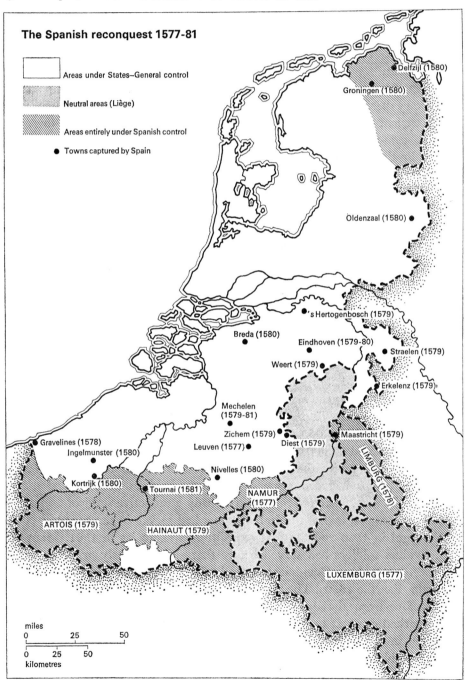

The Spanish reconquest 1577-81

- Areas under States–General control
- Neutral areas (Liège)
- Areas entirely under Spanish control
- ● Towns captured by Spain

Delfzijl (1580)
Groningen (1580)
Oldenzaal (1580) ●
's Hertogenbosch (1579)
Breda (1580)
Eindhoven (1579-80)
Straelen (1579)
Weert (1579)
Erkelenz (1579)
Mechelen (1579-81)
Zichem (1579)
Maastricht (1579)
Leuven (1577)
Diest (1579)
Gravelines (1578)
Ingelmunster (1580)
Nivelles (1580)
LIMBURG (1578)
Kortrijk (1580)
Tournai (1581)
NAMUR (1577)
ARTOIS (1579)
HAINAUT (1579)
LUXEMBURG (1577)

miles
0   25   50

0   25   50
kilometres

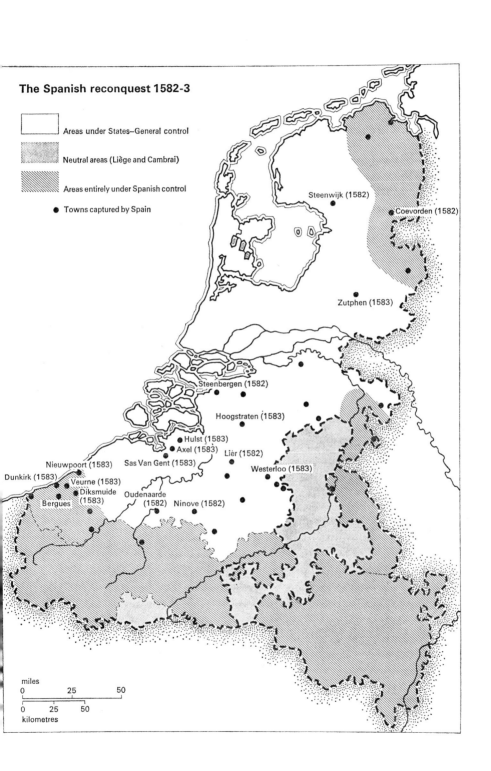

The Spanish reconquest 1582-3

Areas under States–General control

Neutral areas (Liège and Cambrai)

Areas entirely under Spanish control

● Towns captured by Spain

Steenwijk (1582)

Coevorden (1582)

Zutphen (1583)

Steenbergen (1582)

Hoogstraten (1583)

Hulst (1583)

Axel (1583)

Liêr (1582)

Sas Van Gent (1583)

Westerloo (1583)

Nieuwpoort (1583)

Dunkirk (1583)

Veurne (1583)

Diksmuide

(1583)

Bergues

Oudenaarde

(1582)

Ninove (1582)

miles

0   25   50

0   25   50

kilometres

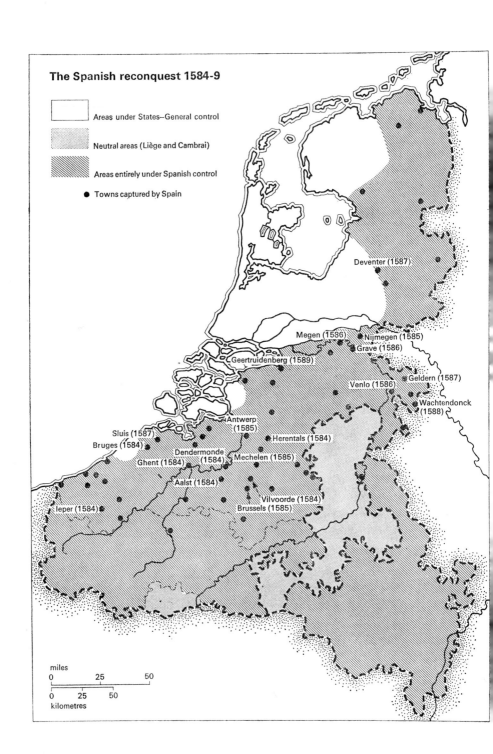

The Spanish reconquest 1584-9

Areas under States–General control

Neutral areas (Liège and Cambrai)

Areas entirely under Spanish control

● Towns captured by Spain

Deventer (1587)

Megen (1586) Nijmegen (1585)
Grave (1586)

Geertruidenberg (1589)

Geldern (1587)

Venlo (1586)

Wachtendonck
(1588)

Antwerp
(1585)

Sluis (1587) Herentals (1584)

Bruges (1584)

Dendermonde
(1584) Mechelen (1585)

Ghent (1584)

Aalst (1584)

Vilvoorde (1584)

Ieper (1584) Brussels (1585)

miles
0   25   50

0   25   50
kilometres

The Spaniards and Italians in the Low Countries were at least 700 and sometimes over 1,000 miles from home. After 1582 these 'asphalt soldiers' of the sixteenth century, 'tough, disciplined and born to fight with the people of the Netherlands' (in Parma's words), were to form the spearhead of all future military operations.

Long before the Spaniards returned, the prince of Parma knew precisely how he was going to employ them. Already in January 1581 he had described to the king how he could bring all the great towns of Brabant and Flanders, the industrial heart of the Netherlands, to their knees if he could only occupy the Flemish coast and block the Scheldt above Antwerp. The towns depended on the sea and the rivers to export their manufactures; if they could be cut off from all water-borne communications, they would be compelled to surrender. The remainder of 1582 was spent in building up the strength of the army of Flanders, so that in 1583 a major offensive could be mounted to capture the Flemish sea-ports. The maps on pp. 210–12 show the broad pattern of the reconquest. In July and August 1583 Dunkirk, Nieuw-poort, Veurne, Diksmuide and Bergues were forced to surrender. Only Ostend remained to the States, saved by the timely arrival of reinforcements aboard an Orangist fleet. Cheated of this prize, Parma swung north-east in October 1583 and captured the major towns along the Scheldt estuary: Sas van Gent, Eeklo, Hulst, Axel, and – farther inland – Rupelmonde. At the same time a skeleton royalist force under Colonel Verdugo in Friesland managed to seize Steenwijk in 1582 and Zutphen in 1583, thus linking Friesland with the rest of the Spanish Netherlands. Also in the east, Parma's forces intervened in a civil war which broke out in the archbishopric of Cologne in 1583 and managed to capture Bonn and other places along the Rhine which were sub-sequently to be of strategic importance in the struggle against the Dutch.

These victories could not fail to impress Philip II. Having annexed Portugal and beaten off attempts by a French fleet to seize the Azores, the king decided to increase his financial commitment to the reconquest of the Low Countries. In June 1583 he instructed his senior finance minister to send 500,000 ducats (about 1,250,000 florins) to Parma forthwith and to arrange for a provision of 200,000 ducats to be sent regularly every month. Aided by the arrival of over 3,000,000 ducats on the Indies fleet of that year, this commitment was honoured and the money began to arrive in the Netherlands in December 1583. It continued to flow with fair regularity, although still in modest quantities, throughout 1584.

Parma's campaign for 1584 concentrated on starving out the great towns on the Scheldt and its tributaries. In February the town of Aalst was betrayed to Parma by its English garrison (for 128,250 florins, paid by Parma in cash). On 7 April, after almost six months' siege, Ieper surrendered. This made the position of Bruges untenable and its magistrates, who had always been predominantly Catholic, surrendered on 24 May without awaiting the inevitable siege. On 17 August Dendermonde surrendered after a desperate (but unsuccessful) Spanish assault. This completed the encirclement of Ghent. Although not a shot was actually fired against its walls, the town gradually weakened with starvation and its leaders began to negotiate. On 17 September it too surrendered.

With all of Flanders (except Ostend) now in his hands, Parma moved on to the great towns of Brabant. Vilvoorde, just north of Brussels was captured in September 1584, completing a network of royalist strongholds around the surviving rebel cities, and Parma began to build his famous bridge across the Scheldt below Antwerp in order to cut the metropolis off from the sea. Although the city fathers opened the sea-dikes and flooded the surrounding countryside – as at Leiden a decade before – the dikes themselves still stood above the water and each became the scene of bitter and bloody encounters between picked men of the two sides. On the whole the Spaniards had the better of the fighting. They spent the winter of 1584–5 quartered in small redoubts and forts along the dikes (many of them still visible today) and by the spring of 1585 their lonely vigil began to bear fruit. The blockade of Brussels became so complete that food began to run short and the large Catholic population became so restless that the Calvinist magistrates could no longer control them. On 28 February negotiations with Parma began and the city surrendered on very favourable terms on 10 March. On 25 February, thirty miles to the north, the great bridge over the Scheldt was completed: 2,400 feet long and resting on piles 75 feet deep drilled by a specially invented machine. It was defended by almost 200 siege guns. The whole enterprise was almost miraculous for its day and Parma had staked everything upon it: it was to be, he averred, either 'his sepulchre or his pathway into Antwerp'.[11] On 5 April it was very nearly the former, for a flotilla of fire ships floated down the stream and blew up a 200-foot span of the bridge, killing 800 Spaniards and dazing Parma who was only a few yards away when the main 'infernal machine' exploded. Incredibly, however, this success remained unexploited and the breach was closed before a relief expedition from the States could get through. This failure was decisive. Antwerp, like Brussels, contained a large number of Catholics – around a third of the total population. After the failure of the 'infernal machine' the pressure of the Catholics for an end to the siege grew, and early in June talks were begun. On 19 July Mechelen surrendered and on 17 August Antwerp too signed its capitulation with Parma. The prince made a ceremonial entry into the subdued and starving city ten days later and ordered the payment of the arrears of his magnificent Spanish veterans. Every man received his due in person and in full: almost a million florins changed hands. The troops then had a well-earned rest.

The prince of Parma had achieved a great deal in a short time. In three years he had doubled the area obedient to the king, his master, and most of these gains were never lost. Parma was, in the words of Justus Lipsius, *conditor Belgii*, the founder of Belgium, and in large measure his success stemmed from his own military ability. Thanks to his grasp of geography and strategy he was able to force the reduction of powerful towns which his troops could not even see, by means of distant blockades. Antwerp was one of the best-defended towns in Europe, its walls five miles in circumference, but it fell without a shot being fired against the city. Also crucial for success were the 'military virtues' of Parma's troops, who withstood hunger, danger and cold with equal fortitude. But for every town which succumbed to military pressure, there was another which surrendered before its time through treachery: Breda and Mechelen in 1579, Lier in 1581, Zutphen and Bergues in 1583, Aalst in 1584, Nijmegen in 1585 . . . Moreover the towns which had strained every muscle to resist the Spaniards had not been relieved. A bitter remonstrance from the burghers of Brussels in 1584, as they starved rather than surrender, pointed out that over thirty towns once loyal to the States-General had fallen to Spain without a finger being lifted in their defence. In September 1584 the States of Brabant wrote to the States of Holland in much the same vein:

'Everyone knows the excellent resources . . . which God has put in
our hands to safeguard our liberty, to protect us one and all against
the attack of our enemies, to reconcile our religious quarrels and end
them with honour. How many admirable oaths, alliances and unions
have we formed and sworn to! If they have not borne fruit, the reason
is clearly that each province, preferring its own particular interest,
has scarcely bothered about the fate of its neighbours and allies,
thinking it enough to make fine promises on paper without following
them up or giving them any effect . . . That is how the fair and powerful
province of Flanders has been lost.'[12]

Any casual observer might assume that the Spanish tide of conquest
would continue north of the great rivers. Parma, like Alva before
him and Spinola after him, experienced little difficulty in throwing
his forces across Rhine and Maas; his troops had proved themselves
equal to even the most daunting challenge, and they had been over a
decade in the field without a major mutiny. They appeared to be invincible. 'The best soldyers at this day in Christendom', unsurpassed
'for discipline and good order' – that was how the army of Flanders
appeared to the English.[13] And it was this exaggerated respect for the
Spanish troops which, against all expectations, determined Queen
Elizabeth and her ministers to intervene openly in the Low Countries'
wars in order to stop Parma from subduing the rest of the United
Provinces.

War or Peace?

The contacts between Queen Elizabeth and the Dutch rebels made up
a long and sorry story of vows of support solemnly made and casually
broken, of assistance promised but never sent, of encouragement offered
and then disowned. In spite of everything that Orange and his friends
could do to move the queen to action, all they got in material terms
was a few hundred soldiers in 1572 (soon to be recalled) and about
one million florins in 1578–9 (some of it provided not in cash but in
alum, a dye-fixer used in textile-manufacture). And even that aid had
been provided clandestinely, grudgingly and tardily. Elizabeth had
no wish to antagonize the king of Spain; she had enough problems
of her own. England settled her trade war with Spain in 1574, and for

a decade after that Elizabeth refrained from patronizing piracy in the Caribbean and she hesitated to support rebellion in the Spanish Netherlands. But everything changed in 1584.

Queen Elizabeth was seriously alarmed by Parma's successes in Flanders and Brabant and by the prospect of a strong Spanish government being restored in the Netherlands: her memories of Alva's 'forward policy' in 1570–71, during his years of supremacy, were still fresh and they were kept green by the discovery of Throckmorton's plot to murder the queen in 1584, a conspiracy in which Spain was clearly implicated and which resulted in the expulsion of the Spanish ambassador, Mendoza. Following this event, and news of the death of both Orange and Anjou, the English Privy Council decided in October 1584 that military aid should be offered to the Dutch in their struggle against Spain: there was to be an attack on the Spanish Indies and an expeditionary force to defend Holland. This offer was conveyed to the States-General in December 1584, but at that time they still hoped that Henry III of France would take up the mantle of his late brother Anjou and become their official protector. The States therefore politely refused Elizabeth's offer, but on 9 March 1585 Henry III equally politely refused them. The fate of Antwerp hung in the balance, and the States realized that an English relief force might yet save the city. On 12 May they therefore decided to offer Elizabeth the sovereignty of the Netherlands or, if she would not accept that, to induce her to send financial and military aid on a regular basis. On 9 August agreement was reached – despite the hostility of Zealand to the deal – by which the queen would send 4,000 foot and 400 horse forthwith to relieve Antwerp and, in addition, would pay the States-General 600,000 florins a year (estimated as one quarter of the total cost of the war). England would also provide a governor-general, to be advised by a new Council of State, who would direct the war and coordinate government. In return (and this was why Zealand objected) the Dutch were to surrender Flushing and Rammekens (in Zealand) and the Brill (in Holland) to England as sureties until all the queen's expenses were repaid after the war.

The Treaty of Nonsuch, embodying the terms agreed, was signed on 20 August and troop-raising began at once. Elizabeth eventually agreed to contribute 1,000 horse and 6,350 foot to the Dutch war-effort and, in order to raise the troops in time, nobles like the earl of

Leicester (who was to command the force) resorted to a virtual feudal levy on their lands. Leicester's Welsh lands were combed for volunteers. By 14 September, thanks to such expedients, there were 4,100 soldiers of the English relief force (the *secours*) at Flushing. Unfortunately they were too late: Antwerp surrendered on 17 August. The barracking of the Zealanders had led to the loss of Zealand's great rival. Undaunted, however, the English presence in Holland increased until there were 7,350 men in the Netherlands paid by the queen in November and 8,000 by December 1585. Just before Christmas the earl of Leicester, Elizabeth's favourite, arrived in Flushing with an impressive following of English noblemen. He also brought ready money from the queen and the promise of more to come.

The decision to grant open aid to the Dutch was, in effect, a declaration of war on Spain. The queen recognized this in her pamphlet, published in November in several languages, which explained why she had abandoned her traditional stance of neutrality, laying great emphasis on the numerous conspiracies and invasion-projects mounted against her, most of which manifestly enjoyed Spanish connivance or Spanish support. Shortly after Nonsuch the queen gave permission to Francis Drake to collect and equip a fleet of twenty vessels with which to plunder Spanish shipping in the Caribbean. The expedition left Plymouth for the West Indies on 14 September, just as the English *secours* reached Flushing.

Philip II reacted swiftly to these acts of aggression. On December 1585 he seized all English and Dutch shipping in Spanish ports and in January 1586 he ordered his ministers to prepare a feasibility study on an invasion of England. The depredations of Drake in the Indies in 1586 (where he burnt Santo Domingo and Cartagena) and the heavy fighting in the Netherlands in which the English were involved strengthened Philip's determination to attack England directly and at once. It seemed as though only the arrival of the English *secours* in the autumn of 1585 had given the Dutch the strength to soldier on. The king was aware of the strength of feeling in Holland, centred on Gouda and Dordrecht, in favour of a negotiated settlement and he knew that the estates of the landward provinces urgently desired an end to the destruction and depopulation caused by the war. Yet all the war-weariness appeared to evaporate when news of Nonsuch arrived. The 'appeasers' were discredited; magistrates in favour of peace were purged from the town councils; the States put their largest army for years into the field in 1586 and actually made a serious effort to relieve a town under siege (Grave – although, characteristically, its governor betrayed it first). It seemed not only to Philip but also to Parma and the other field commanders in the Netherlands that the reconquest of the rebellious provinces could proceed no further until English support was withdrawn. Preparations for a seaborne attack on England therefore proceeded with almost reckless haste. Spain's military machine was decidedly unready, but the king would countenance no delay. The summer of 1587 was spent in amassing men and munitions, ships and provisions, while in the Netherlands Parma's army took the deep-water harbour of Sluis by siege and the important inland town Deventer was betrayed to him by its Anglo–Irish garrison.

At last, in the spring of 1588, all seemed ready and Philip II signed his final instructions for the Armada's commander. The duke of Medina Sidonia was to take his fleet of 130 vessels, carrying 30,000 men, north from Spain to the coast of Flanders where he was to effect a junction with certain small ships and barges assembled by Parma to ferry his army of 17,000 men across to the North Foreland near Margate together with about 6,000 soldiers and a siege-train of twenty-four heavy guns brought by the Armada. Parma was then to march on London. At that point Philip II envisaged two possibilities: in the first scenario the English Catholics would rise, the Tudor regime would be overthrown and a pro-Spanish government would come to power, make peace, restore Catholicism and pull out of the Netherlands. But Philip realized that this admirable course of events was, despite the assurances of Jesuit and other English exiles at his Court, highly unlikely. He therefore foresaw a second and more probable scenario in which Parma would land and occupy a good part of Kent, hopefully London as well, but no more. There would be no Catholic rising and Parma would use his territorial gains as bargaining counters only to be relinquished when the English had agreed to tolerate Catholicism at home and pulled their forces out of the Netherlands.[14]

As a strategy the Armada project had much to recommend it. Even before it sailed, it began to achieve its objective of dividing the English from the Dutch and the Dutch provinces from each other. In truth Elizabeth and the Netherlanders had never had the same aims or outlook. The queen wanted to restore in the Low Countries the constitutional balance of the 1560s, with a weak central government under Philip II's suzerainty. She wanted to expel the Spanish troops but she wanted to conserve Spanish overlordship. After 1581 of course the States were no longer prepared to recognize the king, but Elizabeth refused to countenance their new political stance. In February 1587 she took serious steps towards finding a negotiated settlement for the Low Countries, beginning informal discussions with Parma, and she put very heavy pressure on the States-General to join her in the talks. In this she was considerably aided by the chaos which the earl of Leicester had created amongst the once-united provinces.

The earl was sworn in as governor-general in January 1586 with wide but undefined powers. The treaty of Nonsuch had called for the creation of an effective central authority in the Netherlands, but it left the exact nature of this authority to be worked out by Leicester and the States. This was easier said than done, since the various provincial delegations wanted different things. On the whole the inland provinces – or what was left of them – favoured a stronger executive to protect them from invasion, while Holland and Zealand were opposed to any new authority which might diminish provincial independence. However, every province was divided within itself on the issue: even in Holland the towns of Waterland supported Leicester, as did the towns of Friesland (in both areas the towns were relatively underrepresented in the existing political system). Leicester could also count on the support of most of the Calvinist ministers and most of the refugees from Flanders and Brabant, many of them men of considerable political skill (although again excluded from the prevailing system). In the spring of 1586 Leicester tried hard to establish a stronger executive in the Union with the aid of this disparate band of supporters: he attempted to create a war treasury with new taxes independent of the States and he proposed an embargo on all trade with Spain and the south Netherlands, the lands of the enemy. Both measures were opposed by the States of Holland. Leicester therefore tried, in the summer of 1586, to win over the States of all the other provinces and thus freeze out Holland: in October, aided by southern exiles, his agents purged the magistrates and the States of Utrecht, where Leicester made his headquarters. But just as he appeared to be making progress, the earl was summoned home to advise the queen on whether or not to execute Mary Stuart. He departed in November, leaving the provinces completely deadlocked until, in February 1587, two of Leicester's commanders betrayed Deventer and an important fort near Zutphen to Spain. Leicester was totally discredited and 'there grew a wonderful alteration in the hartes and affections of the people againste the Englishe. They uttered lewde and irreverent speaches of His Excellencie and the whole nation.'[15]

Undismayed, Leicester returned to the Netherlands in March 1587 this time with instructions to persuade the States to join in negotiating with Parma. This completed the confusion, for Leicester's remaining supporters – especially the *predikanten* and the exiles – wanted a strong central authority in order to reconquer the south, not in order to preside over a sell-out. However, Elizabeth was becoming more and more worried by the reports of the Armada assembling in Spain and she became desperate for a settlement of the Netherlands problem. In February 1588 she began formal talks with Parma at Bourbourg; in May she gave orders that her troops in Holland should return and defend the English coasts. The mistrust between England and the Dutch was now complete. In June 1588 Elizabeth's request that some Dutch ships should come over to help defend England from attack was contemptuously ignored. At first the Dutch scarcely believed the news, at the end of July, that the great fleet was in the Channel and that the English were actually fighting against it.

In view of all this, it has been suggested that had the Armada merely sailed up and down the Channel, 'beating its chest before England's gates', it would have achieved rather more than it did by carrying out Philip II's design.[16] This is probably true but, in the event, the English took the initiative and attacked first, initially with guns and then with fire ships. Dutch and English squadrons (operating, typically, independently of each other) kept Parma's barges confined in port until the Armada had gone by, heading for destruction on the coasts of Scotland and Ireland.

The defeat of the Spanish Armada marked a turning-point in the Dutch Revolt. It fatally weakened the prestige of Philip II and it put an end to Parma's impressive string of victories. As soon as it became clear that the great fleet was gone for ever, the duke led his troops to besiege Bergen-op-Zoom, the only major town of Brabant not reconquered. The siege lasted from mid-September until 13 November, but at length the Spaniards had to retreat: they had never managed to complete their encirclement of the town and the garrison put up a good defence. It was Parma's first major failure. More were to follow. In 1589, although the mutinous English garrison of St Geertruidenberg sold their town to Spain in April, Parma's main effort for the year was the invasion of the Isle of Bommel, between the Maas and the Waal. At first all went well, but in September all gains had to be abandoned because the spearhead of the operation, the Spanish *tercio* of Lombardy, mutinied on 30 August. It was the first of over forty mutinies which paralysed the army of Flanders between 1589 and 1607.

'God will grow weary of working miracles for us,' Parma had warned the king in February 1586.[17] Almost all of his great victories, as so often in war, had hung by a thread, and the exhaustion and penury of his own troops always made him fearful of massive desertion or a mutiny which would undermine all his efforts. However, until 1587 Parma's luck held and the rebels succumbed before his own men rebelled. But it could not go on for ever, and once Parma ceased to win victories, criticism of his style of government mounted: had he done all he could to prepare the army of Flanders for the Armada or was he responsible for its failure? Was he squandering the king's treasure on himself and his entourage instead of paying his near-mutinous troops? Was he soft on heretics? Was he not dangerously prone to disobey or disregard the king's commands? All these suggestions were made at some stage by enemies and discontented subordinates of Parma; some had been made before the Armada, but the king had not listened. After 1588, as military failure followed mutiny, Philip II began to doubt his nephew. And Parma knew it. He became anxious to resign while his reputation was still more or less intact.

It was perhaps in this spirit of trying to save his professional skin that in October 1589 Parma sent his trusted adviser, Jean Richardot, to lay before the king a proposal for peace with the Dutch. The plan was submitted to Philip on 11 November 1589. It involved the key concession that Calvinist worship would be permitted in private in certain towns of Holland and Zealand for an indefinite period. In return, Catholic worship would have to be allowed in public in Holland and Zealand, and the rebels would have to disarm and recognize royal authority again.

There was much sense in this proposal. The religious question had undoubtedly sabotaged the talks at Breda in 1575 and at Cologne in

1579; here was a formula which, had it been applied then, might have brought about peace. Philip II, however, was not impressed. He remembered all too vividly the consequences of his last admission of limited toleration in August 1566 and he therefore viewed with considerable misgivings the religious concessions made by Parma to the great towns which surrendered in 1584–5. On 17 August 1585 he informed his nephew:

'In spite of everything I would regret very much to see this toleration conceded without limits. The first step [for Holland and Zealand] must be to admit and maintain the exercise of the Catholic religion alone, and to subject themselves to the Roman Church, without allowing or permitting in any agreement the exercise of any other faith whatever in any town, farm or special place set aside in the fields or inside a village . . . And in this there is to be no exception, no change, no concession by any treaty of freedom of conscience or *Religionsfried* or anything like it. They are all to embrace the Roman Catholic faith and the exercise of that alone is to be permitted.'[18]

King Philip had not changed his spots by 1589. Richardot's proposal met with a frosty reception. The king's principal advisers ruled out the idea of some sort of 'Interim' like the one attempted by Charles V in Germany in 1548. To concede any toleration, they claimed, would be to forfeit 'the claim His Majesty has made and the reputation he has won at the cost of so much treasure and so many lives not to concede one jot or tittle in matters of religion'. On the other hand they realized that the alternative was not easy: 'to attempt to conquer the rebellious provinces by force', they sighed, 'is to speak of a war without end [*una guerra inmortal*]'. The king shared in this dilemma and, as on previous occasions, he turned to the pope for help: if His Holiness wanted the king to keep on fighting, let him put his hand in the pontifical purse 'since this war is being waged solely for religion'. Pending the pope's reply, Parma was authorized to approach the rebels in order to discover whether they would be willing to open discussions or not.[19]

As time passed the king's opposition to the idea of a negotiated settlement waned somewhat. Consulting the pope took longer than expected – Sixtus V was ill and testy until his death in August 1590; his successor Urban VII only lasted a fortnight and a new pope was only elected in December – but by the beginning of 1591 the papal nuncio in Cologne had been named as official intermediary between Spain and the Dutch. The emperor took a hand in the preliminary negotiations, proposing a peace conference at Frankfurt or Cologne, and Philip II duly appointed representatives. He even declared, in a confidential letter to his ambassador in Rome, that he would be prepared to concede toleration for a limited time to the rebellious provinces if they agreed to be reconciled.[20] But in 1591, as in 1566, this major concession by the king came just too late. The failure of the Armada and of Parma's siege of Bergen had indicated the limits of Spanish power; the lack of any effective resistance to the Anglo–Dutch seaborne attack on Corunna and Lisbon in 1589 revealed that Spain herself was vulnerable.

'What makes the Spaniards' discipline to be so famous as it is? their good order; otherwise it is well knowne, the Nation is the basest and [most] cowardlie sort of people of most others; so base, that I perswade my selfe, ten thousand of our Nation would beate thirtie of theirs out of the field, let them be chosen where they list; saving some three thousand which is in the Low Countries.'[21]

The new contempt for Spanish power was shared by the Dutch. The papal and imperial mediators noticed a steady hardening in the attitude of the Dutch towards compromise. The key to this new confidence, however, and to Philip II's change of heart on the question of toleration, was the outbreak of a new and critical civil war between the French Catholics and Protestants in which Spanish resources became extensively committed. The future of the Dutch Revolt was to be decided in France in the 1590s.

[6]

CONSOLIDATION AND
SETTLEMENT

The war to 1609

The death of the duke of Anjou in June 1584 plunged not only the
Netherlands but also France into a constitutional dilemma. Besides
being 'prince and absolute lord' of the Low Countries, at least in name,
Anjou was also the heir to the throne of France, the last male of the
house of Valois. Henry II's four sons all failed to produce a legitimate
male heir and so, according to the Salic Law, when Henry III, the
last of the Valois brood, died, the royal succession would go to his
nearest male survivors. These were clearly the family of Bourbon,
descended from the fourth son of St Louis (d.1270). But the family
had two claimants: Henry, king of Navarre (later King Henry IV) and
his uncle, Charles, cardinal of Bourbon. There was no doubt that
Navarre had the best title on genealogical grounds, but he was a
Protestant – indeed the leader of the French Protestants – and as such
the Catholic majority of the political nation regarded him as incapable
of succeeding to the throne. To prevent a Protestant succession, the

French Catholic leaders therefore formed an alliance, the Sainte Union or League, and they looked to Spain to underpin their efforts with financial and (if necessary) military assistance.

Philip II was not slow to see the danger which a Protestant succession in France would constitute for his own empire and, six months after Anjou's death, he signed a secret agreement with the duke of Guise, the head of the Catholic League, by which he promised to provide the League with 50,000 crowns (almost 150,000 florins) every month – the secret treaty of Joinville, 31 December 1584. Henry III could not withstand this new alliance: in July 1585 he agreed to repeal the edicts of toleration and to exclude Navarre from the succession (Edict and Treaty of Nemours) and in August 1588, as the Armada sailed up the Channel, he recognized the cardinal of Bourbon as *'le plus proche parent de mon sang'* (my closest male relative). Spanish gold and Catholic political pressure had achieved a great deal. However, the situation was transformed by the defeat of the Armada, which entirely discredited the League. In December 1588 King Henry had his revenge: Guise and his brother were murdered and the cardinal of Bourbon arrested. Shortly afterwards he recognized Navarre as his heir. This was tantamount to a declaration of war, and the Catholics immediately mobilized their forces; the Protestants did likewise. Civil war began. Then, by another twist of fate, on 1 August 1589 a Catholic fanatic murdered Henry III, leaving the royal succession wide open.

Henry of Navarre possessed a number of advantages. In the first place he was undoubtedly, apart from his religion, the legitimate heir to the throne. Secondly, his only real competitor (his uncle the cardinal) was in his power, under arrest. Thirdly, he could mobilize the resources of the Huguenots in the south and west of France and he could count on the support of the Huguenots' allies, England and the Dutch (the States of Holland provided their first subsidy to Navarre in April 1588: 90,000 florins). Fourthly, and perhaps most important of all, Henry of Navarre with his *'panache blanche'* had undoubted military flair, which he proceeded to demonstrate by scoring crushing victories over the Catholic League at Arques (21 September 1589) and again at Ivry (14 March 1590).

It was these victories which forced Philip II to intervene openly in France, but he moved into the new policy with great reluctance. In January 1589 he refused to be provoked into an open break with Henry

III following the murder of his allies the Guise. In September 1589 he reacted with evident restraint to the murder of Henry III, ordering Parma to call off the offensive against the Dutch in order to be ready to aid the French Catholics if necessary – but forbidding him to invade until further orders. It was only on 4 April 1590, after hearing of Navarre's great victories, that he informed his nephew that 'although the method by which we have aided the French Catholics has been correct until now, it will not be so any longer'. Parma was to invade France at once with 20,000 men.[1] The duke left the Netherlands on 27 July with a large army and entered Paris in triumph on 19 September. This was a military feat of paramount significance since, had Paris fallen, Navarre would have been crowned at St Denis and the civil war would have been over.

Thanks to Parma's success, the war did not come to an end. Philip II was therefore compelled to continue pouring men and money into the Catholic cause for another eight years. In subsidies to the League alone at least 1,000,000 crowns (about 3,000,000 florins) were provided by Spain between 1582 and 1587; another 2,000,000 in 1588–90; and a further 2,500,000 at least in 1591–5. There was also the subsidy to the duke of Savoy after 1589 (5,000 crowns a month) and the cost of the Spanish troops maintained for the benefit of the League in Savoy, Languedoc, Brittany, Franche-Comté, and northern France (including a garrison of 1,000 in Paris).[2] For the rest of Philip II's life, France came first in all things.

Although many contemporaries, followed by later historians, realized that there was a clear connection between Philip II's intervention in France and the emergence of the Dutch Republic, the States-General were somewhat slow to appreciate their advantage. In 1589 their efforts were diverted to a joint Anglo–Dutch expedition to Portugal. A suggestion made by the stadholder of Friesland that they mount an offensive in the north-east was turned down: the States announced that they preferred

'to use the cessation of hostilities and rest that the enemy had given them to their advantage, with the building of necessary fortifications and putting everything in good order; contenting themselves with retaining what they still had and preventing the enemy's further invasion. They said also that by doing otherwise and seeking out the enemy they would arouse a sleeping dog and bring the war, now averted, upon themselves again.'[3]

Admittedly at that moment the States were still recovering from the loss of St Geertruidenburg and the invasion of Bommel, but in the event their overcautious reluctance to 'arouse a sleeping dog' meant that they were totally unable to exploit Parma's departure for France in July 1590. The best that could be done was a sort of *chevauchée* through Brabant by the Dutch army, reminiscent of the aimless actions of the Hundred Years War, and the construction of some new fortresses in Friesland. The only real success of the year was the surprise capture of Breda in March, the first major town to be captured by the rebels since 1580.

The Dutch leaders, however, realized that Parma would be ordered to return to France in 1591 and that this offered an opportunity too good to miss. They determined to mount a major campaign across the IJssel in order to recover the towns in the north-east captured by Parma in the 1580s. Count Maurice of Nassau, Orange's second son, took personal charge of the States' field army, some 10,000 men with large-scale artillery support, and he captured Zutphen after five days' siege in May 1591 and Deventer after ten days' siege in June. Parma was powerless to stop the Dutch advance. He had left 6,000 of his best men in France to fight for the League, and 2,000 more – one of the crack Spanish regiments – mutinied for their wage-arrears; with a supreme effort, the duke managed to collect 6,000 men and relieve Nijmegen, but he dared not challenge Maurice's superior forces openly. In August 1591, broken in spirit and in body, the duke went to Spa for medical treatment. In November he was back in Brussels, paying off the mutineers (at a cost of 800,000 florins) and collecting an army of 20,000 men with which to raise Henry of Navarre's siege of Rouen, but again the Dutch profited from Parma's absence in France, taking Hulst in north Flanders, Nijmegen in Gelderland and Steenwijk and Coevorden in Overijssel, with a series of rapid and energetic movements.

Parma returned from France in late November 1592 to die at Arras (6 December). He thus spared himself the ignominy of being dismissed, arrested and sent back to Spain – the fate which Philip II's personal representative, the count of Fuentes, had in store for him. The accusations of insubordination and corruption levelled against Parma from

10. *The Dutch reconquest*

The army of the States-General, commanded by Maurice of Nassau, recovered the whole of the north-east in 1591–4 and in the remarkably successful campaign of 1597. After that there were some further gains in the south and some losses in the east, but the heartland of the Dutch Republic was now safeguarded. The fortunes of the war after 1597 never again jeopardized the security of Holland and Zealand, although the invasion of the Veluwe and the capture of Amersfoort in 1629 came dangerously close.

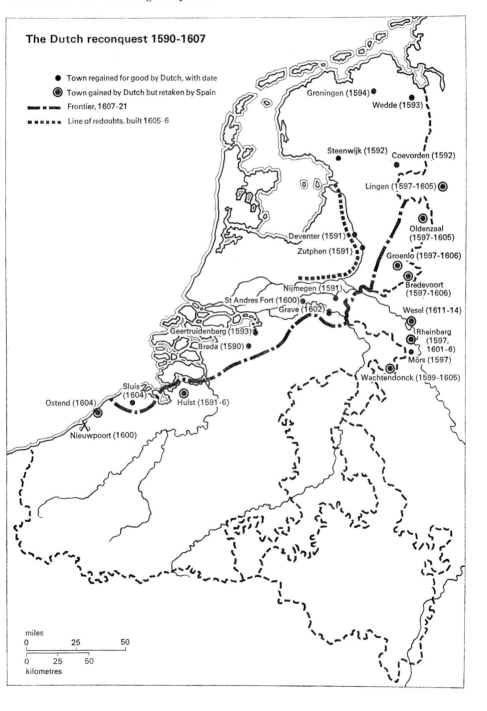

The Dutch reconquest 1590-1607

● Town regained for good by Dutch, with date
◉ Town gained by Dutch but retaken by Spain
▬ ▪ ▬ Frontier, 1607-21
▪ ▪ ▪ ▪ ▪ Line of redoubts, built 1605-6

Groningen (1594) ●
Wedde (1593) ●
Steenwijk (1592) ●
Coevorden (1592)
Lingen (1597-1605) ◉
Oldenzaal (1597-1605) ◉
Groenlo (1597-1606) ◉
Deventer (1591) ●
Zutphen (1591) ●
Bredevoort (1597-1606) ◉
Nijmegen (1591) ●
St Andres Fort (1600) ●
Grave (1602) ●
Wesel (1611-14) ●
Geertruidenberg (1593) ●
Rheinberg (1597, 1601-6) ◉
Breda (1590) ●
Mörs (1597) ◉
Wachtendonck (1599-1605) ◉
Sluis (1604) ●
Ostend (1604) ●
Hulst (1591-6) ◉
Nieuwpoort (1600)

miles
0   25   50

0   25   50
kilometres

all sides had made some impression on Philip II, but he was more conscious still of the fact that, on the one hand, the thirty-two million florins which he had sent to his nephew in 1590–91 had produced only mutiny and defeats, while on the other his orders for Parma to return to France (made with increasing insistence since January 1591, as soon as the king learned of Parma's departure from Paris) had been blatantly disregarded. The king therefore decided to replace his nephew with someone more amenable to his wishes and to cut off all financial supply until Parma had been removed. During 1592 the military treasury of the army of Flanders received just under four and a half million florins in place of the eighteen million of 1590 and the fourteen million of 1591.

Parma's death, however, created more problems than it solved. In particular it left two men with claims to succeed him: Fuentes, sent by the king to replace Parma as commander-in-chief, and Count Mansfelt (now aged seventy-five) who had been left as Parma's deputy in Brussels. Each man refused to recognize the other and the Spanish government in Brussels degenerated into almost total anarchy. Contradictory commands were issued to the same bodies of troops; different bodies of troops were ordered to perform the same functions; different officers were appointed to the same post. At the same time there was mounting opposition by the south Netherlanders to the diversion (as they saw it) of resources from fighting the Dutch to fighting the French. In Brussels Mansfelt, Champagney and others tried to halt the flow of money to the Catholic League, while in the countryside the populace, already armed to the teeth for protection against the Dutch freebooters, became restless. In 1593 there were a number of riots when new taxes were decreed to pay for the war in France – and discontent mounted with the knowledge that the army there was largely inactive: in April 1593 it managed to take Noyon, but the troops did not have enough food or munitions and so they simply abandoned the town and marched back to the Netherlands. As they did so, 3,000 of the front-line troops (Spaniards and Italians) mutinied for their wages and seized the towns of St Pol and Pont-sur-Sambre. There they defied the government for over a year: only in August 1594 were they bought back into service for just under a million florins. These events forced the Brussels regime to conclude a truce with Henry of Navarre (13 July 1593) which was prolonged until April 1594 simply because there was neither the money nor the men to undertake further military action. Navarre made good use of this respite to buy over or subdue the leading French Catholic nobles and cities.

The truce of 1593–4 was the turning-point of the war. Navarre announced his conversion to Catholicism on 25 July 1593, was crowned at Chartres on 27 February 1594 and captured Paris on 22 March. At the same time the Dutch profited from the mutinous impotence of the Spanish army to recapture St Geertruidenberg (in north Brabant) in June 1593 and Wedde (near Groningen) in August. The arrival of a new and more dutiful nephew of Philip II, the Archduke Ernest, in February 1594 did nothing to improve the situation: almost at once 4,000 more veterans from the army of Flanders mutinied while the Dutch laid siege to Groningen, the last royalist stronghold in the north. They captured it on 23 July 1594.

The years after the capture of Groningen were less fortunate for the Dutch, even though Henry of Navarre formally declared war on Spain in January 1595 and promptly invaded Artois. The forces of the United Provinces invaded the neutral principality of Liège in an attempt to create a secure corridor between the Republic and France. Success seemed certain with the death of Archduke Ernest in February 1595, which created another deadlock in Brussels with Mansfelt and Fuentes again vying for recognition as supreme governor, but Fuentes was an able general and the invasion was defeated. The Dutch also failed to capture Rheinberg and Groenlo, even though the main Spanish field army was occupied on the French frontier, where in September Fuentes captured the strongholds of Doullens and Cambrai (the latter held by the French since 1580). In 1596 another of Philip II's nephews, the Archduke Albert, arrived from Spain as governor-general and captured first Calais and Ardres from the French and then Hulst (in northern Flanders) from the Dutch – their first loss since 1589. In 1596 the Dutch formed a triple alliance with France and England (the Treaty of Greenwich) which led to their forces being sent on Essex's fruitless attack on Cadiz and on an expedition to France. In 1597 they took part in another equally fruitless joint expedition to the Azores.

Philip II, however, had broken credit with his bankers again on 29 November 1596 (his third Decree of Bankruptcy) and, although he also confiscated the treasure which arrived from the Indies the same month, his action sapped the confidence of the business community (most members of which were no longer able to lend or transfer money for the king). The troops in the Netherlands despaired; many of them mutinied. Not surprisingly the Archduke Albert was able to achieve little of note in 1597: a surprise attack on the great French city of Amiens succeeded (21 March), but it could not be held and the Spanish garrison capitulated on 25 September. The archduke was powerless to prevent a small Dutch army under Count Maurice from starving out Rheinberg, Groenlo and Lingen in the north-east, and on 21 October he felt compelled to issue a general order to all commanders, authorizing them to surrender if they came under heavy attack, since there was no possibility of relieving them.[4] The king's forces in the Netherlands were fast disintegrating. Francisco Verdugo, the commander of Spanish Friesland, fought a magnificent rearguard action against the Dutch, but what could he hope to achieve when one 'company' in his force was allegedly reduced to ten people? There were three gunners in the van, three pikemen in the middle, and three women and a clerk at the rear. All of them were starving.

The perpetual hunger of the Spanish troops runs as a constant refrain through the correspondence of almost all local commanders of the army of Flanders to headquarters during the 1590s. From Gelderland Count Herman van den Berg painted a sombre canvas of the 'misery and desperation of the poor soldiers' and wondered 'how much courage they will have to resist the enemy's forces with starving bellies'. From Artois, at the other end of the Spanish dominion, the marquis of Varambon's troops 'are almost all falling ill from the hunger and poverty which they endure'.[5] The wonder is that such troops, unpaid and unfed, should have put up any resistance at all to the Dutch. Of course, some of them did not: Nijmegen surrendered to Maurice in October 1591 without waiting for the arrival of siege artillery. Other towns followed suit, leading a prominent minister of the Brussels government to observe: 'If our towns are going to surrender like this, no power on earth can save them.' Even Spanish soldiers deserted to the Dutch and became, outwardly at least, Calvinists.[6] As the papal legate in Brussels remarked in July 1593: 'We can say that this progress of the Protestants stems more from their diligence and energy than from military strength; but even more it stems from the absence of any obstacle.'[7] Spain had never previously appeared so impotent.

At last, his own life nearing its end, Philip II reconciled himself to failure in his French policy. Late in 1597 serious negotiations began with Henry of Navarre, now master of his country and anxious to buy a few years of peace for recovery and reconstruction. Despite the efforts of England and the Dutch to keep France fighting, the Peace of Vervins was signed on 2 May 1598. Philip II, who had concluded a new agreement with his bankers on 14 February, was again free to turn full resources against England and the Dutch. Spanish troops invaded the duchy of Cleves and captured a number of towns which commanded crossing-places over the Rhine.

The death of Philip II in September 1598 made no difference to the new determination to defeat the Dutch rebels, because his son and successor, Philip III, was resolved to begin his reign with a major military effort to demonstrate his firmness to the world. The trouble was that he tried to do it in two ways at once: not content with ordering a new offensive in the Netherlands – the invasion of the island of Bommel between Maas and Waal – he organized and dispatched a fleet to invade Ireland. Alas neither venture was adequately financed: the new Armada (100 ships and 25,000 men) only got as far as the Azores, where over twenty of the unseaworthy ships foundered; the army on Bommel (and elsewhere in the Netherlands) mutinied for lack of pay and the conquests of 1599 were all sold back to the Dutch for cash by their mutinous garrisons.

These Spanish failures brought little comfort to the Archduke Albert, whose powers in the Netherlands had significantly increased after the death of Philip II. The old king had decreed that, although Spain and his other territories were to go to Philip III, the Netherlands were to be the dowry of his daughter, Isabella, who was to marry her cousin Albert, already governor-general in Brussels. The marriage took place in May 1599 and 'the archdukes' (as Albert and Isabella were always known) returned to Brussels as sovereign rulers in September. Of course the archdukes were still partly dependent on Spain – they could not make peace or war without Spanish consent; Spanish garrisons, controlled from Madrid, were permanently maintained in the key towns of the Low Countries – but they still had considerable freedom of action. The Archduke Albert, who was the dominant partner, had long experience of the ways of the Spanish Court. Born in 1559 he had lived in Spain since 1571 and had served as viceroy of Portugal for Philip II from 1583. From 1593 he represented the ageing king at audiences and he sat regularly on the Council of State and on the *junta de gobierno*, the committee of government which dealt with the papers referred by the central councils to the king. In 1595 he was appointed governor-general of the Netherlands. Albert was thus well qualified both to govern the Low Countries and to manipulate their dependence on Spain in his own interests. One of his earliest actions after returning to Brussels in 1599 was to resume peace-talks with the Dutch.

The Dutch, however, were not interested in peace. The leader of the States of Holland, Johan van Oldenbarnevelt, had devised a plan which (he felt sure) would keep England interested in the struggle and would reduce piracy against Dutch shipping from the south Netherlands ports as well. An army of 10,000 men would be landed in Flanders to capture the pirate strongholds of Nieuwpoort and Dunkirk (Ostend was already in the hands of the States-General). The invasion force landed on 22 June 1600, confident that a major mutiny of the Spanish veterans and a rising of the 'oppressed' peoples of Flanders against Spanish tyranny would paralyse all opposition. The Dutch army was ridiculously careless: there was no reconnaissance and no real attempt to sound out Flemish feeling towards their 'brothers' from Zealand who for fifteen years had been relentlessly plundering, looting and killing the people of the province. On 30 June the archduke suddenly appeared, having persuaded 3,000 mutinous but superbly experienced veterans to join his army, and pinned down Count Maurice and his troops on the beach at Nieuwpoort. They inflicted heavy losses on the Dutch and, although the archduke's forces could not destroy or drive off the invaders immediately, the blow was fatal: by the end of the month Maurice had led his men back to Zealand.

The abortive Flanders campaign of 1600 achieved a number of things. First and foremost it put paid to the idea that the south and north Netherlands could be reunited under the rule of the States-General. Secondly, it poisoned relations between Maurice and Oldenbarnevelt, between the Orangist courtiers and the States of Holland and Zealand. A private letter written by one of Count Maurice's entourage is probably representative of the feeling among the army commanders that they had been allowed to fall into a trap: 'Oldenbarnevelt and the longcoats [sc. the deputies of the States] led us to the edge of the precipice; God, however, did not wish us to be destroyed.'[8] On the

Spanish side the invasion of Flanders and its eventual defeat convinced the south Netherlands government of two things: first, that they would have to raise more money for their own defence (on 14 July 1600 the States-General of the southern provinces agreed to provide a regular monthly sum large enough to pay 21,450 soldiers in garrisons), and second, that the Dutch enclave of Ostend would have to be destroyed. Accordingly the siege of Ostend began on 15 July 1601. The operation was mistimed, however: Spain lacked the resources to secure rapid success and the siege dragged on for three years and seventy-seven days – one contemporary called it, with only slight exaggeration, 'the new Troy' – while the Dutch blockaded and captured Rheinburg (1601) and Grave (1602) and laid siege to 's Hertogenbosch (1603).

The archdukes' position was pitiful. Spain refused to make peace, and yet could not provide enough money to win the war. A run of bad harvests in the 1590s was followed in 1599–1600 by the worst outbreak of bubonic plague ever experienced by Habsburg Spain. Perhaps 600,000 people died; around 10 per cent of the total population was carried off. 'The hunger which rose from Andalucia met the plague which came down from Castile,' wrote Mateo Alemán in his famous novel, *El Guzmán de Alfarache*, set in the ailing Spain of the 1590s. It took some time for the country to recover. The English merchants who returned to Spain in 1604 for the first time since the outbreak of war in 1585, were appalled to find that they were only able to sell 'the commodities which are the basest and coarsest that our kingdom yields, that do scarcely find utterance in any other parts of the world.'[9] Inevitably these developments reduced the money which was available for dispatch to the Low Countries. Spain's effective resources were reduced yet further in 1600–1601 by Henry IV's invasion of Savoy, which blocked the 'Spanish Road'. This was the military corridor, running through Savoy, Franche-Comté and Lorraine, which linked the Netherlands with Spanish Italy and brought the élite Spanish and Italian troops to the war in the Low Countries. Without the Spanish Road there could be no victory over the Dutch. Henry IV's invasion of Savoy disrupted the movement of Spanish troops for almost a year; the principal supply-route of the Habsburg empire lay at the mercy of France.

Other humiliations and failures followed for Spain. In 1601 Philip III resolved to send one expeditionary force to Ireland (which was routed at Kinsale) and another to Algiers (seventy ships and 10,000 men; it barely caught sight of its objective). Without funds from Spain, the situation of the soldiers on active service against the Dutch became desperate. In 1602 one of the army commanders found it 'incredible that our soldiers could carry on' with no pay, no clothes and no food.[10] At this time the mutiny of 2,000 veterans at Weert (July 1600–May 1602) was just ending, at a cost to the government of 400,000 florins, and the mutiny of 3,200 more men at Hoogstraten (September 1602–May 1605) was just beginning, which was to cost 1,000,000 florins.

This seemingly hopeless situation was saved for Spain quite unexpectedly by the arrival in the Netherlands of the first of the great military entrepreneurs of the seventeenth century, Ambrogio Spinola. The son and grandson of Genoese bankers and a millionaire in his own right, Spinola had no military experience and no formal military training, but he was a superb organizer, he learned quickly and, above all, (as a fellow Genoese put it) he could always raise 5,000,000 florins, if he needed it, more quickly and cheaply than anyone else.[11] In 1602 he led an expedition of 9,000 men, some raised at his own expense, to join the army of Flanders. In September 1603 he offered to finance the siege of Ostend for the archdukes, serving as their personal banker in return for appointment as commander of the operations. This was agreed and Spinola took over. He refused to be distracted when, in May 1604, the Dutch again invaded the province of Flanders and laid siege to the deep-water harbour of Sluis. Although they captured it on 20 August, the Dutch garrison of Ostend surrendered on 22 September.

After so much effort, to some it might seem a hollow victory; but the fall of Ostend was extremely important. It was popular with the people of Flanders, who were at last free of the pillaging enemy in their midst, and it impressed Philip III with the calibre of his new servant, Spinola. Taken in conjunction with the Treaty of London, which put an end to twenty years of war between England and Spain in August 1604, it gave encouragement to the king and those of his advisers who still believed that the Dutch might be compelled to recognize Spanish sovereignty again. Spinola spent the winter of 1604–5 at the Spanish Court, returning as commander-in-chief of the army of Flanders and superintendent of the treasury: he now had complete control over the troops and over the money to pay them. In 1605 he led an army across the 'great rivers barrier' and captured the important fortresses of Wachtendonck, Lingen and Oldenzaal. After these successes Spinola visited the Spanish Court once more, early in 1606, and emerged with new powers and plans to invade the Dutch heartland in a new and decisive campaign.

The States-General, already worried by the campaign of 1605, had taken precautionary measures: a chain of wooden fortresses linked by earthen ramparts were constructed from Schoterzijl, on the border of Friesland by the Zuider Zee down the left bank of the IJssel to Arnhem, then westwards along the Waal to Gorinchem, a distance of over 150 miles (see p. 229). These remarkable defences proved to be a serious obstacle. Although Spinola managed to throw his forces across the IJssel, the Spanish army was not able to penetrate as deeply as he had hoped, and the only material results of the campaign were the capture of Groenlo (Grol) and Rheinberg (see the map on p. 229). Nevertheless the campaign of 1606 was extremely important: it thoroughly alarmed the States-General, which had imagined that their chain of *houten redoubten* (wooden forts) would prove impregnable.[12]

The Dutch were already less enthusiastic about continuing the war with Spain. The conclusion of peace between Philip III and James I in August 1604 had come as a heavy blow, depriving the Dutch of financial support and opening the Channel to Spanish shipping. As early as June 1605 Spanish troops were sent to the Netherlands directly by sea and, when they took refuge from Dutch pursuit off the English coast, the attackers were driven back by the guns of Dover castle; in the same year the archdukes were allowed to recruit some 5,000 men in England. As it happened, the Gunpowder Plot, hatched and attempted by veterans of the army of Flanders, nipped this burgeoning Anglo–Spanish entente in the bud, but with France and England at peace the Dutch began to feel dangerously isolated. The cost of war was also becoming excessively onerous. From an average cost of under five million florins in the 1590s, the military budget of the Republic rose to an annual ten million in 1604–6. Although the annual French subsidy of around one million florins eased the burden somewhat, the United Provinces had to pay high interest on short-term debts of over ten million florins. In July 1606 Oldenbarnevelt confided to the English agent, Ralph Winwood, that he was reduced 'to seek all artifices and to use sophistries and fallacies to keep them from despair . . . their wants being so great that they live from day to day'. There were riots in Amersfoort and Utrecht against the prolonged taxation, and an English observer commented, 'I see no appearance of how these men can long subsist of themselves'.[13]

Much the same thing was being said – even by the same people – about the Spaniards. It was clear to everyone that Philip III's resources were unequal to all his commitments. When in February 1606 a personal emissary from the archdukes pleaded with the duke of Lerma, the king's favourite, to send more money to the Netherlands, he was answered with a long list of Spain's other pressing commitments: a fleet to defend the Indies and escort the Indies fleet, wages for garrisons everywhere, subsidies to finance the emperor's war in Hungary and the Archduke Ferdinand's war against the Uscocs of Croatia, and bribes to preserve the peace between Venice and the papacy. Lerma 'could not see how more could be spared'.[14] Even after Spinola's successes, some Spanish ministers favoured talks with the Dutch to end the war for the simple reason that there seemed little likelihood of achieving total victory by force of arms, while the cost to Spain of fighting on was appalling: five million florins a year, plus the exorbitant charges claimed by the bankers who loaned and transferred the money sent from Spain to the Low Countries. At the same time expenditure on the Court was claiming an ever-larger slice of available resources: where Philip II had run his household on a shoestring of 500,000 florins, his son in 1608–9 required over two million. Philip III, like James I, seemed incapable of refusing to gratify his own desires and those of his courtiers, and this was serious in a war where (in the words of one experienced royal councillor) victory would go to 'whoever is left with the last escudo'.[15] Even Spinola could not keep an army of 70,000 men going indefinitely without full support from Spain, and another mutiny broke out on 11 December 1606, involving over 4,000 veterans who fortified the town of Diest. It was the largest single mutiny since 1576 and the arrears of the participants came to over one million florins. As soon as these restive troops were paid (and promptly outlawed), the Spanish treasury issued another decree of bankruptcy on 9 November 1607, compulsorily converting its high-interest, short-term debts into low-interest, permanent ones.

It was clear that some respite in the war was essential if the whole Spanish monarchy were not to collapse, and on 14 December 1606 the king sanctioned plans for a drastic reduction in the provisions sent from

Spain to the Low Countries: the war in the Netherlands was to become a purely defensive operation. Before this measure took effect, however, letters arrived from Brussels announcing that the Dutch were prepared to begin serious talks about ending the war.

Although the Council of State professed amazement at the news that the Dutch were willing to talk – it was said to be 'a miracle' – there had been some careful preparations. Apart from the semi-constant dialogue between the two sides – with formal negotiations in 1598 and 1600 – in April 1606 Spinola had been instructed by the king to indicate to the Dutch Spain's willingness to negotiate. The Dutch response to this initiative, after Spain's successful campaign in Overijssel, was soon followed up. In February 1607 an accredited negotiator was dispatched by the Brussels government with the assurance that the independence of the United Provinces would be accepted by Spain as the basis of a settlement and on 29 March a ceasefire for eight months was agreed, coming into force a month later. It brought to an end thirty years of continuous fighting.

The States-General had scored a great success in securing Spain's willingness to recognize Dutch independence. As a burgomaster of Rotterdam said: 'To whatt ende shold we make warrs, for if we shold continue them yett 40 yeares, what cold we have more than to be acknowledged for a free commonwealth?'[16] There was still some hard bargaining ahead, however. Spain wished to secure an explicit guarantee of toleration for all Catholics living in the Dutch Republic; she insisted that the blockade of the Scheldt and the Flemish coast should be lifted; and she required an end to all Dutch trade with the East and West Indies (which Spain regarded as the exclusive preserve of herself and Portugal). This 'deal' proved unacceptable to Holland and Zealand (although the war-weariness of the inland provinces made them, at least, amenable) and it was rejected on 25 August 1608. The French and English mediators then intervened to propose a long truce instead, which made no mention of the Catholics and allowed hostilities to continue outside Europe. Spain, the States-General and the archdukes eventually accepted this formula and a truce for twelve years – the 'truce of Antwerp' – was signed on 9 April 1609.

Spain had made many sacrifices: there was no mention of the Dutch Catholics or the Indies – the Republic was left free to do as it wished. The Scheldt remained blockaded. Above all, the rebels were accorded immediate diplomatic recognition by the other states of Europe. The envoys of the States-General were henceforth treated as full ambassadors by England, France and Venice, and in October 1609 James VI and I promoted his envoy in The Hague to the rank of ambassador. Other potentates soon followed suit.[17]

After forty years of bitter struggle, the north Netherlands had thus at last won *de facto* independence and religious freedom. The achievement was considerable, and yet was it not perhaps a disappointing return for so much effort, blood and treasure? *'Cleyne glorie en groote schade'* (Little glory and great expense) was Oldenbarnevelt's verdict on the campaigns and 'actions' of the Low Countries' Wars in the years preceding the ceasefire of 1607, and he was right. The south Netherlands after Parma's recall were an easy prey for the Dutch; they were left relatively undefended while Spain's formidable resources were tied down elsewhere. The conditions for a rapid Dutch advance would never be as favourable again . . . and yet little was done. The reasons for this failure to exploit a temporary advantage are not hard to find. They lie in the nature of the emerging Dutch Republic which was still paralysed by particularism, and groped only slowly and uncertainly towards a workable constitution.

The Dutch Republic as a great power

The provinces in revolt against Spain were not, for the most part, united by history or tradition. Friesland and Gelderland had spent much of the fifteenth century fighting Holland and Zealand, with Overijssel and Utrecht as both prize and battleground. The landward provinces had only come under Habsburg rule during the reign of Charles V and they all brought their local rights, laws and liberties with them. As noted above (pp. 35–6), they even had their own languages: whereas the western provinces spoke Dutch, Friesland had (and still has) its own language, and the other eastern provinces spoke either 'Oosters' (which Hollanders could understand only with great difficulty) or Low German. The family of Orange-Nassau and their entourage spoke mainly French or German, as did many of the refugees who arrived in the north Netherlands from the south. In 1607 arrangements for a National Synod of the Reformed church were made in 'the two

languages of the Netherlands, French and Dutch'; in 1613 Maurice of
Nassau built a special theatre for the company of resident French actors
who entertained his Court. The religious complexion of the Republic
was as varied as its languages. In a sweeping but famous generalization,
a Swiss observer in 1672 estimated that one third of the population of
the United Provinces was Calvinist, another third was Catholic, and the
rest were either Anabaptist or indifferent. There was doubtless some
truth in this, but the strength of the various religious (and irreligious)
groups was not the same in all areas. The Anabaptists, for example,
constituted more than half the total population in some areas of Friesland, and in 1580 it was estimated that 25 per cent of the whole province
was Anabaptist. In 1660 the Anabaptists still numbered 13 per cent of
the Frisian population, and the Catholics only 10. In the town of
Rotterdam in 1622 there were 20,000 people of whom about 1,500
were Catholics ($7\frac{1}{2}$ per cent), and the rest either Calvinists, atheists,
Jews or something else – in seventeenth-century Rotterdam there were
ten different religions, and there were still many people who belonged
to none of them! Thus neither religion nor language nor history could
provide a basis for the lasting union of the north Netherlands provinces.
Survival depended on the participants finding some concrete political
advantage in their continued association.

To a considerable extent the provinces of the Netherlands had rebelled
in 1572 against the 'tyranny' of the duke of Alva and again in 1576–7
against the 'tyranny' of Don John of Austria and his Spanish troops.
They had opposed, and had eventually deposed, their sovereign prince
because he had failed to respect their laws and privileges. The nobles
and patricians of each province had not staked everything in this
defiance simply to surrender their lives and properties to another
absolute lord. Although they needed a figurehead – Matthias, Anjou,
Leicester – they did not want an effective ruler. On the other hand, even
after Leicester's demise, there was a manifest need for a champion who
could provide an effective defence against a Spanish reconquest. The
events of the 1580s had made it clear that the States-General alone
could not be relied on to provide protection; nor could the Union of
Utrecht (now identical in area with the lands left to the States). Hence
Friesland, Overijssel, Utrecht and Gelderland, the provinces which
were directly threatened by the Spaniards, tended to favour Leicester's
attempts to create a centralized government. However, after Leicester's

resignation (made public in March 1588), first the Armada and then the intervention in France reduced the pressure on the Dutch and made it less imperative to create a strong central executive. In any case some cohesion was already provided by the house of Orange-Nassau. William the Silent's second son, Count Maurice of Nassau, was already stadholder of Holland and Zealand. In 1590–91 he was elected stadholder of Gelderland, Overijssel and Utrecht as well, thus creating anew a measure of unity at the top of the administrative hierarchy (in addition Maurice's cousin William-Louis was stadholder of Friesland and, from 1594 onwards, of Groningen and Drenthe too). Leicester had also left behind him a Council of State, a body created in 1585 at Queen Elizabeth's behest as part of the treaty of Nonsuch. It included two English members, the two stadholders and twelve delegates from the provincial States together with the treasurer-general and other principal officeholders of the Republic. Decisions were taken by majority vote, which meant that no single province (Holland, for example) could veto a decision. Here was another potential source of unity, but in May 1588, with Leicester safely out of the way, the States-General drastically reduced the powers of the Council (known as the Raad van State): its activities were restricted to carrying out the orders of the States. Although it dealt with a considerable volume of business connected with military administration, all the Council's powers were delegated by the States-General and it had no more autonomy than the Mint Office (created in 1579), the Admiralty Board (reorganized into five 'colleges' in 1597) or the Audit Office (set up in 1602).

The seven provinces represented in the States-General in 1588 – Gelderland, Holland, Zealand, Friesland, Overijssel, Utrecht and the Ommelanden – thus held all the levers of power in the Republic, and they were determined not to share their authority with others. They had excluded the representatives of what remained of Flanders and Brabant in 1586; in the 1590s they refused to grant separate representation to Drenthe. Areas annexed afterwards – north Brabant, Limburg and areas along the German border (Emden, for instance, which had a Dutch garrison from 1603 until 1744) – were also denied representation. The States of the seven provinces of 1587–8 retained overall control of all things for themselves. They were in effect the sovereigns in the Republic and this fact was made explicit for the first time in 1587, following the fall of Deventer. The States took a number of emergency steps to repair the damage caused by the defection of Stanley and Yorke, acting as if they were a sovereign power. Their right to do so in the absence of Leicester, who had been vested with 'absolute' power only a year before, was immediately challenged by Thomas Wilkes, an English lawyer who sat on the Raad van State. In March 1587 he delivered a 'Remonstrance' which argued that sovereignty in fact belonged to the people and had been delegated by them to Leicester, not to the States. Wilkes even quoted Bodin in his evidence: 'Sovereignty is limited neither in power nor in time' he told the States, so that if the people had once given Leicester his authority, only the people could take it away again. The States of Holland, however, rejoined that they alone exercised the sovereign power of the people in their province, by virtue of their role as official representatives of the nobles and the magistrates who administered the law of the land. As such they were entitled to make binding contracts with third parties concerning the exercise of that sovereign power. In October 1587 this view was given a more elegant expression by another lawyer, François Vranck, who demolished Wilkes's case by pointing out that since the death of Anjou the States had acted as sovereign and that even Queen Elizabeth had accepted this, since she had treated them as an equal during the negotiations of 1585–6. To question that now, Vranck pointed out, would be to question the validity of the treaties with the queen and with Leicester, and his short treatise concluded with the unequivocal statement:

'The sovereignty of the country resides with the States; . . . the States are now no less sovereign than under the rule of the former princes.'

The formula was endorsed by a resolution of the States-General on 25 July 1590, which declared that the assembly was 'the sovereign institution of the country, and has no overlord except the deputies of the provincial estates themselves'.[18]

These justifications of the new political order in the north Netherlands were convincing and well argued, and in 1602 they were given an even longer defence in Althusius's *Politica methodice digesta* (469 pages; the third edition, in 1614, covered 968 pages). But all these apologia were mute on one important point: how precisely did the States of the seven provinces, whose delegates sat in the States-General, represent and speak for the population at large? Like the other republics of sixteenth-century Europe – Venice and the Swiss cantons – the new

Dutch state was run by a tightly knit oligarchy. Only the provincial government of Friesland had a democratic base which was, by sixteenth-century standards, reasonably wide: there were thirty administrative areas (known as *grietenijen*) which sent two deputies each to a *landdag* or assembly which actually governed the province. These elected deputies, together with the church and community officials of the various localities, were elected by about 10,000 'votes'. There were not, however, 10,000 voters: certain farms were enfranchised in each area, and the local oligarchs endeavoured to buy up more than one 'voting farm'. By 1640 the small regent class of the province already held 26 per cent of the total votes, and they controlled a majority of the votes in 20 per cent of the villages of Friesland (by 1698 these percentages had increased to 38 and 50 respectively). To ensure the smooth exchange of offices among the various patrician families, the oligarchs arranged a fixed rotation between themselves (normally laid down in a legal act known as an *almanach*).

Even with these restrictive practices, however, the government of Friesland was considerably more democratic than that of any other province, where the ordinary freeholders had no voice in elections at all. The ruling class in the Republic was made up of the 2,000 or so men who had seats in the provincial States – the 'regent class'. Their power was particularly strong in Holland and Zealand, the core of the new polity, where the provincial assembly of the first comprised eighteen towns and one deputy from the nobility, and of the second six towns and one representative of the nobles. Each of the major towns resembled a small oligarchic city-state ruled by its exclusive corps of magistrates. These were made up of the *schout* or sheriff and the *schepenen* or aldermen, who were entrusted with enforcing the law, and the burgomasters, who took care of the daily problems of government. The magistrates, except for the *schout*, were usually appointed from the members of the city council, or *vroedschap*, composed of between twenty and fifty local patricians. When a place on the *vroedschap* fell vacant, the rest of the council chose another patrician to fill the gap. Although in one or two places – Dordrecht, for example – the guilds had some voice in the appointment of magistrates, those with such rights often themselves became members of the *vroedschap*. The government of each town was thus a closed oligarchy and although at first there were factions within its ranks, in the course of time the rival groups came to terms with each other. By the mid-seventeenth century family agreements and even formal contracts (known as *almanachs* in Friesland and as *contracten van correspondentie* elsewhere) were signed by the various faction leaders to ensure that all offices were kept within the closed circle, rotating between the groups in a fixed order. This meant that in many towns a particular family grouping, such as the Valckeniers at Amsterdam or the Vrijbergens at Tholen, gained permanent control of urban affairs, broken only at times of crisis by purges instituted by the central government. Thus, at Amsterdam seven new men were appointed to the *vroedschap* in 1618, following the fall of Oldenbarnevelt, and ten new men came to office in 1672 after the fall of Johan de Witt. Since there were only four such crises in the entire life of the Dutch Republic – in 1618, 1672, 1748 and 1787 – at other times the closed oligarchies in each town were able to tighten their grip on the levers of power. If the number of eligible families in a town fell short of the number of offices to be filled, as it began to do in many towns in the mid-seventeenth century, the *vroedschap* decreed a reduction in its own size: thus, in 1650, Gouda reduced its council from forty to twenty-eight seats rather than see new families enter the patriciate, and many other towns soon followed this precedent.

This closed ruling caste endeavoured to defend its position against interference both from above and from below. The town councils stated repeatedly that they 'represented the whole body of the town', a view which was endorsed by the resolution of the States of Holland of 23 March 1581 which forbade all town councils in the province to consult guilds, militia companies or other groups of citizens on any matter of domestic policy, and this injunction was obeyed with very few exceptions until the crisis of 1672. There was, however, an influential body of opinion which was opposed to the oligarchy's monopoly of power, led by the guilds and *schutters* (the militia) who had previously opposed the oligarchs when allied with the Brussels government in 1566 and 1572, and sometimes before. This nascent hostility was exploited by Hembyze and the other Calvinist leaders in the towns of Flanders after 1578, and by the earl of Leicester in the north in 1586–7. Both attempted to create a new type of urban government with the aid of the *schutters* and other groups who resented the power of the regents, but both failed, as we have seen, and thereafter the regent class was relatively safe from the threat of democracy.

For different reasons the regents were also safe from the risk of central autocracy, once Leicester had left, because the sovereign States were entirely responsible to the towns they represented. Each of the towns which possessed the right to send delegates to the States sent a deputation of two or more to each meeting of the provincial assembly, and they sent them with full instructions on how to vote on the various issues likely to be discussed. If these instructions proved to be impracticable or insufficient, or if they contradicted the instructions drafted by other towns, it inevitably produced deadlock in the States. Unanimity was required for all binding decisions. The offending deputation was then obliged to report back to its *vroedschap* for a new brief. It was not allowed to depart from its instructions. Only in the direst emergency (for example, after the assassination of the prince of Orange in 1584) were the inflexible practices of referring back (known as *ruggespraak*) and unanimity abandoned; and even then they were not abandoned for very long.

Thus the oligarchs of the *stemhebbende steden*, of the 'voting towns' which had the right to send representatives to the provincial States, controlled the affairs of their own provinces; and the same oligarchs automatically also controlled the States-General, which consisted of deputies from each of the seven provincial assemblies. Before any decision was taken in the supreme body, the representatives of each province had to refer back to the States which had sent them, and the States in turn had to refer back to the oligarchs and nobles who had mandated them. Because of this rigid control, the States-General became a very small body: seldom more than twelve deputies attended at any one time, and sometimes there were no more than four or five. The average attendance in the 1590s was eight or nine. Because of the unequal economic and political strength of the seven provinces – some, like Gelderland, were partly occupied by enemy troops; others, like Overijssel, were underpopulated and impoverished – their voices in the States-General were of unequal weight. It was above all the opinion of Holland which predominated, partly because the States-General after 1588 sat permanently in The Hague (the capital of Holland) and after 1593 met in the same building as the States of Holland, partly because Holland always paid over one half and sometimes as much as two thirds of the federal budget. The province which paid the piper was normally allowed to call the tune.

The sovereignty described by François Vranck thus resided, in many matters, with the *vroedschappen* of the eighteen 'voting towns' of Holland, a body of about 700 men who were not elected by, or responsible to, anyone outside their own closed group. Each regent could be sure that no major decision in the Republic would be taken without his express knowledge and assent.

Here, indeed, was a world made safe for oligarchs. It was a world for which the leaders of the revolt, in Holland at least, had been fighting since 1572. Unfortunately, however, such a decentralized system was not at all conducive to winning a war. In the 1590s the deputies of the States-General still felt it reasonable to exert direct control over their armed forces, ordering the commander-in-chief, the stadholder Maurice of Nassau, to campaign in Gelderland at once and refusing to send him money or baggage-carts when he stayed instead to lay siege to another town in Overijssel (1592). On another occasion they peremptorily forbade him to sail in person to the relief of Calais (1596). On both occasions, Maurice blandly disobeyed orders – it was the only way to achieve results – and in time, when several victories had been won by the young commander, the States came to recognize that once they had decided on the theatre of operations and the campaign budget, the field commander had to be left a considerable degree of executive responsibility. A similar tacit agreement, a sort of division of powers, was reached between the States-General and the provincial assemblies. It became accepted that the former, with their administrative 'colleges', would deal with public finance, military affairs and foreign policy but would not attempt to legislate or intervene in the domestic affairs of individual provinces. That was left to the various States.

Nevertheless this division of authority within the Republic could produce intense friction over several delicate issues, and the harmonization of the various organs of government could take a very long time to achieve. The Dutch system required a reservoir of men with sound political sense and monumental patience if it was to work at all. Although the experienced politicians from Flanders and Brabant who fled to the north with the States-General in the 1580s were valuable, the man who did most to create a workable political system in the Republic after the death of William of Orange was born in Amersfoort in the province of Utrecht: Johan van Oldenbarnevelt.

Oldenbarnevelt was a lawyer by training. Born in 1547, he studied

at Leuven, Bourges, Heidelberg and Padua and started to practise in
The Hague in 1570. By 1576 he was so successful that, although young,
he was appointed town clerk ('pensionary') of Rotterdam. As such he
was normally chosen by the town council to be one of their representatives in the States of Holland and he began to serve on their committees.
In 1585 he was one of the Dutch delegation sent to negotiate the Treaty
of Nonsuch, and there he established a reputation for capacity, common
sense, and cool calculation. During the clash with Leicester the States
of Holland therefore elected Oldenbarnevelt to serve as their 'advocate',
or leader, an office he was to hold from March 1586 until his death in
May 1619.

The advocate's powers were considerable. He represented the nobles
of Holland in the States-General and he cast their single 'vote'; he
formulated and proposed policies to the States and he was their spokesman to the outside world, whether to foreign powers or to the other
provinces of the Union. Oldenbarnevelt himself also held a number of
minor offices in the province – Lord Privy Seal, registrar of land tenures
and so on – which brought him into contact with a wide circle of important people and, thanks to this powerful combination of offices and
contacts, coupled with a strong personality and an amazing capacity for
sustained hard work, Oldenbarnevelt was able to impose a considerable
degree of cohesion upon the loose federation of Netherlands provinces
still in revolt against Spain. No sooner had Leicester departed than
Oldenbarnevelt, who had played a leading role in his defeat, emerged
as the coordinating force in the Republic. Lord Willoughby, Leicester's
successor as lord general, referred to the advocate as 'Beelzebub' and
saw his hand in everything. In 1589, Sir Thomas Bodley, an English
member of the Raad van State, observed that nothing was done 'unless
those of Holland and especially the Advocate are present'; in a more
positive vein he noted that 'all here is directed by Holland and Holland
is carried away by Barnevelt'. As the Dutch began to score victories
and reconquer territories in the 1590s, Oldenbarnevelt and the system
which he laboured so hard to operate became acceptable both inside and
outside the Republic.

But the advocate had his problems. In foreign affairs he could not
prevent first France (1598) and then England (1604) from making
peace with Spain; at home he could not manage to prevent Holland
and Zealand from large-scale trading with Spain and Spanish-held

territories. Although he managed to squeeze considerable financial subsidies from France long after she had made peace, and although he managed to browbeat the provinces into unanimity on most issues sooner or later, he was always an agent, a factor. His power stemmed not from any dictatorial authority inherent in his office (as Leicester's had done) nor from any advantage of birth or breeding (as Orange's had done). 'Mr Barnfield', as the English knew him, was powerful because he was the spokesman of the richest province in the Union, and his authority reflected the commercial wealth and well-being of Holland.

During the 1590s the trade of the north Netherlands, and especially of Holland, burgeoned. Dutch ships sailed in increasing numbers to the Baltic, to the Mediterranean, to France, and to the European colonies overseas. Between 1598 and 1605, on average twenty-five ships sailed to West Africa, twenty to Brazil, ten to the East Indies and 150 to the Caribbean every year. Sovereign colonies were founded at Amboina in 1605 and Ternate in 1607; factories and trading posts were established around the Indian Ocean, near the mouth of the Amazon and (in 1609) in Japan. Such an expansion of trade overseas was accompanied by a growth in population, trade and industrial activity at home, especially in Holland. Even the size of the province increased. Between 1500 and 1650 the land under cultivation in north Holland increased by around 45 per cent; in south Holland, where a survey of 1514 had described much land as *pro derelicto* because it was habitually flooded or covered by sand-dunes or peat-diggings, by 1650 vast tracts had been drained or otherwise brought back into cultivation. Taking the province as a whole, the average amount of land reclaimed annually rose from 128 acres in the 1580s to 580 acres between 1590 and 1614 and 713 acres between 1615 and 1639. By 1650 most of the lakes of north Holland and many of those farther south had been drained and were yielding crops. Between 1632 and 1654, some 343 acres were recovered along the coast from the sand dunes.

There is little doubt about the motive for this impressive reclamation of land, almost all of it achieved by private enterprise: the value of agricultural land was rising steadily, in response to growing population and growing prosperity. In 1514 north Holland had 79,000 people and south Holland had 194,000; in 1622 the north had 188,000 (an increase of 138 per cent) and the south had 482,000 people (an increase of 156 per cent). The combined population in 1622 was thus 670,000 people, of whom 44 per cent lived in 425 villages and 56 per cent lived in twenty-eight towns. The second-largest town in the province was Leiden, where the population rose from 12,000 in the 1570s to about 65,000 in the 1640s. This spectacular growth was closely related to the booming textile industry in the town, which produced only around 500 pieces of cloth annually in the 1570s but 35,000 pieces the following decade and over 100,000 in the 1620s. We know that immigration played a crucial role both in the demographic growth and in the textile bonanza. Well over 10,000 emigrants arrived in the town between 1580 and 1630 and almost half of them came from the south Netherlands, in particular from the cloth-weaving towns of Flanders. Already in the 1580s surveys of the Leiden population show a strong immigrant minority – indeed, 40 per cent of all the men listed in a survey of 1581 came from outside the town – and on the whole the newcomers tended to be living in better houses and to have larger families than the native population (which was perhaps still suffering from the privations of the great siege of 1574).

Other towns besides Leiden benefited from the influx of well-to-do refugees from the southern provinces. Many specialists of all kinds fled from the Spanish advance. Thus of 364 publishers and booksellers who are known to have been active in the north Netherlands between 1570 and 1630, 248 (68 per cent) were southern immigrants. Likewise, of 127 teachers known to have been active in the schools and the university of Leiden between 1575 and 1630, 82 (67 per cent) were southern immigrants. Over the same period no less than 442 teachers came to the north Netherlands from the south, many of them persons of distinction who wrote books about their speciality or about teaching methods. The contribution of an intellectual élite like this to their adopted new country is impossible to quantify, but clearly their influence extended into every corner of Dutch life.

Although on the whole the immigrant teachers tended to avoid the city (only fifty-five of the 442 went there), Amsterdam with its population of 120,000 or so attracted a large number of refugees from the south. An analysis of marriages celebrated in the city between 1586 and 1601 reveals that 1,478 bridegrooms, 16 per cent of all men married in Amsterdam in those years, came from the south (788 of them came from Antwerp alone). Many of these and other newcomers were persons of considerable wealth: of the 320 largest depositors in the Amsterdam

Exchange Bank in 1611, over half were southern refugees; surviving tax registers from 1631 reveal that about one third of the richest Amsterdammers were of south Netherlands origin; some 27 per cent of the shareholders of the Amsterdam chamber of the Dutch East India Company in 1602, including the three largest subscribers, were Walloon or Flemish exiles, and they provided almost 40 per cent of the Company's total capital. The southerners were not the only men with money in their pockets, however: many Hollanders also made their fortunes. Of the 685 citizens of Amsterdam who in 1631 declared that their personal wealth exceeded 25,000 florins, only 160, or one quarter, came from the south. About half were native Hollanders who had grown rich in spite of the war – or even because of it.[19]

The Revolt undoubtedly brought greater prosperity to Amsterdam and some other towns of Holland than could possibly have accrued under Spanish rule, but the cost of independence was high. The inland provinces were ravaged, their populations scarcely holding their own between 1580 and 1640. Moreover all citizens had to pay for the cost of the armed forces. The conquests of Count Maurice after 1590 may have been achieved on a shoestring by Spanish standards, but the cost of offence and defence was a heavy burden on the young Republic and especially upon Holland which had to meet half the cost. While the province had to provide 960,000 florins for the war in 1579, twenty years later it had to find 5,384,968 florins. Even with the new prosperity of the Indies, tax increases on this scale hurt, and the provincial authorities failed to collect over 750,000 florins of the 1599 quota. Travellers noticed the penny-pinching of public authorities during the war-years in many small ways. In 1592 Fynes Morison visited Delft and remarked that the monument to William of Orange in the church there was 'the poorest that ever I saw for such a person, being onely of rough stones and morter with postes of wood, coloured over with black, and very little erected from the ground'.[20] Until the coming of peace in 1609, however, there was neither time nor money for unnecessary ostentation, nor for disagreement between the provinces. Even the Orangists' disenchantment with Oldenbarnevelt after Nieuwpoort was kept in the background as long as the war with Spain continued.

It was the same in the Dutch Reformed church. Profound differences had developed among the Calvinist faithful, particularly about predestination and about the right of civil magistrates to mediate in clerical disputes. At the centre of the controversy was one of the Amsterdam pastors, Jacob Hermans or Arminius. In 1592, in 1602 and again in 1608 he was accused of heterodoxy and challenged to a public disputation, but on each occasion the quarrel was settled by the civil authorities, who felt that an open schism in wartime was to be avoided at all costs. In 1609 Arminius died peacefully in his bed, but the coming of peace in the same year removed much of the restraint from the other protagonists in the dispute. The 'Arminian debate' became far more passionate and almost everyone of political consequence was eventually forced to choose a side. The discussions over whether or not there should be a truce with Spain had already created two determined political parties: Oldenbarnevelt, who favoured a settlement, was supported by most of the regent class of Holland; Maurice, who did not wish for peace, was supported by the Calvinists, the southern exiles and the city of Amsterdam. This division of opinion was kept alive and made sharper by the barrage of pamphlets issued by the supporters and opponents of the late Arminius, all appealing for support. On the whole the Calvinist establishment, the House of Orange, the exiles from the south, and the landward provinces sided with the anti-Arminians (known as Counter-Remonstrants or Gomarists), while the regent class of Holland sided with the Remonstrants (as the Arminians were known). The situation steadily worsened. The writings of Catholic theologians like Bellarmine against predestination (which Arminians had also attacked) opened the Remonstrants to accusations of treason. Their churches were attacked and their ministers mobbed.

In August 1617 the States of Holland, led by Oldenbarnevelt, decided to authorize any town to raise any troops of its own which it judged to be necessary to preserve law and order; these troops, known as *waardgelders*, were to swear allegiance to the town which raised them. This move, although justified by the refusal of both Maurice and the militia companies to protect the Arminians from attack, proved unpopular with the other provinces and with the House of Orange. From September 1617 onwards Maurice took a personal role in the controversy, purging the landward provinces of their Remonstrant magistrates and isolating Holland. By August 1618 the States General, directed by Maurice, decreed that all the *waardgelder* units should be disbanded, and every town complied. Oldenbarnevelt and those who had ordered the levy were arrested. Next Maurice purged the Holland towns of all Remonstrants (although he took care not to introduce non-patricians into the magistracy) and the anti-Arminian States-General had Oldenbarnevelt tried and executed for treason in 1619.

'Mr Barnfield' was thus expendable in peacetime, but only because Holland's importance in the Republic naturally diminished when she was no longer providing 50 per cent of the war budget. The predominance of Oldenbarnevelt's successor, Johan de Witt, after 1650, was to show that the Republic needed the leadership of the Advocate of Holland if it was to prosper. The *waardgelder* crisis of 1617–19 was serious, but it never really threatened the survival of the independent Dutch state. Its true importance lay in diverting the Republic from foreign affairs: a crucial opportunity to enmesh the Habsburgs in central Europe was missed because Oldenbarnevelt was not there in 1618 to secure massive Dutch support for the revolt of Bohemia. Perhaps more important, although less dramatic, the Arminian controversy prevented the Republic from opposing and undermining the growth of an independent and resilient political community in the south Netherlands. If the Truce of 1609 marked the establishment of an independent northern state, the twelve years of peace which followed permitted the emergence of a separate southern one which made permanent the division of the Netherlands created by the campaigns of Parma, Maurice and Spinola.

The survival of the Spanish Netherlands

'As soon as I entered into the Archduke's country, which begins after Lillow [Lilloo], presently I beheld . . . a Province distressed with war. The people heartless; and rather repining against their Governors than revengeful against their enemies. The bravery of that gentry which was left, and the industry of the merchant, quite decayed. The husbandman labouring only to live, without desire to be rich to another's use. The towns (whatsoever concerned not the strength of them) ruinous. And, to conclude, the people here growing poor with less taxes, than they flourish with on the States' side.'[21]

Sir Thomas Overbury's depressing picture of the south Netherlands on the morrow of the Twelve Years' Truce was confirmed by others. There had been a massive emigration of capital and population from the south Netherlands in the period 1567–1609. Perhaps 100,000 people abandoned the southern provinces, many of them seeking refuge in the north. Beyond this there was the widespread destruction of people and property effected by the war, particularly during the 1580s (with the prince of Parma's advance through Flanders and Brabant) and the 1590s (while the bulk of the Spanish army was absent in France, leaving the 'obedient provinces' undefended). A considerable number of communities in the south appear to have lost between one half and one third of their population between 1570 and 1600 and several villages were abandoned altogether, some through the flooding of large areas during the siege of Antwerp, others through poverty and destruction. The income of the town of Ieper, which in 1574–7 was around 20,000 florins annually, had fallen to 386 florins in 1584–6 and even in 1607–8 was only 5,000. In southern Flanders it has been estimated that only 1 per cent of the farming population remained on their land throughout the crisis decade of the 1580s, while farther north, around Ghent, the area under cultivation fell by 92 per cent over the ten years. It was the same story in Brabant where farms were destroyed, crops burned and entire families of peasants murdered by the soldiers and freebooters. Wolves roamed everywhere in large packs. A plea of 1596 from the 'Brugse Vrij' – the area between Bruges and the Scheldt and once the richest agricultural land in the Netherlands – conveys a clear picture of the general devastation. The Vrij sought permission to pay 'contributions' (protection money) to the Dutch, in order to be spared further wanton destruction and allow the inhabitants 'to return to their accustomed occupations, after having been confined to walled towns, exhausted, and subjected to so many miseries, including the death of over two thirds of their number'.[22] No doubt a good number of the survivors had fled to Holland as well: Bruges's loss was Leiden's gain.

The proximity of heavy fighting also had an adverse effect on industrial production. Heavy capital equipment was wantonly destroyed by the troops of both sides. The clothworks of Hondschoote, by far the largest in the Netherlands, changed hands six times between 1578 and 1582, when they were burnt to the ground by French soldiers. The town's population fell from 18,000 in the 1560s to 385 in 1584. Cloth production fell from 90,000 pieces annually in the 1560s to 9,000 pieces in 1587–8 (see figure on p. 256). Other textile centres virtually ceased production during the 1580s; some of them never recovered. The Spanish army in the Low Countries was driven to buy its clothes in England, since the native textile producers could not supply the troops' needs. The burden of taxation, in addition to the contributions paid to the Dutch in return for a measure of 'protection', crippled economic recovery. The province of Namur, which had paid 3,000 florins a year in taxes at the beginning of the sixteenth century, was paying 7,000 florins a *month* at the end.

The author of all these misfortunes was the war. Up to 1609 the government of the south Netherlands needed to devote all its resources and all its attention to the military operations against the Dutch. Only after the signature of the Twelve Years' Truce in April 1609 was there time or money to spare for reconstruction. With peace, 'contributions' and mutinies came to an end; there was a drastic reduction in the armed forces, from 60,000 to 15,000 men; and taxes were reduced. The population of the south began to increase once more, at least in the towns, as the following table makes clear:[23]

Town	Decade	Total Baptisms	Decade	Total Baptisms	% Increase
Ghent	1606–15	11,185	1686–95	19,729	76
Mechelen	1596–1605	5,050	1676–85	9,176	82
Leuven	1586–95	2,785	1660–75	5,427	95
Lier	1586–95	1,761	1626–35	3,473	97

The population of Antwerp, over the same period, increased from some 42,000 in 1589 to around 57,000 in 1645. It is true that these were all communities which had suffered particularly severe devastation during the war and were therefore ripe for recovery, but the rate of increase – especially in the case of Lier (97 per cent in forty years) – is still spectacular.

Trade and industry also recovered. Antwerp merchants began to trade again with Italy and Spain and even with the Spanish and Portuguese overseas empires. Almost 600 south Netherlands merchants are known to have traded with the Iberian powers and their empires between 1598 and 1648. Silk, sugar and other 'colonial'

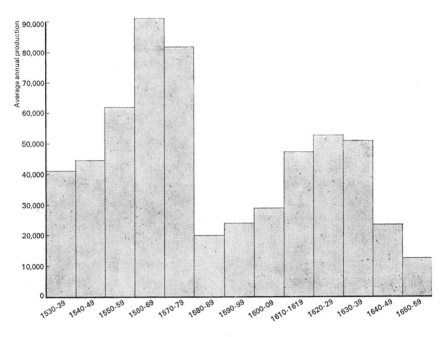

11. *Production of the serge cloth industry of Hondschoote, 1530–1659: number of serge cloths produced for export*

The dramatic rise in production up to the 1560s was followed by an equally dramatic fall during the 1580s: almost 83,000 pieces of cloth were exported in 1579, but only 9,475 in the year August 1587–August 1588. The total for 1584, when the clothworks were burned down, was doubtless lower still. The steady recovery of production under the archdukes is striking, reaching a peak of almost 61,000 cloths in 1630, but the war with France after 1635 dealt the 'new draperies' of Hondschoote a fatal blow.

Source: E. Coornaert, *Un centre industriel d'autrefois. La draperie-sayetterie d'Hondschoote* (*XIVe–XVIIIe siècles*) (Paris, 1930), 493–5.

goods flowed into Antwerp in considerable quantities after 1589, while the vast sums spent by the king of Spain on his army in the Netherlands, most of it sent from Castile, also brought prosperity to some bankers, sutlers and military contractors in the 'obedient provinces'. There was considerable industrial recovery too. Even Hondschoote produced almost as many broad-cloths in the 1620s as in the 1550s: almost 60,000 pieces were turned out in some years, most of them exported to Spain through Ostend and Dunkirk (see the figure above). Ghent too produced large quantities and many varieties of textiles in the first half of the seventeenth century: 29,000 linen cloths were brought to market in 1636, of which 20,000 were exported to Spain. In many towns new activities grew up to compensate for the demise of the old – silk, lace, tapestries, glass-making, jewellery, diamond cutting and printing – while in general there was a shift of emphasis from quantity to quality. The profits made from these enterprises are reflected to this day in the rich town houses of Antwerp, Ghent, Brussels, Bergues and elsewhere constructed between 1600 and 1670. One eighth of Ghent – 1,260 houses – was rebuilt or refaced in stone during this period. In the countryside too there was recovery (possibly aided by the enforced 'fallow' of the 1590s). The improvements in farming methods became legendary and an English observer, Sir Richard Weston, wrote that in 1644–5, between Dunkirk and Bruges 'I saw as rich a countrie as ever my eies beheld, stokt with goodly wheat and barlie, and excellent meadow and pasture.'[24]

When hostilities recommenced in 1621, the degree of devastation was not the same. The 'protection system' was immediately reintroduced: communities paid a regular sum to the enemy in return for immunity from attack, and their evident security soon encouraged an influx of peasants from neighbouring 'unprotected' communities. By 1640 a senior officer in the Spanish army complained: 'The majority of our villages in the "contribution land" [north Flanders and north Brabant] are harbouring enemy soldiers sent to protect them . . . This means that our scouting parties cannot go to collect information in these villages, because the "protection men" arrest them as spies.'[25] The letter went on to comment on the prosperity of these 'protected villages', thanks to their 'aid and assistance' to the enemy. The stabilization of the military frontier along the Maas after 1621 meant that only a limited area of the south Netherlands was a prey to the Dutch; the frontier of France had always been better protected, and French raiding was not a serious threat until the 1640s.

Yet neither the degree nor the duration of the recovery must be exaggerated. The war continued to take its toll. Considerable areas of the archdukes' possessions in 1609 were lost over the succeeding fifty years: parts of north Flanders, the area around Maastricht and, most important, the stronghold of 's Hertogenbosch with almost 200 villages in its vicinity, were lost to the Dutch; most of Artois, parts of Hainaut and parts of Luxemburg were lost to the French. From the provinces which remained, taxes were required in ever-increasing quantities to finance the war – about four million florins a year between 1600 and 1640 – diverting capital from productive investment and impoverishing the taxpayers. The 70,000 and more troops who regularly fought for Spain in the south Netherlands, mainly foreigners, were expensive in other ways, too: quite apart from the malicious damage they so often committed, the soldiers all had to be fed and lodged in billets at the Netherlanders' expense. Finally, some devastation by enemy forces was inescapable. In Luxemburg Condé's invasion of 1636 'caused people to die miserably in their hundreds and thousands through famine, plague and illness; not one person in ten was left alive'.[26] The areas near to the theatre of military operations therefore recovered very slowly, and some industries, such as the cloth works at Diksmuide, Eecke, Menen, Poperinghe and other lesser centres never fully recovered from the destruction of the 1580s. Farther south, the city of Mons, which had weathered the storms of the later sixteenth century with relatively little loss, began to decline fairly rapidly after 1600. Its population in 1593 was 17,239, but it had fallen to 13,944 by 1625, some of the people seeking greater security and prosperity in Amiens and other towns across the border in France. For Mons and the other large towns along the southern border, the war which broke out between Spain and France in 1635 brought widespread devastation and industrial collapse.

Economics, however, does not explain everything. The areas conquered by the Dutch after 1621 remain to this day solidly Catholic enclaves within a predominantly Calvinist state; the areas annexed by France after 1640 retained for a long period a distinctive 'nationality' – a loyalty to Burgundy and the south Netherlands. The 50,000 inhabitants of Lille, for example, who were taken over by Louis XIV in 1667, remained reluctant Frenchmen until at least 1700, drinking the king of Spain's health, celebrating the births and marriages of the House of Habsburg, aiding French garrison soldiers to desert to join the Spanish forces. This new 'south Netherlands identity', religious and political, was born under the archdukes and above all during the Truce.

The Catholic Church had not been exempt from the ravages of the Dutch. On the contrary, clerical property had been the prime target and many areas were left for many years with virtually no religious provision at all. In 1590 in north Brabant the deanery of Herenthals had only thirty resident priests in place of 150 and the deanery of Breda (overrun by the Dutch later the same year) had only forty priests when the full establishment stood at 200. As late as 1610 the twenty-two parishes of the rural deanery of Tielt in Flanders had only thirteen priests. The few clerics in residence were very much on their own. No bishop visited some parishes to hold, for example, confirmation services for twenty, thirty or even forty years. Without supervision the standards, both moral and intellectual, of the clergy were not high and this unfavourable situation did not change overnight.

The improvements in clerical standards registered during the 1560s and 1570s, at least in the south, were all lost during the years of war which followed. In 1630 the deanery of Tielt still only had twenty-one pastors for its twenty-two parishes (with almost 11,000 communicants), of whom only two or three bothered to give sermons on holy days. Instead the traditional temptations of alcohol (in five cases) and sex (two or three cases) kept the clergy otherwise occupied. In 1625 the archbishop of Cambrai informed the Vatican that he had deprived 100 priests of their livings for sundry irregularities – equivalent to almost one sixth of the total diocesan clergy. Only gradually were the priests persuaded to heed the advice of their bishops who encouraged them to sublimate their worldlier desires in the building up of libraries and the cultivation of large gardens (for flowers, vegetables and fruit) in their leisure time. The improvement in standards came from above, not below, in the south Netherlands. A permanent papal nuncio was in residence from 1596 onwards and he and other papal visitors made efforts to improve episcopal standards, while the bishops in turn organized seminaries, discussion groups (*capitulae pastorum*) and visitations for their clergy, New churches were constructed; old ones were restored. The regular clergy likewise improved: the Jesuits increased from seventeen convents in 1598 to forty-six by 1640 (when they were teaching some 32,000 children in the *provincia Flandro–Belgica*); the Capuchins increased from twelve houses in 1595 to forty-two in 1626. Both Orders played a major part in running the seminaries established in each diocese to train priests and this played an important part in providing a more educated and more respectable class of priest. Equally important, the material conditions of the clergy were significantly improved: between 1632 and 1682, at least in Flanders, the average income of the pastors increased by around 40 per cent, to about six times the wage of agricultural workers, while prices remained about the same. A better class of ordinand became evident from the 1640s onwards.

By that time, the struggle against Protestantism had been won. An edict of the archdukes issued on 31 December 1609 ordered the expulsion of all non-Catholics, and over the years the covert Protestant minorities that remained dwindled into insignificance in most places. There were exceptions – especially near the Dutch border, where the Republic prevented any priests from residing in some twelve Catholic villages north of Antwerp – but on the whole the problem of the Catholic clergy in the seventeenth century was, as in Protestant areas, to combat the superstition, indifference and ignorance of their parishioners, not to ward off the seducers from another faith.

Nevertheless the Catholic clerical élite expended a great deal of missionary zeal, and some of their best men, in the 'Hollandse Zending', an attempt by about 200 'missionaries' to supply the Catholics of the north with priests, services and religious literature. Presses all over the south Netherlands printed pamphlets and history books, as well as Bibles and devotional manuals, to set out what a good Catholic should believe in politics as well as in religion. The Revolt was portrayed as the work of a few wicked men, the disasters of the war were seen merely as God's punishment on the Netherlands for their former opulence and luxury. Every deed of the Protestants was calumnied and ridiculed. At first only Netherlands affairs were covered, but after 1609 events elsewhere came in for scrutiny: the revolt of Bohemia in 1618–20, the war with England in 1624–30 and so on. Gradually a consistent attitude emerged, a sort of 'collective identity' which was distinct and able to resist the inroads, intellectual as well as military, of both the Dutch (especially during the crisis of 1632) and the French.

This embryonic 'national identity' was an impressive monument to the government of the archdukes, and it survived almost forty years of gruelling warfare (1621–59) and the invasions of Louis XIV until, in 1700, the Spanish Habsburgs died out. This endurance was undoubtedly in part the work of Albert and Isabella; but it was also the fruit of Spain's determination to defend the Catholic Netherlands, whatever the cost.

The cession of the 'obedient provinces' to the archdukes in 1598 was never intended to be permanent: Philip II had good reason for believing that his daughter, Isabella, could bear no children and, if she died childless, the Netherlands were to revert to Spain. If there should be a child, it was to marry back into the royal family. Philip II always intended Spain and the Low Countries to remain united. It was for this reason that Philip III followed his father's example and poured Spanish men and money into the Low Countries' struggle from 1598 until 1607. Only bankruptcy and the demoralization of his generals induced him to make a truce with the rebels after that. Spain had no intention of abandoning the Netherlands.

The Truce of Antwerp, however, initiated a decade of reverses, defeats and humiliations for Spanish power abroad which inevitably weakened her position in the Low Countries. There had been some at Philip III's Court who predicted that a compromise with the Dutch would lead to trouble in Spanish Italy and elsewhere. They argued that if Spain failed to stand up for her rights in Brussels she would prove unable to stand up for them in Milan, Naples and Vienna.[27] Subsequent events lent some support to this point of view. The Dutch got the better of the scramble for Cleve-Jülich in 1611 (although Spain won back some of her losses in 1614); Spain twice failed to defeat the duke of Savoy (1614–15 and 1616–17); the Spanish and Portuguese navies proved hopelessly inadequate to contain Dutch colonial expansion in the East and West Indies. The same period saw equally serious reverses for Habsburg power in eastern Europe: first Hungary (1604–6) and then Bohemia (1609 and 1611) rebelled successfully against the authority of the Emperor Rudolf II (Philip III's uncle). In 1615–17 there was a degrading struggle between Archduke Ferdinand of Styria (later to be Holy Roman Emperor) and Venice, which rapidly escalated until almost all Spain's enemies were involved: 4,000 Dutch troops arrived in Venice and fought against the archduke, and it was rumoured that more would be sent to Savoy if the duke declared war against Spain.

This succession of disasters alarmed Spain's leaders. Particularly disturbing was the tendency for their enemies in one area to offer assistance to other enemies elsewhere. Late in 1616 the Council of

War in Madrid therefore decided that, if the Dutch actually sent military support to Savoy, it would justify reopening hostilities in the Netherlands: if the Dutch army could be tied down at home, the Council argued, it could not interfere in areas like Italy which were closer and more important to Spain. As it happened, French mediation settled these disputes in the course of 1617–18 (Treaties of Madrid, 9 October 1617, and Wiener Neustadt, 1 February 1618), but almost at once a new crisis broke out: in May 1618 Bohemia defied the authority of the emperor for the third time, claiming that the concessions won in 1609 and 1611 were not being observed. At once the Bohemian rebels approached the Dutch States-General and the Protestant princes of Germany for support: the former sent money and later some troops; the head of the Union of German Protestants, Frederick Elector Palatine, agreed to become the rebels' leader and in August 1619 he was formally elected king by the estates of Bohemia.

The third Bohemian revolt was the most severe challenge to Habsburg power to date: apart from the fact that the family had ruled the kingdom since 1526 and that the Archduke Ferdinand had been recognized as king-designate in October 1617, Bohemia held the crucial seventh vote in the elections which chose the Holy Roman Emperor. If the Habsburgs lost Bohemia they would also lose the empire. The Archduke Ferdinand who became emperor in August 1619, just before his 'deposition' by the Bohemians, manifestly lacked the resources to cope with a major revolt backed by hostile foreign powers, but he could count on support from at least two quarters. The league of German Catholic States, formed in 1609 to counter the Protestant Union made the previous year, was opposed to a Protestant (the Elector Palatine) gaining control of Bohemia and (perhaps) of the empire too. Spain, also, was alarmed at the prospect of a Protestant emperor who, as suzerain of Lombardy and the Netherlands, could soon challenge Spanish control there. In July 1618 therefore Philip III authorized the dispatch of 750,000 florins to Vienna to pay for mobilization against the rebels. More money followed, and the papacy also provided subsidies. Then in the course of 1619 troops were sent from Spanish Italy and the Spanish Netherlands to the emperor until Philip III had some 10,000 men on the frontiers of Bohemia. It was agreed that in 1620 the forces of the Catholic League would invade the Upper Palatinate, sandwiched between Bavaria and Bohemia, while an army from the

Low Countries would overrun the Lower Palatinate on the Rhine, and the emperor would conquer Bohemia. Each of the victors would be left with what they managed to capture.

The Habsburgs' opponents could not match this display of strength. Although the Dutch sent about 5,000 men and promised one million florins to Bohemia in 1619–20 and a further 500,000 to the Protestant Union, it was too little and too late. The crisis of authority between Maurice and Oldenbarnevelt distracted Dutch politicians for a crucial period. The largest German Protestant states, Saxony and Brandenburg, kept neutral; so did the king of England. Unharassed by outside interference, the Habsburg campaign of 1620 was a total success: Spinola and his troops captured the Rhine Palatinate (the operation went so smoothly, wrote one Spanish officer, that it was like a country ride near Toledo); the Bavarians overran the Upper Palatinate; and the joint Spanish–Imperial army smashed the forces of the Bohemians and their allies at the Battle of the White Mountain, outside Prague, on 8 November 1620.

Spain's international position had suddenly improved. The allies of the Dutch had been defeated and Spanish arms had scored two notable victories. In addition Spanish troops from Milan had taken advantage of the disturbed situation to occupy the Valtelline, the valuable military corridor which connected Lombardy with Austria and blocked communications between Venice and France. France was in no position to object because in 1619 there was a rebellion by a group of disaffected Court nobles, followed in 1620 by a new Huguenot revolt.

Such a favourable conjuncture naturally influenced Spain's views on the appropriate policy to be followed in the Netherlands when the Truce expired in April 1621. The question had been debated both in Brussels and Madrid since 1618, and opinion appears to have been unanimous, in Spain at least, that the Truce should not be renewed on the same terms: clause 4 of the Truce of Antwerp, which permitted war to continue outside European waters, had proved particularly damaging to the overseas dominions of Spain and Portugal and it was generally agreed that no further accommodation with the Dutch could be considered which failed to curtail Dutch activity in America and Asia. There was less unanimity about the alternatives; the archdukes in Brussels were invincibly opposed to renewing the war in the Netherlands as long as a large part of their forces were tied down in Bohemia and the Palatinate. The Council of Finance in Spain was hostile to any move, such as a declaration of war, which might involve the expenditure of more money. But the Council and the archdukes were overruled. Philip III made up his mind to allow the truce to run out unless the Dutch agreed to make concessions on the Indies question. On 29 March 1621, two days before his death, the ailing king ordered that from 9 April, when the Truce expired, the Dutch were to be treated 'in the form and manner that obtained before the Truce'.

This did not mean, however, that Spain had embarked upon another attempt to end the Dutch Revolt by force. In April 1619 Philip III's chief policy adviser, Don Balthasar de Zúñiga, made Spain's position clear in an internal memorandum: 'We cannot, by force of arms, reduce those provinces to their former obedience . . . To promise ourselves that we can conquer the Dutch is to seek the impossible, to delude ourselves.'[28] Zúñiga, who retained control of Spanish foreign and defence policy until his death in October 1622, remained convinced that reconquest was out of the question, but he felt that nothing would be lost by a little brinkmanship. By allowing time to run out, and perhaps even mounting one brisk campaign to remind the Dutch that Spinola was still undefeated, he believed that the terms agreed in 1609 might be improved. But Zúñiga misread the signs of the times. He mistakenly believed that the divisions in the Republic would make the Dutch more favourably disposed towards peace, whereas in fact the triumph of Maurice and the Gomarists gave the upper hand to the war-party. As early as August 1619 the States-General began to make plans for a direct attack on Peru in case Spain should decide not to renew the Truce. Zúñiga was also totally misled about the attitude of France to the renewal of the Truce. All through 1620 and 1621 French agents made every effort to appear pro-Spanish, promising to put pressure on the Dutch to make further concessions in the interests of peace. In fact they did nothing of the sort; they merely deluded Spain into increasing her demands for a new settlement, which the Dutch angrily rejected. Although negotiations continued throughout 1621, and beyond, the French had achieved their objective of ensuring a renewal of war in the Low Countries which would prevent Spain from intervening in the new civil war in France.[29]

At no time, however, did Zúñiga and his successor (and nephew) the count-duke of Olivares imagine that the war with the Dutch was likely to bring about the collapse or conquest of the Republic. Even following the capture of Breda and the recovery of Brazil in 1625, which seemed to some to presage general Dutch prostration, Spain made it clear that her aim was not to force the unconditional surrender of her adversary, but merely to improve the relations (especially the overseas economic relations) between the two powers, and to secure better terms for the south Netherlands. The debates of the Spanish Council of State in September 1628, concerning the need to make peace with the Dutch, are revealing. Even though Spain was winning the war (Piet Heyn's capture of the silver fleet was not yet known in Europe; the Dutch capture of 's Hertogenbosch in Brabant and Pernambuco in Brazil still lay in the future), Philip IV's ministers all favoured negotiations on the basis of equality between sovereign powers. Ambrogio Spinola, who had defeated the Dutch for over twenty years, counselled peace-talks because 'the experience of sixty years of war with the Dutch has shown how impossible it is to conquer those provinces by force'. Spain could continue fighting for years, he pointed out, taking one or two cities each campaigning season, but this would 'only serve to further our prestige [*reputación*], not to finish the war'. Spinola was supported by all the five veterans of the Flanders war who belonged to the Council. One of them, Don Fernando Girón, was particularly strong in his support for Spinola's pessimism: 'The experience of sixty years' fighting [he told the Council] has shown that the Low Countries' Wars have been and will continue to be the longest, the most expensive, the most bloody and most interminable of any war in History.' He counselled a new settlement. The marquis of Montesclaros pointed out that the Dutch behaved like a world power, making alliances and treaties, discovering new lands and founding overseas colonies. It was ridiculous to pretend that they were mere rebels. Even Philip IV's chief minister, the count-duke of Olivares, agreed: for him it was simply a matter of getting the best terms for Spain and the south Netherlands in the inevitable negotiated settlement; it was a question of 'reducing the Dutch to friendship with us', not of reducing the Dutch to subservience.[30] The final settlement of the Low Countries' Wars, in January 1648, merely formalized these attitudes. The peace of Münster expressly recognized the sovereign authority of the Dutch over all the lands they held in the Low Countries (almost exactly the same as the present kingdom of the Netherlands) and overseas (mostly gained from the Portuguese). A Spanish official ambassador was sent to The Hague as a symbol of Philip IV's recognition of Dutch independence. The Dutch also retained their blockade of the Scheldt. The only gain made by Spain was an undertaking that the Dutch would keep out of Spanish America and cease hostilities against Spanish shipping in American waters.

The peace of Münster thus put an end to the war between Spain and the Dutch, a war which had come to be seen, even in Madrid, as little different from Spain's wars against other foreign powers. For the Spanish Habsburgs, as for the rest of Europe, the Revolt of the Netherlands had come to an end in 1609.

Postscript: the Netherlands divided

'By God, I think the Devil shits Dutchmen,' wrote a harassed Samuel
Pepys in 1667, as the navy of the United Provinces sailed up the
Medway and burned a considerable part of the British fleet at anchor.[1]
The seventeenth century is full of Dutchmen, trading, draining lakes,
colonizing new lands, planting gardens, establishing new towns . . .
and making war – with Sweden, France, Portugal and England as
well as with the 'arch-enemy', Spain.

The seventeenth century was, as Professor Charles Wilson has
pointed out, profoundly 'anti-Dutch' and yet the political hostility
of much of Europe, which led the Republic into war so often, was
almost always tinged with envy or admiration. 'The United Provinces
are the envy of some, the fear of others and the wonder of all their
neighbours,' wrote Sir William Temple in his famous *Observations*
of 1673.[2] Even the most seasoned world travellers paused in Holland,
their hardened sensitivity touched by the achievement of the Dutch
in turning their inhospitable land into a civilized paradise. Peter

Mundy, who visited most parts of the known world in the 1630s and 1640s, apologized to his readers for devoting so much space to a description of the Netherlands. 'I have bin the longer aboutt the discription of this place', he explained, 'because there are soe many particularities wherein it differs (and in som excells) other parts, allsoe beeing myselff somewhatt affectionated and enclined to the manner of the countrie.' Mundy, like others before and after him, was captivated by the ingenuity of the Dutch, with their houses built on piles forty feet deep, their sawmills, their street-lighting, their land-reclamation schemes and their clockwork devices. 'They are as ingenious both for al manuary arts, and also for the ingenuous disciplines, as any people whatsoever in all Christendom,' wrote a captivated Thomas Coryat in 1611. He was particularly impressed by the things which we now take for granted, like paved streets: at Gorinchem he marvelled at the streets 'very delicately paved with bricke, which is composed after that artificiall manner that a man may walke there presently after an exceeding shower of raine, and never wet his shoes'. Later visitors were entertained by special houses like the Mennisten Bruyloft (the Anabaptists' wedding) in Amsterdam which were full of machines and toys powered by water or clockwork.[3] The Dutch in the seventeenth century had an unmistakable cultured polish, reflected in the cleanliness of their streets and houses, in their artistic appreciation ('many tymes blacksmithes, coblers, etc., will have some picture or other by their Forge and in their stalle') and in the 'little gardens' and 'flower potts' everywhere. This well-organized society was epitomized by its transport-system: regular and cheap canal-boats ran once an hour between Delft and Haarlem, once every half-hour between Delft and The Hague, and so on, many of them provided with special song books so that the travellers could spend the journey agreeably; fast stage coaches also maintained a regular service between inland towns, running on the Republic's well-paved roads.

It was not merely the 'sights' which impressed visitors in the seventeenth century as they had impressed Philip II and his entourage nearly a hundred years before. There was also the tolerant attitude of the Dutch towards others. The Dutch practice of trading openly with Spain in wartime, even allowing money for the army of Flanders (the very troops who were trying to attack them!) to be sent from

Spain through the banks of Amsterdam, baffled almost everyone. Likewise Dutch toleration of Jews and atheists impressed most foreigners, whether hostile like Andrew Marvell:

'Hence Amsterdam – Turk, Christian, Pagan, Jew,
Staple of Sects and Mint of Schism grew'

or well disposed like the Leveller leader, William Walwyn:

'It is more than evident by the prosperity of our neighbours in Holland, that the severall wayes of our brethren in matters of Religion hinder not, but that they may live peaceably one amongst an other, and the Spaniard will witnesse for them that they unite sufficiently in the defence of their common liberties and opposition of their common enemies . . .'[4]

A persecuted Leveller like Walwyn might also cast an envious eye on the freedom of political expression which prevailed in the Dutch Republic. There was virtually no censorship and most controversial issues were debated publicly and discussed in pamphlets. Some 20,000 political pamphlets published in the north Netherlands between 1560 and 1795 have survived, dealing with almost every conceivable topic. Current affairs were also reported almost as they happened in the weekly newspapers, or *corantos*, which began to appear regularly from the 1620s (two rival papers were published in Amsterdam every Saturday from 1624). They carried home and overseas news, some of it sent in by special reporters like the first ever 'war correspondent' who followed the Dutch army on campaign (the *'courantier in 't Legher van sijn princelijke Excellentie'*). For those who could not read, news could be gathered from the political ballads, or Sea Beggar songs, which were popular at the time. A collection of Dutch songs made in about 1700 (the *Oude en nieuwe Hollandsche boerenlietjes en contradansen*) contained 996 different melodies from the sixteenth and seventeenth centuries; many of them were used for political ballads like *'Merckt toch hoe sterck'* ('See how strong the siege', composed over the winter of 1622–3 in honour of Spinola's unsuccessful siege of Bergen-op-Zoom the same year) or Piet Heyn's song of triumph (composed in 1629 in honour of the man who captured an entire Spanish treasure fleet) which is still sung today by supporters of victorious Dutch football teams! Most ballads, being intended for popular consumption, were coarse and vulgar – the Spaniards were habitually referred to as *maraens* (*marranos* or pigs) and *spekken* (bits of bacon), origin of the present Americanism 'spik' – but their appeal was considerable. Freedom to say or to sing what one liked was a distinctive feature of life in the Dutch Republic. As a French ambassador, Buzenval, once observed, the Dutch were 'a people who believe that freedom of speech is a part of liberty'.

To most people in the seventeenth century therefore the Dutch appeared:

'In some sorte Gods, for they set bounds to the Sea: and when they list let it pass them. Even their dwelling is a miracle. They live lower than the fishes. In the very lap of the floods, and incircled in their watry Arms. They are the *Israelites* passing through the Red Sea . . . They have struggled long with *Spains Pharaoh*, and they have at length inforced him to let them go . . . They are the wane of that Empire, which increas d in *Isabella* and in *Charles* the 5th was at full.'[5]

Genealogical Table I — WEST NETHERLANDS FAMILIES

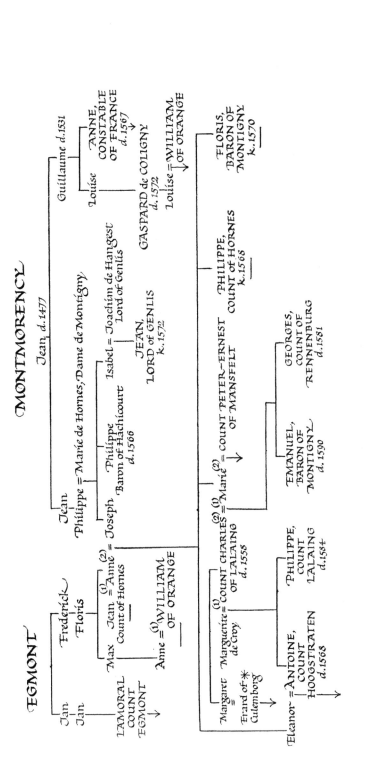

EGMONT

Jan
Jan

Frederick
Floris

Max = Anne (1) (2) Jean, Count of Hornes

Anne = (1) WILLIAM OF ORANGE

LAMORAL, COUNT EGMONT

Margaret = (1) COUNT CHARLES (2) (1) Marie (2) = COUNT PETER-ERNEST OF MANSFELT
OF LALAING d.1558

Margaret = Erard of Culemborg

Eleanor = ANTOINE, COUNT HOOGSTRATEN d.1568

PHILIPPE, COUNT LALAING d.1584

EMANUEL, BARON OF MONTIGNY d.1590

GEORGES, COUNT OF RENNENBURG d.1581

PHILIPPE, COUNT OF HORNES k.1568

MONTMORENCY

Jean, d.1477

Jean
Philippe = Marie de Hornes, Dame de Montigny

Philippe = Joseph

Philippe, Baron of Hachicourt d.1566

Isabel = Joachim de Hangest, Lord of Genlis

JEAN, LORD OF GENLIS k.1572

Guillaume d.1531

Louise

ANNE, CONSTABLE OF FRANCE d.1567

Louise = WILLIAM OF ORANGE

GASPARD de COLIGNY d.1572

FLORIS, BARON OF MONTIGNY k.1570

* See Table II

Genealogical Table II—EAST NETHERLANDS FAMILIES

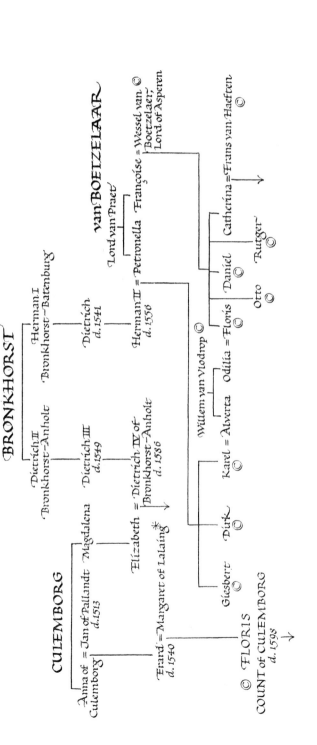

* See Table I.

◎ Signed the 'Compromise of the Nobility' in 1565–6.

Genealogical Table III — ORANGE-NASSAU

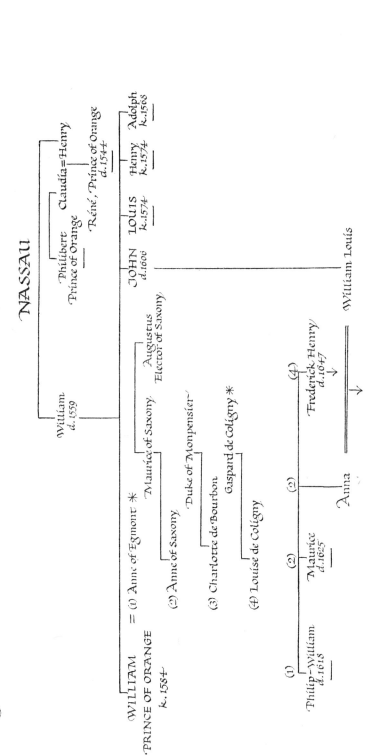

NASSAU

William
d. 1559

Philibert
Prince of Orange

Claudia = Henry

René, Prince of Orange
d. 1544

JOHN
d. 1606

LOUIS
k. 1574

Henry
k. 1574

Adolph
k. 1568

WILLIAM
PRINCE OF ORANGE
k. 1584

= (1) Anne of Egmont *

(2) Anne of Saxony
— Maurice of Saxony

(3) Charlotte de Bourbon
— Duke of Monpensier

(4) Louise de Coligny
— Gaspard de Coligny *

Augustus
Elector of Saxony

Anne of Saxony

William Louis

(1)
Philip-William
d. 1618

(2)
Maurice
d. 1625

(2)
Anna

(4)
Frederick-Henry
d. 1647

* See Table I

Bibliography and notes

ABBREVIATIONS USED IN BIBLIOGRAPHY AND NOTES

AA	Archivo de la Casa de los duques de Alba, Madrid
A.D.E.	*Archivo Documental Español*, vols. I–IX, XIV and XVI, publishing the correspondence of the Spanish ambassadors in France, 1560–68
AGRB *Audience*	Archives Générales du Royaume, Brussels (Algemeen Rijksarchief, Brussel), *Papiers d'État et d'Audience (Papieren van Staat en Audientië)*
AGRB *SEG*	ibid., *Secrétairerie d'État et de Guerre (Sekretarie van Staat en Oorlog)*
AD *Nord B*	Archives départementales du Nord, Lille, *série B.*
AGS *CJH*	Archivo General de Simancas, (Valladolid), *Consejos y Juntas de Hacienda*
AGS *CMC 2a*	ibid., *Contaduría Mayor de Cuentas, 2a época*
AGS *Estado*	ibid., *Papeles de la secretaría de estado*
AGS *GA*	ibid., *Guerra Antigua*
AHN *Estado*	Archivo Histórico Nacional, Madrid, *sección de Estado*
ARA	Algemeen Rijksarchief, The Hague
AS	Archivio di Stato
ASEB	*Annales de la Société d'Émulation de Bruges*
ASV	Archivio di Stato del Vaticano, Rome

BCRH	*Bulletin de la Commission royale d'Histoire* (Brussels)
BM *Addl*	British Library (formerly British Museum Library), department of manuscripts, Additional Manuscripts
BMB	Bibliothèque municipale, Besançon (manuscripts from the *Collection de Granvelle*)
BMHG	*Bijdragen en Mededelingen van het Historisch Genootschap* (Utrecht)
BMGN	*Bijdragen en Mededelingen betreffende de Geschiedenis der Nederlanden* (Leuven)
BNM MS	Biblioteca Nacional de Madrid, sección de manuscritos
BNP MS	Bibliothèque Nationale de Paris, section des manuscrits
BPM MS	Biblioteca del Palacio Real, Palacio de Oriente, Madrid, manuscritos
BSHPF	*Bulletin de la Société d'Histoire du protestantisme français* (Paris)
BtG	*Bijdragen tot de Geschiedenis en inzonderheid in het oud hertogdom Brabant* (Antwerp)
BVGO	*Bijdragen voor Vaderlandsche Geschiedenis en Oudheidkunde*
Co.Do.In.	*Colección de Documentos Inéditos para la historia de España* (112 vols., Madrid)
EHR	*English Historical Review* (London)
Epistolario	Duque de Alba, *Epistolario del III duque de Alba, Don Fernando Alvarez de Toledo* (3 vols., Madrid, 1952)
ESR	*European Studies Review* (London)
HHStA	Oesterreichisches HauptStaatarchiv: Haus- Hof- und Staatsarchiv, Vienna (with *repertorium* and *abteilung*)
HMC	*Historical Manuscript Commission Reports*
HMGOG	*Handelingen der Maatschappij voor Geschiedenis en Oudheidkunde te Gent* (Ghent)
IVdeDJ	Instituto de Valencia de Don Juan, Madrid, manuscript collection (with *envio* and folio)
Nueva Co.Do.In.	*Nueva Colección de Documentos Inéditos para la historia de España* (6 vols., Madrid)
NAK	*Nederlands Archief voor Kerkgeschiedenis*
RA	Rijksarchief (in a province of the Netherlands)
RBPH	*Revue belge de Philologie et d'Histoire*
TvG	*Tijdschrift voor Geschiedenis* (Groningen)
UB	Universiteits bibliotheek
van der Essen, *Cahier*,	reference to one of the notebooks made by Professor Léon van der Essen in the Farnese archives of Naples. The notebooks are in private hands.

GENERAL SOURCES

'The rise of the Dutch Republic must ever be regarded as one of the leading events of modern times. Without the birth of this great commonwealth, the various historical phenomena of the sixteenth and following centuries must have either not existed, or have presented themselves under essential modifications.'

The opening lines of John Lothrop Motley's *Rise of the Dutch Republic*, written over a century ago, pay elegant tribute to the central importance of the Dutch Revolt in human history. It is this importance above all else which explains why the literature on the subject is so enormous. Even while the struggle with Spain was in full swing, contemporaries recognized that the Netherlands were the hinge of Europe and that the outcome of the struggle would decide the direction in which the history of the continent would develop. Many men therefore tried to explain how the situation had come about and, in some cases (such as the *De leone belgico* published by Michael von Aitzing in 1583), tried to predict how it would end. Thirty-four contemporary histories of the Revolt, all written before 1648, are listed in the admirable guide to the historical literature of the North Netherlands: H. de Buck, *Bibliografie der Geschiedenis van Nederland* nos. 2268–301 (Leiden, 1968). The complete list of books and articles covering the period of the 'Eighty Years' War' runs to over 300 titles (nos. 2260–594, covering pp. 181–205). And de Buck only includes the items published up to 1968 and concerning the north Netherlands. Publications dealing with the south are listed in H. Pirenne, *Bibliographie de l'histoire de la Belgique* (3rd edn, Brussels, 1931), while more recent items are listed in the bibliographical sections of the journals *Revue du Nord* (annually from 1947) and *Revue belge de philologie et d'histoire* (annually from 1952). The latter has now expanded into the excellent and indispensable *Bulletin critique d'histoire de Belgique et du Grand-Duché de Luxembourg* (published by the Seminaris voor Geschiedenis of the University of Ghent, 5 vols. to date, covering publications 1966–73). Recent publications on the history of the Netherlands are catalogued and discussed briefly each year in *Tijdschrift voor Geschiedenis* and, for English readers, there is the 'Survey of recent historical works on Belgium and the Netherlands', prepared by the Anglo–Dutch seminar of the Institute of Historical Research, London, which appears in each issue of the *Acta Historiae Neerlandicae*.

But, in spite of all the literature, a great deal of the crucial evidence concerning the revolt of the Netherlands remains in manuscripts, much of it little used and some of it hitherto unseen. The archives of most countries of western Europe have considerable materials which shed light on the Dutch 'war of independence', starting of course with the public archives of the Netherlands themselves. Those of the north are described in the recent survey of L. P. L. Pirenne *et al.*, *De rijksarchieven in Nederland*, 2 vols. (The Hague, 1973) and W. J. Formsma, *Gids voor de Nederlandse archieven* (Bussem, 1967). There is a list of collections and inventories in W. J. Formsma and B. van 't Hoff, *Repertorium van inventaristen van Nederlandse archieven* (2nd edn, Groningen, 1965). There is a similar guide for Belgium: J. Nicodème, *Répertoire des inventaires des archives conservées en Belgique, parus avant le 1er janvier 1969* (Brussels, 1970). However, many of the papers of the Brussels government are now in the Haus- Hof- und Staatsarchiv in Vienna, section 'Belgien' (see L. Bittner, *Gesamtinventar des Wiener Haus- Hof- und Staatsarchiv*, IV, Vienna, 1940), and in the Archivo General de Simancas (see M. van Durme, *Les archives de Simancas et l'histoire de la Belgique* (Brussels, 1964 onwards, four vols. to date). For the present location and the nature of the archives of the Spanish organs of government, see G. Parker, *Guide to the Archives of the Spanish institutions in or concerned with the Netherlands (1556–1706)* (Brussels, 1971). The collections of documents in all languages concerning Netherlands history scattered in other European countries are described in P. J. Blok, *Verslag aangaande een onderzoek in Duitschland naar archivalia belangrijk voor de geschiedenis van Nederland* (The Hague, 1888); ibid., *Verslag . . . Duitschland en Oostenrijk* (The Hague, 1889); ibid., *Verslag . . . Engeland* (The Hague, 1891), ibid., *Verslag . . . Parijs* (The Hague, 1897); and G. Brom, *Archivalia in Italië belangrijk voor de geschiedenis van de Nederlanden*, 3 vols. (The Hague, 1908–14).

The systematic exploitation of these archives began in the middle of the nineteenth century as, one after another, they were thrown open to scholars. The publications of sources which followed tended at first to concentrate around the leading figures of the revolt: the correspondence of Granvelle (published by Weiss, Poullet and Piot), of Margaret of Parma (published by Gachard, Theissen, and Enno van Gelder), of William of Orange (by Groen van Prinsterer and Gachard), of Leicester (by Bruce, Blok and Brugmans), of the duke of Alva (by the late duke of Berwick y Alba), of Don Luis de Requesens (in the *Colección* and the *Nueva colección de documentos inéditos para la historia de España*). Later there were publications concerning foreign policy (such as Kervijn de Lettenhove, *Relations politiques des Pays-Bas et de l'Angleterre*, 11 vols.), concerning the link with Spain (with the *Correspondance de Philippe II sur les affaires des Pays-Bas* of Gachard and Lefèvre, 9 vols., and the *Correspondance de la Cour d'Espagne sur les affaires des Pays-Bas au 17e siècle* of Lonchay, Cuvelier and Lefèvre, 6 vols.), and concerning the work of the States-General (the *Resolutiën der Staten Generaal van 1576 tot 1609* edited by Japikse and Rijperman). Diaries, chronicles, price series and parish account books have been edited and printed by learned societies or by the historical manuscript commissions of Belgium, Britain and the Netherlands. There is so much in print that it is almost impossible for a single scholar to digest it all – and yet the effort must be made, for recent research has given a new significance to work previously neglected after publication and the printed material must be read and re-read before its full value is appreciated.

Nor do manuscripts and printed manuscripts exhaust the sources which exist for the Dutch Revolt and the Netherlands in early modern times. There are the thousands of pamphlets published at the time (a selection of which, together with certain key documents, has been published in English translation: E. H. Kossmann and A. F. Mellink, *Texts concerning the revolt of the Netherlands* (Cambridge, 1975). There are the medals struck to commemorate the leading events of the struggle (see H. van Loon, *Histoire métallique des XVII provinces* (The Hague, 1720–40); H. Enno van Gelder and J. van Kuyk, *De penningen en de Munten van de Tachtigjarigen Oorlog* (The Hague, 1948); and H. Enno van Gelder, *De Nederlandse noodmunten van de Tachtigjarige Oorlog* (The Hague, 1955). There are also the 'Sea Beggar Songs' which were written to celebrate the chief event of the war (see F. van Duyse, *Het oude Nederlandsche Lied. Wereldlijke en Geestelijke liederen uit vroegeren tijd. Teksten en Melodieën*, II (Antwerp, 1905, pp. 1578 onwards). The art of the period, one of the great ages of Dutch painting, is best approached through the vast but fascinating study of R. H. Wilenski, *Flemish Painters*, 2 vols. (London, 1960). Finally, there is a good atlas of the period which shows the precise terrain on which the Revolt took place: S. J. Fockema Andreae and B. van 't Hoff, eds., *Christiaan Sgroten's kaarten van de Nederlanden*, 2 vols. (Leiden, 1961). There is also the useful compilation of P. J. Blok, ed., *Geschiedkundige Atlas van Nederland*, VIII, 2 parts (The Hague 1917–18), IX (The Hague, 1922), and XI (The Hague, 1919).

The problem of overabundant source material on the Dutch Revolt only exists, however, for those able to read the languages of all the governments involved in the struggle: Spanish, Dutch, English, French and German. For the English reader the situation with regard to sources is enormously simplified: there is scarcely anything left. An indication of what one is missing may be gained from: J. W. Smit, 'The present position of studies regarding the revolt of the Netherlands' in *Britain and the Netherlands*, I, ed. J. S. Bromley and E. H. Kossmann, (London, 1960), 11–28; and P. de Vries, 'The writing and study of history in the Netherlands in the 19th century', *Acta Historiae Neerlandicae*, III (1968), 247–65. The *Acta*, which now appears annually, contains translations (mostly into English) of articles in Dutch as well as the review of recent literature – both in English and in Dutch – concerning the history of the Netherlands noted above. This is an invaluable tool for all those interested in Dutch history. For those who wish to discover what the Eighty Years' War was about with a minimum of effort, the following four items may be suggested: G. N. Clark 'The birth of the Dutch

Republic', *Proceedings of the British Academy*, XXXII (1946), 189–217; G. Parker, 'Spain, her enemies and the revolt of the Netherlands, 1559–1648'; *Past and Present*, XLIX (1970), 72–95; E. H. Kossmann and A. F. Mellink, *Texts concerning the revolt of the Netherlands* (Cambridge, 1975), 1–51; G. Parker, 'Why did the Dutch Revolt last eighty years?', *Transactions of the Royal Historical Society*, XXVI (1976), 53–72. The standard accounts in English remain, however, Motley's *Rise of the Dutch Republic*, first published in 1856, and Pieter Geyl's *The Revolt of the Netherlands, 1555–1609*, first published in Dutch in 1931 and in an abridged English translation in 1932. Both books have their failings – most notably an absence of any economic considerations and, in Geyl's case, a lack of any real attempt to understand Spain's policies and aspirations – and the conclusions of both have inevitably been modified by subsequent research. But both are still well worth reading and no book to date, including this one, can supersede them. For the world viewed through the eyes of the King of Spain, see G. Parker, *The private world of Philip II* (Boston, Mass. 1977).,

NOTES TO THE FOREWORD

1. J. W. Smit, 'The present position of studies regarding the revolt of the Netherlands', in J. S. Bromley and E. H. Kossmann, eds., *Britain and the Netherlands*, I (London, 1960), 28; a paper given at the first Anglo–Dutch Historical Conference in 1959.

2. R. C. Bakhuizen van den Brink, *Les Archives du Royaume des Pays-Bas* (The Hague, 1857), 39 (resolution of 20 July 1572).

3. Examples taken from the illustrated article of E. M. Braekman, 'L'armée des gueux', *Revue belge d'histoire militaire*, XIX (1971), 32–5.

4. AGS *Estado* 554/146, Requesens to the king, 30 Dec. 1573; IVdeDJ 67/1, Requesens to Andrés Ponce de León, Jan. 1574, and many others. BMB *Ms. Granvelle* 28/219–27, 'Discours sur l'Estat des Pays-Bas'.

5. H. G. Koenigsberger, *Estates and Revolutions* (Ithaca, New York, 1971), 234n. Cf. also chapter 2 of the present work.

6. H. Lonchay, 'Étude sur les emprunts des souveraines belges au XVIe et XVIIe siècles', *Bulletin de l'Académie royale de Belgique. Classe des Lettres, année* 1907, 995. Cf. J. J. Woltjer, *Kleine oorzaken, grote gevolgen*, Inaugural Lecture (Leiden, 1975).

7. Owen Feltham, *A brief character of the Low-Countries* (London, 1652), 85.

8. J. J. Poelhekke in *BMGN*, LXXXVIII (1973), 479–82, especially p. 481.

9. J. Romein, 'Het vergruisde beeld. Over het onderzoek naar de motieven van onze Opstand', an Inaugural Lecture delivered and printed in 1939; reprinted in J. Romein, *In opdracht van de tijd*, (Amsterdam, 1946).

BIBLIOGRAPHY FOR CHAPTER 1: PRELUDE

There are many descriptions of the Low Countries during the Golden Age written by contemporaries. There is a useful guide to them in K. W. Swart, *The miracle of the Dutch Republic as seen in the seventeenth century* (London, 1967), 21 n.1. In the sixteenth century the accounts of Vicente Alvarez and Lodovico Guicciardini, cited in n.1 below, stand out. (See, for the latter, of which there are fifty-eight editions to date, R. H. Touwaide, 'La description des Pays-Bas par Lodovico Guicciardini', *Archives et Bibliothèques de Belgique*, XLV (1974), 106–84.) There is also the outstanding narrative of prince Philip's journey by C. Calvete de Estrella, *El felicissimo viaje del mvy alto y mvy poderoso principe don Phelipe* (Antwerp, 1552;

critical edn, 2 vols., Madrid 1930). For more modern descriptions, see J. de Vries, *The Dutch rural economy in the Golden Age, 1500–1700* (New Haven & London, 1974); A. Lambert, *The making of the Dutch landscape: an historical geography of the Netherlands* (London, 1971); and G. Parker and C. H. Wilson, eds., *Introduction to the sources of European economic history*, I (London, 1977), chap. 1. In more detail, see J. J. Murray, *Antwerp in the age of Plantin and Breughel* (Newton Abbot, 1972), and the regional studies discussed in A. van der Woude, 'The A.A.G. Bijdragen and the study of Dutch rural history', *Journal of European Economic History*, IV (1975), 215–45. For the standard of living in the Netherlands, see the article of E. Scholliers, 'Le pouvoir d'achat dans les Pays-Bas au XVIe siècle', in *Album Charles Verlinden*, I (Ghent, 1975), 305–30.

On Philip II's early years, see K. J. W. Verhofstad, *De regeering der Nederlanden in de jaren 1555–1559* (Nijmegen, 1937); M. Dierickx, 'De eerste jaren van Filips II, 1555–67', in *Algemene geschiedenis der Nederlanden*, IV (Utrecht – Antwerp, 1952), 305–49; and P. Rosenfeld, 'The provincial governors of the Netherlands from the minority of Charles V until the Revolt', *Standen en Landen*, XVII (1959). The early history of Protestantism in the Netherlands is in the process of being rewritten and there is no reliable overall survey (except the useful article of A. C. Duke mentioned in n.12 below). See the exciting new work of J. Decavele (n.2 below) and of G. Moreau, *Histoire du Protestantisme à Tournai jusqu'à la veille de la révolution des Pays-Bas* (Paris, 1962); E. Mahieu, 'Le Protestantisme à Mons, des origines à 1575', *Annales du cercle archéologique de Mons*, LXVI (1965–7), 129–247; and M.-P. Willems-Closset, 'Le Protestantisme à Lille jusqu'à la veille de la révolution des Pays-Bas (1521–65)', *Revue du Nord*, LII (1970), 199–216. In the north Netherlands, the outstanding study is by J. J. Woltjer, *Friesland in hervormingstijd* (Leiden, 1962). The same author's article, 'Het conflict tussen Willem Bardes en Hendrik Dirkszoon', *BMGN*, LXXXVI (1971), 178–99, is also important because it shows how difficult it was for the Inquisition to apprehend and convict heretics when the civil authorities were uncooperative. In the province of Holland no death sentence was passed for heresy after 1553, because the magistrates were not prepared to enforce the full rigour of the laws on religious conformity.

NOTES TO CHAPTER 1

1. Vincente Alvarez, *Relación del camino y buen viage que hizo el príncipe de España Don Felipe* (Brussels, 1551; critical edition in French translation, ed. M. T. Dovillée, Brussels, 1964), 123–9, and L. Guicciardini, *Description de tous les Pays-Bas* (Antwerp, 1567; 2nd edn, Antwerp 1582), 48–57: both give fascinating accounts of the local customs and manners of the Netherlanders in the mid-sixteenth century. For the situation a century later, see W. Temple, *Observations upon the United Provinces* (London, 1673; critical edn by G. N. Clark, Oxford, 1972), 88–9, and indeed all of chap. 4. Although 'cold', Dutch girls in the seventeenth century gave some observers many free kisses: R. C. Latham and F. Mathews, *The diary of Samuel Pepys*, I (London, 1970), 138 and notes.

2. Information drawn from J. G. C. A. Briels, 'Zuidnederlandse onderwijskrachten in Noord Nederland, 1570–1630. Een bijdrage tot de kennis van het schoolwezen in de republiek', *Archief voor de geschiedenis van de katholieke kerk in Nederland*, XIV (1972), 89–169 and 277–98; R. Hoven, 'Écoles primaires et écoles latines dans le diocèse de Tournai en 1569' in *Horae Tornacenses: Recueil d'études d'histoire* (Tournai, 1971), 177–93; E. Coornaert, *La Flandre française de langue flamande* (Paris, 1970), 126–31; J. Decavele, *De dageraad van de Reformatie in Vlaanderen*, I (Brussels, 1975), 106–9;

F. de Potter, *Dagboek van Cornelis en Philips van Campene* (Ghent, 1870), 316–17; and E. H. Waterbolk, 'Aspects of the Frisian contribution to the culture of the Low Countries in the early modern period', in *Britain and the Netherlands*, IV, ed., J. S. Bromley and E. H. Kossmann (The Hague, 1971), 113–32, at p. 119.

3. The quotation from Plantin comes from J. J. Murray, *Antwerp in the age of Plantin and Breughel* (Newton Abbot, 1972), 3–4. On Plantin's commercial operations see L. Voet, *The Golden Compasses. A history and evaluation of the printing and publishing activities of the 'Officina Plantiniana' at Antwerp*, 2 vols. (Amsterdam, 1969) – a most important study. For publishing in the Netherlands as a whole, see J. G. C. A. Briels, *Zuidnederlandse boekdrukkers en boekverkopers in de Republiek der Vereenigde Nederlanden omstreeks 1570–1630* (The Hague, 1974).

4. Susato, who died in 1564, was the first man to print music from moveable type. He published fourteen books of French songs and dances in four-part harmonies between 1543 and 1550, and three books of *amoureuse liedekens* in Dutch in 1551. Some of his music has been recorded recently: *Danceries de la Renaissance*, by the *Mvsica Avrea* consort of Liège (Record No. MBM 9A); and *Two Renaissance Dance Bands*, by the Early Music Consort of London (Record No. HQS 1249). See also the bibliographical study of U. Meissner, *Der Antwerpener Notendrucker Tylman Susato*, 2 vols. (Berlin, 1967).

5. Papal election lotteries noted by G. D. Ramsay, *The City of London in international politics at the accession of Elizabeth Tudor* (Manchester, 1975), 8–9; other lotteries and gambles recorded in H. van der Wee, *The growth of the Antwerp market and the European economy (14th–16th centuries)*, II (The Hague, 1963), 364–5.

6. For further information on the 'spectacles' which accompanied prince Philip's tour of the Netherlands in 1549, see J. Jacquot, ed., *Fêtes et cérémonies au temps de Charles-Quint* (Paris, 1960), 297–342 (with illustrations).

7. The political situation of the Netherlands after 1548 is discussed by H. A. Enno van Gelder, *Van Beeldenstorm tot Pacificatie. Acht Opstellen* (Amsterdam, 1964), chap. 1; and F. Postma, 'De visie van de Nederlandse regering op het verdrag van Augsburg aan de vooravond van de 80-jarige oorlog', *BMHG*, LXXX (1966), 141–51. The nature of the link with the empire is discussed at length by P. J. Nève, *Het Rijkskamergerecht en de Nederlanden* (Assen, 1972), and P. J. van Winter, *De Zeven Provinciën* (Haarlem, 1954), 15–19. See also C. A. Rutgers, 'Gelre: een deel van Nederland?', *TvG*, LXXXVIII (1975), 27–38.

8. The question of 'national' sentiment and 'national' identity in the sixteenth-century Netherlands is vexed. There is considerable evidence that Netherlanders abroad began to refer to all the provinces as their '*patrie*' or '*vaderland*' (see examples in G. J. Hoogewerff, 'Uit de geschiedenis van het Nederlandsch nationaal besef', *TvG*, XLIV (1929), 113–34; and J. H. Hessels, *Ecclesiae Londino-Batavae Archivum* – the correspondence of the Dutch Church in London – which is full of references to 'the whole Fatherland', e.g. vol. II, Cambridge 1889, nos. 113, 156 and vol. III part 1, Cambridge 1897, nos. 388, 804 and so on). There were also some groups in the Netherlands who used '*patrie*' in this way: see the examples in P. Rosenfeld, 'The provincial governors', *Standen en Landen*, XVII (1959), 13–15; and A. Louant, *Le 'Livre de Ballades' de Jehan et Charles Bocquet, bourgeois de Mons au 16e siècle* (Brussels, 1954), introduction. However, many other people, even educated persons such as ministers and schoolmasters, referred only to their province when they said or wrote 'fatherland'. Thus in the 1580s it was common for refugees from Flanders, Brabant and Friesland who took employment in Holland to insert into their contract a clause which freed them from their obligations should the

'Spanish yoke be removed from their *vaderland*' (see the article by Briels cited in n.2, pp. 103 and 280). See also J. J. Poelhekke, 'The nameless homeland of Erasmus', *Acta Historiae Neerlandicae*, VII (1974), 54–87.

9.　C. Piot, *Correspondance du Cardinal de Granvelle*, IV (Brussels, 1884), 463. Morillon to Granvelle, 17 Oct. 1572 (Morillon was the vicar-general of the archbishopric of Mechelen; Granvelle was the absentee archbishop).

10.　BM Addl MS., 28,388/68, Requesens to Gaspar de Quiroga, Inquisitor-general and councillor of Philip II, Aug. 1575. Requesens contrasted the effects of the rebellions in the Low Countries with those of the *comunero* revolt in Castile, 1520–21.

11.　The celebrated Dutch historian, Professor Pieter Geyl, insisted that by 1550 a binary linguistic structure existed in the Netherlands: only the 'linguistic frontier' between French and Dutch was shown on his famous map in *The Revolt of the Netherlands* (London, 1958 edn) p. 22. Such a simplistic view of the linguistic situation cannot now be maintained. Cf. H. Baetens Beardsmore, *Le français regional de Bruxelles* (Brussels, 1970), chap. 1 (for French-based dialects); A. van Loey, 'L'action de la langue écrite sur la langue parlée commune néérlandaise', *Bulletin de l'Académie royale de Belgique*, XLIII (1957), 180–91 (for Dutch variations); B. H. Slicher van Bath, ed., *Geschiedenis van Overijssel* (Deventer, 1970), 236–53; and A. C. F. Koch, 'Tussen Saksen en Hollanders: de wording van Oost-Nederland', *Akademiedagen. Koninklijke Nederlandse Akademie van Wetenschappen*, XVIII (1966), 59–85 (for Oosters). On p. 300 n.36 I have presented some evidence which indicates that those who spoke West-Dutch could not understand Oosters; certainly the reverse was also true. My research student, Mr J. S. Coonan, has also shown me documents from the 1560s proving that the gentry of Gelderland could not understand Latin '*sonder duijtsche expositie*' ('without a Dutch explanation').

12.　A. C. Duke, 'The face of popular religious dissent in the Low Countries, 1520–1530', *Journal of ecclesiastical history*, XXVI (1975), 41–3.

13.　M.-A. Arnould, 'L'incidence de l'impôt sur les finances d'un village a l'époque bourguignonne: Boussoit-sur-Haine, 1400–1555', *Contributions à l'histoire économique et sociale*, I (1962), 39–105; F. Braudel, 'Les emprunts de Charles-Quint sur la place d'Anvers', in *Colloque: Charles-Quint et son temps* (Paris, 1958), 191–201.

14.　L. P. Gachard, 'Le 2e remonstrance de Emanuel Philibert', *BCRH*, 2nd series, VIII (1856), 125; AGS *Estado* 513/174, reply of the king to this; A. Louant, 'Charles de Lalaing et les remonstrances de Emanuel-Philibert', *BCRH*, XCVII (1933), 268–9. On Philip II's first struggle with the States-General, see A. Louant, 'Les nations de Bruxelles et les États de Brabant de 1556–1557', *BCRH*, XCIX (1935), 223–50.

15.　On depopulation: M. A. Arnould, *Les dénombrements de foyers dans le Comté de Hainaut (XIVe–XVIe siècles)* (Brussels, 1956), *passim*; on the wolves, AGRB *Audience* 778/187, minutes of the debate of the Council of State for 9 Oct. 1562.

16.　BPM MS. II-2320, fo. 6, Perrenot to Juan Vázquez de Molina, minute, 29 May 1559.

17.　ibid., fo. 124, Perrenot to Juan Vázquez, minute, 21 July 1559; cf. also ibid., fo. 122, to Alva, 20 June 1559; and AGS *Estado* 137/95–7, 'Apuntamientos para embiar a España', discussed by F. Braudel, *The Mediterranean and the Mediterranean world in the age of Philip II*, II (London, 1973), 947–9.

18.　AGS *Estado* 1210/94, Philip II to the duke of Sessa, 8 Apr. 1559; *Estado* 1124/257 and 278, papers concerning Don Bernat de Guimerau, knight of Malta, who proposed the Tripoli expedition to Philip II, and fo. 271, Don Sancho Martínez de Leiva to the king, 30 Nov. 1559, predicting the outcome. See also the richly documented discussion of J. F. Guilmartin, *Gunpowder and galleys* (Cambridge, 1975), 123–34.

19. C. Weiss *Papiers d'État du Cardinal de Granvelle*, V (Paris, 1844), 673, Philip II to Perrenot, 27 Dec. 1559. See also the king's admission in July of the same year: '*Han reydo alla harto*' (They had a good laugh over there at my expense – misquoted from AGS *Estado* 137/227 in F. Braudel, *The Mediterranean*, II, 965).

20. L. Paris, *Négociations de Sebastian de l'Aubespine . . . relatives au règne de François II* (Paris, 1841), 66, letter to Francis II, 4 Aug. 1559.

21. G. Groen van Prinsterer, *Archives ou correspondance de la maison d'Orange-Nassau, 1ère série*, I (2nd edn, Leiden, 1841), 152. Granvelle to the king, 10 Mar. 1563. See also the suspicious tone of Egmont: 'The king is totally determined to retain the Spanish infantry and demobilize all other troops; I leave you to guess his reasons' (N. Japikse, *Correspondentie van Willem I, prins van Oranje*, I (Haarlem, 1933), 143–4: Egmont to Orange, 1 July 1559).

22. BPM *Ms.* II-2249, unfol., Gonzalo Pérez to Perrenot, 19 Nov. 1560; Weiss, *Papiers . . . de Granvelle*, VI, 166, Perrenot to the king, 12 Sep. 1560. For a 'case study' of the Spanish troops in a Netherlands town at this time, see E. van Autenboer, 'De houding der Nederlanders en bijzonder der Mechelaars tegenover de Spaansche troepen in 1560', *Mechelse Bijdragen*, III (1943), 87–98.

23. The complete episcopal structure was to be as follows (new bishoprics in italics): *Groningen, Leeuwarden, Haarlem, Deventer* and *Middelburg* under the archbishop of Utrecht – all Dutch, Oosters and Frisian speaking; *Roermond, 'sHertogenbosch, Antwerp, Bruges* and *Ieper* under the archbishop of *Mechelen* – all Dutch speaking; *St Omer, Namur*, Arras and Tournai under the archbishop of Cambrai – all Walloon speaking. The diocese of Liège remained separate ecclesiastically as well as politically, losing much of its extensive jurisdiction in adjacent Namur, Limburg and Brabant. On the new bishoprics scheme see the definitive studies of M. Dierickx: *Documents inédits sur l'érection des nouveaux diocèses aux Pays-Bas (1521–1570)*, 3 vols. (Louvain, 1960–62), especially the introduction in vol. I, and *De oprichting der nieuwe bisdommen in de Nederlanden onder Filips II* (Antwerp & Utrecht, 1950). More recently, there has been a detailed study of one new diocese: F. Jacques, *Le diocèse de Namur en mars 1561. Etude de géographie historique* (Brussels, 1968).

24. On Granvelle, see the biography of M. van Durme, *El cardenal Granvela (1517–1586)*. *Imperio y revolución bajo Carlos V y Felipe II* (revised and augmented edn, Barcelona, 1957), 225–71 (on this period, p. 170 n.151 is of particular interest). There has been much discussion of whether Granvelle and the central government *intended* to 'pack' the States of Brabant with abbot-bishops. At the time this unworthy suggestion was hotly denied by all involved with the scheme; however, a confidential holograph letter written many years later by Cardinal Granvelle expressly acknowledged that this was indeed the government's intention. He reminded the king that the principal reason for the incorporation 'was because the abbots of Brabant are the men who cause the most trouble in the deliberations of the States of Brabant, and if three experienced bishops, zealous in Your Majesty's service, were to intervene in the discussions with the authority of their rank . . . they would command greater respect'. (IVdeDJ 47/49, Granvelle to Philip II, 12 May 1576 – a most interesting and hitherto unknown letter.)

25. B. van 't Hooft, 'Dr Faust in Gelderland', *Gelre*, XXXIII (1930), 70; I owe this reference to the kindness of my research student, Mr James S. Coonan.

26. N. Japikse, *Correspondentie*, 311–15, Egmont and Orange to the king, 23 July 1561; AGS *Estado* 521/80, 81, Egmont to Erasso, 27 July and 15 Aug. 1561 and 15 Aug. 1561. On Egmont's role in the early opposition to Philip II see P. B. de Troeyer,

Lamoraal van Egmont: een kritische studie over zijn rol in de jaren 1559–1564 (Brussels, 1961).

27. L. Febvre, *Philippe II et la Franche-Comté* (Paris, 1911), 411–18, put forward the idea that Orange was turned against Granvelle by contact with the cardinal's old enemies from Franche-Comté, Simon Renard and the Rye family. While it is true that the gentry of the Comté were deeply committed to opposing Philip II's policies in the 1560s (expertly described by Febvre), Orange seems to have had little to do with the process. The humiliation of the king's opposition to his marriage seems to have been the catalyst; Renard played upon a hatred which was already hot (see van Durme, *Granvela*, 243–5 and notes). There is surprisingly still no definitive biography of William of Orange, nor a complete edition of his letters and papers. Happily the first will soon be provided by Professor K. W. Swart, the second by Professor B. A. Vermaseren. In the meantime, a shrewd analysis of Orange's aims during this period, and of his 'aristocratic constitutionalism', is given by J. K. Oudendijk, 'Den coninck van Hispaengien heb ick altijt gheeert', in *Dancwerc: opstellen aangeboden aan Prof. Dr D. Th. Enklaar* (Groningen, 1959), 264–78.

28. *Supplément a l'histoire des guerres civiles de Flandre sous Philippe II du Père Famian Strada*, II (Amsterdam, 1729), 267–8, Hornes to 'Grasso' (= Erasso), 19 Dec. 1561. This letter was shown to the king and was mentioned in his letter to Hornes of 9 Feb. 1562. (Preserved in AGRB *Audience* 478/3, a volume of Hornes's letters seized by the Council of Troubles, in 1567. Several items in it shed light on Hornes's grievances. See, for example, fos. 59–63, his Instructions to Alonso de Laloo, 12 Jan. 1567; 'His Majesty told me [in 1559] . . . that he wished me to go to Spain to serve about his person, and that when I was there he would make me superintendent of the affairs of these provinces . . . However, when I arrived at the Court of His Majesty I was there six months before I was informed of any business of these provinces . . . ' Hornes also lamented that when he left Court in 1561 his pension of 6,000 florins a year was stopped.)

29. C. Weiss, *Papiers de Granvelle*, VI, 156–65 (the budget was sent by the king on 7 Sep. 1560); IVdeDJ 68/309 *bis*, 'Cuenta con Jeronimo de Curiel y Francisco de Lixalde' gives the remittances to the Netherlands.

30. AGRB *Audience* 475/84, Josse de Courtewille to Viglius, 24 May 1563: 'L'on ne parle icy que du siège d'Oran . . . Erasso m'a dit que le fait d'Oran a jà cousté plus de vjc mil ducatz'.

31. BNP MS. *fonds français* 15,587/3–7, Memoire of the bishop of Limoges to Catherine de Medici, autumn 1563, citing the view of François Baudouin on the Netherlands: '*L'accroissement et perseverance des Seigneurs en cette rancune est fondée sur la partialité et division qui est en la Cour d'Espagne . . . Le duc d'Alve et Ruigomes . . . estendent leurs aisles aux terres plus longtaines comme en flandres ou ledit duc supporte le Cardenal de Granvelle et Ruigomes, qui dès le temps de l'Empereur dernier [Charles V] luy est ennemi, favorise au contraire ceux-cy.*' The relationship between events in the Netherlands and the interplay of factions at the Spanish Court has been definitively dealt with by P. D. Lagomarsino, 'Court factions and the formation of Spanish policy towards the Netherlands, 1559–67' (Cambridge University Ph.D. thesis, 1973). This entire thesis is extremely important and should be published. I am very grateful to Dr Lagomarsino for allowing me to read his work and for saving me from many errors.

32. See L. P. Gachard, *Études et notices historiques concernant l'histoire des Pays-Bas*, I (Brussels, 1890), 107–29 (article entitled 'La chute du Cardinal de Granvelle' and based upon the state papers in Simancas). See also the copies of the letters sent by Armenteros

to Margaret of Parma from Spain in van der Essen, *Cahier* IX fos. 8–34 and X fos. 1–17. *Cahier* IX/21–3 analyses the letter of 23 Sep. 1563, in which Armenteros assessed the state of the factions at the Court and their bearing on the success of his mission.

33. Magistrates of Bruges quoted by J. Decavele, *De Dageraad van de Reformatie in Vlaanderen, 1521–1566*, 1 (Brussels, 1975), 354; States of Holland quoted by E. G. Brünne, 'Die dänische Verkehrssperre und der Bildersturm in den Niederlanden im Jahre 1566', *Hansische Geschichtblätter*, XXXIII (1928), 107; secretary Bave to Cardinal Granvelle, 4 Dec. 1565, quoted by E. Poullet, *Correspondance . . . de Granvelle*, I, 27.

34. Example taken from Decavele, *Dageraad*, I, 502–6.

35. ibid., 445.

36. One must not overestimate the appeal of Calvinism to the *marranos*, however: for many of them it was no more than a façade for crypto-judaism. It is significant that few *marranos* became Protestants in 1577–84 when it was easy but there was no persecution: see I. S. Révah, 'Pour l'histoire des marranes à Anvers: recensements de la nation portugaise de 1571 à 1666', *Revue des études juives*, 4th series, II (1963), 123–47; and B. A. Vermaseren, 'De Antwerpse koopman Martin Lopez en zijn familie', *BtG*, LVI (1973), 3–79 (with an English summary). On the Chambers of Rhetoric, see H. A. Enno van Gelder, 'Erasmus, schilders en rederijkers: het wezen der Reformatie', *TvG*, LXXI (1958), 1–15, 206–42 and 289–331; J. Decavele, op. cit., I, 193–220, and references there. Nineteen Flemish *rederrijkers* were tried for heresy between 1520 and 1566.

37. Based on the table in Decavele, *Dageraad*, I, 549. Because fewer cases were brought against gentlemen, the upper class support for Protestantism is underrepresented.

38. The traditional source for the story of a secret Spanish–French pact to extirpate heresy comes from the *Apologie* of William of Orange (ed. A. Lacroix, Brussels, 1858, 88–9), supported by most Protestant writers of the time – cf. V. de Caprariis, *Propaganda e pensiero politico in Francia durante le guerre di religione (1559–72)* (Naples, 1959), 463–4. Such a secret pact was certainly proposed by the Spanish negotiators at Cateau-Cambrésis: cf. AGS *Estado* 8334/186, '*Praticado y conferido por los del consejo de estado de castilla cerca de los puntos de la paz*' (January 1559) – '*Assymesmo que se restituyesen presos los hereges que del un reyno se pasasen al otro para que fuesen castigados*'.

39. Figures on Titelman's activities, based in part on the audited accounts which he submitted annually to the government, drawn from Decavele, *Dageraad*, I, 14–31. For a good general survey of the Netherlands Inquisition see J. Scheerder, *De Inquisitie in de Nederlanden in de XVIe eeuw* (Antwerp, 1944). On the overall pattern of persecution in the Netherlands (and not just in Flanders, which is covered in such detail by Decavele), see G. Güldner, *Das Toleranz-Problem in den Niederlanden im Ausgang des 16 Jahrhunderts* (Lubeck and Hamburg, 1968), table facing p. 36.

40. All quoted by Decavele, *Dageraad*, I, 229. It is interesting to note that twenty-three street-singers were tried for heresy in the province of Flanders between 1520 and 1566 (ibid., 551.)

41. H. A. Enno van Gelder, *Correspondance française de Marguerite de Parme. Supplément*, II (Utrecht, 1942), 272, Philip II to Margaret of Parma, 31 July 1566.

42. AGS *Estado* 527/5, Philip II to Gonzalo Pérez, undated, telling him how to draw up Egmont's instructions: '*Ya tendréis entendida mi intención q[ue] es de no resolver agora estas cosas q[ue e]l C[ond]e pretende, ni desengañarle dellas, porq[ue] nos mataría y nunca acabariamos con él*'. This document is difficult to interpret, and I gratefully acknowledge the assistance of Dr P. D. Lagomarsino in doing so. Dr Lagomarsino also established in his thesis (cf. n. 31 above), 88–120, that the document was composed on 24 Mar. 1565.

43.　A. Wauters, *Mémoires de Viglius et Hopperus* (Brussels, 1858), 268. Hopperus was present at the council when Egmont addressed it on 5 May 1565; his account is the only one available, because the official minute for that session has been lost.

44.　Groen van Prinsterer, *Archives*, I, 342, Brederode to Orange, Dec. 1564.

45.　The situation was reported to the king: AGS *Estado, 527/59*, Margaret to the king, 22 July 1565. The duchess defended the 'usurpation of power' by the nobles, citing as precedents the pre-eminence of Lalaing and de Praet in the 1550s and of Granvelle, Viglius and Berlaymont in the early 1560s. She made out a good case, but the king never read her letter, which ran to twenty-one sides of her angular Italian script. Instead he read an abstract (*Estado 527/70*) made by Gonzalo Pérez, which made no mention of Margaret's arguments. The king's insistence on seeing everything for himself thus produced a distorted and incomplete picture. For a less favourable account of the nobles' usurpation of power, cf. Weiss, *Papiers . . . de Granvelle*, IX (Paris, 1852), 279–80, Viglius to Granvelle, 14 June 1565.

46.　Groen van Prinsterer, *Archives*, I, 369, Orange to Count Louis, 3 Apr. 1565; Gachard, *Correspondance de Philippe II sur les affaires des Pays-Bas*, I (Brussels, 1848), 367, Armenteros to Gonzalo Pérez, 20 Aug. 1565, and 376, Granvelle to the king, 30 Oct. 1565. There are many other references by contemporaries to the connection between Philip II's Mediterranean commitments and his policy towards the Netherlands. See, by way of example: Groen, op. cit., I, 440, Orange, Nov. 1565; Weiss, *Papiers d'État*, IX, 503–10 (Alonso del Canto, 12 Sep. 1565) and 578–9 (Bave, 7 Oct. 1565); Poullet, *Correspondance de . . . Granvelle*, I (Brussels, 1877), 65, 226, 322, 334, 342; and *A.D.E.*, VIII (Madrid, 1954), 350–51, Don Francés de Alava to the king, 7 May 1566. There are, of course, many more references in unpublished sources. The realization that developments in the Netherlands and in the Mediterranean were closely connected may well have come to the Netherlands leaders from the king himself: see his letters to the Regent and others cited in n. 15 to chapter 2 below and the discussions of the Council of State in Brussels (*Audience* 779 fos. 120 for 26 Jan. 1565, 178 for 28 June, 225 for 3 Oct; *Audience* 780 fos. 30 for 18 Feb. 1566, 34 for 28 Feb, and so on).

47.　The labyrinthine process by which these crucial letters were prepared, a process which lasted from 12 Aug. until 20 Oct. 1565, was correctly unravelled and masterfully described in the thesis of Dr Lagomarsino (n. 31 above), pp. 168–206, to which my account here is indebted. There were, in all, four letters in French signed on 17 Oct. and two in Spanish signed on the 20 Oct.

BIBLIOGRAPHY FOR CHAPTER 2: THE FIRST REVOLT

There are three outstanding accounts of the 'first revolt': R. Fruin, 'Het voorspel van de 80-jarige oorlog', in *Verspreide Geschriften*, I (The Hague, 1900, first published in 1860), 266–449; J. van Vloten, *Nederlands Opstand tegen Spanje in zijn beginselen, aard en strekking geschetst, 1564–67* (Haarlem, 1856); and F. Rachfahl, *Wilhelm von Oranien und der Niederländische Aufstand*, 3 vols. (Halle and The Hague, 1906–24). The last, with over 2,200 pages covering the period to 1569, is the best – and it is the best because it makes use of the archives of the Spanish government, both in Brussels and in Madrid, to determine not only what the aims of the 'rebels' of 1566–8 were, but also what the government *thought* they were. A proper examination of the records collected by the Council of Troubles, the body created in 1567 to deal with those involved in the rebellion, is imperative if we are to understand the first revolt of the Netherlands aright. Nevertheless, these papers have never been published.

There is the archive of the Council itself (AGRB *Raad van Beroerten*: printed inventory by A. Jamees), which contains the interrogation of Egmont: *Raad van Beroerten* 156, in Spanish; the French transcript of this document, which contains many inaccuracies, was published in F. de Reiffenberg, *Correspondance de Marguerite d'Autriche, duchesse de Parme, avec Philippe II* (Brussels, 1842), 297–349. The original interrogation of Hornes has, it seems, been lost but a copy has been published in *Supplément à l'histoire des guerres civiles de Flandre sous Philippe II du père Famian Strada*, I (Amsterdam, 1729), 103–210. Most of the documents printed in this rare but important two-vol. work concern Hornes's trial. The interrogation of Hornes's brother, Montigny, was published in *Co.Do.In.* V, 5–74. The interrogations of several lesser nobles were printed as appendices to monographs and collections of correspondence, e.g.: G. van Hasselt, *Stukken voor Vaderlandsche Historie*, I (Arnhem, 1792), 215–24, 251–61, 356–75, and II, 87–104; E. Poullet, *Correspondance de . . . Granvelle*, II (Brussels, 1880), 648–76 and III (Brussels, 1881), 611–25. This, however, only represents a fraction of the surviving records of the efficient Council. In Simancas there are two fat bundles of Montigny's correspondence (*Estado* 533 and 534) and an enormous register of the Council's deliberations (*Secretarías provinciales* 1413) and much more. In Brussels there is the *Raad van Beroerten* series, and more in the collection *Audience* (for instance nos. 477 and 478, the papers of Berghes and Hornes respectively). The series *Audience* also contains the minutes of the meetings of the Council of State held between 1560 and 1567, a unique record, which even gives the gist of the speeches made by the various councillors, see J. Lefèvre, 'Les notules du Conseil d'État', *Archives, Bibliothèques et Musées de Belgique*, XXIII (1952), 13–24. The originals are at AGRB *Audience* 778–85; the most important minutes of meetings in 1566 were published by L. P. Gachard, *Correspondance de Guillaume le Taciturne, prince d'Orange*, VI (Brussels, 1857), 355–444.

The importance of these government documents was first pointed out in 1849 by the great Dutch archivist and historian, R. C. Bakhuizen van den Brink: see his *Studiën en Karakterschetsen over Vaderlandsche Geschiedenis*, III (The Hague, 1913), 1–250, especially his 'Brief aan Groen van Prinsterer over de Spaansche-Belgische bronnen van den Nederlandschen Opstand', pp. 209–50. In my account of the 'first revolt' I have tried to follow the path indicated by Bakhuizen, even though the result (which he did not foresee) is to damn the rebels out of their own mouths.

NOTES TO CHAPTER 2

1. Minutes of the debate of the Council of State printed in L. P. Gachard, *Correspondance de Guillaume le Taciturne*, VI (Brussels, 1857), 374–6. Montigny was paid handsomely for his travelling expenses to the Spanish Court – 12,400 florins paid: AGS *CJH* 70 *antiguo* (46 *moderna*), unfol., 'Cuenta de Mos. de Montigny', 29 May–31 Dec. 1566 – but he was arrested there for treason on 19 Sep. 1567 and secretly strangled in the castle of Simancas, at Philip II's express command, on 16 Oct. 1570.

2. L. P. Gachard, 'Extraits des registres des consaux de Tournai', *BCRH*, 1st series XI (1846), 82–3. Almost exactly the same thing happened at Amsterdam: A. C. Duke and D. H. A. Kolff, 'The time of troubles in the country of Holland, 1566–7', *TvG* LXXXII (1969), 316–37, at p. 330.

3. They had originally intended to meet in Antwerp, but Orange had dissuaded them. The four leaders of the Confederacy – Brederode, Culemborg, van den Berg (Orange's brother-in-law) and Count Louis of Nassau – met at Lier, just outside Antwerp, on 4 July and resolved to call a general assembly at St Truiden for the 14 July. On the

history of the Compromise and the Confederates see the richly documented study of J. W. Te Water, *Historie van het verbond en de smeekschriften der Nederlandsche edelen . . . 1565–1567*, 4 vols. (Middelburg, 1779–96).

4. AGRB *Audience* 282/256, F. de la Baze to Margaret, 17 July 1566; ibid., fo. 261, G. Mattaeu to Margaret 22 July 1566.

5. M. de Ram, 'Lettres de Viglius à Josse de Courtewille', *BCRH*, 1st series XVI (1849–50), 207–8. The connection between unemployment and religious mischief in 1566 was frequently noted: 'All trade has come to a standstill, so that there are 100,000 men begging for their bread who used to earn it . . . which is an important change since poverty can often force people to do things which otherwise they would never think of doing' – Count Egmont to Philip II, 29 Aug. 1566, quoted in C. Gilles de Pélichy, 'Contribution à l'histoire des troubles politico-religieuses des Pays-Bas au XVIe siècle', *ASEB*, LXXXVI (1949), 105–6; 'All trade and industry has ceased, so that poverty will increase the temerity of the people' AGRB *Audience* 476/144, Viglius to Charles de Tisnacq, 9 Sep. 1566.

6. The connection between the bread riots at Ghent on 21 Aug. and the iconoclasm which began there the following day was noted by both the city's chroniclers: H. van Duyse, *Mémoires d'un patricien gantois*, I (Ghent, 1905), 87, and F. de Potter, *Dagboek van Cornelis en Philips van Campene* (Ghent, 1870), 10–11. The shortage of grain was also recorded in R. van Roosbroeck, ed., *De kroniek van Godevaert van Haecht over de troebelen van 1565 tot 1574 te Antwerpen en elders*, I (Antwerp, 1929), 14, 17; H. van der Wee, *The growth of the Antwerp market and the European economy*, I (The Hague, 1963), 177–8, 187–8; and C. Verlinden, et al., *Documenten voor de geschiedenis van prijzen en lonen in Vlaanderen en Brabant*, I (Bruges, 1959), 57, 59–61 and so on. For an attempt to relate political events to the economic conjuncture, see H. van der Wee, 'The economy as a factor in the beginning of the revolt of the Netherlands', *Acta Historiae Neerlandicae*, V (Leiden, 1971), 52–67.

7. The iconoclasts were definitely hired for a daily wage at Antwerp, Axel, Hulst, Tournai and Mechelen, which suggests that this was the norm in the southern provinces, see M. Dierickx, 'Beeldenstorm in de Nederlanden in 1566', *Streven*, XIX (1966) 1040–48; J. Decavele, 'De reformatorische beweging te Axel en Hulst (1556–66)', *BMGN*, XXII (1968–9), 1–42; and O. J. de Jong, *Beeldenstorm in de Nederlanden* (Groningen, 1964 – a short but brilliant inaugural lecture). More remarkable still, a single group of 'professional' iconoclasts seems to have gone all the way from west Flanders to Breda smashing images: cf. M. Backhouse, *Beeldenstorm en Bosgeuzen in het Westkwartier (1566–8)* (Kortrijk, 1971), 91–111; and Backhouse, 'Dokumenten betreffende de godsdiensttroebelen in het Westkwartier: Jan Camerlynck en tien zijner gezellen voor de Ieperse vierschaar (1968–9)', *BCRH*, CXXXVIII (1972), 79–381 (especially pp. 100, 139 and 218–20). There are two other outstanding studies of the Iconoclastic Fury: J. Scheerder, *De Beeldenstorm* (Bussum, 1974 – with maps and illustrations) and E. van Autenboer, 'Uit de Geschiedenis van Turnhout in de 16e eeuw: voorbereiding, uitbarsting en gevolgen van de Beeldenstorm (1566)', *Taxandria*, XL–XLI (1968–9), also published as a separatum of 275 pages.

8. J. W. Burgon, *The Life and times of Sir Thomas Gresham*, II (London, 1839), 139: R. Clough to Gresham, Antwerp, 31 Aug, 1566. J. van Vloten, *Onderzoek van 's Konings Wege ingesteld omtrent de Middelburgsche beroerten van 1566 en 1567* (Utrecht, 1873), 160 and 229; M. Delmotte, 'Het Calvinisme in de verschillende bevolkingslagen te Gent (1566–7)', *TvG*, LXXVI (1963), 145–76.

9. J. van Vloten, op cit., 209–10; Duke and Kolff, op. cit., 322; W. Troost and J. J.

Woltjer, 'Brielle in hervormingstijd', *BMGN*, LXXXVII (1972), 307–53, at pp. 328 and 331.

10. M. van Vaernewijck, *Van die beroerlijcke tijden in die Nederlanden*, I (ed. F. van der Haeghen, Ghent, 1872), 128. Near Groningen, the local schoolmaster led 'the poor scholars out of the school to help smash the images' – J. C. J. Kleintjens, 'Beeldenstorm in Groningen en in de Ommelanden', *Archief voor de Geschiedenis van het Aartsbisdom Utrecht*, LXVII (1948), 212; twenty-two Antwerp schoolmasters lost their jobs in 1568 because they had taught their charges Protestant psalms and catechisms and had encouraged them to defy authority (J. G. C. A. Briels, 'Zuidnederlandse onderwijs-krachten in Noord-Nederland, 1570–1630', *Archief voor de geschiedenis van de katholieke kerk in Nederland*, XIV (1972), 92.

11. Enno van Gelder, *Correspondance de Marguerite d'Autriche, Supplément*, II, 326–32, Margaret to the king, 29 Aug. 1566; AGS *Estado* 530, unfol., 27 Aug. 1566. On 29 Aug. Egmont wrote to the king that 'At present all Catholic worship in the province of Flanders has ceased except in Bruges, in the areas around Aalst and Dendermonde, and in the "Land van Waas" ' (document cited in n. 5 above).

12. UB Leiden, *Hs. Pap.* 3, fo. 3, Laloo to Hornes, Segovia, 13 Aug. 1566, received 13 Sep. Hornes underlined the passage about the 'Three seigneurs'; AGS *Estado* 531/11, French translation of 'Alava' to 'Margaret', 29 Aug. 1566.

13. UB Leiden, *Hs Pap.* 3, fos. 4 and 5, Laloo to Hornes, Segovia, 20 and 26 Sep. 1566; Groen van Prinsterer, *Archives*, II, 364, Montigny to Orange, 4 Oct. 1566. The accuracy of Montigny's information is intriguing in view of the fact that he was expressly excluded from the meetings of the Council of State which took the decisions which he described. It seems clear that someone was 'leaking' the king's secrets, and the principal suspect was Jean Vandenesse, the Flemish groom of Philip II's chamber. He was accused and interrogated in 1569 on the orders of the duke of Alva (who claimed to have proof of his guilt: see his *Requisitoria* in AGS *Estado* 542-122); but Vandenesse died before the case could be concluded.

14. AD Nord, *B* 19280, *pièce* 47432, 'Interrogation à faire de par Msgr le prince d'Orenges au conseiller del Rio'. The answers of del Rio, despite his exclusion from some of the crucial council debates, are nonetheless fascinating.

15. J. Theissen, *Correspondance française de Marguerite de Parme*, 142–6, king to Margaret, 6 May 1566; AGRB *Audience* 1185/3, king to magistrates of Valenciennes, 6 May 1566: '*comme . . . nous avons entendu que le principal effort desdicts turcqz se dressoit par terre, nous semblant que tantmoins y avoit-il que redoubter par mer, nous véans de ce costel-là plus libre pour entendre à aultres choses, sommes délibérez d'aller bien tost pardelà.*'

16. Poullet, *Correspondance . . . de Granvelle*, I, 314–18, Granvelle to the king, 19 Jun. 1566; the debate of the council was reported by Miguel de Mendivil, Margaret of Parma's agent, who was present for part of the proceedings – cf. his letter to Margaret of 22 Sep. 1566, noted in van der Essen, *Cahier* XXXIV, pp. 18–19 (from AS Napoli, *Carte Farnesiane, fascio* 1706, now destroyed); AGS *Estado* 1055/257, king to the viceroy of Naples, 26 Sep. 1566, ordering him to send the 7,000 Spanish veterans aboard the Mediterranean galleys to Lombardy 'for a certain effect very important to our service', and *Estado* 1219/261, Philip II to the governor of Lombardy, 30 Oct. 1566. Foreign ambassadors at the Spanish Court were not slow to get wind of the main decisions when they occurred: C. Douais, *Dépêches de . . . Fourquevaux*, I, 138–42 (*avis* of 6 Nov.); HHStA, *Spanien: Diplomatische Correspondenz* 7, bundle for 1566, fos. 46–51 (letter of Dietrichstein, 4 Nov.); BNM MS. 8246/183–6 (Letter of Rossano, papal ambassador, 2 Nov.); AS Firenze, *Mediceo* 4898/4–6 (letter of Nobili, 6 Nov.);

AS Genova, *Negoziazione Spagna* 3a (letters of Sauli, 29 and 30 Oct. – the first man with the news); *Calendar of State Papers, Foreign Series, 1566–1568*, no. 786 (letter of Dr Man, 5 Nov.); AS Venezia, *Senato: Dispacci Spagna* 6, ff. 16–17, letters of Tiepolo, 30 Oct. and 6 Nov. Between them these ambassadorial dispatches give an almost comprehensive picture of developments at the Spanish Court. They form the basis of my account, supplemented by the printed versions of L. Cabrera de Córdoba, *Historia de Felipe II, rey de España*, I (Madrid 1619; reprinted 1876), book VII, chap. 6–7; A. Ossorio, *Vida y Hazañas de Don Fernando Alvarez de Toledo, duque de Alba* (Madrid, 1669; reprinted 1945), 331–42; and A. Wauters, ed., *Mémoires de Viglius et d'Hopperus sur le commencement des troubles des Pays-Bas* (Brussels, 1858), 320–33 and 337–63. The account of Hopperus, who was in Spain when the decisions were taken, was accepted by the Council of Troubles as the standard account of the events leading up to the first revolt (see AGS *S.P. libro* 1413 fo. 7v–8, description of the '*bref receuil*' read out on 22 Sep. 1567). Hopperus was also the main source for Cabrera de Córdoba's account of the debates of Sep. and Oct. 1566.

17. Orange's attitude towards the use of force against the king in 1566–8 was not consistent. In January 1566 he was prepared to explore the possibility of raising troops in Germany (Groen van Prinsterer, *Archives*, II, 23–5, Orange to Count Louis, 25 Jan. 1566); but by August it was Louis who held the initiative and made contact with German military enterprisers on his own authority (ibid., 205–9, Louis to John of Nassau, 10 Aug. 1566, and 257–8, '*Bestallungsbrief*' to Colonel Westerholdt, 30 Aug. – irrefutable evidence that the confederates would stop at nothing in their resistance). By December 1566, however, Orange was lending artillery to Brederode to help him to fortify his castle of Vianen – Gachard, *Correspondance de Guillaume le Taciturne*, II (Brussels, 1850), 328–31 and 337–41, Margaret of Parma to Orange and Orange to Margaret, 13 and 21 Jan. 1567; two guns later listed in an inventory in Vianen in 1567 bore Orange's motto *Maintiendray*: J. J. Salverda de Grave, 'Twee inventarissen van het huis Brederode', *BMHG*, XXXIX (1918), 1–172, at pp. 93 and 105. The reasons for this vacillating behaviour, ending in dangerous defiance of the government, may have something to do with Louis of Nassau. The count's influence on his brother is uncertain, but it is perhaps significant that they normally lived under the same roof, both at Breda (the family palace) and at Brussels, where Louis had a personal suite of two rooms: S. W. A. Drossaers and T. H. Lunsingh-Scheurleer, *Inventarissen van de inboedels in de verblijven van de Oranjes*, I (The Hague, 1974), 35–6. The count also tried deliberately to influence his brother, bringing him a treatise '*touchant les causes pour lesquelles l'inférieur Magistrat peult prendre les armes quant le supérieur dort ou tyranize*' ('concerning the reasons for which the Inferior Magistrate may take up arms when the Superior is negligent or a tyrant') (Groen, *Archives*, II, 37–8, Hames to Louis, 27 Feb. 1566). This was undoubtedly the *Bekenntnis* of Magdeburg, written in 1551, and in fact not only the book but also its co-author, Matheus Flacius Illyrius, came to the Netherlands in 1566, see O. K. Olson, 'Theology of revolution: Magdeburg, 1550–51', *The Sixteenth-Century Journal*, III (1973), 65–79.

18. M. Koch, *Quellen zur Geschichte des Kaisers Maximilian II*, II (Leipzig, 1861), 36–7, prints a letter from the imperial army around Gotha, dated 19 Feb. 1567, and stating that '*Der Graf Ludwig von Nassau war dieser Tage hier im Lager, um mehr Leute auf die Beine und herbei zu bringen*'. A Spanish translation of this letter was sent to Philip II by the emperor (AGS *Estado* 657/20).

19. AGRB *Raad van Beroerten*, 156, Interrogation of Egmont on 15 Nov. 1567, supplementary questions 37 and 38. Egmont was not tortured: he incriminated his former

colleagues voluntarily and more or less signed their death warrants. He corroborated the insinuations and suspicions of the Spanish ambassador in Paris at the time, Don Francés de Alava: *A. D. E.*, VIII, 348–54, Alava to the king, 7 May 1566 (especially page 349), ibid., 374–81, 5 June 1566. ibid., 389–93, 14 June, and ibid., 434–5, 9 July. Not surprisingly Montigny denied all charges (*Co.Do.In.*, V, 53) but in vain.

20. For details on these contacts, see: W. Hollweg, *Der Augsburger Reichstag von 1566 und seine Bedeutung für die Entstehung der Reformierten Kirche und ihres Bekenntnisses* (Neukirchen, 1964); J. V. Polišenský, *Nizozemská politika a Bílá Hora* (Prague, 1958), 94; N. Mout, *Bohemen en de Nederlanden in de 16e eeuw* (Leiden, 1975), 28–32; and B. Chudoba, *Spain and the Empire, 1519–1648* (Chicago, 1954), 134–8. Again it is important to remember that both Margaret and Philip II were fully informed (and extremely worried) about these developments: see AGS *Estado* 654/73, Chantonnay to Margaret, 21 Sep. 1566 (copy).

21. Confession of Mathieu Wattepatte, chief collector of the funds for the Request, quoted in J. Scheerder, 'Het drie miljoen goudguldens rekwest' in *Miscellanea historica in honorem Leonis van der Essen*, I (Louvain, 1947), 559–66. Wattepatte was arrested by the government with his money: see H. A. Enno van Gelder, *Gegevens betreffende roerend en onroerend bezit in de Nederlanden in de 16e eeuw*, I (The Hague, 1972), 335. It seems possible that the idea of offering money in return for toleration was suggested by the *marranos* (the Jewish exiles of Iberian descent) who were prominent in the Antwerp Calvinist consistory: the same technique had been employed by the Jews in fifteenth-century Spain and by the *moriscos* of Granada until 1568.

22. See the unequivocal letter of Gilles Le Clercq to the consistory of Valenciennes, 1 Oct. 1566, printed in *Bulletin de la commission de l'histoire des églises wallonnes*, V (1893), 190–91, and the compromising papers of Le Clercq found after the fall of Valenciennes listed in Enno van Gelder. *Correspondance française de Marguerite de Parme: supplément*, II (Utrecht, 1942), 319–29. Le Clercq and Hornes were incriminated by the confession of Guy de Brès: C. Paillard, 'Interrogatoires politiques de Guy de Bray', *BSHPF*, XXVIII (1879), 56–67, at pp. 62–3. William of Orange also seems to have promised support to Valenciennes: Gachard, *Correspondance de Guillaume le Taciturne*, II, cxlix n. 1.

23. *A.D.E.*, IX, 136, Don Francés de Alava to the king, 13 Feb. 1567, writing from the French court where '*han andado . . . vendiendo retratos de Bredoroda, como si fueran de Escipion*'. The Beggars' organization, like the idea of a 'Compromise' which preceded it, was probably taken from the 'act of association' and the first organization of the French Huguenots in the spring of 1562. On the personality of the *Grand Gueux* – who has not yet been the subject of a worthy biography – there is the suggestive study of Enno van Gelder, 'Bailleul, Bronkhorst, Brederode', in *Van Beeldenstorm tot Pacificatie* (Amsterdam, 1964), 40–79. See also the inventory mentioned in n. 17 above, which lists Brederode's possessions in 1567 (including 219 books, eight of them Lutheran and five Calvinist). On the printing press of Vianen – which cost Plantin 500 florins – see H. de la Fontaine Verwey, 'Le siège de Valenciennes et l'imprimerie clandestine de Plantin à Vianen en 1566–67,' *Revue française d'histoire du livre*, I (1971), 9–25.

24. Granvelle's regular correspondents Morillon and Cornet, for example, both later hostile to the duke of Alva, recognized that the foreknowledge of the duke's approach did a great deal to pacify the Netherlands: Poullet, *Correspondance . . . de Granvelle*, II. 424–36 (Morillon to Granvelle, 9 May 1567), and 490–91 (Cornet to Granvelle, 14 June 1567).

25. The standard account of the prince's career is L. P. Gachard, *Don Carlos et Philippe II* (2nd edn, Paris, 1867). On pp. 365–7, Gachard dismisses as bogus the various accounts

of the intrigues of Berghes and Montigny with Don Carlos, despite the testimony of such pro-Spanish authors as Strada, Campana and, especially, Cabrera de Córdoba (*Historia de Felipe II*, I, vii, 22). However, the prince was already taking a part in government in 1566–7, and he received regular letters on Netherlands affairs from Margaret of Parma (see *Cahier van der Essen* XXVI fos. 20–21 – a crucial and hitherto unnoticed piece of evidence). As such he was a potential governor of the Netherlands, and worth the while of the Netherlands seigneurs to cultivate. See further my forthcoming biography of Philip II, chap. 5.

26. These and other details are taken from AA *caja* 165/23, 'Relación del viaje que su excelencia hizo de Italia a Brusselas, 1567', an eye-witness diary probably compiled by Francisco de Ibarra. On the creation of the 'Spanish Road', see G. Parker, *The Army of Flanders and the Spanish Road*, chap. 2, but note that the itinerary through Savoy, Franche-Comté and Lorraine was first suggested by Cardinal Granvelle to the king on 10 March 1563 (see AGS *Estado* 524/4).

27. AGRB *Audience* 244/67, Alva to Margaret, 8 Aug. 1567. In fact this letter was drafted a month before while the duke was at Lons-le-Saunier (10–13 July). None of Margaret's pleas could persuade him to change his mind.

28. Cynics at the Court of Spain were convinced throughout that the preparations of the king to go to the Netherlands in 1567 were an elaborate sham. After all, Philip II had promised to go every year since 1563 and every year he had failed to do so. Although the decision not to go in 1567 was only made public on 23 Sep. the papal ambassador had known of it since the beginning of the month and the king warned Alva that he would not go that year on 7 Aug. (AA *caja* 5/69), and already on 10 Aug. the English ambassador, Dr Man, had sensed that there would be no voyage (Cambridge University Library, MS. MM-3-8 fo. 89, Man to Cecil, 10 Aug. 1567). This is not to say, however, that the king had *never* intended to go: later claims to this effect might be no more than attempts to save face. Over 200,000 ducats had been spent on preparations, according to Ruy Gómez, quoted in A. González de Amezúa, *Isabella de Valois*, II (Madrid, 1949), 413, along with a wealth of other fascinating documents. Some of these preparations were so minute that they suggest a genuine intention to be ready (at least) to go if need arose: see 'Relación de los estandartes, banderas y gallarderes de la nave en que el rey don Felipe II había de ir a Flandes', in *Revista de archivos, bibliotecas y museos*, IV (1874), 406–8 (these great pennants intended for the fleet – thirty-one of them – were used in 1568 for Don John of Austria and the Mediterranean fleet: IVdeDJ 60/205, Philip II note to Antonio Pérez). Documents were sought out from the archives of Spain ready to take to the Netherlands (IVdeDJ 60/321v, Pérez to the king and reply). A fleet was collected at Santander, and provisions for the voyage were even loaded aboard – a remarkable precaution if the king never intended to sail (see Escorial, MS. P.1.20, fos. 192–240, '*Partidas de dinero . . . para el gasto del descargo de los vastimientos de la armada de Su Magestad en Santander*', Sep. 1567). There is thus every reason to suppose that, had Alva reached Brussels in mid-July as planned and found everything pacified, the king would have left Spain as he had done previously in 1548 and 1554.

29. The German troops had been raised on the assurance that their services would be required by Philip II not 'for the sake of religion' but 'only to reduce his subjects to their proper obedience' (AGRB *Audience* 2811, unfol., 'Sommaire de la lettre de Hans Engelpart', commissioned to raise the government's troops in Germany, 20 Nov. 1566). Some of the troops thus raised were therefore Lutherans, and held Lutheran services while on active service against the (Calvinists) rebels (AGRB *Audience*

265/446, Colonel Eberstein to Margaret, May 1567, claiming that 'His Majesty would have recruited very few troops' if it had been known in advance that only Catholics would do). See in general L. van der Essen, 'Croisade contre les hérétiques ou guerre contre les rebelles?' *Revue d'histoire ecclésiastique*, LI (1956), 42–78.

30. Were these controversial arrests premeditated? Motley, following many Dutch writers of the time, suggested that Philip II had signed blank death-warrants in advance for Alva to take with him. This seems unlikely, but since knights of the Golden Fleece enjoyed special judicial privileges (the right to trial by their peers and so on) the king foresaw the difficulties which might arise if it became necessary to arrest any knight involved in the Troubles. On 24 Mar. 1567 he therefore signed a commission which gave Alva express authority to try and sentence any knight accused of sacrilege or treason, notwithstanding the privileges of their Order (IVdeDJ, *envío 6* carpeta 1, no. 4, patent).

31. *Co.Do.In.*, XXXVII, 84: Alva to the king, 6 Jan. 1568, '*Si V.M. mira bien lo que hay que hacer, verá que es plantar un mundo nuevo*'; BMB *MS Granvelle*, XXV fos. 325–7, protonotario Castillo to Granvelle, 28 Dec. 1567: Courtewille and del Rio were serving Alva '*para su consejo de cámara que reciveran todas las requestas y supplicationes para hazer el raport y distribuyrlas a cada consejo segun las materias*'; BNM MS. 18,672, fo. 69, Don Hernando de Toledo to Albornoz, 14 Nov. 1569: '*la excellencia del duque haze buscar y llamar de ytallia algunos letrados para servirse dellos en magistrado y otros oficios destos estados*'. The legal changes are discussed in J. Gilissen, 'Les phases de la codification et de l'homologation des coutumes . . . des Pays-Bas', *Tijdschrift voor Rechtsgeschiedenis*, XVIII (1950), 36–67 and 239–90.

32. AGS *Estado 556/173*, Alva to the king, 15 May 1573; *Estado 545/69*, same to same, 9 July 1570 ('*estos estados . . . hanse de governar desde ay y no de aqui*').

33. G. Moreau, 'Catalogue des livres brûlés à Tournai par ordre du duc d'Albe (16 juin 1569)', *Horae Tornacenses* (Tournai, 1971), 194–213.

34. Groen van Prinsterer, *Archives*, III, 321–2, Meghen to Assonleville, 26 July 1569; Poullet, *Correspondance de Granvelle*, III, 23, Morillon to Granvelle, 21 Sep. 1567.

35. Most accounts of the Dutch Revolt have exaggerated the 'blood-thirstiness' of the Council. The total of those condemned was certainly large, and perhaps excessive, but it hardly amounted to the 'blood torrent' of Motley (based on Dutch polemics such as the 'Advice of the Inquisition', forged in 1570 – Motley, *Rise*, 364–5). In fact only those who had broken images or sheltered iconoclasts, who were Calvinist ministers or elders, or who had borne arms against the government were proceeded against – as they would have been in almost every Catholic state. The true scale of the Council's activities has been established by A. L. E. Verheyden, *Le Conseil des Troubles. Liste des condamnés, 1567–1573* (Brussels, 1961). Unfortunately the list is not definitive. (1) There are several cases of double (or more) entries for the same plaintiff (thus the 127 'persons' listed from Turnhout only refer to 103 real people; the rest were double, or more, entries). (2) Some plaintiffs who were eventually acquitted are included among the condemned. (3) Those tried before Sep. 1567, when the Council was established, are omitted. Despite these three objections, however, there can be no doubt that the scale of the repression reflected in Verheyden's figures is correct.

36. Poullet, *Correspondance de Granvelle*, III, 611–25 prints the confession of Villers. It was said that Villers's revelations sealed the fate of Egmont and Hornes, executed on 5 June (ibid., 266, Morillon to Granvelle, 7 June 1658). It is true that Villers stated that Hornes's relatives had provided money for the 1568 campaign, and that the whole 1568 campaign discredited the claims of the two counts that they had never intended to use

force. But the government already had enough evidence to support the charge of treason against all the nobles. Apart from the contacts with France and Germany (ns. 19 and 20 above) which the government knew all about, the king had been informed that Egmont had been intriguing with Queen Elizabeth and her councillors to procure the fall of Granvelle in 1562–3: see G. D. Ramsay, *The City of London and international politics at the accession of Elizabeth* (London, 1975), 182–3. Even if some of these suspicious dealings were not treasonable, they amounted to an impressive indictment taken all together. And in Hornes's case there was also the collaboration with the Calvinists of Valenciennes and perhaps elsewhere (n. 22 above). This explains the different treatment in prison accorded to the two counts: Egmont was allowed his own servants and meals, Hornes was not (see Poullet, op. cit., III, 3, n. 2, 4, n. 3, and 20 for observations on this point). Under the circumstances, with the counts' former allies mounting a triple armed invasion with considerable foreign support, it is hard to see how Egmont and Hornes could have been spared in the summer of 1568.

37. AA *caja* 6, fo. 12, the king to Alva, 13 May 1568; A. W. Lovett, 'A new governor for the Netherlands', *ESR*, I (1971), 90: Espinosa to Alva, 2 Mar. 1569; cf. also AA *caja* 165, fo. 44, 'Tanteo del gasto ordinario para el entretenimiento destos estados de flandes.'

38. The calculation was ingenious: the average rent for a house was taken to be equivalent to $6\frac{1}{4}$ per cent of its capital value, so that one had to multiply by sixteen to arrive at its true market value ($6\frac{1}{4} \times 16 = 100$). Thus a house, for example, which was rented for sixty-two and a half florins a year was valued by the tax inspectors at 1,000 florins. The tax was collected at the rate of 16 per cent on the annual rent which in this case – sixty-two and a half florins – would yield just ten florins, or precisely the 'hundredth penny' of the capital value. Income from investments other than houses was taken as $4\frac{1}{2}$ per cent on average, and the multiplier and the rate of tax to produce the 'hundredth penny' was therefore twenty-two instead of sixteen. The advantage of this method of calculation (as far as the Treasury was concerned) was that it provided an estimate of the value of investments at market prices, not at a price artificially reduced by the owner for fiscal purposes. As such it was probably the most 'modern' tax ever levied in early modern times.

39. On Alva's intimidation tactics in 1569 see J. Craeybeckx, 'De moeizame definitieve afschaffing van Alva's tiende penning', in *Album Charles Verlinden*, I (Ghent, 1975), 63–94, at pp. 83–6.

40. Piot, *Correspondance . . . de Granvelle*, IV, 594–5, minute of the king to Alva written by Hopperus, Feb. 1572, and the even more insistent AGS *Estado 553/40*, king to Alva, 16 Mar. 1572.

41. Piot, op. cit., 146–52, Morillon to Granvelle, 24 Mar. 1572.

42. The literature on Alva's hated taxes is extensive. There is a good general survey of the duke's government, which reviews previous work, by M. Dierickx, 'Nieuwe gegevens over het bestuur van de hertog van Alva in de Nederlanden', *BGN*, XVIII (1964), 167–92. Since then, there is the article cited in n. 39 above, and J. Craeybeckx, 'La portée fiscale et politique du 100e denier du duc d'Albe', in *Acta Historica Bruxellensia*, I (Brussels, 1967), 342–74: G. Janssens, 'Brabant in verzet tegen Alva's tiende en twintigste penning', *BMGN*, LXXXIX (1974), 16–31; and Janssens, 'Een gezantschap naar Filips II in 1572', *Spiegel historiael*, VIII (1973), 82–7.

BIBLIOGRAPHY FOR CHAPTER 3: THE SECOND REVOLT

The book which has done most in recent years to illuminate the second revolt of the Netherlands is undoubtedly N. M. Sutherland, *The massacre of St Bartholomew and the European Conflict 1559–1572* (London, 1973). It is now possible to establish the events which led up to the invasion of 1572 and which determined its outcome, events which took place far outside the Netherlands. The diplomatic efforts of William of Orange and his friends extended even further than Dr Sutherland suggests, however: for ramifications involving Algiers and the Turks, see J. C. Devos, 'Un projet de cession d'Alger à la France en 1572', *Bulletin philologique et historique*, LXXVIII (1953–4), 339–48; for plans to involve Sweden and Denmark see P. J. van Herwerden, *Het verblijf van Lodewijk van Nassau in Frankrijk: Hugenoten en Geuzen, 1568–1572* (Assen, 1932), *passim*, especially pp. 162–3; and C. F. Bricka, *Inberetninger fra Charles de Dançay til det franske hof om forholdene i Norden, 1567–1573* (Copenhagen, 1901), the letters of Dançay are printed in French.

On the organization of the rebels for the invasion of 1572, see J. C. A. de Meij, *De watergeuzen en de Nederlanden, 1568–1572* (Amsterdam, 1972), and B. Dietz, 'Privateering in north-west European waters, 1568 to 1572' (University of London Ph.D. thesis, 1959). See also R. Glawishnig, *Niederlande, Kalvinismus und Reichsgrafenstand, 1559–1584. Nassau-Dillenburg unter Graf Johan VI* (Marburg, 1973). The numbers and organization of the refugees is covered by H. Schilling, *Niederländische Exulanten im 16. Jahrhundert. Ihre Stellung im Socialgefüge und im religiosen Leben deutscher und englischer Städte* (Gutersloh, 1972); and R. van Roosbroeck, *Emigranten: nederlandse vluchtelingen in Duitsland, 1550–1600* (Leuven, 1968). The 'churches under the cross' are covered by D. Nauta, 'Les réformés aux Pays-Bas et les Huguenots' in *Actes du Colloque: l'Amiral de Coligny et son temps* (Paris, 1974), 577–600. Despite the 'military' organization of the Dutch Calvinists, their leaders were far more restrained in politics than their French brethren: where the French Synod of La Rochelle pledged full support to Coligny and the political leadership of the movement, the Synod of Emden tried to keep away from any political commitment. The precise role of religion in the early stages of the Dutch Revolt has caused much discussion, some of it partisan and impassioned. The available evidence is judiciously presented and reviewed by A. C. Duke and R. L. Jones, 'Towards a reformed polity in Holland, 1572–1578', *TvG*, LXXXIX (1976), 373–93. The political structure in the early years of the Revolt is discussed by H. Lademacher, *Die Stellung des Prinzen von Oranien als Statthalter in die Niederlanden von 1572 bis 1584. Beitrag zur Verfassungsgeschichte der Niederlande* (Bonn, 1958). The military organization of the rebels is covered by J. W. Wijn, 'Het Noord Hollandse regiment in de eerste jaren van de opstand tegen Spanje', *TvG*, LXII(1949), 235–61, and E. M. Braekman, 'L'armée des Gueux', *Revue belge d'histoire militaire*, XIX (1971), 5–46. The best accounts of the war at this time were composed by two Englishmen: Roger Williams, *The actions of the Low Countries* in J. X. Evans, ed., *The Works of Sir Roger Williams* (Oxford, 1972); and Walter Morgan, All Souls' College, Oxford, Library MS. CXXIX: see C. W. C. Oman, 'Walter Morgan's illustrated chronicle of the war in the Low Countries', *Archaeological Journal*, LXXXVII (1930), 1–15 and also n. 39 below.

Finally, for the South Netherlands under Spanish rule, there is the important report of Don Francés de Alava in January 1572 (printed in Gachard, *Correspondance de Philippe II sur les affaires des Pays-Bas*, IV, 215–19) and the suggestive study of F. Barado y Font, *Don Luis de Requesens y la política española en les Países Bajos* (Madrid, 1906). More recently, Dr A. W. Lovett has written some useful articles about the Requesens years: 'A new governor for the Netherlands: the appointment of Don Luis de Requesens', *ESR*, I (1971), 89–103; 'The governorship of Don Luis de Requesens, 1573–76. A Spanish view', *ESR*, II (1972), 187–99;

'Some Spanish attitudes to the Netherlands, 1572–78', *TvG*, LXXXV (1972), 17–30; and 'Francisco de Lixalde: a Spanish paymaster in the Netherlands, 1567–77', *TvG*, LXXXIV (1971), 14–23. For further information on the Lixalde case, see G. Parker, 'Francisco de Lixalde and the Spanish Netherlands: some new evidence', *TvG*, LXXXIX (1976), 1–14. The chief obstacle to a proper assessment of the Spanish regime in the Low Countries, however, still remains prejudice: anti-Spanish feeling both at the time and subsequently makes it very hard to separate fact from fiction and myth from legend in determining what happened and why. See the penetrating article of K. W. Swart, 'The Black Legend during the Eighty Years' War', in J. S. Bromley and E. H. Kossmann, eds., *Britain and the Netherlands*, V (The Hague, 1975), 36–57.

NOTES TO CHAPTER 3

1. W. J. C. Moens, *The Walloons and their church at Norwich: their history and registers*, I (Lymington, 1887), 217–18.
2. AGS *Estado* 823/150–58, minute of the debate of the council of state in Spain, 7 July 1571; AA *caja* 7, fo. 58, king to Alva, 14 July 1571 (ordering him to invade England in Aug. or Sep., using the Spanish troops previously moved into Holland and Zealand for defence against the pirates); AGS *Estado* 547/3, king to Alva, 14 Sep. 1571 (repeating the earlier order).
3. IVdeDJ 67/1, Requesens to Andrés Ponce, January 1574.
4. AGRB *Audience* 404/139, Zweveghem to Alva, 25 March 1572. On the question of whether Orange and Count Louis knew about the descent on the Brill before it happened, see P. J. van Herwerden, *Het verblijf van Lodewijk van Nassau in Frankrijk* (Assen, 1932), 175, letter of Count Louis to the Beggars, 22 Apr. 1572, which clearly suggests that he was not privy to their initiative.
5. Piot, *Correspondance . . . de Granvelle*, IV, 148, Morillon to Granvelle, 24 Mar. 1572.
6. The '*Gentsch Vaderonze*' was printed with an English translation (on which the above is based) at the end of part III of Motley's *Rise* (1882 edn) p. 544. The '*briefkin*' can be dated from the entry for 16 Mar. 1572 in F. de Potter, ed., *Dagboek van Cornelis en Philips van Campene* (Ghent, 1870), 388–9. The 'hard times' of 1571–2 are recorded in the letters of Morillon to Granvelle with particular vividness (Piot, *Correspondance*, IV, 139–43 and 146–65), and in the *Dagboek van Jan de Pottre* (ed. J. de St Genois, Ghent, 1861), 37–42, and the *Kroniek van Godevaert van Haecht*, II, 150–52. E. Autenboer, 'Uit de Geschiedenis van Turnhout', *Taxandria*, XL–XLI (1968–9), 12n., records the flight of most of the clergy from the town in 1571–2 on account of the plague, so that hardly any masses were said or sung for a year.
7. R. van Roosbroeck, *De kroniek van Godevaert van Haecht*, II, 157, mentions the children's game; Piot, *Correspondance . . . de Granvelle*, IV, 176, Morillon to Granvelle, 13 Apr. 1572, noted the impotence of the magistrates; L. Devillers, *Inventaire analytique des archives des États de Hainaut*, I (Mons, 1864,) 178, for the pusillanimous attitude of some tribunes of the people. See n. 42 to chap. 2 above for sources on the duke of Alva's new taxes.
8. The equation was not always quite so simple however. At Gouda, for example, the magistrates kept control in 1566–7 and prevented any iconoclasm; they therefore remained in office in 1572, putting up a strident opposition to the Tenth Penny. In March 1572, however, they failed to prevent the appointment of collectors for the tax. See Meerkamp van Embden, 'Gousdche vroedschapresoluties 1565–72', *BMHG*,

XXXIX (1918), 341–407. The arrangements to collect the tax could not have come at a better time from the rebels' point of view. The assertion that the 'oligarchization' of town government was deliberate Habsburg policy is confirmed by the changes made to the constitution of dozens of German cities by Charles V in 1550–52, see C. R. Friedrichs, 'Capitalism, mobility and class formation in the early modern German city', *Past and Present*, LXIX (1975). 24–49, at p. 35.

9. On the defence of Brill, see de Meij, *Watergeuzen*, 84–5; AGRB *Audience* 339/169–71, Order to withdraw the garrison, 28 Oct. 1571; and W. Troost and J. J. Woltjer, 'Brielle in Hervormingstijd', *BMGN*, LXXXVII (1972), 307–53. On the Beggars' difficulties on Vlie, see AGRB *Audience* 340, fos. 3 (Bossu to Alva, 9 Jan. 1572), 15 (reply, 23 Jan.), 19 (Bossu to Alva, 30 Jan.) and 22 (reply, 4 Feb.); and *Audience* 297, fos. 38 (Gaspar de Robles, governor of Friesland, to Alva, 24 Jan.), 40 (reply, 4 Feb.), 55, 66, and 81 (Robles to Alva, 6, 8 and 23 Mar.).

10. AGRB *Audience* 340/26 Bossu to Alva, 7 Feb. 1572, and f. 31, Alva to Bossu, 13 Feb.; AGS *Estado* 551/94, 'Relación de lo que se trato en el consejo que se tuvo en Bruselas a 1º de Abril, 1572'.

11. AGRB *Audience* 344/1 and 48, Bossu to Alva, 16 and 28 May, 1572.

12. AGRB *Audience* 344/83, Alva to Bossu, 15 June 1572, minute.

13. E. Gachet, 'Rapport . . . sur ses recherches dans plusieurs dépôts littéraires de France', *Compte rendu de la Commission royale d'Histoire*, 2nd series IV (1852), 342–3.

14. Groen van Prinsterer, *Archives*, III, 505, Orange to Count John, 21 Sep. 1572, and IV, cii, decypherment of same letter. Royalists like Morillon agreed that Alva's position had been saved by the massacre: 'If God had not permitted the destruction of Coligny and his followers, this country would have been lost': Piot, *Correspondance . . . de Granvelle*, IV, 428, Morillon to Granvelle, 16 Sep. 1572. Needless to say, the duke of Alva also got the point: '*Je vous envoye* [he wrote to Count Bossu] *avec ceste la relation des choses succedées à Paris et en France qui sont admirables et vrayement significatives que dieu s'est servi de changer et reduyre les choses comme il cognoit convenir pour la conservation de la Sainte Foy et augmentation de son sainct service et sa gloire. Et après tout cela, ces choses viegnent si merveilleusement à propos en ceste conioncture pour les affaires du Roy nostre maistre que plus ne pourriont, dont ne pouvons assez remerchier sa divine bonté . . .*' (AGRB *Audience* 1728/2, fo. 77, Alva to Bossu, 29 Aug. 1572).

15. L. Didier, *Lettres et négociations de Claude de Mondoucet*, I, 20, letter of Sep. 1572; Piot, op. cit., IV, 427, letter cited in preceding note.

16. B. H. Slicher van Bath, *Een Fries landbouwbedrijf in de 2e helft van de 16e eeuw* (Wageningen, 1958), 77. This study is based on the 'Rekenboeck off Memoriael' of Rienck Hemmema, a Friesland farmer, between 1569 and 1573, and it provides a fascinating insight on what it was like to live through the tempestuous events of 1572.

17. Richardot, quoted by L. P. Gachard, *Rapport sur les différents séries de documents concernant l'histoire de la Belgique qui sont conservés dans les archives . . . à Lille* (Brussels 1841), 234. The French ambassador Mondoucet was particularly appreciative of the success of the massacre at Mechelen, cf. L. Didier, *Lettres et négociations de Claude de Mondoucet*, I, 55–7, letters to Charles IX dated 2 and 5 Oct. 1572. William of Orange agreed: 'After the sack of Mechelen [he told his brother John] the garrisons of the other towns were so terrified that one after another they have abandoned the places entrusted to them. In short, forty companies of soldiers have made a base and ignominious flight, without cause and even without having any news of the enemy's approach. If this continues, I see no way of continuing the struggle.' (Groen, *Archives*, IV, 3,

letter of 18 Oct. 1572). It is worth insisting upon the success of Alva's policy of 'beastliness' because it explains why he continued to use it.

18. Groen, *Archives*, IV, 2–6, letter cited in preceding note.

19. ibid., 29, Count Neuenar to Count Louis of Nassau, 17 Nov. 1572: '*Dimenche passé on a ouy ung grand jamergeschrey et tuerie dedans Zutphen, mais on ne sçait ce que c'est.*'

20. Didier, *Lettres et négociations*, I, 106–10, Mondoucet to Charles IX, 25 Nov. 1572.

21. *Epistolario*, III, 261, Alva to the king, 19 Dec. 1572: '*la infantería española les ganó la muralla y degollaron burgueses y soldados sin escaparse hombre nacido*'.

22. There is a transcript of the resolutions taken at this crucial 'rebellious' first assembly of the States of Holland in R. C. Bakhuizen van den Brink, *Les Archives du Royaume des Pays-Bas*, I (The Hague, 1847), 32–46. It was attended by representatives from Dordrecht, Haarlem, Leiden, Gouda, Gorinchem, Alkmaar, Oudewater, Hoorn, Enkhuizen, Medemblik, Edam and Monnikendam; deputies from Rotterdam joined on 25 July, deputies from Delft two days later. During the 1560s the States of Holland had claimed – and on occasion had exercised – the right to convene themselves. This practice, condemned by Orange when stadholder under Philip II, was welcomed by him in 1572.

23. J. C. Boogman, 'De overgang van Gouda, Dordrecht, Leiden en Delft in de zomer van het jaar 1572', *TvG*, LVII (1942), 81–112, at pp. 93, 98.

24. ibid., 107.

25. J. Hessels, *Ecclesiae Londino-Batavae Archivum*, III, part 1 (Cambridge, 1897), 200–204, Jan van der Beke to Dutch Church at London, 15 Feb. 1573.

26. Kervijn de Lettenhove, *Relations politiques*, VI, 483–6, Elizabeth's Instruction to Captain Pickman, *c.* 8 Aug. 1572; J. H. Burton, ed., *Register of the Privy Council of Scotland*, II (Edinburgh, 1878), 148.

27. H. van Grol, 'Het Zeeuwse prijzenhof te Vlissingen', *BVGO*, 5th series IV (1917), 1–46.

28. E. Charrière, *Négociations de la France dans le Levant*, III (Paris, 1853), 477–82, bishop of Dax (French ambassador at the Porte) to Charles IX, 8 May 1574, referred to the 100,000 écus which the French king had been sending to Orange for the 'past eighteen months' (sc. since Nov. 1572). This seems improbable, in view of the parlous state of the French treasury. It is true that Orange wrote about '*l'argent de France*' arriving (Groen, *Archives*, IV, 245, Orange to his brothers 17 Nov. 1573), but this almost certainly referred to a *single* payment of 100,000 écus provided by Charles IX at this time (Groen, op. cit., IV, 193–8; T. Juste, *Les Valois et les Nassau 1572–74*, Brussels, n.d.; and R. Glawishnig, *Niederlande, Kalvinismus und Reichsgrafenstand*, 95, 103–4). The contribution of the tiny county of Nassau to the Dutch cause may well have been worth more than the subsidies from France: Nassau provided 600,000 florins (300,000 Rheingulden) from 1568 to 1573 (see Glawishnig, op. cit., 94).

29. J. H. Van Dijk, 'De geldelijke druk op de Delftsche burgerij in de jaren 1572–1576', *BVGO*, 7th series, V (1935), 169–86. There is, as yet, no proper study of the war finance of the rebels in these early years, but see: N. J. M. Dresch, 'Rekeningen van Marten Ruyschaver, thesaurier in het Noorderkwartier, 1572–3', *BMHG*, XLIX (1928), 45–127; and K. Heeringa, 'Stukken betreffende de inkomsten van Zeeland in 1572 en volgende jaren', *BMHG*, XLVI (1943), 1–44. On annuities, see D. Houtzager, *Hollands lijf en losrentelening voor 1672* (Schiedam, 1950), chap. 4.

30. Figures of population loss from A. M. van der Woude, *Het Noorderkwartier, A. A. G. Bijdragen*, XVI (1972), 3 vols., I, 154–6; and F. Daelemans, 'Leiden 1581: een sociodemografisch onderzoek', *A. A. G. Bijdragen*, XIX (1975), 137–215. It is perhaps worth noting the only available estimate of the size of the principal Dutch towns at

this time, since so much of the revolt's success depended upon them. The following figures are suggested for the 1560s, before the war reduced population, on the basis of partial censuses and town-maps. All are probably a little too high.

Large towns		Small towns	
Amsterdam	30,900	The Hague	9,300
Leiden	22,600	Alkmaar	5,500
Haarlem	14,700	Hoorn	4,600
Delft	14,000	Schiedam	4,100
Dordrecht	12,700	Enkhuizen	3,500
Gouda	12,500	Vlaardingen	2,800
Rotterdam	12,500	Den Brielle	2,500

Source: J. C. Ramaer, 'Middelpunten van bewoning in Nederland', *Tijdschrift der Aardrijkskundige Genootschap*, XXXVIII (1921), 1–38 and 174–214, at p. 181.

31. Kossman and Mellink, *Texts*, 115: Orange to Count John, 7 May 1574.
32. H. A. Enno van Gelder, *Vrijheid en ontvrijheid in de Republiek: geschiedenis der vrijheid van drukpers en godsdienst van 1572 tot 1798*, I (Haarlem, 1947), chap. 3; P. de Jong, 'Can political factors account for the fact that Calvinism rather than Anabaptism came to dominate the Dutch Reformation?', *Church History*, XXXIII (1964), 392–417.
33. H. ten Boom, 'De diaconie der gereformeerde kerk te Tiel van 1578 tot 1795', *NAK*, LV (1974–5), 32–69, at p. 47.
34. H. J. Jaanus, *Hervormde Delft ten tijde van Arent Cornelisz (1573–1603)* (Amsterdam, 1950), 33; J. H. Hessels, *Ecclesiae Londino-Batavae Archivum*, II (Cambridge, 1889), 433, Lieven de Herde to Dutch Church at London, Oct. 1572: '*De kercke hier* [Flushing] *eerstmael zeer flauwelick begonst, ghemerct hier het volck nae den aert der visschers ende scippers zeer wilt en woest es.*'
35. The data in this paragraph, including the estimate of 'one tenth' (reported in P. Bor, *Oorsprongk*, II, 975–6) is taken from the article of A. C. Duke and R. L. Jones, 'Towards a Reformed Polity in Holland, 1572–78', *TvG*, LXXXIX (1976), 373–93. A comparison between the strength of the Roman church before 1572 and the Reformed church afterwards is extremely difficult. Catholic historians – most notably L. J. Rogier, *Geschiedenis van het Katholicisme in Noord-Nederland*, 3 vols. (Amsterdam, 1945–7); and J. A. de Kok, *Nederland op de breuklijn Rome-Reformatie* (Assen, 1964) – have tended to compare total priests with total ministers. This is misleading. In the first place, by no means all of the Catholic clergy were actively engaged in pastoral work: as many as 90 per cent of the Roman clergy in a given area might be chaplains, monks or other non-pastoral priests. Many of them might also not reside in their living. Even when they did, they might be poorly deployed: Rotterdam, with perhaps 5,000 people, had only one priest in 1520; Amsterdam, with perhaps 20,000 people, had but two and so on. This changed with the coming of the Reformation: there was a considerable redistribution of church resources, especially in the towns, and parish boundaries were redrawn to give more equal cover to each community. At the same time much of the administrative and social work of the parish was taken over by the elders and deacons, leaving the clergyman to become a full-time preacher and teacher of the Word. The Reformed minister thus received far more help from his lay officers than the Catholic priest; a straight comparison of the numbers of clergy is thus not meaningful. The same may be said about comparing the communicants in the two religions: there was

considerable social pressure on the local population to attend Mass before 1572 but after that there was no pressure to attend any church at all. As noted in the text, attendance at the Reformed church was in some ways unattractive and in some places downright dangerous. Only the devout and courageous were counted.

36. C. A. Tukker, 'The recruitment and training of Protestant ministers in the Netherlands in the sixteenth century' in *Miscellanea Historiae Ecclesiasticae*, III, ed. D. Baker (Leuven, 1970), 198–215; A. C. Duke, 'Nieuwe Niedorp in Hervormingstijd', *NAK*, XLVIII (1967), 60–71, at p. 69, for the *'duytsche wijse'* speech of the minister of Winkel in west Friesland; Hessels, op. cit., III, 278–9, consistory of Rotterdam to Dutch Church at London, 4 Jan. 1575, asking for a second minister to serve the new congregation, warning that *'den Oosterschen ofte Vrieschen Predicanten en worden zo byons van het slechte volck niet verstaen'*. The archives of the Dutch Church at London pullulate with pleas from the new Reformed communities in the Netherlands for more ministers.

37. R. L. Jones, 'Reformed church and civil authorities in the United Provinces', *Journal of the Society of Archivists*, IV (1970), 109–23, at pp. 121–2; and Jones, 'De nederduits gereformeerde gemeente te Leiden in de jaren 1572–76', *Leids Jaarboekje*, 1974, 126–44, at pp. 138–9. This whole section on the religious situation in the young Republic relies heavily on the important work of Ms Jones and of her husband Alastair Duke.

38. Owen Feltham, *A brief character of the Low Countries* (London, 1652), 1–2, 5.

39. See D. Caldecott-Baird, *The expedition in Holland 1572–74. From the manuscript of Walter Morgan* (London, 1976), 152–3.

40. J. X. Evans, ed., *The works of Sir Roger Williams* (Oxford, 1972), 33.

41. P. Geyl, *The revolt of the Netherlands, 1555–1609* (2nd edn, London, 1958), 134, quoting from P. Bor, *Oorspronck, begin ende vervolgh der Nederlandsch Oorlogen*, I (Amsterdam, 1621), 327.

42. BNM MS. 783/469–71, Granvelle to Don Juan of Austria, 28 Aug. 1573 (Granvelle did not argue that the Haarlem garrison should have been spared: he merely felt that 'it was not wise to dispose of them before the end of the war; there would have been plenty of time to dispose of them afterwards'), IVdeDJ, 32/139, Medina Celi to Mateo Vázquez, 20 July 1573.

43. A. Henricpetri, *Tragicall Historie*, trans. T. Stocker (London, 1583), fos. 128–9. Professor K. W. Swart informs me that this piece of rhetoric was first published in the contemporary account of the siege by J. Fruytiers, *Corte beschryvinghe van de strenghe belegheringhe ende wonderbaerlijcke verlossinghe der Stadt Leyden* (Delft, 1574), 20.

44. Alva's hostility to compromise appears in: *Epistolario*, III, 502–4, Alva to the king, 31 Aug. 1573; AGS *Estado* 554/146, Requesens to the king, 30 Dec. 1573; *Epistolario*, III, 474–8, Alva to the king, 29 July 1573. For the proposal to flood or burn out the rebels, see Parker, *Army of Flanders*, 134–5. This passage, in which I refer to Philip II's personal reluctance to sanction wholesale flooding, has been criticized by the distinguished Dutch historian, J. J. Poelhekke, as 'gullible' (*BMGN*, LXXXVIII (1973), 480–81). This view flies in the face of the available evidence. Although perhaps the correspondence between the king and his governor-general might not reflect the realities of the situation in the field (see the letters printed in Gachard, *Correspondance de Philippe II*, III, 174–7 and 191–2), the letters of the field commanders cannot be pure imagination. See therefore Gachard, op. cit., III, 158–9, Francisco de Valdés to Requesens, 18 Sep. 1574; AGRB *Audience* 1723/1, fo. 163, Baron Hierges to Alva, 4 Aug. 1573 (saying that his men had begun systematically to destroy crops – cutting them down rather than burning them because the corn was still green); and *Audience*

1723/2, fo. 411, Hierges to Requesens, 29 Nov. 1574 (saying that Valdés's Spaniards had already begun to burst the dikes, but that Hierges had stopped them in order to prevent the province of Holland being lost for ever: see extract in Piot, *Correspondance de Granvelle*, V, 526). The correspondence of Hierges, governor of Gelderland and Holland, is full of passages about dike-breaking and crop-destruction by both sides. It seems certain that, had the Spaniards not mutinied in the winter of 1574, they would have laid waste most of the *platteland* of Holland: it was well within their power.

45. Based on Parker, *Army of Flanders*, 287.
46. Letter of Requesens to Andrés Ponce, 21 Feb. 1574, quoted in A. W. Lovett, 'The governorship of Don Luis de Requesens, 1573–76. A Spanish view', *ESR*, II (1972), 196.
47. Henricpetri, *Tragicall Historie*, fo. 100v.
48. AGS *Estado* 559/104, Requesens to the king, 11 Dec. 1574; BM Addl MS. 28,388/ 70v–71, Requesens to Don Gaspar de Quiroga, Aug. 1575; *Nueva Co.Do.In.*, V, 368, Requesens to the king, 6 Oct. 1574.
49. Didier, *Lettres et Négociations*, II, 338–9, Mondoucet to Henry III, 23 Oct. 1574.
50. IVdeDJ 51/31, Vázquez to the king, with royal reply: 31 May 1574 (*'Es fuerte cosa y se sombra cada día en tal punto'*); 51/33, 20 June 1574 (*'Creo que todo es tiempo perdido según como va lo de Flandes'*); 53, carpeta 3, fo. 87, 4 July 1574; 53 carpeta 3, fo. 77, 18 July 1574 (*'Todas las cosas nos van faltando y tan a priesa que no sé que me diga dello'*). Some of these extracts were cited – but in an unacceptably loose translation – by A. W. Lovett, 'Some Spanish attitudes to the revolt of the Netherlands', *TvG* LXXXV (1973), 24–5.
51. Kossmann and Mellink, *Texts*, 115: letter to Count John of Nassau, 7 May 1574.
52. Groen van Prinsterer, *Archives*, V, 379–81, Orange to Count John, 16 July 1576.

BIBLIOGRAPHY FOR CHAPTER 4: THE THIRD REVOLT

The central event in the Dutch Revolt was, after the capture of the Brill in 1572, the sack of Antwerp in 1576. Although many documents concerning the preliminaries to the sack perished during the holocaust, there is a fine collection of material – 728 pages of it – in P. Genard, 'La furie espagnole. Documents pour servir à l'histoire du sac d'Anvers en 1576', *Annales de l'Académie royale d'archéologie de Belgique*, XXXII (1876). On the connection between the sack and the Pacification of Ghent, see H. van der Linden, 'La pacification de Gand et les États-Généraux de 1576' in *Études d'histoire dediées à la mémoire de Henri Pirenne* (Brussels, 1937), 357–65. The history of the States-General has been written by J. Gilissen, 'Les États-Généraux des Pays de Par Deçà, 1464–1632', *Standen en Landen*, XXXIII (1965), 263–321. The acts and resolutions of the States-General have also been published from 1576 onwards: L. P. Gachard, *Actes des États-Généraux des Pays-Bas*, 2 vols. covering 1576–80 (Brussels, 1861–6); and N. Japikse, *Resolutiën der Staten Generaal van 1576 tot 1609*, 14 vols. (The Hague, 1917–70). The introductions to the relevant volumes of the correspondence of William of Orange, the key personage in this period, are also illuminating: L. P. Gachard, *Correspondance de Guillaume le Taciturne, prince d'Orange*, III (Brussels, 1851) and IV (Brussels, 1854); G. Groen van Prinsterer, *Archives ou correspondance inédite de la maison d'Orange-Nassau*, 1st series V (Leiden, 1838) and VI (Leiden, 1839).

The various attempts to establish an effective government in the rebel provinces are described by J. C. H. de Pater, *De Raad van State nevens Matthias, 1578–81* (The Hague, 1917); L. Delfos, *Die Anfänge von der Utrechter Union, 1577–1587* (Berlin, 1941); and

P. J. van Winter, 'De ontwerpen van de Unie van Utrecht'; *BMHG*, XLVI (1943), 108–79. There is also a most interesting article by A. A. van Schelven, 'De staatsvorm van het Zwitsersche Eedgenootschap der Nederlanden ter navolging aanbevolen', in *Miscellanea historica in honorem Leonis van der Essen*, II (Louvain, 1947), 747–56.

The 'defection' of the Walloons from the States-General is best approached through vols. I and II of L. van der Essen, *Alexandre Farnèse, prince de Parme* (Brussels, 1933–4). In addition there is the published correspondence of the leading nobles, letters which were destroyed in 1914 in the town archives of Ieper: J. B. Blaes, ed., *Mémoires sur Emanuel de Lalaing, baron de Montigny* (Brussels – The Hague, 1862); I. L. A. Diegerick, *Correspondance de Valentin de Pardieu, seigneur de La Motte* (Bruges, 1857); Diegerick, 'Lettres inédites de Philippe, comte de Lalaing', *BCRH*, 2nd series, VIII (1856), 428–503; Diegerick, 'Lettres inédites de Emanuel de Lalaing', *BCRH*, 2nd series, IX (1857), 320–79; and Diegerick, 'Lettres inédites de Georges de Lalaing, comte de Rennenbourg', *BCRH*, 2nd series, X (1858), 107–64. The 'defections' of Groningen and 's Hertogenbosch are discussed by F. U. Ros, *Rennenburg en de Groningse Malcontenten* (Groningen, 1964), and L. P. L. Pirenne, *'s Hertogenbosch tussen Atrecht en Utrecht. Staatkundige geschiedenis, 1576–1579* (Tongerlo, 1959).

Most of the studies which deal with the collapse of the States-General party after 1578 suffer from a partisan approach, whether from the point of view of the States or the point of view of modern Belgium. But it was not so easy at the time for a Catholic like Rennenburg to see that there was no place for him in the camp of John of Nassau and the Calvinists. The accusation of *verraad*, treason, which is so often levelled against Rennenburg and his fellows is anachronistic: to whom or to what were they traitors? Certainly not to their Catholic faith, and probably not to the ideals and principles enshrined in the Pacification of Ghent either. See L. J. Rogier, 'Rennenburgs Afval', *Annalen van het Thijmgenootschap*, XLV (1957), 125-34, and J. J. Woltjer, *Friesland in hervormingstijd* (Leiden, 1962), 307–8. For a later incidence of 'treason', see J. J. Poelhekke, 'Het verraad van de Pistoletten?', *Verhandelingen der Koninklijke Nederlandse Akademie voor Wetenschappen, afd. Letterkunde*, new series, LXXXVIII (1975).

NOTES TO CHAPTER 4

1. IVdeDJ 37/72, Requesens to Don Juan de Zúñiga (his brother), 12 Nov. 1575. Cf. also ibid., 67/121, same to same, 30 Oct. 1575: 'I am well aware that those who advised and arranged the Decree have lost these provinces for the Roman Catholic Church.'
2. IVdeDJ 68/170, Requesens to Andrés Ponce de León, 24 Feb. 1574.
3. AGS *Estado* 559/104, Requesens to the king, 12 Dec. 1574.
4. IVdeDJ 36/38, Royal apostil to a billet of Antonio Pérez, 16 June 1576.
5. Gachard, *Correspondance de Philippe II*, IV, 425–6, note written by Philip II and given to Don John before he left Madrid on 18 October 1576. The main points were also in Don John's Instruction and Patent drawn up at the same time but only signed on 30 October (ibid., 453–64). Philip II's rather different letter to Roda on 11 Sep. is in ibid., 369–71. It was intercepted and published by Orange on 13 Oct.
6. Gachard, *Correspondance de Philippe II*, V, 109; Don John to the king, 22 Dec. 1575. On a later occasion Don John compared himself to a tennis ball, now picked up, now set down; now in one court, now in another . . .
7. Quoted by Gachard, op. cit., V, xii.
8. AGS *Estado* 574/137, Don John to the king, 28 July 1577.

9. G. Griffiths, *Representative government in western Europe in the sixteenth century* (Oxford, 1968), 460; extract from an Orangist account of the St Geertruidenberg conference which appears to give verbatim accounts of the heated discussion between Orange and the royalist negotiators – a discussion which Orange, for once, lost.

10. AGS *Estado* 573/193, Don John to the king, 31 July 1577.

11. IVdeDJ 36/21, Don John to Don Juan de Zúñiga, 30 Sep. 1577.

12. Bor, *Oorsprong*, I, 711a: undated letter from Marnix to Sonoy, governor of north Holland, Oct. 1576.

13. All noted in the journal of Laurence Metsius, a member of the States of Brabant, which was printed by Gachard, *Correspondance de Philippe II*, IV, 759–94, see pp. 761–2 and 770. This 'democratic' coup was repeated by the Paris *sans-culottes* when on 20 May 1795 they invaded the National Convention in order to secure the implementation of the policies they desired.

14. Quoted by F. Braudel, *The Mediterranean*, II, 1140, Granvelle to the king, 6 Dec. 1574.

15. Details on this ultimatum are in Gachard, *Correspondance de Guillaume le Taciturne*, IV, xv–xxiii. Don John's own account may be found in IVdeDJ 36/21, Don John to Don Juan de Zúñiga, 30 Sep. 1577.

16. Philip II took the decision to renew the struggle in the Netherlands at some point between 28 August (when he ordered the governor of Lombardy *not* to send the Spaniards back: AGS *Estado* 1247/133) and 31 August (when he signed a series of orders announcing that they would return: IVdeDJ 47/16, and 6/8/12, to governor of Lombardy and duke of Savoy respectively). For an attempt to deny the existence of the Turkish Truce even to other government ministers, cf. AGS *Estado K* 1543/74, Gabriel de Zayas, secretary of state, to Diego Maldonado, acting Spanish ambassador in Paris, 7 Oct. 1577: '*La voz que por allá ha corrido de que Su Magestad haze tregua con el Turco tiene tan poco fundamento que creo se havra reydo v.m. . . . Es un gran burlería.* ('The reports which have circulated over there that His Majesty is making a truce with the Turks are so unfounded that I expect you laughed at them . . . It is a big joke.')

17. IVdeDJ 60/18, apostil of the king on a billet of Antonio Pérez referring to letters from Flanders dated 30 Oct. 1577. The Council of State was still bitterly divided over whether or not to go ahead with the truce in May 1578 (IVdeDJ 60/127–9, report of Pérez on a Council debate, 10 May 1578).

18. I. H. van Eeghen, *Dagboek van Broeder Wouter Jacobszoon*, II, 717 (entry for 21 April 1578). There are other references to the symbolic behaviour and games of the children – a fascinating subject – on pp. 327, 329 and 559. Cf. also above, pp. 80 and 130.

19. AGS *Estado* 2843/1, Council of State *consulta*, 11 Sep. 1577 against allowing Parma to go to the Netherlands, but the king overruled them '*porque creo le* [Don John] *podra ayudar segun lo que he entendido antes de agora de su persona*' ('Because I believe the prince may assist him [Don John], according to what I already know of him'). Cf. also HHStA *Belgien DD* 233/1 fo. 207, commission of Don John appointing Parma to succeed him, 29 Sep. 1578. (The signature on this order is barely legible, Don John being crippled with plague; he died two days later.) Philip II approved of the transfer of power on 13 October.

20. Compare the onerous conditions imposed upon Anjou in 1581 with the more moderate ones exacted from Matthias in 1577 and the *carte blanche* accorded to Don John (Griffiths, *Representative government*, 463–8 and 492–504).

BIBLIOGRAPHY FOR CHAPTER 5: INDEPENDENCE AND SURVIVAL

Two biographies offer the best introduction to this impossibly complicated period in the history of the Netherlands: L. van der Essen, *Alexandre Farnèse, prince de Parme, gouverneur-général des Pays-Bas, 1545–1592*, 5 vols. (Brussels, 1933–7); and J. den Tex, *Oldenbarnevelt*, 5 vols. Dutch edition (Haarlem – Groningen, 1960–72), 2 vols. abridged English edition (Cambridge, 1973). There are also two very fine but unfortunately unpublished doctoral theses which throw much light on developments: F. G. Oosterhoff, 'The earl of Leicester's governorship of the Netherlands 1586–87', (University of London Ph.D. thesis, 1967); and H. de Schepper, 'De kollaterale Raden in de katolieke Nederlanden van 1579 tot 1609' (Leuven University Ph.D. thesis, 1972).

One of the reasons why the history of the Netherlands in the 1580s is so hard to write stems from the particularism of the various provinces, towns and social groups. On this theme, see the excellent studies of: G. Malengreau, *L'esprit particulariste et la révolution des Pays-Bas au 16e siècle, 1578–1584* (Louvain, 1936); T. Wittmann, *Les gueux dans les 'bonnes villes' de Flandre (1577–1584)* (Budapest, 1969); F. Prims, *Beelden uit den Cultuurstrijd der jaren 1577–1585*, 2 vols. (Antwerp, 1942–3); A. Despretz, 'De instauratie van der Gentse Calvinistische Republiek, 1577–79', *HMGOG*, XVII (1963), 119–229, together with the trenchant criticisms of P. Rogghé, 'De orangistische putsch van 28 oktober 1577 te Gent', *Appeltjes van het Meetjesland* (1967), 143–81.

The efforts of the Dutch to obtain foreign support are reviewed in G. Parker, 'The Dutch Revolt and the polarization of world politics', *TvG*, LXXXIX (1976), 429–43. For further details on the English 'secours', see: Charles Wilson, *Queen Elizabeth and the revolt of the Netherlands* (London, 1970): and R. B. Wernham, *Before the Armada: the growth of English foreign policy, 1488–1588* (Oxford, 1966). The military assistance is described by C. G. Cruickshank, *Elizabeth's Army* (2nd edn, Oxford, 1966); and S. L. Adams, 'The gentry of North Wales and the earl of Leicester's expedition to the Netherlands, 1585–86', *The Welsh History Review*, VII (1974), 129–47. For French aid, there is nothing better than the vintage study of Kervijn de Lettenhove, *Les Huguenots et les Gueux, 1560–1585*, 6 vols. (Bruges, 1883–5). The most interesting introduction to the involvement of the French and English Courts with the cause of William of Orange is undoubtedly the delightful study of Frances A. Yates, *The Valois Tapestries* (2nd edn, London, 1975).

Finally, on the crisis of Orange's death and the Armada, see: A. M. van der Woude, 'De crisis in de Opstand na de val van Antwerpen', *BVGN*, XIV (1959–60), 38–57 and 81–104; and G. Parker, 'If the Armada had landed . . . ', *History*, LXI (1976), 358–68.

NOTES TO CHAPTER 5

1. Act of Abjuration, 26 July 1581, quoted by H. H. Rowen, *The Low Countries in early modern times* (New York, 1972), 102; the accompanying oath was printed by P. Bor, *Oorsprong*, II, 280a.
2. Accord of 5 July 1581 printed in Bor, op. cit., II, 183–5.
3. Censorship decree quoted by H. A. Enno van Gelder, *Vrijheid en onvrijheid in de Republiek: geschiedenis der vrijheid der drukpers en godsdienst van 1572 tot 1798*, I (Haarlem, 1947), 104. Data on congregation sizes from L. J. Rogier, *Geschiedenis van het Katholicisme in Noord Nederland*, I, 520, 525–8, 545, 550, 566–7 and so on.
4. Data from J. H. Hessels, *Ecclesiae Londino-Batavae Archivum*, III part 1, 560–61 (Dutch church at Antwerp to Dutch church at London, 3 Sep. 1579), 570–71 (Dutch

church at Brussels to same, 7 Apr. 1580), 599–600 (Dutch church at Bruges to same, 31 Dec. 1580), 713–14 (Daniel de Dieu to same, from Brussels, 8 June 1583), and many others. Hessels's collection includes many letters from the 'churches under the cross' in Flanders and Brabant which prove the survival of organized Calvinist cells there throughout the Spanish regime (cf. ibid., 222–3, 355–6, 365–6 and others).

5. Data in this paragraph taken from J. van Roey, 'De correlatie tussen het sociale-beroepsmilieu en de godsdienstkeuze te Antwerpen op het einde der XVIe eeuw', in *Sources de l'histoire religieuse en Belgique* (Louvain, 1968), 239–58. It is worth remembering that these Antwerp figures are unique because they reflect the *free* choice of the population: nowhere else in sixteenth-century Europe do we have such a large sample from an area which tolerated almost all forms of religion.

6. Hessels, III, 679–81, Daniel de Dieu to the Dutch church at London, Brussels, 9 Aug. 1582. See also ibid., II, 625–8, Jacobus Regius to same, Ghent, 30 Aug. 1578, expressing the conviction that most of the magistrates were *'van geene religie'* ('of no religion') and the fear that most of the people *'zonder Gods woort leven'* ('live without the Gospel'). It is of course impossible to prove conclusively that 'dechristianization' was a consequence of the Reformation. Among other things, the multiplicity of religions in the tolerant Dutch Republic makes it almost impossible to work out just how many people 'went to church'. There were no less than ten religions practised in Rotterdam during the seventeenth century: A. M. van der Woude and G. J. Mentink, 'La population de Rotterdam au XVIIe et XVIIIe siècles', *Population*, XXI (1966), 1165–90. And then there is the difficulty of defining who precisely was a believer. Throughout the seventeenth century the old Catholic shrines continued to attract an impressive number of pilgrims, but no doubt not all of them were practising Catholics: W. Frijhoff, 'La fonction du miracle dans une minorité catholique: les Provinces Unies au XVIIe siècle', *Revue d'histoire de la spiritualité*, XLVIII (1972), 151–78. However, 'dechristianization' is what the surviving evidence suggests and, with Catholicism suppressed and Protestantism unable to fill the gap for some time, it is what one might expect to find. It is certainly what one finds elsewhere: see J. Delumeau, *Le Catholicisme entre Luther et Voltaire* (Paris, 1971), 293–330; G. Strauss, 'Success and failure in the German Reformation', *Past and Present*, LXVII (1975), 30–63; S. K. Boles, 'The economic position of Lutheran pastors in Ernestine Thuringia, 1521–55', *Archiv für Reformationsgeschichte*, LXIII (1972), 94–125; and R. B. Manning, 'The spread of the popular reformation in England', *Sixteenth-century essays and studies*, I (1971), 35–52.

7. *Calendar of State Papers, of the reign of Elizabeth, Foreign Series, 1581–82* (London, 1907), 346 (22 Oct. 1581), 415 (24 Dec. 1581) and 466 (28 Jan. 1582), and many more.

8. *Memoriën en adviezen van C. P. Hooft*, ed. H. A. Enno van Gelder, II (Utrecht, 1925), 7. This discourse, delivered on 9 June 1584, is the earliest of Hooft's known writings and is a fine example of his powerful style. Amsterdam had only come under Calvinist control in 1578 and from the first it opposed substituting Orange's sovereignty for that of Philip II.

9. Motley, *Rise*, 904. This moving phrase is, in fact, the last in his epic account and it is taken from the official report of Orange's death sent by the States-General to the town council of Brussels: *'dont par toute la ville l'on est en si grand duil tellement que les petits enfans en pleurent par les rues'*.

10. ibid., 881, and Rowen, *The Low Countries*, 261, asserted that the Spanish troops never left. There is, however, a copious correspondence in Simancas and in the various archives of the 'Spanish Road' which proves that they did!

11. F. Strada, quoted by Motley, *History of the United Provinces 1584–1609*, I (London, 1869), 176.

12. The complaint of Brussels was quoted by L. P. Gachard, 'Analectes Historiques', *BCRH*, 3rd series, VIII (1866), 247; the protest of the States of Brabant by Bor, *Oorsprong*, III, 475.

13. The earl of Leicester, quoted in H. Brugmans, ed., *Correspondentie van Robert Dudley, graaf van Leycester*, III (Utrecht, 1931), 284–6 (letter of 15 Nov. 1587); Sir Roger Williams, quoted J. X. Evans, ed., *The works of Sir Roger Williams* (Oxford, 1972), 14 (from *A briefe discourse of Warre*, published 1590).

14. AGS *Estado* 165/175–7, Instruction of Philip II to Parma, 1 and 3 Apr. 1588, abridged translation in M. A. S. Hume, *Calendar of letters and state papers relating to English affairs preserved principally in the archives of Simancas*, IV (London, 1899), 250–52.

15. 'Discours' of Thomas Wilkes, 1587, printed *apud* H. Brugmans, ed., *Correspondentie van Robert Dudley, graaf van Leycester*, II (Utrecht, 1931), 447.

16. I. A. A. Thompson, 'The appointment of the duke of Medina Sidonia to command the Spanish Armada', *Historical Journal*, XII (1969), 201.

17. AGS *Estado* 590/22, Parma to the king, 28 Feb. 1586.

18. AGS *Estado* 589/33, Philip II to Parma, 17 Aug. 1585, imperfectly printed in Piot, *Correspondance . . . de Granvelle*, XII, 339–43, and quoted by Motley, *History of the United Provinces*, I (London, 1869), 244.

19. AGS *Estado* 2855, unfol., 'Sumario de los 4 papeles principales que dio el presidente Richardot' and 'Lo que Su Magestad es servido que se responda a los 4 papeles principales'. Paper 3 dealt with a possible compromise solution to the Dutch Revolt.

20. AGS *Estado* 2220/1, fo. 6, Philip II to Count Olivares, 12 Nov. 1590. Cf. the rest of the letters exchanged between the king and his ambassador in Rome in 1589–91 about a negotiated settlement in *Estado 956, 957* and *958*.

21. J. X. Evans, ed., *The Works of Sir Roger Williams*, 12.

BIBLIOGRAPHY FOR CHAPTER 6: CONSOLIDATION AND SETTLEMENT

The standard account of the decade of Dutch victories which followed the Armada is by Robert Fruin, *Tien jaren uit de 80 jarige oorlog (1588–89)* (Leiden, 1857). It is, however, marred by Fruin's neglect of the French commitments of Philip II, as was pointed out by P. van Isacker, 'De Spaanse tussenkomst in Frankrijk en de Nederlanden' (University of Leuven Ph.D. thesis, 1914: I am very grateful to Fr. Karel van Isacker, S. J., for allowing me to consult the only surviving copy of his father's invaluable work). On the Dutch campaign in Friesland, see G. Overdiep, *De Groningen schansenkrijg: de strategie van graaf Willem Lodewijk;. Drenthe als strijdtoneel* (Groningen, 1970). This otherwise excellent work overlooks the fact that the Dutch army was at all times during the 1590s outnumbered by the Spanish army of Flanders and that only the mutinies of the latter prevented the relief of the key 'conquests' of Steenwijk in 1592 and Groningen in 1594. On the organization of the mutinies see G. Parker, *The Army of Flanders*, chap. 8; and 'Mutiny and discontent in the Spanish Army of Flanders, 1572–1609', *Past and Present*, LVIII (1973), 38–52. On the forms of warfare at this time, see G. Parker, 'The "Military Revolution, 1560–1660" – a myth?', *Journal of Modern History*, XLVIII (1976), 195–214. The narrative accounts of Carnero, Coloma, Croy, Giustiniano, Verdugo and other contemporaries mentioned in the notes which follow are all interesting and valuable sources for the period. For the limitation of warfare in Germany as well as in the Low Countries, see :G. Benecke, 'The problem of death and destruction in Germany during the Thirty Years' War', *ESR*, II (1972), 239–53; and I. Bog, *Die bauerliche Wirtschaft im 30-jahrigen Krieg* (Coburg, 1952), 142–54.

On Dutch constitutional developments see P. F. M. Fontaine, *De Raad van Staat: zijn taak, organisatie en werkzaamheden in de jaren 1588–1590* (Groningen, 1954); A. T. van Deursen, 'De Raad van Staat en de Generaliteit, 1590–1606', *BMGN*, XIX (1964–5), 1–48; S. J. Fockema Andreae, *De Nederlandse Staat onder de Republiek* (Amsterdam, 1961); R. J. Fruin and H. T. Colenbrander, *Geschiedenis der Staatsinstellingen in Nederland tot den val der Republiek* (2nd edn, The Hague, 1922). Recent research has concentrated on the sort of political analysis favoured by Sir Lewis Namier, concentrating on family and faction as the mainsprings of politics: D. J. Roorda, *Partij en factie. De oproeren van 1672 in de steden van Holland en Zeeland: een krachtmeting tussen partijen en factien* (Groningen, 1961); D. J. Roorda and H. van Dijk, 'Sociale mobiliteit onder regenten van de Republiek', *TvG* LXXXIV (1971), 306–28; and J. A. Faber, 'De oligarchisering van Friesland in de tweede helft van de 17e eeuw', *A. A. G. Bijdragen*, XV (1970), 39–64. Two older studies may also be recommended on the oligarchic tendency in the Republic: J. de Witte van Citters, *Contracten van correspondentie en andere bijdragen tot de geschiedenis van het ambtsbejag in de Republiek der Vereenigde Nederlanden* (The Hague, 1873); and C. J. Guibal, *Democratie en oligarchie in Friesland tijdens de Republiek* (Assen, 1935). The central personage in the government of the Republic until 1618, however, was Oldenbarnevelt and on him the magnificent biography of Den Tex, noted on p. 304 above is indispensible. On the reasons for his fall, see (apart from Den Tex) the interesting study of C. Bangs, 'Dutch theology, trade and war, 1590–1610', *Church history*, XXXIX (1970), 470–82.

The most memorable (and surprisingly accurate) picture of everyday life in the Spanish Netherlands during the early seventeenth century is given in Jacques Feyder's brilliant film *La Kermesse Héroique* (1935). Likewise the genre paintings of Teniers (with over 2,000 pictures attributed to him) and Jan Breughel (with almost as many to his credit) reveal the pleasures and sorrows of popular life, while those of Vranckx and Snaeyers capture the brutality of Low Countries warfare in the first half of the seventeenth century (see the descriptive catalogue of R. H. Wilenski, *Flemish Painters, 1400–1800*, 2 vols. London, 1960). The destruction of the war is discussed by G. Parker, 'War and economic change: the economic costs of the Dutch Revolt' in J. M. Winter, ed., *War and economic development* (Cambridge, 1975), 49–71; and A. Cosemans, 'Het uitzicht van Brabant op het einde der XVIe eeuw', *BtG*, XXVII (1936), 285–351 (especially the list of devastated communities on pp. 327–51). On the archdukes' methods of government see: H. de Schepper and G. Parker, 'The formation of government policy in the Catholic Netherlands under "the Archdukes", 1596–1621', *English Historical Review*, XCI (1976), 241–54. There is unfortunately no adequate biography either of the Archduke Albert or of Ambrogio Spinola, although the materials for both are abundant (see Parker, *Guide to the Archives*, 54–8 and 97–9 for listings of their papers).

On the crucial religious revival in the south Netherlands, the best study is undoubtedly that of M. Cloet, *Het kerkelijk leven in een landelijke dekenij van Vlaanderen tijdens de XVIIe eeuw: Tielt van 1609 tot 1700* (Louvain, 1968) – there is an English summary of this important study in *Acta Historiae Neerlandicae*, V (1971), 135–58. Other recent work which examines the precise nature of the Catholic revival includes: P. de Clerck, 'De priesteropleiding in het bisdom Ieper (1565–1626)', *ASEB*, C (1963), 7–67: and J. Roegiers, 'De oprichting en de beginjaren van het bisschoppelijk seminarie te Gent (1569–1623)', *HMGOG*, XXVII (1973), 3–192. Probably the most useful general study is E. de Moreau, 'Het katholiek herstel in de Zuidelijke Nederlanden' in *Algemene Geschiedenis der Nederlanden,*

VI (Utrecht–Antwerp, 1953), chap. 10. On the decline of Protestantism see the three different views of A. Pasture, 'Le déclin du protestantisme dans les Pays-Bas méridionaux au XVIIe siècle' in *Hommage à D. Ursmer Berlière* (Brussels, 1931), 183–96 (claiming that most of them became Catholics); C. de Rammelaere, 'Bijdrage tot de geschiedenis van het protestantisme in het Oudenaardse gedurende de moderne periode', *HMGOG*, XIV (1960), 103–15 (about one Protestant community that refused to die: Ste Maria Horebeke, with thirty Calvinist communicants in 1660 and fifty in 1680); and G. A. C. van Vooren, 'Westvlaamse uitwijking naar Aardenburg in de 17e eeuw' in *Album Joseph Delbaere* (Rumbeke, 1968), 207–17 (showing that many Protestants chose to emigrate just across the Dutch border). Finally, for the abuses which the Counter-Reformation strove to overcome, see J. Toussaert, *Le sentiment religieux, la vie et la pratique religieuse des laics en Flandre* (Paris, 1958–9 and 1963), which covers the period to 1570; and a series of articles on specific abuses, by E. Brouette: *RBPH*, XXXIII (1955), 327–32 and XXXIV (1956), 1067–72; and P. Muret and P. Vandermissen: *RBPH*, XXXVII (1959), 941–9.

The 'national feeling' of the south is recorded in A. Lottin, *Vie et mentalité d'un Lillois sous Louis XIV* (Lille, 1968), chap. 4; M. Sabbe, *Brabant in 't verweer. Bijdrage tot de studie der Zuid-Nederlandsche strijdliteratuur in de eerste helft der 17e eeuw* (Antwerp, 1933); B. Knipping, *De iconografie van de contra-reformatie in de Nederlanden* (Hilversum, 1939); and W. J. C. Buitendijk, *Het Calvinisme in de spiegel van de Zuid-Nederlandse literatuur der Contra-reformatie* (Groningen, 1942).

NOTES TO CHAPTER 6

1. AGS *Estado* 2855, unfol., *consultas* of the Council of State, 10 Jan. and 2 Sep. 1589; *Estado* 2219/197, king to Parma, 7 Sep. 1589; *Estado* 2220/1, fo. 157, king to Parma, 4 Apr. 1590.

2. AGS *Estado K* 1573, fos. 12, 21, 24, 35, 40–42, sundry receipts signed by the duke of Guise for Spanish subsidies paid; AGS *CMC*, 2a/23, unfol., 'Cuenta y relación jurada de Gabriel de Alegría', paymaster for Spanish subsidies to the League, Mar. 1587–Sep. 1590; *CMC* 2a/840, 'Cuenta con Gabriel de Santesteban' (paymaster-general 1590–95), section 'lo pagado en dinero a las cosas de Francia'. In 1593 the duke of Feria, Spanish envoy in Paris, estimated that Philip II had spent more than six million escudos on France; in March 1594 the papal nuncio in France put the figure at seven million. Both were probably more or less correct. (A. Bernard, *Procès verbaux des États-Généraux de 1593* (Paris, 1842), 128; ASV *Nunz. Fiandra*, 3/310, Malvasia to Aldobrandino, 6 Mar. 1594). It seems likely that the Dutch actually spent more money than Philip II *in the Netherlands war*: the States-General voted 42,500,000 florins during the 1590s, and spent almost all of it locally; the paymaster-general of the army of Flanders received 100,000,000 florins during the decade, but spent up to two thirds of it in France.

3. Quoted by J. den Tex, *Oldenbarnevelt*, I (Cambridge, 1973), 193.

4. RA Arnhem, *Archief van het Huis Bergh*, 604, unfol., Archduke Albert to Count Frederick van den Berg, Arras, 21 Oct. 1597.

5. F. Verdugo, *Comentario de la guerra en Frisa* (1610; republished by H. Lonchay, Brussels, 1899), 141; RA Arnhem, *Archief . . . Berg*, 530, unfol., Count Herman van den Berg to Fuentes, 24 June 1595; BNP MS. *Lorraine*, 525/142, Varembon to Parma (undated, but clearly from 1591). See also the accounts of these events by the eyewitnesses: Antonio Carnero, *Historia de las guerras civiles que ha avido en los estados de*

Flandes (Brussels, 1625), and Carlos Coloma, *Las guerras de los Estados Baxos* (Antwerp, 1625).

6. BNP MS. *Lorraine*, 526/127, Moriensart to Varembon, 28 Oct. 1592; AHN *Inquisición: espontáneos* 1150/24–6, confession of Francisco López, native of Toledo, who deserted to the Dutch during the 1590s, attended Calvinist services and served in the Dutch army for about five years before returning voluntarily to Spain (and the Inquisition – who pardoned him). It was Spanish renegades in the Dutch army who recognized and captured the Spanish commander-in-chief, the admiral of Aragon, at the battle of Nieuwpoort in 1600.

7. ASV *Nunz. Fiandra*, 3/155, Malvasia to Aldobrandino, 30 July 1593.

8. E. van Reyd (the historian) to E. Stöver, 26 June 1600, quoted by J. den Tex, 'Maurits en Oldenbarnevelt voor en na Nieuwpoort', *BMGN*, LXXXV (1970), 67.

9. Quoted by H. W. Taylor, 'Price revolution or price revision? The English and Spanish trade after 1604', *Renaissance and Modern Studies published for the University of Nottingham*, XII (1968), 29.

10. C.-A. de Croy, *Mémoires guerriers de ce qu'y c'est passé aux Pays-Bas* (Antwerp 1642), 71.

11. AGS *Estado* 634/73, paper of Juan Andrea Doria on the Netherlands, 1605. In the event Spinola needed all his financial resources to keep Philip III's armies in being: he advanced five million florins to the king in 1603–5, for which he was not repaid until 1619 (AGRB *SEG* 27/8 and 26v–27, orders of 2 Oct, and 9 Dec. 1619 to reimburse Spinola; AGRB *Audience* 1465/1, unfol., Spinola's memorial to the Spanish treasury, 8 Nov. 1607).

12. P. Giustiniano, *Delle guerre di Fiandra, libri VI* (Antwerp, 1609), 228–9 and figures 14 and 25 describe and illustrate the redoubts. There is also a brief description of them in English in T. Coryate, *Coryat's Crudities* (London, 1611), 640–41.

13. Sir William Browne to Sir Robert Sydney, 24 Aug. 1606: *Report on the Manuscripts of the Lord de Lisle and Dudley*, III (ed. W. A. Shaw, London, 1936), 307–8; Winwood's letter quoted J. den Tex, *Oldenbarnevelt*, I, 352. The military budgets of the Dutch Republic are recorded in ARA *Raad van State* 1499 and 1500; the French subsidies are printed by D. Buisseret, *Sully and the growth of centralized government in France 1598–1610* (London, 1968), 82.

14. AGRB *Audience* 643bis, unfol., Luis Verreycken to Archduke Albert, 10 Feb. 1606.

15. '*Desde que começo la guerra de flandes oyó dezir que él que se quedase con el postrer escudo saldría con su intento*' – AGS *Estado*, 2023/134, vote of the count of Olivares at the Council of State, 6 Jan. 1605, apparently quoting from Don Bernardino de Mendoza's *Teoría y práctica de la guerra* (Madrid, 1595): '*el triunfo será de quien posea el último escudo*'.

16. *De Lisle and Dudley*, III, 363–4, Sir W. Browne to Sir R. Sydney, 19 Mar. 1607. The burgomaster spoke more truly than he knew: the Dutch did in the end fight until 1647 – and gained little extra.

17. J. Heringa, *De eer en hoogheid van de staat. Over de plaats der Verenigde Nederlanden in het diplomatieke leven van de 17e eeuw* (Groningen, 1961), 252–3; Rowen, *Low Countries*, 112–13.

18. The quotation from Vranck's *Corte Verthoninge* (composed in April and published in October 1587) comes from Kossmann and Mellink, *Texts concerning the revolt of the Netherlands* (Cambridge, 1974), 281; the resolution of 1590 comes from N. Japikse (ed.), *Resolutiën der Staten-Generaal*, VII (The Hague, 1923), 79–80. Even before the revolt the town council of Gouda in Holland claimed to be '*Die burgermeesters, regierders, schepenen ende ghemeen vroetsschap der stede vander Goude representerende 't corpus vande*

stadt' ('The burgomasters, governors, magistrates and common council of the town of Gouda, representing the whole town') (Reference from 1571 kindly provided by Mr A. C. Duke). François Vranck was the pensionary of Gouda.

19. Information from G. Parker, 'War and economic change: the economic costs of the Dutch Revolt' in J. M. Winter, ed., *War and economic development* (Cambridge, 1975), 59–60. Perhaps the author exaggerates the extent to which the war may have held back the growth of Amsterdam and some other great towns of Holland.

20. F. Morison, *Itinerary*, I (London, 1617), 47. The magnificent monument which stands today in the Nieuwe Kerk at Delft was built by Hendrik de Keyser between 1614 and 1622.

21. Sir T. Overbury, 'Observations upon the State of the Archduke's Country, 1609' in *Stuart Tracts, 1603–1693*, ed. C. H. Firth (Westminster, 1903), 218–20. Cf. also Bodleian Library, North MS, b. 12, fos. 85–90, Lord Dudley North's bleak account of the south Netherlands in 1605.

22. K. Maddens, 'Het uitzicht van het Brugse Vrij op het einde van de XVIe eeuw', *ASEB*, XCVII (1960), 72.

23. From J. Verbeemen, 'De werking van economische factoren op de stedelijke demografie der XVIIe en XVIIIe eeuw in de Zuidelijke Nederlanden', *RBPH*, XXIV (1956), 695.

24. R. Weston, *A discours of husbandrie used in Brabant and Flanders* (London, 1650), 2, quoted with the other data in this section in G. Parker, 'War and economic change: the economic costs of the Dutch Revolt', 49–71.

25. AHN *Estado, libro* 972, unfol., Marquis Sfondrato to Don Miguel de Salamanca, 4 June 1640.

26. Report of the Council of Luxemburg to the central government in 1648, quoted by A. Cosemans, 'Het uitzicht van Brabant', *BtG*, XXVII (1936), 289.

27. Cf. the views of the count of Fuentes quoted in Parker, *The Army of Flanders*, 133–4. Cf. also the instructions of Philip III to Don Diego de Ibarra, 17 May 1607, urging him to sabotage the Truce because 'it is so damaging to our reputation', in duque de Berwick y Alba, *Noticias históricas y genealógicas de los estados de Montijo y Teba segun los documentos de sus archivos* (Madrid, 1915), 129–33.

28. AGRB *SEG* 183/169–71, Don Balthasar de Zúñiga to Juan de Ciriza, secretary of state, 7 Apr. 1619, cited by P. Brightwell, 'The Spanish system and the Twelve Years' Truce', *EHR*, LXXXIX (1974), 289. He continued: 'To those who lay all the blame for our troubles on the Truce and foresee great benefits from breaking it, we can say for certain that whether we end it or not we shall always be at a disadvantage. Affairs can reach a certain stage where every decision taken is for the worse, not through lack of good advice but because the situation is so desperate that no remedy can conceivably be found.'

29. On the decision not to renew the truce in 1621 see, apart from the article by Brightwell noted above: J. J. Poelhekke, *'T Uytgaen van den Treves. Spanje en de Nederlanden in 1621* (Groningen, 1960); and H. J. Elias, 'Le renouvellement de la Trève de Douze Ans', in *Hommage à Dom Ursmer Berlière* (Brussels, 1931), 105–16. For Dutch preparations to attack Spain in the colonies if the Truce was not renewed, see: W. Voorbeijtel Cannenburg, *De reis om de wereld van de Nassausche Vloot, 1623–1626* (The Hague, 1964), xx; and L. van Aitzema, *Saken van Staat en Oorlogh*, I (The Hague, 1669), 3–5.

30. AHN *Estado, libro* 720 (formerly *legajo* 3285), unfol., *consulta* of the Council of State, 1 Sep. 1628 (parts of this crucial document were printed in footnotes by J. J. Poelhekke, *De Vrede van Munster* (The Hague, 1948), 30–34.

BIBLIOGRAPHY FOR THE POSTSCRIPT

There are many excellent studies of the Dutch Republic in its Golden Age. The five best available in English are: K. H. D. Haley, *The Dutch in the Seventeenth Century* (London, 1972); J. H. Huizinga, *Dutch civilization in the seventeenth century* (London, 1968); C. H. Wilson, *The Dutch Republic and the civilization of the seventeenth century* (London, 1968); P. A. Zumthor, *Daily life in Rembrandt's Holland* (London, 1962); and J. L. Price, *Culture and Society in the Dutch Republic During the 17th Century* (London, 1974). There is also a useful review of literature in the inaugural lecture of K. W. Swart, *The miracle of the Dutch Republic as seen in the seventeenth century* (London, 1967). For the Dutch overseas there is the excellent collection of essays by C. R. Boxer, *The Dutch Seaborne Empire, 1600–1800* (London, 1965). But perhaps the best guide to Dutch history during this period is P. Geyl, *The Dutch in the seventeenth century*, 2 vols. (London, 1936 and 1964).

NOTES TO THE POSTSCRIPT

1. Sir William Batten, Surveyor of the Navy, on 19 July 1667 recorded in R. C. Latham and F. Mathews, *The Diary of Samuel Pepys*, VIII (London, 1974), 345.
2. W. Temple, quoted by K. W. Swart, *The miracle of the Dutch Republic as seen in the seventeenth century* (London, 1967), 6.
3. T. Coryat, *Coryat's crudities* (London, 1611), 638–9; R. C. Temple, ed., *The Travels of Peter Mundy*, IV (Hackluyt Society, London, 1924), 81. The Mennisten Bruyloft was visited and described by Mundy (op. cit., 76–7); John Evelyn in E. S. de Beer, ed., *The diary of John Evelyn*, II (Oxford, 1955), 46–7; and Sir William Brereton, *Travels in Holland . . . 1634–5* (London, 1844), 57–8.
4. Andrew Marvell, *The character of Holland* (London, 1672); William Walwyn, *The Compassionate samaritane* (London 1644, reprinted in W. Haller, *Tracts on Liberty in the Puritan Revolution*, III, New York, 1934, 87b). Other Levellers, like Richard Overton who had lived in Holland, also cited Dutch examples in favour of toleration in England during the civil war.
5. Owen Feltham, *A briefe character of the Low-Countries under the States* (London, 1652), 91–2.

Index of authors cited in the notes

Guides to works used and to further reading are provided in the references to each chapter. The following list gives the page and note where the work of each author is referred to for the first time and given a full citation. Where more than one work by the same author has been used, the year of each publication is given as well as the page on which it is first cited.

The list is, of course, not exhaustive. For full bibliographical data see the items noted on p. 277 above.

Index

Aalst (town in Flanders): sacked by Spanish troops (1576), 173; captured by Parma (1584), 214

Accord, the, between the Brussels government and the Calvinists (23 August 1566), 81–2, 93, 97

Act of Abjuration (26 July 1581), 197–200

Aerschot, Philippe de Croy, duke of (1526–1595), Netherlands nobleman: member of council of state (1565), 67; supports *Moderation* (1566), 71; opposes Spanish policy, 163, 170–71, 175–6; intrigues against Orange, 183–6

Afflighem, abbey of (in Brabant), 47–8

Alava, Don Francés de (d. 1586), Spanish ambassador in Paris (1565–71), 83, 91–2, 98

Albert, archduke of Austria (1559–1621), ruler of the Netherlands (1595–1621): early years, 231–2; career and government, 233–4; campaigns of (1599–1607),

234; achievements, 258; opposes renewal of war (1621), 263–4

Alençon, duke of, *see* Anjou, duke of

Alkmaar (town in Holland): Protestantism in, 153, 154; siege of (1573), 158, 162

Alva, Fernando Alvarez de Toledo, duke of (1510–82), councillor of Philip II and captain-general in the Netherlands (1567–1573): mentioned, 15, 16, 23, 54–5, 66–7; chosen to suppress 'first revolt', 84–90, 99–105; march to the Netherlands in 1567, 102–4; policies implemented in the Netherlands, 105–17, 293 n. 31; and the invasion of 1572, 131–42; and St Bartholomew massacre (1572), 297 n. 14; opposes negotiated settlement, 161–4; military failure of, 161–3

Alvarez, Vicente, author and household officer of Philip II in 1548, 21, 25, 280 n. 1

ambassadorial reports, value of, 289 n. 16